Soviet-Chinese Relations, 1945–1970

O. B. Borisov and B. T. Koloskov

Soviet-Chinese Relations, 1945–1970

EDITED WITH AN INTRODUCTORY ESSAY BY

VLADIMIR PETROV

Indiana University Press

Bloomington & London

This book has been published with the
assistance of a grant from the EARHART FOUNDATION.

Published in Canada by Fitzhenry & Whiteside Limited,
Don Mills, Ontario

Manufactured in the United States of America

Library of Congress Cataloging in Publication Data

Borisov, Oleg Borisovich.
  Soviet-Chinese relations, 1945-1970.

    Translation of Sovetsko-kitaĭskie otnosheniia.
    Includes bibliographical references and index.
    1. Russia--Foreign relations--China. 2. China--
Foreign relations--Russia. I. Koloskov, Boris
Trofimovich, joint author. II. Title.
DK68.7.C5B6313 1975 327.47'051 74-31443
ISBN 0-253-35410-2   1 2 3 4 5 79 78 77 76 75

*There is nothing more difficult to take in hand, more perilous to
conduct, or more uncertain in its success, than to take
the lead in the introduction of a new order of things.*
NICCOLÒ MACHIAVELLI, *The Prince*

Contents

Acronyms

CC CCP	Central Committee of the Communist Party of China
CC CPSU	Central Committee of the Communist Party of the Soviet Union
CCP	Chinese Communist Party
CPSU	Communist Party of the Soviet Union
PLA	People's Liberation Army
PRC	People's Republic of China
UDA	United Democratic Army

Foreword

The study of Soviet-Chinese relations by O. B. Borisov and B. T. Koloskov which constitutes the bulk of this volume is a unique document. To all intents and purposes, it is the official Soviet record of conflict with the People's Republic of China (PRC) as seen from the perspective of Moscow in 1971, the year in which it was published. There is no "Borisov" or "Koloskov" in real life: these are pseudonyms of two high-ranking specialists in Chinese affairs. Neither one is an academic scholar; both have been intimately acquainted with the convolutions of Soviet-Chinese relations over a long period of time, and both had unlimited access to secret party and government archives as they were writing their book. Who they actually are is irrelevant. Their desire to remain anonymous is valid, for a disclosure of their identities would preclude their participation in negotiations with the PRC or service at the Soviet Embassy in Peking. They wrote their study on instructions from the people directly concerned with Soviet policies toward China, who then carefully reviewed it: it took an unusually long time—almost nine months—for the book to be approved for publication after the completion of the manuscript.

Somewhat puzzling is the period which Borisov and Koloskov chose to cover in their work: from 1945 to 1970. If their purpose was to analyze Soviet relations with the Chinese Communist Party (CCP), they should have started with an earlier date, say with the late 1930s, when the CCP, on Moscow's bidding, formed a united front with the Kuomintang (KMT) to fight the Japanese, who were then threatening the Soviet Union as well as conquering China. If their purpose was to study state relations with the PRC, they should have started with 1949, when it was formed: during the years 1945–1949 "Soviet-Chinese relations" were relations between the Soviet Union and the government of the Republic of China headed by Chiang Kai-shek.

We can surmise that the year 1945 was selected as a starting point because it was then that the Soviet Union, having taken part in defeating Japan, occupied Manchuria and emerged as a powerful factor in the affairs of China, maintaining relations with its legitimate government while enabling the CCP to use Manchuria as a staging area for its future offensive against KMT forces. Since Borisov and Koloskov do not explore the background of Stalin's attitudes and policies toward the Chinese Communists, crucial for the understanding of subsequent developments, I have preceded their book by an introductory essay, "The Soviets and World Communism: Sources of the Sino-Soviet Dispute."

Borisov and Koloskov's reluctance to go into the background of Moscow's relations with the CCP is understandable. With the partial rehabilitation of Stalin in recent Soviet historiography, his statemanship is acknowledged only in the general area of Soviet relations with "imperialist" countries. His internal policies receive scant attention, while his attitudes toward foreign Communist parties, from the 1930s to his death, are given a uniformly silent treatment: Stalin's name has become anathema to all ruling and many nonruling Communist parties, to all, that is, except the Chinese. For reasons of their own—quite obnoxious to the present Soviet leadership—they have allocated to Stalin a place of honor in the Communist Pantheon. The introductory essay seeks, in part, to explain this phenomenon.

Apart from this gap, *Soviet-Chinese Relations, 1945–1970* represents the most detailed and informative account of the Sino-Soviet conflict ever published anywhere and, as of 1971, also the most definitive Soviet statement on the subject. It is by no means an objective study in the Western sense. Surveys of this kind always have one paramount purpose in the Soviet Union: to serve the current needs of Soviet foreign policy, to provide those interested in the subject, whether professionally or academically, with guidance as well as with information. Unlike "bourgeois objectivist" studies in the West, Soviet studies leave no doubt as to where The Truth lies and who is to blame for an unfortunate turn of events in Soviet relations with other countries. No book or article has ever appeared in a Communist country which directly or indirectly criticized one or another aspect of its foreign policy.

Yet it would be erroneous to assume, in spite of its consistently annoying self-righteous tone, that *Soviet-Chinese Relations* is merely an indictment of the Maoist heresy. Since the book is by necessity polemical, the authors not only heap charges against the adversary but also answer, even if by implication, Chinese accusations of Soviet leadership. A Western scholar familiar with the Sino-Soviet dispute would have no difficulty in establishing the adequacy of these rebuttals by reviewing the record of CCP attacks against the Soviets.

Borisov and Koloskov concentrate on broader aspects of the history of Chinese Communism and CCP-CPSU (and PRC-USSR) relations rather than on machinations of "Mao Tse-tung's clique," and generally avoid overstating their case. For instance, they make a major point, that without victory over Japan and Soviet occupation of Manchuria, the CCP would never have succeeded in defeating the KMT. Yet they are careful not to say that the *objective* of Soviet occupation was to assist the CCP in seizure of power in China. And although they recite at length all forms of aid given the CCP in Manchuria which helped to convert it into a Communist stronghold by the end of 1947, they make no claim whatsoever that the Soviet Union continued to assist the CCP with operations against the KMT after the Communist offensive got under way.

Soviet-Chinese Relations is a study of both party-to-party and state-to-state relations, although the former are assumed to have been terminated by the end of 1963. However, ideological CCP-CPSU debates which surfaced after 1960 are treated primarily as affecting adversely USSR-PRC state relations. The authors do not bother to answer CCP doctrinal charges, nor do they attempt to view them as "legitimate" even within the specific context of CCP politics. They constantly stress that the attacks were always initiated by the Maoists, reflecting the increasingly anti-Soviet orientation of the CCP leadership, but they do not adequately explain the *causes* of this orientation.

Needless to say, the authors consistently present Soviet policies toward the PRC as uniformly benign and Soviet intentions as impeccable. The deterioration of Soviet-Chinese relations, the undermining of the basic foundations of socialist unity, are presented exclusively as a responsibility of the chauvinist elements in the CCP led by Mao, who, in the end, triumphed over the internationalist (i.e. pro-Soviet) wing of the party.

The principal roots of the conflict, as they are described in the Borisov/Koloskov study, appear as follows:

1. Mao's "cult of personality," which allowed him to distort the fundamentally healthy CCP and push China toward an ultra-nationalist course, inevitably leading to its anti-Soviet stance.

2. Maoist opposition to the Soviet "peaceful coexistence" policy toward the imperialist world, first and foremost toward the United States; Mao's attempts, beginning with 1957, to press for a more militant Soviet international posture, which could have provoked a Soviet-American nuclear confrontation—e.g., over the Taiwan Straits crisis or the Sino-Indian border dispute—seem to have been at the very foundation of Soviet hostility to the PRC.

3. Maoist ingratitude for Soviet aid and Soviet efforts to advance PRC interests internationally, eventually leading to CCP determination to develop China independently from the Soviet Union and other socialist states.

4. Violations by the Peking leadership of the most basic rules of behavior, mandatory in relations with other socialist states, such as refusal to coordinate its foreign policy with Moscow in the name of socialist unity, or insistence on continuing open polemics in which the most sensitive party and state secrets were aired to the delight of imperialist enemies.

5. The growth of anti-Soviet sentiments in China, fomented and cultivated by the Maoists, culminating in the anti-Soviet orgy of the "cultural revolution" and armed clashes along the Sino-Soviet frontier. Externally, the CCP anti-Soviet line manifested itself in efforts to split the international Communist movement by casting the Soviet Union in the role of a reactionary revisionist state, colluding with the imperialist United States against revolutionary national liberation forces.

Borisov and Koloskov end their story with the events of 1970, before rapprochement between the PRC and the United States took place and before President Nixon's spectacular trip to Peking. This development, of great political and strategic importance for the Soviet Union, has since been dealt with in numerous Soviet articles and official statements. But if *Soviet-Chinese Relations* were to be updated to include the later period, changes in the study, if any, would probably be minimal: there has always been an implicit assumption in Moscow that enemies of the Soviet Union tend to gravitate toward each other. Once China had cut itself loose from the rest of the socialist commonwealth (save for Albania) and actively embarked on an anti-Soviet course internationally, there was no natural limit to how far it might go.

Yet there remains a strange ambivalence in the Soviet view of the PRC because in doctrinal terms China remains a socialist country. As one recent Soviet theoretical study states,

> No country should be "excommunicated" from socialism just on the basis of certain ideological or political differences. Disagreements on separate questions of a political and ideological nature, if they do not lead to attempts to restore bourgeois social relations or to an actual alliance of a particular country with the imperialist powers against the other socialist countries, do not put any socialist state outside the world socialist system. . . . If a country remains socialist from the point of view of the dominant system of social relations, objectively it belongs to the system of world socialism. No one can decree its "exclusion" or "withdrawal" from this system.*

* A. Butenko, ed., *The World Socialist System and Anti-Communism* (Moscow, 1972), pp. 136–137.

Thus the People's Republic of China, whether anyone likes it or not, is bound to remain part of the "socialist system" unless it restores capitalism or enters a formal alliance with, say, the United States (or Japan) against the Soviet Union. Until either or both of these conditions are met, other socialist states would continue to regard the PRC as a fraternal nation. This postulate, of course, does not preclude certain pragmatic precautions on the part of the Soviet government, such as stationing impressive military forces along the border with China or intensive diplomatic maneuvers aimed at preventing it from getting too close to the principal enemy, "imperialism."

The text of the Borisov-Koloskov book for the present publication (translated by machine and verified by David Chavchavadze) was rather heavily edited in order to (a) reduce its size and (b) make the translation no less readable than the original. Both tasks were approached with the utmost care. Nothing of substance was eliminated. Cuts were made mainly at the expense of excessively numerous "episodes" used by the authors to illustrate causes and consequences of changing policies; detailed recitations of scientific-cultural USSR-PRC exchanges; lengthy quotations from minor Chinese publications and from speeches in various Communist conclaves, supporting and reiterating Soviet positions; developments in obscure plants and factories bearing upon more significant events; and not inconsiderable redundancies, common in Soviet political writings.

Daggers (†) in the text indicate information which has not been published before in the Soviet Union. In many instances, especially where the authors rely on documents deposited in secret party and government archives or on debriefings of Soviet officials who had served in China, this information appears for the first time in any language. The length of such new material is usually one or two sentences.

In trying to assure readability, no attempt was made to alter the original text. Not a sentence was added, even if it could have provided a smoother transition between paragraphs. The style, the language, were preserved faithfully. Editing affected exclusively sentence structure and choice of words, to correspond to modern American usage, and on occasion saying in five sentences what the authors tried to say in ten. As a result of the total editorial effort, the length of the original translation was reduced by about fifteen percent.

In cutting the text, I relied on my own judgment based on the general knowledge of the subject. I also heeded the advice of Dr. Boris

Zanegin, a Soviet Sinologist, currently with the Institute USA of the Academy of Sciences of the USSR, whose familiarity with Soviet studies of the People's Republic of China was far superior to my own and who pointed out to me the passages in the Borisov-Koloskov book containing original and theretofore unpublished information. The main burden of improving the readability of the text and tracking down redundancies was borne by Sally G. Bunting. To her, as well as to Dr. Zanegin, I express my heartfelt gratitude.

VLADIMIR PETROV

INSTITUTE FOR SINO-SOVIET STUDIES
GEORGE WASHINGTON UNIVERSITY
OCTOBER 1974

The Soviets and World Communism: Sources of the Sino-Soviet Dispute

Vladimir Petrov

In their international relations governments deal with other governments: heads of state with heads of state, foreign ministers with foreign ministers, central bankers with central bankers, etc. In alliances, such as NATO, there are direct communications between defense ministers, intelligence chiefs, and the military. The nature and the closeness of relations are determined by national interests and by perceptions of common threat. Among democratic societies there is also a degree of mutuality, based on historical factors and economic interdependence. These affinities, however, do not preclude conflicts, sometimes bitter, with mutual grievances aired freely in speeches of politicians and in the national press.

Relations among states ruled by Communist parties are conducted on an entirely different basis. National interests are superseded by imperatives of ideological unity, both against the perceived common enemy, "imperialism," and as reinsurance against attempts to dislodge Communist leadership from within. Day-by-day affairs of state are also conducted on a government-to-government level. But all major policy decisions are made by party leaders who maintain continuous liaison through separate party channels. It is through these channels that Communist states coordinate their common foreign policy positions, their trade policies, and even their educational systems, which stress Communist values based on Marxist-Leninist teachings. A party-controlled press may on occasion offer original interpretations of national and international events but only rarely can one discern actual contradictions with interpretations of similar events in other Communist countries. In addition, Communists make an effort to cultivate people-to-people relations. They exchange motion pictures, scholars, and stage performers; all sorts of delegations go in every direction; and, partially because of hard-

1

currency shortage, tourist traffic among Communist countries is much more extensive than between Communist and non-Communist countries.

Theoretical foundations for Communist (socialist) unity had been developed in the Soviet Union long before other socialist states came into being at the end of the Second World War. The primacy of the Soviet Union, as the only power able to withstand the pressures emanating from the hostile "imperialist" environment, was recognized by all Communist parties, whose sacred duty was to protect and advance Soviet interests, assumed to be in the interest of all, a *sine qua non* for survival and success of the Communist cause. This basic assumption has been and remains at the very core of Soviet foreign policy, if not always shared to the same extent by leaders of other socialist states.

Seen from Moscow's perspective, the world as it has evolved since the Second World War consists of two categories of states: socialist, comprising those ruled by Communist parties, and nonsocialist, which encompasses the rest. The principal characteristic of the former is that they had all undergone a socialist revolution in which the old capitalist ruling classes lost power to Communists, who then transformed their respective societies politically and economically according to Marxist-Leninist principles. Having formed a "socialist camp" by the mid-1950s, these states in their foreign policies have one common denominator: they oppose "imperialism" and favor national liberation movements struggling against it. Ideally, in Soviet theory—and for a while in actual practice—it is the Central Committee of the CPSU that is called upon to provide members of the socialist camp, as they conduct their relations with the outside world, with general guidelines and day-by-day coordination.

Socialist unity was first broken in 1948 as Tito resisted Stalin's attempts to direct Yugoslav internal affairs. In the post-Stalin years, Moscow's declining authority in the socialist camp was on occasion challenged by others, but only the People's Republic of China and Albania openly defied the Soviet Union, proclaiming their unalterable opposition to Soviet leadership. This opposition does not mean that they had forfeited their membership in the socialist camp.[1] At least in doctrinal terms, the quarrel has been seen as temporary not only in Belgrade, Peking, and Tirana, but also in Moscow. The conflicts are ascribed not to clashing national interests but to erroneous views and policies of the leaders currently in power. Socialist unity in confronting imperialism remains everybody's professed objective.

Maintaining this unity has been a major preoccupation of Stalin's heirs, absorbing a great deal of their time and energies and, since the late 1950s, calling increasingly for outlays of resources to prop up the sometimes shaky economies of fraternal states. While some of this effort has been dictated by ideological considerations, socialist unity has had its primary value to Moscow in proving to "imperialist" adversaries that the Soviet Union commands a consistently loyal international following representing a major factor in international relations and that the "socialist camp" must be reckoned with more than ever.

According to the Soviet concept, relations among socialist states are qualitatively different from their relations with the outside world. Structurally, in the CC CPSU, they are supervised by a separate department, that of Liaison with Communist and Workers' Parties, as distinct from the International Department watching relations with other states. In their studies of foreign policies of their government, Soviet scholars maintain the same distinction: relations among socialist states are implicitly assumed to be nonconflicting while their relations with nonsocialist states are seen as inherently conflicting, reflecting the international "class struggle." This otherwise convenient and neatly arranged approach has developed—at least so it seems to outsiders—one major flaw: the lasting and bitter Soviet-Chinese conflict, challenging not only practitioners but also theoreticians of Soviet foreign policy. In order to appreciate the full significance of this challenge, it ought to be put into a broader context of Soviet *Weltanschauung* and the peculiar Soviet ways of interrelating ideological and pragmatic (or "strategic" and "tactical") aspects in their policies toward the outside world. These, in turn, need to be analyzed by taking into account the Soviets' perceptions of their own and their adversaries' strengths and weaknesses, by no means an easy task. The intricate interplay between the evolving doctrine and the impact of developments outside Soviet control, and between Moscow's "strategy" and specific "tactics," has always been so obscured from public view as to defy the skills of Sovietologists. Even well-informed Soviet insiders are often unable to judge, except in retrospect, whether or not the cumulative effect of certain "tactics" suggested a qualitative change in policy amounting to a new strategy.

Soviet relations with socialist states presumably rest on solid ideological foundations. Yet understanding them is impossible without retracing Soviet relations with foreign Communist parties in the prewar years, and certainly without considering the general context of Soviet foreign policy during and after the war. Such an analysis is admittedly complex, particularly given the paucity of documentation. In this, Soviet historians are of little help. They are adamant in separating the history of the Comintern from that of Soviet foreign policy, perpetuating the fiction of Stalin's era that the Soviet leadership had little to do with the former and implicitly denying the fact that foreign Communist parties served Soviet interests. Perhaps because of overspecialization, Western historians of Soviet foreign policy pay scant attention to this Comintern function while students of Communism only perfunctorily relate Communist activities to Soviet external objectives.

We know, however, that at higher levels of the Soviet party hierarchy no distinction has been made between "state" and "party" international affairs and that since Lenin's time the interests of the Soviet state have always taken precedence over particular aspirations of foreign Communist parties. For this reason, Soviet perceptions of the hostile outside world provide a logical framework for Moscow's relations with the Communist movement.

Soviet foreign policy itself is not an easy subject to study. In tracking down its convolutions one cannot rely on contemporary official statements, which are themselves acts of policy rather than explanatory documents. Various recorded conversations between Soviet leaders and foreign dignitaries and diplomatic correspondence are of limited utility because candor and diplomacy tend to be mutually exclusive. Soviet historical studies are nearly worthless for this purpose since their authors—including those few who may have had a genuine insight into the workings of the top policy-making circles—do not have the privilege of critically examining their party's and government's policies. The very nature of Soviet policy-making is such that short of detailed minutes of Politburo meetings there is nothing that can *document* the leaders' hopes and fears, intentions and calculations upon which policy is founded. Thus a Western historian is reduced to piecing together a jigsaw puzzle with many facets missing, the quality of his reconstruction depending heavily on his own calculations.

Evolution of Soviet Foreign Policy in the Second World War

Soviet foreign policy doctrine provides adequately for conflict situations under the conditions of capitalist encirclement; it provides for exploitation of contradictions among capitalist states; and it leaves room for "peaceful coexistence" between the Soviet Union and its imperialist adversaries. It does not, however, provide for alliances with one imperialist power against another. Alliances imply a degree of mutual trust and understanding which the Soviets cannot tolerate in dealing with the "class enemy." This peculiarity of the doctrine largely accounted for the fact that the Nazi-Soviet Pact, concluded in August 1939, never evolved into a base for a viable alliance. To the protagonists the arrangement appeared advantageous in the specific circumstances of the time. It created no lasting bonds, and once the circumstances had changed, the arrangement dissolved in the ferocity of the German onslaught. This painful lesson Stalin kept in mind as Russia entered into a new relationship with Great Britain and the United States.

To Stalin, the crucial test of his partners' intentions was the issue of the second front. Because they failed to undertake a landing in France at a time when the German armies were at the gates of Moscow and Leningrad and rolling toward the Volga and Caucasus, crushing one Soviet army after another, he concluded that Russia's value to the allies was limited to deflecting the Nazi forces which otherwise would have been directed against England. He regarded Lend-Lease as a minimal contribution by the United States in order to prevent the collapse of the Soviet front and avert the possibility of a separate Soviet-German peace. The utter devastation of most of European Russia, the colossal dislocations of population and the economy, the millions of casualties sustained by the Soviet armies may have evoked the sympathy of the English-speaking peoples. This sympathy, however, was insufficient to induce the allies to risk the blood of their own people in order to relieve Russia's plight. As Stalin saw it, they were resolved to wage war with the least possible sacrifice and content—if not actually anxious—to see Russia bled white. This looked like a callous and fundamentally hostile policy which certainly absolved him of any need to be grateful for whatever assistance they rendered.

Given Stalin's *Weltanschauung,* this was fair enough: imperialists were merely true to themselves, leaving the Soviets no choice but to assume by far the greatest burden in fighting the common enemy. There was, however, a way to capitalize on this role since Russia's heroic struggle could be presented as its great contribution to the allied cause, the claim widely accepted in the United States and even in England. Under the pressure of public opinion, Roosevelt and Churchill were forced to constantly apologize for not doing enough and to promise efforts which they knew they could not or would not make.

Stalin was determined to translate this psychological advantage over his partners into tangible gains. He barely bothered to conceal his suspiciousness, repeatedly and forcefully accusing them of reneging on their solemn promises to open the second front. At the same time, Stalin realized the need to find some kind of *modus vivendi* with Roosevelt and Churchill, for upon their good will depended the terms of the postwar settlement and the future Soviet role in world affairs.

Stalin sometimes touched upon the issue of "war aims" in conversations with British and American emissaries, but usually avoided the appearance of being anxious. He temporized for a full year after the tide of the war had turned at Stalingrad, and only when he was sure he had some high cards to play did he consent to meet his partners at Teheran.

The conference opened late in November of 1943. The issue of the second front was still high on Stalin's agenda. Although the German armies were in retreat and large areas of Russia had been liberated, massive Soviet attacks were carried out with enormous human losses; the ability of the enemy to resume the offensive could not be discounted. The terms of the peace settlement, however, were uppermost in Stalin's mind. After two years of disastrous war, his objective had crystallized: to make Russia and his regime so strong and powerful as to discourage future enemies from following Hitler's example. As the costs of waging war mounted, craving for total security had become his obsession. With the demise of Germany and Japan, only the United States and Great Britain loomed as potential enemies, and Stalin could very well interpret Roosevelt's and Churchill's reluctance to discuss the postwar settlement as a perfidious stratagem: to defer crucial decisions until after victory, when they would not need Russia—and then short-change Soviet interests.

He played his hand cautiously at Teheran. He did not downgrade Soviet difficulties at the front and was firm in his demand for Operation Overlord. But he appeared confident in ultimate victory. He reaffirmed his promise to take part in the war against Japan, presenting it as yet another sacrifice by Russia to the common cause. Only then he came to the subject that concerned him most, wanting to learn whether his allies, who were so reluctant to come to Russia's rescue in the moment of its greatest peril, would now quibble in rewarding it after the war at the expense of the Axis and the nations not in the forefront of the gigantic struggle.

Stalin's first impression was favorable. Roosevelt stressed Russia's "right" to have access to warm seas. Churchill proposed to consign to the Soviet Union nearly one-half of prewar Poland. Roosevelt made no formal commitment, pleading that he did not want to alienate Polish-American voters in an election year, but privately told Stalin he would go along with this alteration of the map. Both partners accepted Stalin's claim to Koenigsberg, the Kurile Islands, and southern Sakhalin; Roosevelt also felt certain he could persuade Chiang Kai-shek to grant the Soviet Union special rights in Manchuria. Finally, although neither Stalin nor Churchill appeared very enthusiastic about it, the three partners agreed in principle to consider partitioning of Germany, Roosevelt's pet idea.

It all looked like a good beginning. The atmosphere was friendly and Stalin clearly enjoyed being host to the leaders of the foremost imperialist nations. As all three discussed transfer of territories and other issues affecting the destinies of millions of people, Stalin felt equal, if not superior, to his partners. In this exciting imperialist game, there was no need for rhetoric; everything was businesslike. The future peace settlement looked more and more like another repartitioning of the world among the victors, much as the Versailles settlement was after the First World War. Stalin could reasonably expect that the Soviet share of the spoils would be commensurate with Russia's contribution to the war effort.

Teheran marked the beginning of a brief period of ambivalence in Stalin's attitude toward the Western powers. The cautious optimism and the degree of trust born at that meeting, however, never fully displaced Stalin's suspicion that the affability and cooperativeness of his partners were merely a passing phase. The now proven might of Russia, and its ability to roll back the German tide singlehanded, was one factor the allies had to reckon with. Another was the presence of a strongly pro-Russian sentiment in their countries; yet we may safely assume that looking forward, Stalin realized that in recarving the world and filling the vacuum left after the defeat of the Axis, the Soviet Union would eventually collide with its erstwhile allies. Stalin was not looking forward to clashing with the United States and Great Britain, but he was determined to secure, by Soviet power and Soviet power alone, the gains made and legitimized in agreement with them.

It has often been suggested that at some point Stalin ceased to be a good Communist and turned into an old-fashioned nationalist, bent on the restoration and expansion of his empire. This was true but only insofar as imperial expansionism could be judged to be incompatible with the Communist doctrine, which stresses that Communism must come as a result of an internal social revolution, carried out by a native proletariat. Stalin's preoccupation with the expansion of Soviet influence by force and through secret agreements with imperialists was contrary to this basic principle.

Stalin probably could justify—even in Communist terms—some outright annexations, either presenting Soviet Russia of 1917–1920 as a victim of hostile powers which took undue advantage of its temporary weakness, or by regarding the territories to be annexed as a reward due the Soviet Union for its great sacrifices in the war against the Axis. Roosevelt and Churchill essentially accepted this rationalization as they sanctioned Soviet acquisition of parts of Finland, Poland, East Prussia, and Romania, and acquiesced in the absorption of the Baltic states. They regarded Soviet claims to the Kurile Islands and Southern Sakhalin as a just payment for Stalin's willingness to enter the war against Japan, historical enemy of Russia and currently at war with the United States and China. Soviet demands for special rights and bases in Manchuria which Imperial Russia once possessed presented some problems, since they infringed upon China's sovereignty, but Roosevelt felt he could pressure Chiang Kai-shek to grant these demands. And neither he nor Churchill noticed that one country, Tannu Tuva, quietly changed its independent status to that of a Soviet province.

But if Roosevelt and Churchill—or their successors after 1945— thought that direct territorial acquisitions ought to have adequately compensated the Soviet Union for its war effort, they displayed rank ignorance of Stalin's ideas about the Soviet role in the postwar world. To him, an enlarged Russia would remain in danger of hostile capitalist encirclement until it had secured additional power positions. It was in the struggle for these positions that, from Teheran on, he relentlessly pressed and tested his partners, trying to extract as many concessions as possible, probing their resistance to his demands. And it was in the process of this struggle that the image of the United States as the principal enemy of the Soviet Union eventually emerged, firming as the Cold War swept away the wartime affinities.

The allies succeeded in frustrating Soviet attempts to annex the Turkish provinces of Kars and Ardahan and, later, Iranian Azerbaijan. They did not give Stalin either a military base in the Dardanelles or the trusteeship of Tripolitania, former Italian colony, which he demanded. At Potsdam, Stalin probably did not envision the eventual emergence of the Soviet zone of occupation as a separate German state. But the disappearance of East Prussia and the *de facto* transfer of the Oder-Neisse territories to Poland meant that future Germany would be a much smaller nation.

Unhappy as Stalin might have been in having some of his territorial claims unsatisfied, he probably accepted the outcome. His partners had to draw the line somewhere, now that the war was over and they didn't need the Soviet Union. But he looked quite differently at their reaction to Soviet *political* claims.

From Stalin's point of view, the Soviet Union could not become a truly great power without a number of lesser countries in its orbit. Eastern Europe, which fell under Soviet control as Soviet armies advanced into Germany, was a natural part of the Soviet sphere. Stalin knew that traditional nationalistic elites of these countries had been bitterly anti-Communist and anti-Soviet before the war and, if permitted to regain power, would inevitably take a hostile position toward the Soviet Union. Since almost all East Europeans claimed to be outposts of Western civilization, granting them genuine independence meant that they would gravitate toward the imperialist West. In the end, as Stalin saw it, a new *cordon sanitaire,* a hotbed of anti-Soviet intrigue, and an eventual springboard for a new imperialist attack on Russia would form. In order to forestall this development, Stalin proceeded to implement a violent revolutionary transformation of their societies under the aegis of, and with unlimited assistance from, Soviet occupation authorities. Thanks to Tito's Communist regime, there was no need for Soviet intervention in Yugoslavia. Communization of the others was completed by 1948. Former Axis satellites—Romania, Bulgaria, and Hungary—and the erstwhile victims of the Nazis, Poland and Czechoslovakia, found themselves in the same predicament: all became Soviet satellites.

The doctrinal announcement of the emergence of "two hostile camps"—the "imperialist" headed by the United States and the "peace-loving" headed by the Soviet Union—was officially made at the launching of the Cominform in September 1947. There is no doubt, however, that this vision of the division of the world had firmed in Stalin's mind much earlier. It has been suggested by many students of Soviet affairs abroad, and by Khrushchev in his secret speech at the 20th CPSU Congress, that in his later years Stalin was a victim of paranoia and that this personal misfortune somehow explained the general paranoid direction of Soviet policies.

Needless to say, this explanation is much too primitive to be convincing. Political paranoia, if this is what it was, had characterized the Soviet elite since the Revolution. The experiences of the Civil War; foreign intervention and blockade of the Soviet state; the all-too-real international isolation of Soviet Russia in the twenties and thirties; and finally the tragic sequence of events following Munich and the Nazi-Soviet Pact, ending in the catastrophe of the German invasion—all this experience had enormous cumulative impact on the formation of Soviet attitudes toward the outside world. Ingrained suspiciousness; an inferiority complex resulting from painful awareness of their own weaknesses; verbal aggressiveness; irritatingly stubborn haggling over minor issues in international negotiations and rejection of compromise, so common in relations among Western states; all these features have become part and parcel of Soviet foreign policy. The ultimate brilliant victory over Germany and Japan did not result in self-confidence or magnanimity. It could not erase from Soviet memory the utter devastation of the war, colossal human and material losses, and the near-defeat from the German onslaught in 1941–1942.

True, the war was over. The Soviet Union had been recognized as a great power. Its huge military machine commanded awe and respect. But there was no return to normality in dealing with the outside world. Eastern Europe seethed under the iron rule of Soviet occupation, and there was no certainty that it could be held subdued indefinitely. And Stalin perceived the erstwhile partners in common struggle against the Axis, the United States and Great Britain, as already plotting against the Soviet Union.

The greatest impact upon the formation of the "two hostile camps" doctrine was probably made by the change in the political climate in East-West relations. As the violence of the East European revolution became public knowledge in the West, and as the European Communist parties went into opposition (the process was completed by the summer of 1946), agitating against the unstable governments and plunging their ruined and starving countries into chaos in a series of political strikes, "Communism" again became a dirty word. At first, the conservative and right-wing politicians, and eventually liberal statesmen of the former anti-Axis coalition, began openly to subscribe to the view that Communists, guided and aided by the Soviet Union, were on the move to seize power and to destroy democracy and other values of the Western world.

Stalin may have disapproved some of the tactics of West European Communists who were attempting to strengthen their power positions within their respective countries: the degree of actual Soviet control over them is a subject of legitimate debate. But Stalin could not divorce the Soviet Union from their activities because the image of the Communist monolith was too important for him to maintain in his conflict with the West. Yet it was this very image which largely accounted for the wave of anti-Sovietism which started swelling in the United States and Western Europe.

Stalin's primary concern was Germany, the nation which came dangerously close to defeating Russia a few years earlier. He noted that rather than withdraw from Germany—as Roosevelt had suggested as inevitable within a year or two after the war—the United States was getting more involved there. Instead of consistently implementing the Morgenthau Plan, General Lucius Clay seemed to be protecting German interests at the expense of the Soviets: in May 1946 he discontinued the shipments of dismantled industrial equipment from the American zone to Russia. In September, Secretary of States James C. Byrnes indicated in his Stuttgart speech a shift in United States policy toward granting the Germans a greater role in managing their own affairs.

A specter of Germany allied with the United States and the American-dominated Western European countries began to arise in the minds of Soviet leaders. Added to this was a constant Western, particularly American, meddling in the affairs of Eastern Europe, which encouraged resistance of nationalistic elements to the Soviet-sponsored Communization. Before long, the Greek civil war (in which the Communists received support and encouragement from Tito's Yugoslavia) introduced American presence in the Balkans. The militantly anti-Communist Truman Doctrine proclaimed in May 1947, and the subsequent "Mr. X" policy statement in *Foreign Affairs* calling for containment of Communism on a global scale, signaled to Stalin that a new "imperialist offensive" had been launched. Grossly overrating the danger of another crusade against the Soviet Union, Stalin accelerated consolidation of his domain. The ferocity with which this operation was executed greatly contributed to the intensification of the Cold War. It may be argued that this ruthlessness was necessary for quick Communization of Eastern Europe and the establishment of firm Soviet control. There is no question, however, that it eroded much of the foundation upon which international Communist solidarity rested. Naked force brought forth enough obedient collaborators to carry out Moscow orders but it was ruinous to the spirit of voluntary cooperation, the only long-term guarantee of cohesiveness of the Soviet bloc.

Stalin and the International Communist Movement

Stalin's early biographers usually depicted him as the man who betrayed the revolution. He bureaucratized the party; he replaced its collective leadership by his own rule, mercilessly crushing all opposition; he submerged Russia's revolutionary spirit in the sea of reaction. There have been differences in emphasis on some particulars among the biographers, but they have essentially agreed that Stalin was, or at some point in history became, a "bad" Communist.

It also has to be remembered that Stalin's critics, from Trotsky to Khrushchev, did not condemn him—or the party under his leadership—for the destruction of religious institutions; for expropriation of even modest private property; for persecution of nationalistic groups and organizations; for the collectivization of farming carried out at the cost of

perpetually crippling Russia's agriculture; or for the enormous dislocations caused by industrialization. Discussing the bloody purges of the
1930s, critics lamented the liquidation of the Communist elite but gave
scant attention to the fate of untold millions who perished in Siberian
exile and concentration camps in the same period.

Such selectivity in compiling Stalin's indictment points out the critics'
terms of reference: their commitment to the cause of the left, to "good"
Communism, "good" Marxism. Believing in the essential goodness of the
Russian revolution, they implicitly assumed that in such a backward
country as Russia, with its heritage of autocracy and misrule, excesses
were all but inevitable.

If we turn to studies of international Communism of Stalin's era, we
find that these also were an exclusive preserve of either socialists or ex-
Communists. Idealistic internationalists themselves, they accused Stalin
of excessive centralization of management of Communist affairs, of arbitrary and capricious administration of the Comintern, of purging his opposition on a global scale, and of subordinating the cause of the world
revolution to the needs of Soviet foreign policy.

It is easy to see how those scholars who would want to study international Communism as an instrument of Soviet foreign policy would
find the utility of the traditional studies of international Communism of
limited value. To pursue this subject fruitfully, they would have to disregard evil qualities of Stalin's political personality or his "subversion"
of Communism. Instead they would have to shift their perspective and
look at the subject in its totality from the vantage point of the Man in
the Kremlin as he tried to utilize all means available to him in order to
protect and advance the interests of the Soviet state. Whatever others
might have thought of him, *he* considered himself a good Communist, a
true disciple and creative interpreter of Lenin. For our purposes, it is
his judgment as to what constituted the right course for the movement as
a whole and for its individual components, major Communist parties,
that truly counts. And the appraisal of his judgment, his accomplishments
and miscalculations, ought to be made within the framework of the Soviet foreign policy needs, as Stalin himself perceived them.

Unlike Trotsky and other Bolshevik internationalists, Stalin was convinced that building the might of the Soviet Union was a *sine qua non*
for the eventual triumph of the world revolution. He deeply mistrusted
excitable revolutionary romantics, particularly intellectuals, who failed
to appreciate this basic task, who were unable to appraise properly the
"objective conditions" and "revolutionary situation" and were inept in
selecting proper tactics in their struggle. This type of revolutionary was

common among Stalin's enemies in the CPSU in fights following Lenin's death. It was even more common among the leaderships of the other Communist parties which were still struggling for power or even for their very existence. While tirelessly praising Stalin's wisdom, they were naturally preoccupied with their own affairs; for this reason they expected more understanding and assistance from Moscow than the Soviets deemed prudent to give.

These expectations posed a difficult dilemma for Stalin. On the one hand, the international Communist movement was the only active force in the world on whose support the weak, encircled, and isolated Soviet Union could count. Quite aside from a very genuine fraternal spirit which probably even Stalin felt on occasion, it was absolutely imperative for the Soviets to back it up politically (and sometimes materially) in many battles Communists waged in the 1920s and 1930s. This unconditional Soviet support added immensely to the Communists' image of strength, to their revolutionary optimism. It also assured their unswerving loyalty to the Soviet Union.

On the other hand, as the Soviets began to establish diplomatic and trade relations with European countries, this remarkable Communist unity frequently emerged as an objective liability to Soviet foreign policy. Fear of revolution within each country cast the Communists in the role of social enemy: following Lenin's teachings they left no doubt that revolution was their objective. On top of it, heavy representation of minority groups in many Communist parties combined with their all-too-visible ties to Moscow enhanced their image of traitors to the national cause. These factors accounted heavily for the anti-Soviet orientation of nationalistic governments which dominated European politics in the interwar period.

The Soviets tried to resolve this dilemma by disclaiming responsibility for Comintern activities, insisting that the "real" Soviet foreign policy was conducted by the Narkomindel, in conventional above-board fashion. In part because of the low status which the formal foreign policy establishment occupied in the Soviet hierarchy—while Communist affairs were at the core of the party attention—these disclaimers were universally rejected. Stalin was not permitted to eat his cake and have it too.

Having usurped the supreme right to judge the best road for the Communists to follow, Stalin sought to bring the movement under his complete control. In this he was only partially successful. It was relatively easy to dominate the central apparat of the Comintern and the Moscow colony of Communist exiles. It was much more difficult to manipulate the affairs of individual parties, but in the end this was accomplished by bureaucratizing the administrations of the principal parties and by wholesale purges of anti-Stalinist elements. Bilateralism established in Soviet relations with other parties made them directly and separately dependent on Moscow's good will. The role of the Comintern's Executive Committee (filled with Stalin's stooges) declined correspondingly. It issued whatever directives Stalin wanted and served as a secondary channel through which foreign Communist leaders communicated their requests and grievances for Soviet consideration.

A great master of bureaucratic management, Stalin concentrated operational functions of the Comintern in the International Department of the CC CPSU, where each party was closely watched and personal dossiers on its prominent leaders were kept. The physical links with individual parties were maintained through the network of the Foreign Department of the GPU-NKVD-MVD, which could be relied upon to keep these links secret and which actually employed a number of important foreign Communists as its agents. The expertise developed in these two departments allowed Stalin to follow closely developments in each party, create and cultivate rivalries, and by manipulating factional struggles, by playing on the fears and ambitions of key individuals, assure their obedience. Once the principle that what's good for the Soviet Union is good for the world Communist movement was firmly established and accepted, Stalin could utilize each party's resources for Soviet needs, be it recruitment of spies, saboteurs, and killers, or launching political strikes at a time of Moscow's choosing.

The streamlining of management of foreign Communist affairs, however, did not and could not convert the movement, responsive as it was to Soviet wishes, into a perfect instrument of Soviet foreign policy. For one thing, there is plenty of evidence that although Soviet intelligence-gathering was quite extensive and information available to Stalin and his associates was plentiful, Soviet comprehension of social and political processes in foreign countries often was defective, not indicating what action by a local Communist party would be most effective. For another, there were natural limits to what Communists could do short of committing political suicide. The parties *had* to remain revolutionary, combatting the "establishments" of their respective countries. They *had* to take strong positions favoring national minorities because these were their natural constituencies in many countries. They *had* to attack social democrats, at whose expense they expanded their popular base: this tactic was predetermined by the very *raison d'être* of the Comintern since its inception. Finally, because conditions varied widely from country to country, the Comintern could never adequately reconcile the contradiction between national interests of the parties and their inter-nationalism. The principle of international solidarity called for unity and strict following of common policy embodied in Comintern resolutions reflecting Soviet foreign policy needs. Aside from this, parties had little in common and their specific interests, subordinated to those of the Soviet Union, frequently suffered from inability to be flexible.

Even the growth of Fascism in Europe did not provide an alternate common denominator. German Communists continued to regard social democrats as their chief enemy until Hitler became Chancellor and turned against both. Good Soviet relations with Mussolini's Italy pre-cluded any substantial activity of Italian Communists. In Romania, Com-munists were for a while *de facto* allies of the Iron Guard, and in Bulgaria of IMRO. And in some countries Fascistic groups were too in-significant for the Communists to fight against, resolutions of the Com-intern's 7th Congress notwithstanding.

As Nazi Germany emerged as the main menace to the Soviet Union, the Comintern called for Popular Fronts against Fascism, to include social democrats and other groups of the left. But the social demo-crats, vividly remembering past Communist hostility and savage attempts to destroy their power, mistrusted the motives and patriotism of the Communists and cooperated with them only half-heartedly. There was also a practical reason for it: even this limited cooperation cost the social democrats heavily in public support. In France in the late 1930s, the popular slogan "Better Hitler than Léon Blum" manifested the break-down of national unity in the face of the external threat.

The Spanish Civil War became a sacred cause for the Communists, in part because many of them were by then secretly disenchanted with Stalinism. Stalin, who understood this and who, besides, did not approve any sacred causes other than upholding Soviet interests, was finally com-pelled to give the Spanish loyalists limited material and military assist-ance. He probably valued the improvement of the Soviet image among European and American liberals, tarnished by the purges in Russia; he also wanted to draw the attention of Western democracies to the Fascist peril and hoped to isolate Germany and Italy, the "bad guys" of the Spanish tragedy. But his real attitude toward the sacred cause itself was better manifested by the activities of the NKVD mission in Spain, which liquidated a number of members of the International Brigade, especially Trotskyites, Mensheviks, and anarchists. Most of the Soviet veterans of Spain were shot shortly after they had returned to Russia. The Spanish Communist Party itself was, of course, decimated after Franco's victory.

Stalin had to conclude that Popular Fronts were a failure. All they did was to polarize politics in a number of countries to Soviet disadvantage. In this polarization, the right gained because Hitler and Mussolini posed as defenders of Western civilization against the Red menace. One outcome of Spain was Munich, which again raised the specter of a European imperialist crusade against the Soviet Union.

We can surmise that in the late 1930s Stalin did not regard European Communists any longer as a valuable arm of Soviet foreign policy. The savagery of the last phase of purge in Russia, in which many foreign Communist leaders who had escaped to the Moscow heaven perished, seems to confirm this conclusion. We may also guess, for instance, that the mysterious dissolution of the Polish Communist Party some time in 1938 was Stalin's belated attempt to reach an understanding with Poland in order to prevent its slipping into the German sphere.

After its last congress in 1935, the Comintern rarely made the news. As European developments accelerated after Munich and Stalin made up his mind to make a compact with Hitler, this symbol of international Communist unity became a liability. Although its Executive Committee still functioned as a liaison with foreign Communist leaders, Stalin probably considered dissolving the Comintern even before Ribbentrop's momentous visit to Moscow in August 1939.

The purges of the 1930s brought about a virtual extinction of whatever had remained of indigenous revolutionary internationalism in Communist parties. With the advent of the Nazi-Soviet collaboration, Communists finally committed political suicide as they were forced to acquiesce in this new twist of Soviet foreign policy. During the two years of collaboration, 1939–1941, Moscow never interceded with Berlin on behalf of hapless Communists who were hounded by Fascist and quasi-Fascist regimes in Nazi-dominated Europe; as if to demonstrate his utter indifference to their lot, in November 1940, in exchange for some minor but tangible concessions, Stalin offered to join the Anti-Comintern Pact, an offer which Hitler did not have enough humor to accept.

After the German invasion of Russia, the surviving Communists resumed their anti-Fascist activities, but this time it was a qualitatively different phenomenon. There was little direction and even less aid from Moscow, and they operated—where they did—within the national contexts of resistance. Their principal objective was not so much to help the Soviet Union in the moment of deadly peril, and sometimes not even to combat the Axis occupiers, but to prepare for the seizure of power in their respective countries at the end of the war. Their principal enemy in Eastern Europe and the Balkans was the nationalist resistance groups connected with governments-in-exile in Cairo and London. All the same, they could pose as *bona fide* anti-Fascists and patriots, thereby laying the foundation for resurrection of their parties.

The expansion of these parties, when it came, brought into the ranks thousands of people who had only a vague notion about Marxism-Leninism or international solidarity; postwar Communism was vastly different from that conceived by Lenin. The aim of the parties was to seize power in their respective countries, and the Soviets alone could help them to attain power and to hold it against internal and external enemies. Communists universally held the Soviet Union in awe and regarded Stalin as a demigod: he demonstrated in Eastern Europe that Soviet might was absolutely indispensable in overturning old ruling classes and giving Communist parties the muscle they needed to carry out revolutionary transformation of their nations.

Stalin was fully aware of this dependence. He resented the handful of surviving old leaders who still clung to the outdated principles of international solidarity. He assisted in the revolutionary transformation of East European states, not out of idealistic notions but because this transformation advanced Soviet interests; in this new setting he saw no room for fraternal reciprocity. All he expected was submissiveness and obedience. But what he apparently had lost sight of was that the links with foreign Communist parties had greatly weakened during the war and so did Moscow's capacity for manipulating them from within, especially in countries where there was no physical Soviet presence.

After the glorious victory over Germany and Japan, Stalin attached even less importance to the Communist movement as an instrument of Soviet foreign policy. This victory secured Eastern Europe for Communism and gave respectability and influence to Communist parties elsewhere. Stalin's old contention that Soviet might was the key to the success of the Communist cause seemed to be justified. The appearance of ideological unity was maintained; no party dared to take a political stand deviating from that of Moscow; in the Cold War years Communists were useful in launching all sorts of peace campaigns, and that appeared sufficient. Stalin made no effort to resurrect the Comintern, dissolved in 1943, to provide an alternate focal point of loyalty for international Communism. Communist solidarity meant only one thing: unswerving devotion to the Soviet Union, which Stalin had every reason to take for granted. But in dealing with "imperialists" he chose to rely on the newly acquired power and prestige of the Soviet Union, reinforced by the image of the monolithic Soviet bloc of nations which Communists ruled by 1948.

Tito's "rebellion" jolted Stalin. Belatedly he discovered that his inability to manipulate the Yugoslav Communist Party from within, to rid it of heretics, made "imperialists" question his power to control the movement, made them talk about "cracks in the Kremlin Wall." Determined to make sure that the challenge would not be repeated elsewhere, he resorted to the old tested tool of intimidation. In the wave of purges unleashed after Tito's defection, most of the old-line leaders, still given to idealistic notions of Communist solidarity, perished. By the time of Stalin's death, Soviet unchallengeable authority seemed re-established. It took his successors three years to conclude that foreign Communists could no longer be taken for granted and to reappraise the nature of Soviet relations with international Communism. The new policy was inaugurated at the 20th CPSU Congress in 1956 and at the Moscow Conference of Communist and Workers' Parties in 1957. "Socialist internationalism" and the abandonment of the Soviet model as mandatory for other Communist states opened a new page in the history of the movement.

Stalin and the Chinese Communists

During two decades following the Revolution, nowhere was the conflict between Soviet commitment to international Communism on the one hand and Soviet state interests on the other as pronounced as in China. The Soviet Far East, underpopulated and underdeveloped, linked with the rest of Russia by thousands of miles of one-track railroad, was the most exposed and vulnerable region of the country. In addition, the Soviets had inherited from the Tsarist period important economic assets in northern Manchuria in the form of the strategic Chinese Eastern Railway (CER) and its many enterprises, which they wanted to preserve. But southern Manchuria was dominated by Japan, a traditional enemy which had defeated Russia in the war of 1904–1905 and attempted to seize the Far East during the Russian civil war. Indigenous Chinese authorities in Manchuria were anti-Communist and pro-Japanese, among other things offering protection to thousands of White Russians who had fought the Reds in the civil war and were bent on causing difficulties to the Soviets.

Fully aware of the precariousness of their position in dealing with the Chinese, the Soviets placed their bets on Sun Yat-sen's nationalist and anti-imperialist party, the Kuomintang (KMT), and very materially helped Sun's successor, Chiang Kai-shek, in his bid for unification of China under KMT rule. But in assisting the KMT, Moscow inevitably had to sacrifice interests of the Chinese Communist Party (CCP), which regarded the KMT, especially after Chiang's violent onslaught against it in April 1927, in which thousands of Communists were slaughtered, as its most hateful enemy.

Stalin's personal involvement in Chinese Communist affairs began in 1924–1925 when he fought Trotsky over the issue of revolution in China. Together with romantic intellectuals, then prevailing in the CCP leadership, Trotsky wanted to concentrate on struggle against the native bourgeoisie—including the KMT—in order to seize power in China. Stalin, already skeptical in his appraisal of revolutionary potential in foreign lands and reflecting pragmatic interests of the Soviet state, won in this debate. The Comintern directed the CCP to cooperate loyally with the KMT while retaining its autonomy and identity. This line did not materially change after the 1927 massacre. The Soviet Union maintained active diplomatic relations with Chiang Kai-shek's government until July 1929, when it broke them because of the increased harassment of Soviet CER personnel in Manchuria by local KMT authorities. Following this diplomatic gesture the Soviets applied military pressure and actually deployed force in Manchuria, and by the end of the year the *status quo ante* on the railroad was restored. Formal diplomatic relations with Chiang's government in Nanking, however, were resumed only in 1932, after Japan had occupied Manchuria and posed a clear and present danger to both China and the Soviet Union.[2]

The Japanese threat to the Soviet Union determined Stalin's (and, conversely, Comintern) attitudes toward Chinese Communists until the end of the Second World War. The Soviet goal was to diminish this threat by diplomatic compromises, avoiding anything which could aggravate the situation, while gradually building up industrial and military strength in the Khabarovsk region bordering on Manchuria. Another goal was to encourage Chiang Kai-shek to resist the Japanese and strengthen his government, constantly challenged by ambitious warlords heading unruly KMT factions. In these circumstances, it was only natural that the Comintern, through its Executive Committee (ECC), consistently tried to dampen CCP revolutionary spirit. The ECC repeatedly rejected CCP appeals to permit it to launch uprisings against the KMT, appeals stemming from the unrealistic assumption, common among foreign Communists, that the Soviet Union would be bound to come to their assistance in any armed struggle against the "class enemy." One CCP "plan" was to start an uprising in Manchuria so as to provoke war between Japan and the Soviet Union in which both the Japanese and the local KMT warlord's forces would presumably be defeated. The Comintern not only condemned this "plan" as dangerous adventurism but also removed its author, Li Li-san, from CCP leadership. It also ordered the CCP not to nurture such plans in the future, concentrating instead on a gradual accumulation of strength in the areas controlled by it.

This line was stressed time and again during the 7th Comintern Congress in August 1935. Although it convened at a time when the ranks of the CCP armies, then moving north in the Long March and constantly attacked by KMT forces, had dwindled to a mere 25–30,000, the Comintern unequivocally placed the "sacred struggle against Japan and for salvation of the Chinese Motherland" ahead of the revolutionary goals.[3] CCP leaders were split over the question as to whom to regard as the principal enemy but dutifully, if grudgingly, approved the Comintern line. In actuality, CCP enmity for the KMT remained unshaken, if only because Chiang was determined to exterminate Communist forces, viewing them as a main obstacle to consolidation of KMT rule in China.

Japan's attack on North China in July 1937 changed the situation substantially and an uneasy alliance between the antagonists was established. Chiang recognized CCP autonomy in the Special Border Area Region, with its capital in Yenan; the CCP, by then led by Mao Tse-tung, renamed its Red Army the 8th National-Revolutionary Army of China, and dropped all the slogans calling for the overthrow of the Kuomintang. This united KMT-CCP front against Japanese aggression was established despite private objections of the "leftist" elements in the CCP. Still anxious to carry out revolutionary struggle against the KMT, Mao himself was known to disagree with the Comintern line, which, to him, amounted to betrayal of revolutionary principles. The watchful Comintern, although recognizing psychological difficulties confronting the Communists in accepting the hated Chiang Kai-shek as an ally in a common struggle, repeatedly condemned "leftist" tendencies. Since questioning Stalin's wisdom was something no Communist could do with impunity, Mao acquiesced. He also accepted Moscow's decision to channel all its aid to China—amounting to $250 million in 1938–1939 alone—through Chiang's government, which, in turn, until 1940 subsidized the 8th (and later the 4th) National-Revolutionary Army operating out of the Special Border Area Region.

The KMT-CCP united front formally lasted until the end of the war but came under increased strain after 1938, as the Japanese progressed in their conquest of China. The KMT leadership felt that the Communists weren't doing enough against the aggressor, that in spite of their numerical growth and expansion of territory they controlled, CCP forces tended to limit themselves to guerrilla activities, leaving it to the KMT armies to combat the enemy in open warfare. Recent Soviet studies indicate that Stalin essentially shared Chiang's view, suspecting—as Chiang did—that the CCP remained relatively passive in the war against Japan in order to conserve and build up its own strength for future battles for the seizure of power in China. It is easy to deduce that the latter task did not rate high among Stalin's priorities.

The significance of Soviet historical writings on relations with the Chinese Communists cannot be overrated because they shed unique light on inner workings of the international Communist system, traditionally veiled in utmost secrecy. Their appearance has been dictated by the imperatives arising from the Sino-Soviet conflict, by the recognized need to explain its antecedents to the Soviet public. While the Maoists, in their attacks on Soviet leadership, have abstained from criticizing Stalin's policies, ascribing Soviet "deviations" to the errors and political degeneration of his successors, the Soviets feel compelled to go further back into history, to expose Maoist perfidy, because China's turnaround had challenged the most fundamental premises of Communist ideology and Soviet statecraft.

One of the most revealing recent documents is a volume of diaries of P. L. Vladimirov, who, disguised as a TASS military correspondent, was *de facto* Soviet representative (initially the "Comintern liaison officer") at Mao Tse-tung's headquarters in Yenan in 1942–1945. His diaries were prepared for publication by his son, Yu. P. Vlasov, no doubt on instructions from the Central Committee of the CPSU.[4]

One cannot assume, of course, that Vladimirov's judgments were identical with those of Stalin and other Soviet leaders. But being, in effect, Moscow's envoy in Yenan for such a long time (he had been to China on sensitive assignments twice before), he can be assumed to reflect rather closely the contemporary views of the Soviet leadership. The importance of his role is further underscored by the fact that although Mao had his own channel of communications to the Comintern, in important matters he preferred to deal through Vladimirov. Regarding him as "Moscow's Eye," Mao spent endless hours in intimate conversations with him, explaining (or "covering up") his actions and policies, almost as if he were explaining them to Stalin himself. The diaries are obviously incomplete—sensitive details of the chain of command allowing Vladimirov to reach the top of the Soviet hierarchy in a few hours, for instance, are omitted—and some entries may have been slightly "doctored" to reflect the Soviet-Chinese clash in the 1960s. Nevertheless, their authenticity seems unquestionable; a good part of what he says has been corroborated by other Soviet authors who had access to secret Comintern and CC CPSU archives,[5] and they deserve most attentive analysis by students of Communist affairs.

There are several major themes in Vladimirov's diaries. First and foremost, there is a deep-seated suspicion of Mao's loyalty to the Soviet Union, which was supposed to be taken for granted in those days. There is great bitterness and indignation at the CCP's failure to do its best in the struggle against the Japanese, who, in Moscow's view, represented an imminent threat to Russia, at least until the tide of the war against Germany had turned after the battles of Stalingrad and Kursk. Not only did Mao fail his "sacred internationalist duty" to do everything to weaken this dangerous enemy of the Soviet Union; Vladimirov reports that during the spectacular German offensive in the first years of the war Mao lost faith in the Soviet Union, expected Germany to win the war, and resolved to attend to CCP particular interests independently of the destiny of world Communism.

Second in importance in Vladimirov's indictment was the prolonged purge which was conducted from the beginning of 1942 in the CCP, the so-called rectification campaign, or the Cheng Feng movement. It was aimed at consolidation of Mao's own power in the party and, remembering Stalin's own purges in the 1930s, Vladimirov would not have attached excessive importance to it had it not been for the fact that among those who came under attack were prominent trusted friends of the Soviet Union, the "true internationalists." Given this circumstance, Vladimirov could not fail to interpret the rectification campaign as an unfriendly, if not altogether hostile act. Almost equally significant appeared to him the systematic efforts of K'ang Sheng, Mao's chief of secret police and a known enemy of the Soviet Union, to isolate him in Yenan and restrict his ability to gather information independently for transmission to Moscow.

Thirdly, there is a peculiar ambivalence in Vladimirov's attitude toward the CCP-KMT conflict, vividly illustrated by one episode. In July 1943, rumors swept Yenan, causing near-panic among CCP leaders, that Kuomintang armies were about to attack the Special Border Area Region. Mao came to see Vladimirov, to request Moscow to discourage Chiang from this action. Vladimirov immediately transmitted the request and appropriate pressure was brought upon Chiang, who then called off the offensive. Yet although Communist solidarity took precedence, one can almost sense that Vladimirov secretly wished that the KMT would teach the CCP a good lesson. Doubtless a good Communist, Stalin's envoy was also a Russian patriot. As such he was more sympathetic to the KMT government of China, which bore the burden of the struggle against the common enemy, than to the CCP; this sympathy did not diminish even during the great Japanese offensive in the summer and fall of 1944, when Chinese resistance virtually collapsed.

Vladimirov records with considerable sarcasm fluctuations of Mao's attitudes toward the Soviet Union. As the Soviet counteroffensive against the Germans progressed, Mao became more and more solicitous in conversations with Vladimirov; manifestations of anti-Sovietism in Yenan, so pronounced earlier, disappeared as if by magic. By late 1944 there was a tantalizing guessing game going on in the CCP headquarters: whether the Soviet Union would or wouldn't, after defeating Germany, turn against Japan. Since such an attack would mean employment of a large Soviet military force in Manchuria and perhaps in North China, Mao's strategy against the KMT, and CCP prospects for gaining power in China, would heavily depend on Moscow. Understanding that, Vladimirov watched with unconcealed disgust the scheming and calculating Maoists, concerned exclusively with their own fortunes and totally indifferent to what, to him, was of paramount importance: Russia's gigantic struggle against German and Japanese imperialism.

With equal mistrust and concern, he recorded how earlier in the year (in July), the arrival of the U.S. Observers' Group in Yenan raised Mao's hopes for establishing direct links with the United States. Mao counted on obtaining American military supplies, to enable the CCP to fight Japan—and if need be, use them later in civil war against the KMT. Aware of American disenchantment with Chiang's government, Mao also counted on U.S. political support, which could assure the CCP power and influence, quite out of proportion to its actual strength, in some future coalition government. These hopes were soon dashed but, needless to say, Vladimirov regarded them as bordering on treason. His conviction that the CCP Chairman was a hypocritical, cunning opportunist, not to be trusted under any circumstances, had firmed.

This conviction probably accounted for Vladimirov's decline upon his return to Moscow late in 1945. Even if Stalin felt the same way about Mao, broad political and strategic considerations required utilization of the CCP in Manchuria, then already occupied by Soviet troops. Stalin didn't feel he had to *trust* Mao: the very presence of an unchallengeable Soviet power in Manchuria would, in his view, greatly restrict Maoist capacity for mischief and strengthen the pro-Soviet, "internationalist" wing of the CCP.

Stalin may have also shared Vladimirov's relatively benign view of the KMT government; in expectation that it would rule China after the war, he concluded with it, in August 1945, the Treaty of Friendship and Alliance, which granted the Soviet Union special rights in Manchuria. But Stalin did not regard Chiang Kai-shek as a free agent, capable of carrying out independent policies. Having assumed that the United States had become the principal enemy of the Soviet Union, Stalin expected it to manipulate Chinese politics to Soviet disadvantage. Sitting in remote Yenan, Vladimirov did not display this awareness; he was too absorbed in local developments to be able to appraise properly a broader picture and the emerging configuration of forces in the world at large.

In the end, however, Vladimirov's unshakable anti-Maoist convictions were appreciated. In 1948, shortly after CCP armies launched their first major offensive against the KMT, he reappeared in China as Soviet consul-general in Shanghai. He stayed there through the rest of the civil war, returning to Moscow only in 1951. In the following year he was sent to Burma as Soviet ambassador. He died, apparently of cancer, in September 1953.

A careful reader of recent Soviet studies dealing with the immediate postwar years gets an impression of considerable uncertainty in Moscow as to how to conduct external affairs in a manner corresponding to the new role of the Soviet Union as a major world power. This uncertainty stemmed, in part, from a shortage of knowledge and experience, but primarily from painful awareness of the enormous inner weakness of the country, only beginning to recover from the consequences of a devastating war and already confronting the hostility of the West, suggesting a possibility of another armed conflict in a not-too-distant future. In the areas physically controlled by Soviet military power, as in Eastern Europe, the Soviets could resort to force and use familiar police methods in attaining their political and security objectives. The situation was quite different in the Far East.

The treaty of August 1945, which left Manchuria under seemingly effective Soviet control, recognized the sovereignty of the KMT government over all of China. The major Manchurian railroads and the naval base in Port Arthur were supposed to be in joint Soviet-Chinese ownership, but were in fact in Soviet hands. The Soviets took possession of all former Japanese property, from the Kwantung army arsenals to plants and factories which they immediately proceeded to dismantle, shipping machinery and equipment to Russia. For a while there was no challenge to Soviet supremacy but KMT armies were moving northward, reclaiming one province after another, and Chiang Kai-shek appeared determined to extend his government to Manchuria.

In order to limit KMT capacity for challenging their dominance, the Soviets resolved to create a political infrastructure favorable to Soviet interests. To that end, they encouraged the Chinese Communists to form local administrations throughout the occupied region. Since there were few native Manchurian Communists, the Soviets had to rely on a few hundred trusted Chinese brought from Russia at the end of the war but primarily on CCP forces, led by Lin Piao and Kao Kan and numbering about 150,000, which penetrated Manchuria from North China before KMT armies had reached it. They were well-trained and disciplined and consisted of dedicated Communists but were poorly armed: two-thirds of the soldiers had no arms whatsoever; each rifle had only 30 rounds of ammunition; there was one machine-gun for every 100 soldiers. Except for a few pieces of artillery captured from the surrendering Japanese, CCP troops had no means for fighting a serious battle.[6] Soviet authorities supplied them with adequate amounts of ammunition and side arms but, for the time being, with little else, assigning them primarily political and police functions. All Communist units and organizations were subordinated to the CCP Northeastern Bureau headed by elements friendly to the Soviet Union and responsive to the needs of the Soviet command in Manchuria. It can be surmised that during the first two postwar years, when Communist forces everywhere were under relentless pressure from the KMT, the CCP leadership from Mao Tsetung down (Mao remained in far-away Yenan until it was captured, in March 1947, by KMT armies and he had to flee to other remote areas of North China) fully realized their dependence on the Soviets and cooperated with them loyally.

"Loyally," of course, did not mean happily. There were doubtless plenty of reservations among CCP leaders about the Soviets' decision to make a compact with Chiang Kai-shek, whose government, now the war was over, the CCP could legitimately claim to be its prime enemy. But the Communists' position was in fact weak, and the areas they had controlled were under attack by vastly superior KMT forces. In these circumstances it was painfully evident that the Soviet Union alone—acting in its own interest rather than out of the ideological motive of Communist solidarity—could help assure the CCP's survival by supplying it with weapons and other essentials and, it was hoped, by trying to restrain Chiang Kai-shek from carrying his anti-Communist campaign to its logical bloody end. Military assistance was in fact given, although, outside Manchuria, it isn't clear how generously. Chiang, however, was more confident than ever that he could unify China under KMT rule and was determined to seek a military, rather than political, solution to the conflict with the CCP. The KMT offensive through 1945 and early in 1946 against CCP-held regions progressed successfully everywhere except in Manchuria, which was still "controlled" by the Soviets.

So long as the Soviet occupation continued, KMT and CCP elements coexisted in southern Manchuria rather peacefully. But in March 1946 the Soviets began withdrawal of their troops, completing it by early May. The six KMT armies, with more following, advanced on their heels, crushing CCP attempts to retain possession of key cities and towns. Suspecting that the KMT operations were conducted with the knowledge and encouragement of the United States and determined to prevent American influence, however indirect, from spreading to the proximity of Russia, Stalin invited Chiang Kai-shek, early in May, to come to Moscow for discussions. Chiang declined.[7] Although he simultaneously rejected United States insistence on formation of a coalition government with the CCP, viewing it as an attempt to "neutralize China," Stalin, who had never trusted the sincerity of the American mediation effort, drew his own conclusions.

The KMT offensive stopped at Mukden. Under pressure of the United States to reach a compromise with the CCP (in July 1946 a U. S. embargo on shipments of military material to China went into effect), and not daring to challenge Soviet authority in northern Manchuria, Chiang abandoned his cherished goal of liquidating CCP military power. Communist forces withdrew behind the Sungari River, where they could regroup and reorganize in safety. The Soviets supplied them with large quantities of Japanese heavy weapons and Lin Piao's army, reinforced by some 100,000 North Korean troops, gradually developed into a formidable force. In the fall of 1947 the Communists launched a counteroffensive on several fronts in Manchuria and North China; all of Manchuria was in their hands by November. Peking fell in January 1949; and by the end of the year the People's Republic of China was an established fact.

An equally established fact is that Stalin derived little satisfaction from the CCP victory and even less from Mao Tse-tung's personal triumph. As Milovan Djilas, the only high-ranking Communist who has candidly relayed his observations of Stalin, remarked, it was not correct to assume that Stalin "was generally against revolutions" only because he abstained, "always in decisive moments, from supporting the Chinese,

Spanish, and in many ways even the Yugoslav revolutions." But, Djilas points out, Stalin opposed revolutions

> conditionally, that is to the degree to which the revolution went beyond interests of the Soviet state. He felt instinctively that the creation of revolutionary centers outside of Moscow could endanger its supremacy in world communism. . . That is why he helped revolutions only up to a certain point—up to where he could control them—but he was always ready to leave them in the lurch whenever they slipped out of his grasp.[8]

In January 1948, discussing with Djilas and others the prospects for a Communist victory in the civil war in Greece, Stalin insisted that "the uprising in Greece must be stopped, and as quickly as possible," because Great Britain and the United States would not permit it to succeed. When someone mentioned the recent successes of the Chinese Communists, Stalin remarked:

> Yes, the Chinese comrades have succeeded [but] China is a different case, relations in the Far East are different. True, we, too, can make a mistake! Here, when the war with Japan ended, we invited the Chinese comrades to reach an agreement as to how a modus vivendi with Chiang Kai-shek might be found. They agreed with us in word, but in deed they did it in their own way when they got home: they mustered their forces and struck. It has been shown that they were right, and not we.[9]

Djilas proceeds to comment that Stalin probably anticipated "future danger to his own work and to his own empire from the new communist great power, especially since there were no prospects of subordinating it internally." And he adds that Stalin "knew that every revolution, simply by virtue of being new, also becomes a separate epicenter and shapes its own government and state."[10]

These were doubtless valid observations. Djilas, however, did not know what Stalin did: that Mao, far from being a good internationalist, had a long record of anti-Soviet tendencies, which included making overtures to the Americans in 1944–1945 and possibly even in 1946, during CCP negotiations with General George C. Marshall. In fact, it can be assumed that until the outbreak of the Korean War Stalin couldn't be certain that Mao would not attempt to collude with the United States against the Soviet Union; he doubtless took notice of suspicious noises in the United States, where important figures spoke in 1949 and 1950 of the desirability of "turning Mao Tse-tung into another Tito."[11] Although many prominent CCP leaders were considered to be friendly to the Soviet Union at that time, Stalin had no means for organizing a plot in order to dislodge Chairman Mao: manipulating CCP politics from within was well beyond Soviet power.

Yet Stalin held a few trump cards up his sleeve even before Korea. The CCP as a whole was firmly committed to the concept of international Communist unity; his own and the Soviet Union's authority in the Communist movement were at their zenith; the People's Republic of China was virtually isolated, in part because of the intense xenophobia widespread among the Chinese; China's economy was in ruins; and the Communists could not be sure that KMT forces in Taiwan, perhaps backed by the United States, would not be able to stage a comeback. These impressive "objective factors" tied the PRC to the Soviet Union, the only power capable of offering it economic assistance and military protection.

Making no attempt to win Mao's affection, Stalin deliberately made the leader of China cool his heels for ten weeks in Moscow (December 1949-February 1950) before the Treaty of Friendship, Alliance and Mutual Assistance between the two Communist states was signed.[12] The terms of the treaty were much less generous than Mao, in his then chronic overrating of Soviet might, had anticipated, but having nowhere else to go, he praised Stalin's wisdom and magnanimity.

Mao's freedom of international maneuver was greatly reduced with the Korean War; the appearance of the U.S. Seventh Fleet in the Formosa Straits made "liberation" of Taiwan impossible and the anti-American posture of the PRC inevitable. At the end of 1950 Mao yielded to Soviet pressure, sending hundreds of thousands of Chinese "volunteers" to fight in Korea, thereby dooming the PRC to nearly two decades of international isolation and continuing dependence on the Soviet Union.

NOTES

1. A comprehensive ideological discussion of the foundations of socialist unity is contained in *The World Socialist System and Anti-Communism*, Moscow, 1972 (in English).

2. For political developments of that period and their latest Soviet interpretation, see *Komintern i Vostok* ("Comintern and the East"), Moscow, 1969; particularly the entries by Glunin, Grigoriev, Kukushkin, and Levinson. See also Richard C. Thornton, *The Comintern and Chinese Communists, 1928–1931,* University of Washington Press, 1969, and Robert C. North, *Moscow and Chinese Communists,* Stanford University Press, 1953.

3. See North, p. 183 note.

4. *Osobyi rayon Kitaya: 1942–1945* ("Special Border Area Region: 1942–1945"), Moscow: Novosti, 1973.

5. Cf., for example, M. I. Sladkovsky, ed., *Noveyshaya istoriya Kitaya* ("Modern History of China"), Moscow, 1972, or O. Vladimirov and V. Ryazantsev, *Stranitsy politicheskoi biografii Mao Tze-duna* ("Pages from Political Biography of Mao Tse-tung"), Moscow, 1969.

6. *Noveyshaya istoriya Kitaya,* p. 210.

7. See Richard C. Thornton, *China: The Struggle for Power, 1917–1972,* Indiana University Press, 1973, pp. 193–195.

8. Milovan Djilas, *Conversations with Stalin,* Harcourt, Brace and World, 1962, p. 132.

9. Ibid., p. 182. Stalin apparently refers to a visit in Moscow in 1945 of a Chinese delegation headed by Kao Kan and Liu Shao-ch'i.

10. Ibid., p. 183.

11. See U.S. Senate, Committee on Foreign Relations, "The United States and Communist China in 1949 and 1950: The Question of Rapprochement and Recognition," GPO, 1973.

12. *Khrushchev Remembers: The Last Testament,* Little, Brown & Co., 1974, pp. 239–244.

Soviet-Chinese Relations, 1945–1970

Introduction

The development of the world revolutionary process shows with increasing clarity the tremendous effect the Great October Socialist Revolution has had on that process, and the tasks of investigating the relations between the first socialist state in the world, born that October, and other countries and peoples is becoming increasingly more important. The task of studying Sino-Soviet relations is of primary importance in this regard, for without such study it is impossible to arrive at an accurate view of the true picture of the modern world.

The history of relations between the Soviet Union and China is not simply a history of interstate ties between two countries. It is inseparable from the chronicles of the national liberation and revolutionary struggle of the Chinese people; the most important facet of that struggle is the theme of help and support rendered by the Soviet Union. Relations with the USSR during the post-October period played an exceptionally important role in the development of China and became an integral factor in the root transformations which occurred in Chinese society. It is here that the Great October Socialist Revolution, which V. I. Lenin called a turning point for the world and a new chapter in world history, found its concrete manifestation in terms of international value.

The October Revolution tore a gigantic hole in the world capitalist system, and to an enormous degree lessened the pressure of imperialist powers on China, thus making immeasurably more simple the struggle of the Chinese people for social and national liberation. The result of the October Revolution was not only to remove Russia from the ranks of imperialist states threatening the national independence of China, but also to convert Russia into a country solidly supporting the national liberation struggle of the Chinese workers; ultimately this was the most important international factor in the successful development of that struggle.

Leading revolutionary figures in China did not hesitate to praise the October Revolution's historical importance to their own country's destiny. One of the founders of the Chinese Communist Party (CCP),

Professor Li Ta-chao, wrote, "A workers' and peasants' state and government was born in the flame of the October Revolution. This state is the motherland, the vanguard, and the great stronghold for workers and peasants throughout the world."[1]

In its relations with China, the Soviet Union has steadfastly held to class positions, constantly proceeding on the basis of interests of revolutionary forces of the Chinese people. Guided by the principles of proletarian internationalism, Soviet Communists considered it to be their duty to help the Chinese working class establish, on the basis of Marxism-Leninism, its political vanguard—the CCP.

From its very beginning the CCP had to function in a complicated and difficult situation. Sharply focused was the task of developing flexible strategy and tactics for a revolutionary struggle responsive to the historical conditions of a semifeudal and semicolonial China. Our Leninist party willingly came to the aid of the young CCP, in helping the training of Marxist cadres and in handing over to the CCP its theoretical legacy and the wealth of practical experience gained in the long struggle of the Russian proletariat.

V. I. Lenin devoted a great deal of attention to the development of the Chinese revolution. His theoretical works on the national-colonial question, his advice to the Communists in the East, and his talks with the Chinese representatives in the Comintern formed the basis for the revolutionary strategy and tactics of the CCP. Such of Lenin's works as *Report to the II All-Russian Congress of Communistic Organizations of the Peoples of the East, Report of the Commission on National and Colonial Questions* to the II Congress of the Comintern, *Better Less, But Better,* and many others, illumined the path of struggle for the Chinese people.

The Comintern was of great theoretical assistance to the CCP, making valuable contributions to solutions of the most important problems surrounding the revolutionary movement in China, including such problems as building the party, hegemony of the working class, questions of allies of the working class, role of the peasantry in China, a unified anti-imperialist front, establishment of revolutionary bases in the countryside, and the building of a Chinese Red Army.

As Chinese Communists have admitted, positions taken on questions of the revolutionary struggle in China, as set forth in our party's documents, and including speeches by J. V. Stalin, during the 1920s and 1930s, were invaluable to the CCP. They touched on the problems of the motivating forces of the Chinese revolution, its peculiarities and basic tasks at various stages. They countained conclusions with respect to the inevitability of development of the bourgeois-democratic revolution in China into a socialist revolution, to the need for transition to an armed struggle against militant counterrevolutionary forces, and to the role of the united front.

Such Chinese Communist-internationalists as Li Ta-chao, P'eng P'ai, Teng Chung-hsia, Ch'ü Ch'iu-pai, Ts'ai Ho-shen, Fang Chih-min, and others were well aware of the magnitude of help and support given by our party and country in the successful development of the revolutionary movement in China. "The Chinese Communist-internationalists, the best sons of the Chinese people," said the greetings from the Central Committee of the Communist Party of the Soviet Union (CC CPSU) on the occasion of the 45th anniversary of the CCP, "have constantly stressed the importance of unity with the working class in the USSR, with the Soviet people, and with the CPSU in the victory of the Chinese revolution."[2] The Chinese Communists-internationalists did much to educate members of the CCP, as well as Chinese workers, in the spirit of loyalty to the ideas of October and to the brotherly friendship between the peoples of China and the Soviet Union.

As early as December 1917 the Soviet government proposed to the government of China that the question of Sino-Soviet relations be reviewed from the standpoint of foreign policy principles of the first socialist state. The Soviet government took the initiative in holding talks with the Peking government, formally considered the national government of China, concerning the annulment of inequitable treaties and the establishment of relations based on the principles of equality and mutual respect for sovereignty. The Soviet government announced the return to the Chinese people of everything that had been taken from them by the Tsarist government independently, or jointly with Japan and other powers.

The workers and peasants of revolutionary Russia declared their brotherly solidarity with the workers of China. The Council of People's Commissars of the RSFSR, led by V. I. Lenin, on July 25, 1919, issued an appeal to the Chinese people, and to the governments of South and North China, which said, "We bring freedom to the people from the yoke of the foreign bayonet and from the yoke of foreign gold, which oppress the enslaved peoples of the East, including in particular the Chinese people. We bring help not only to our working classes, but the Chinese people as well. . . ."[3]

Victorious revolutionary Russia from the very beginning was inseparably linked with the national liberation movement in China, providing it with every conceivable assistance and support. The brightest pages in the history of Sino-Soviet relations were those written during the years of the heroic struggle of the Chinese people against the Japanese aggressors (1937–1945). The truly internationalist position of our country with respect to China was clearly manifested during this period of the most terrible of national trials of the Chinese people. "When the war against the Japanese invaders began in 1937," stated the VII Congress of the CCP, "the Soviet Union once again was the first to come to the aid of China in its struggle against the aggressor."[4]

The rout of the crack Kwantung Army in 1945 by Soviet troops supported by armed forces of the Mongolian People's Republic and the People's Liberation Army of China (PLA) played a decisive role in the defeat of militaristic Japan, and in the complete expulsion of the Japanese occupiers from Chinese soil, and was, as well, the most important international factor in the victory of the Chinese revolution. Manchuria, liberated by Soviet troops, became a dependable military and strategic base of operations for Chinese revolutionary forces. It was from this base that Chinese Communists led the people in the decisive struggle against the corrupt Kuomintang regime.

The formation in October 1949 of the People's Republic of China (PRC), and its embarkation on the path of socialism, opened a new stage in the development of Sino-Soviet relations. The liquidation of the reactionary Kuomintang regime removed obstacles in the path of the Chinese people to establishing close cooperation and friendship with the Soviet people. The historical tendencies toward a close rapprochement between the two countries received a broad base for development. In the USSR, the new China found a dependable friend and ally in the struggle to liquidate economic backwardness, to strengthen its international position, and to build a socialist society.

The first decade of the existence of the PRC provided convincing proof that there were present all of the objective conditions for development of Sino-Soviet relations in this direction, and that this development corresponded to the basic interests of the workers of the Soviet Union, China, and the peoples of all countries. Unswervingly implementing the Leninist internationalist course with respect to China, the CPSU and the Soviet government were tireless in their efforts to develop and strengthen friendship, unity, and all-around cooperation between the USSR and the PRC, between the CPSU and the CCP, and between the peoples of the two countries.

Nevertheless, by the end of the 1950s, negative tendencies became more and more obvious in Sino-Soviet relations, and the fault could not be attributed to our country. These negative tendencies continued to increase and become more pronounced, despite steps taken by the Soviet side. The result was deviation by the PRC from the policy of friendship and cooperation with the Soviet Union and other socialist countries, and a slide into a position of struggle against them. It is quite clear that the interrelationship between the PRC and the Soviet Union not only affects the basic interests of the Soviet and Chinese peoples, but even has a far-reaching influence on the international situation as a whole, seriously affecting the alignment of class forces in the international arena.

In order to justify their splitting course, Chinese leaders distort the real reasons of their hostility toward the USSR and other socialist countries. They want to obliterate from the memory of the Chinese people all good things about the Soviet Union and to indoctrinate them in a spirit of hostility to all things Soviet, while simultaneously preparing conditions that will strengthen the policy of anti-Sovietism in the future. Anti-Soviet forces in Peking grossly distort generally known facts of the history of Sino-Soviet relations, pile up slanderous accusations against our party and country, attempt to pervert the principles of the Soviet Union's foreign policy, distort and slur the true role of the CPSU and of the USSR in the international arena, and cause other peoples to distrust and become hostile to our party and our country. It is no accident that reactionary bourgeois propaganda willingly seizes on these fabrications, for it sees in them important support in the struggle against socialism. Thoroughly falsified conceptions of the development of Sino-Soviet relations have been the basis for popular brochures and multi-volumed "researches" that have so numerously appeared in recent years in the United States, Great Britain, West Germany, and other capitalist countries.

However, any attempts to distort the truth of Sino-Soviet relations or to use various false documents in order to slander the Leninist foreign policy of the world's first socialist state are doomed to failure. The history of Sino-Soviet relations is a bright chronicle of events providing irrefutable evidence that the policy of the CPSU and of the Soviet state with respect to the PRC is faithfully directed at strengthening the brotherly friendship and cooperation between our two countries, and providing every kind of help and support to the Chinese people in their struggle for socialism.

Moreover, history shows that development of Sino-Soviet relations was not a simple and direct matter, as has been depicted in the works of some authors published in the 1940s and 1950s. Rather it was a complex and contradictory process, reflecting the struggle of two lines: the consistent line of the CPSU directed at strengthening friendship and cooperation between our parties, peoples, and countries, and, in opposition to this, the line of the nationalistic and antisocialist forces in China.

Evaluations of the principles and a detailed analysis of the policies of the present Chinese leadership are contained in a series of documents published by our party, in decisions of Plenums of the CC CPSU, and in speeches made by Soviet leaders. These documents reveal the characteristics of the status of Sino-Soviet relations at various stages, review the process by which they developed, and set forth the course of the Soviet Union.

Many moments in the history of Sino-Soviet relations after formation of the PRC are discussed in the works of Soviet authors published in recent years. A great many documents and handbook materials on this question have been published in our country, as well as in foreign countries.

The present study attempts to generalize available data and thus trace the development of Sino-Soviet relations during the period 1945–1970, in order to show the basic directions of international assistance and support given the revolutionary forces in China by the CPSU, the genuine Leninist character of the policy of our party and of the Soviet state with respect to the PRC, and the total correspondence between this policy and the basic interests of the Soviet and Chinese peoples.

NOTES

1. Li Ta-chao, *Izbrannyye stat'i i rechi* (*Collected Articles and Speeches*) (Moscow, 1965), p. 194.

2. *Pravda,* July 1, 1966.

3. *Sovetsko-kitayskiye otnosheniya. 1917–1957. Sbornik dokumentov* (*Sino-Soviet Relations. 1917–1957. A Collection of Documents,* hereinafter referred to as *Sino-Soviet Relations, 1917–1957*) (Moscow, 1959), p. 43.

4. Mao Tse-tung, *Izbrannyye proizvedeniya* (*Selected Works*), Vol. 4 (Moscow, 1953), p. 552.

CHAPTER ONE

The Rout of Japanese Imperialism—One of the Decisive Factors in the Victory of the Chinese Revolution. Sino-Soviet Relations (1945–1949)

The Chinese Revolution was the result of both development of the international situation and deep internal processes, at the basis of which were the ever-increasing aggravation of class contradictions in the country and the intensification of national liberation tendencies. The crux of these contradictions, the basic motivating forces, and the tasks of the revolution determined its antifeudal, anti-imperialistic, democratic character.

At the same time, the Chinese Revolution is a clear indication that in the modern epoch the success of the revolutionary movement in any country, and particularly in a country in which the proletariat is relatively weak and where the party must depend primarily on the revolutionary character of broad, petty bourgeois layers, depends to a tremendous degree on the help and support its movement receives from places where socialism already has triumphed. Without such support, successful development of the revolution and transition to the building of socialism are impossible.

Considering the Chinese revolution from this point of view, it must be emphasized that one of the most decisive factors in its successful development was the victory of the peace-loving, progressive forces in World War II over German Fascism and Japanese militarism, the decisive contribution to that victory having been made by the Soviet Union.

The period 1945–1949 occupies a special place in the history of the Chinese revolution. During this stage of its development, revolutionary forces in China were able to take advantage not only of generally favorable conditions prevailing as a result of liberation by the Soviet Army of Japanese-occupied Manchuria, but also of the direct aid and support of the Soviet Union in the struggle to overthrow the reactionary Chiang

39

Kai-shek domination. At the same time, it is important to note that Yenan was surrendered to the Kuomintang in 1947 and lost its importance as the center of the revolutionary forces. From that time the main stronghold of the Chinese people in the struggle against the Chiang Kai-shek regime and its imperialistic accomplices was the military and revolutionary base in Manchuria.

The period 1945–1949 is important as well because the foundation was laid down for cooperation between the two countries, which after 1949 took on a comprehensive character. This is why the period deserves special consideration as an important prerequisite to the development of Sino-Soviet relations after the formation of the PRC, considering the fact that in Soviet historiography the years 1945–1949 have been dealt with very one-sidedly, and at times even incorrectly.

1. Manchuria in the anti-Soviet plans of Japanese militarism

Japanese militarists in their struggles against Communism, the Soviet Union, and the revolutionary forces of China assigned paramount importance to the establishment of a military and strategic base in Manchuria. Direct aggression was the weapon used for these purposes. In 1932 Japan set up the puppet state of Manchukuo and began feverish exploitation of the military and economic resources of this region, which, in terms of size of territory (1,100,000 square kilometers within the 1944–1945 boundaries), and in specific weight of industrial production (over 20 percent of the industrial production of China as a whole), occupied an important place.

Japanese militarists used fire and sword to put down revolutionary actions of Chinese workers in Manchuria. Dispatching crack troops and police units to the region, they converted Manchuria into one big concentration camp. Japanese militarists, the worst enemies of both the Soviet and Chinese peoples, in cooperation with the Hitlerites, nurtured plans for further expansion of aggression against our peoples, as well as for a campaign against Singapore, Indochina, Thailand, Malaya, Burma, Indonesia, and the Philippines.

The Japanese General Staff, in initiating the war in Southeast Asia, looked forward to an easy victory. Japan made great territorial gains in the area, and far from rejecting the idea of war against the USSR, actually was tireless in preparing for it. The Kwantung Army in Manchuria was in a state of constant readiness to be hurled northward. The Japanese government simply was awaiting a "decisive victory" by Germany, first the "fall of Moscow," then the "fall of Stalingrad." The Japanese press openly demanded annexation of the Soviet Far East. The great Siberian Railroad, together with adjacent regions to the west of Omsk, was to pass to Germany, with those to the east of Omsk going to Japan.

The Japanese General Staff developed "Operation Kantokuan," along the lines of the Fascist "Operation Barbarossa," which was aimed at conquering the USSR. The Japanese command in Manchuria was engaged exclusively in preparing to carry out this plan. The Japanese imperialists believed their conquests in China and in Southeast Asia could not be lasting if the Soviet Union were not defeated, because those initiating partisan warfare against Japanese occupiers regarded the Soviet Union as a base of support.

Japanese imperialists systematically violated the Soviet-Japanese neutrality pact, coordinating with Fascist Germany their plans for attacking the USSR. On May 15, 1942, Ribbentrop, the Minister of Foreign Affairs of the Third Reich, telegraphed Tokyo that concentrations of Japanese forces on the Soviet-Manchurian border helped Germany greatly, "since in any case Russia has to keep troops in Eastern Siberia in order to prevent a Russo-Japanese conflict."[1]

The Japanese command set up military bases in rapid succession along the Soviet and Mongolian borders, built strategically important railroads and highways in Manchuria, and stockpiled rolling stock and fuel. Between 1941 and 1945 Japanese naval forces stopped 178 Soviet merchant ships and sank over 10 Soviet cargo and passenger ships in Far Eastern waters. Diversionary groups constantly made incursions into Soviet territory from Manchuria. Japanese intelligence systematically supplied Berlin with espionage information on the Soviet Union.

After the capitulation of Hitler's Germany, Japanese imperialists continued the war in the Pacific, refusing to lay down their arms and recognize defeat. Their main hope rested on the Kwantung Army, deployed in Manchuria, which as of mid-1945 was fully equipped and manned with crack units. The Japanese militarists believed that this army, with its military and industrial bases in Manchuria untouched by American aviation, would hold out until more favorable conditions enabled it finally to play a decisive role. They also were preparing to use bacteriological weapons in order to turn the war in their favor. This was established irrefutably by materials introduced at the Khabarovsk trial of Japanese war criminals. The Japanese General Staff had organized large-scale production in Manchurian occupied territories of plague, cholera, typhus, and other epidemic bacteria. Mass "tests" of the use of bacteriological warfare were held there over whole populated regions.

The Supreme Command of the United States and England did not plan to conduct "decisive" operations against Japan until 1946–1947. Churchill told the House of Commons on August 16, 1945 that no one could determine how much time would be required to conduct these "decisive" operations.

At the beginning of August 1945 the Kwantung Army comprised the 1st and 3rd Fronts, the 4th Independent, and 2nd Air armies. It later was reinforced with the 17th Front and 5th Air armies. The Kwantung Army had over 1,000 tanks, 5,000 guns of various calibers, and 1,800 aircraft. The Army's personnel had long been indoctrinated in the spirit of samurai militaristic traditions, and hatred of Soviet, Chinese, and Mongol peoples. The Kwantung command also had at its disposal the puppet army of Manchukuo (some 190,000 men) and puppet units in regions in Inner Mongolia and Suiyuan province occupied by the Japanese.*

2. The rout of the Kwantung Army and the capitulation of Japan

The situation that evolved in China during the anti-Japanese war, splitting the nation and damaging the united front, created conditions favorable to Japanese imperialism. China therefore was unable to cope with international reactions threatening the national independence of the country. And that is why efforts of the Soviet Union at the time were devoted to providing armed assistance to the struggling Chinese people, and to rallying them under the flag of a united anti-Japanese front.

The Soviet Union considered the struggle with Japanese imperialism as part of the overall problem of progressive, peace-loving forces coming out against the aggressive plans of extreme imperialist reaction, plans that found their organized formulation in the piratical union of the "Axis countries," Germany, Italy, and Japan. Even before the complete rout of Fascism in Europe, the Soviet government at the Yalta Conference, on February 11, 1945, obligated itself to enter the war against Japan within two to three months after the capitulation of Hitler's Germany.

In assuming this obligation the Soviet Union not only carried out its duties as an ally to the states of the anti-Hitler coalition, but evidenced true internationalism as well, unhesitatingly coming to the assistance of the Chinese and other peoples in their struggle for liberation from Japanese aggressors. At the Yalta Conference the Soviet Union

---

* Dispositions are as given in the text. The nomenclature does not match that listed in John Toland's *The Rising Sun*, 1970, index to Volume II, for example.— Translator's note.

expressed its readiness to conclude a treaty of friendship and alliance with China in order to help, with its armed forces, to liberate China from the Japanese yoke.[2]

Within three months after the victory over Hitlerite Germany the Soviet Union had transferred heavy military forces and equipment to the Far East. At the beginning of military operations against the Japanese militarists the Soviet side had in readiness an army of 1,500,000 men, over 26,000 guns and mortars, over 5,500 tanks and self-propelled artillery pieces, and almost 3,900 combat aircraft.[3] The warships of the Pacific Fleet and of the Red Banner Amur Flotilla were placed on a combat footing as well.

Marshals of the Soviet Union A. M. Vasilevskiy, R. Ya. Malinovskiy, and K. A. Meretskov, as well as other famous Soviet military commanders, supervised the operations for destroying the Kwantung Army.

On August 8, 1945 the Japanese ambassador in Moscow was handed the justified declaration of the Soviet government that as of August 9 the Soviet Union considered itself to be in a state of war with Japan.

On the morning of August 9 Soviet troops launched a simultaneous attack with forces assigned to the three Fronts, the Transbaikal, the First Far Eastern, and the Second Far Eastern. The attack by Soviet troops developed with exceptionally rapid tempo. By August 12 the main body of the 6th Guards Tank Army, part of the Transbaikal Front, had crossed the Bol'shoy Khingan and broken out onto the Manchurian plain.

The entry of the USSR into the war against Japan, and the first successes of Soviet troops, shocked the ruling Japanese clique. On August 9 Prime Minister Suzuki told the members of Japan's Supreme Council that "the Soviet Union's entry in the war against Japan this morning finally has placed us in a hopeless situation, and makes further prolongation of the war impossible."

The Chinese people greeted the Soviet Union's declaration of war against Japan with tremendous enthusiasm. Reflecting these feelings, Mao Tse-tung, on August 9, 1945, wrote that, "on the eighth of August the government of the Soviet Union declared war on Japan. The Chinese people greet this warmly. Thanks to this step on the part of the Soviet Union, the duration of the war with Japan has been considerably shortened. The war with Japan already is in its last stage. The hour has come for the final victory over the Japanese invaders, and all of their stooges."[4]

The brilliant operations conducted by the Soviet Army and elements of the People's Revolutionary Army of the Mongolian People's Republic operating jointly in northeastern China resulted in rapid flight of the Japanese from Inner Mongolia and North China, and served as the signal for the 8th and New 4th armies, under the leadership of the CCP, to mount their offensive.

Stunned by the rout of the Kwantung Army, the Japanese actually yielded the major cities of Kalgan, Chengtu, and Chefoo to the PLA without a struggle. The result was to permit the revolutionary troops to enter Manchuria and make contact with Soviet units. The strongly fortified Japanese regions built along the Amur and Ussuri rivers, and the Bol'shoy Khingan Khrebet [mountain range], were breached at all points. Those Japanese units that did resist were encircled and bypassed. The lightning-like tactics of all branches of Soviet ground troops, airborne troops, and naval ships disrupted the plans of the Japanese militarists to use bacteriological weapons.*

The blows inflicted by the Soviet Army and Navy were so crushing and so swift that the Japanese agreed to unconditional surrender.

The day after military operations were begun by the Soviet Army, Japan's Minister of Foreign Affairs, Shigenori Togo, made the following statement to Soviet Ambassador Ya. A. Malik:

> The Japanese Government is ready to accept the conditions of the Declaration of 26 July of this year [the Potsdam Declaration—author], to which the Soviet Government is a party. The Japanese Government understands that this Declaration contains no demands infringing the prerogatives of the Emperor as the sovereign ruler of Japan. The Japanese government requests definite information as regards this.[5]

Nevertheless, Japanese troops continued to offer stiff resistance.

On August 11, 1945, the governments of the USSR, USA, China, and England demanded that Japan meet conditions for capitulation necessary to carry out the terms of the Potsdam Declaration, and that she

---

* The former Commander-in-Chief of the Japanese Kwantung Army, General Yamada, [Yamada is a direct transliteration from the Russian. The reference could be to General Yoshijiro Umezu, since no source available to the translator lists a General Yamada as commander of the Kwantung Army. Translator's note.] at the Khabarovsk trial said, "The entry of the Soviet Union in the war against Japan and the swift advance of the Soviet Army deep into Manchuria deprived us of the possibility of using bacteriological weapons against the USSR and other countries." (*Materialy sudebnogo protsessa po delu byvshikh voyennosluzhashchikh yaponskoy armii, obvinyayemykh v podgotovke i primenenii bakteriologicheskoyo oruzhiya.* M., 1950, str. 99) (Materials from the trial in the matter of former military personnel of the Japanese Army accused of preparing and using bacteriological weapons. Moscow, 1950 p. 99).

issue orders to Japanese armed forces, wherever found, to cease military operations and lay down their arms.

On August 14 the Japanese government announced that the Emperor of Japan had issued an Imperial proclamation regarding Japan's acceptance of conditions of the Potsdam Declaration, and that he was prepared to ensure the signature of his government and that of Imperial General Headquarters to the conditions for implementation of the Potsdam Declaration provisions.

The "Imperial proclamation," however, was merely a general declaration. In point of fact, no order to cease operations was issued to the Kwantung Army, and, as before, Japanese armed forces continued their resistance, in a number of cases even counterattacking.

On August 17, 1945 the Commander-in-Chief of Soviet Forces in the Far East, Marshal A. M. Vasilevskiy, transmitted the following radio message to the commander of the Kwantung Army.

> Headquarters of Japan's Kwantung Army has radioed headquarters Soviet Forces Far East a proposal to cease military operations, but nothing has been said about the surrender of Japanese armed forces in Manchuria.
>
> At this same time Japanese troops have begun to counterattack along many sectors of the Soviet-Japanese front.
>
> I propose to the commander that the troops of the Kwantung Army cease all combat operations against Soviet troops along the entire front, that they lay down their arms and consider themselves as prisoners, as of 1200 hours on August 20.
>
> The above time is fixed in order to give the headquarters of the Kwantung Army time to issue orders to all its forces to cease resistance and become prisoners.
>
> As soon as Japanese troops begin to give up their arms, Soviet forces will cease combat operations.[6]

The Soviet ultimatum was strengthened by decisive actions on the part of Soviet forces. The airborne units of the Soviet Army were particularly outstanding in Manchuria. Here is one example. On August 18 a big drop was made on Harbin airport, and the whole of its territory was taken in a matter of minutes. The Deputy Chief of Staff of the 1st Far Eastern Front, Major General G. A. Shelakhov, was among those making the drop. The Chief of Staff of the Kwantung Army, Lieutenant General Hata, arrived at the airport shortly thereafter. G. A. Shelakhov demanded assurances of immediate, unconditional surrender of Japanese units in the Harbin area, and proposed to General Hata that he proceed by Soviet aircraft to the 1st Far Eastern Front's command post in order to reach agreement on questions concerned with disarmament and surrender of the Kwantung Army. On August 19 Hata, with accompanying Japanese generals and officers, arrived at the Soviet command point, where they met Marshal Vasilevskiy, who presented the Japanese general with conditions for becoming prisoners and for disarming the Kwantung Army.

At the same time the Soviet landing force in Harbin took the bridges across the Sungari River, as well as some most important objectives in the city. Our forces entered the USSR Consulate General, which was surrounded by Japanese soldiers and police. As it turned out, the Japanese had planned on sending consular employees, headed by Consul General G. I. Pavlychev, to the city of Dal'niy for internment and then on to Japan. Only the arrival of the Soviet troops prevented the Japanese from carrying out this plan.

A Soviet airborne landing in Mukden on August 19 found and captured at the airfield the puppet "Emperor" of Manchukuo, Henry Pu-yi himself. Pu-yi was waiting for an airplane to take him to Japan. Soviet airborne forces occupied Changchun and captured the commander of the Kwantung Army, Lieutenant General Yamada.

Total losses incurred by the Japanese Kwantung Army in Manchuria during the period from August 9 to 20, 1945, in dead and captured, and not counting those missing, numbered some 700,000 officers and men (of whom 594,148 were prisoners). This was considerably in excess of personnel losses inflicted on the Japanese armed forces on all fronts over the preceding four years of World War II. The troops assigned to just two of our Fronts captured 1,565 guns, 2,139 mortars and grenade throwers, 600 tanks, 861 aircraft, and other armaments.

The rout by Soviet forces of the strongest disposition of Japanese ground forces, the Kwantung Army, and not the American atomic bombings of Hiroshima and Nagasaki, predetermined the rapid capitulation of militaristic Japan.

". . . The Soviet Army entered Manchuria and completely routed and destroyed the Kwantung Army," declared Chu Teh, the commander of the armed forces of the Chinese revolution, "thus forcing the Japanese militarists to surrender."[7] Developing this thought, the Chinese press wrote at the time:

> . . . when the Soviet Union moved its army and the Japanese Kwantung Army was smashed, the dreams of the Japanese aggressors of converting Manchuria into a lair for their last fight vanished. No out other than that of unconditional surrender remained. This is persuasive evidence of the fact that only the entrance of the Soviet Union into the war forced Japan

into unconditional surrender, and that only the actions taken by the Soviet Army in liberating the northeastern provinces and Korea helped shorten considerably the period the allies had to wage war against Japan . . .[8]

The act of unconditional surrender by Japan was signed on board the battleship *Missouri,* in Tokyo Bay, on September 2, 1945. An auspicious future for further development of China's struggle for national and social liberation had opened.

The treaty between the USSR and China was signed on August 14, 1945. It not only supported the national liberation struggle of the Chinese people, but also paved the way for the USSR to provide direct assistance to revolutionary and democratic forces in China, and made possible the establishment of conditions favorable for activities of the CCP. This treaty was a definite obstacle in the path of the anti-Soviet policy practiced for so many years by the forces of Chiang Kai-shek. The organ of the National Liberation Army of China, the newspaper *Chien-Fang Jihpao,* on August 27, 1945, wrote:

> The treaty of friendship and union with the USSR is the first equitable treaty with a foreign state in the history of our country. The Chinese and Soviet peoples have united in a friendly, glorious union. We feel that this treaty is yet another manifestation of the policy of equality that the Soviet Union has always displayed in its relations with us. . . .

3. The situation in Manchuria after the rout of militaristic Japan

China continued to be divided into two camps after the capitulation of Japan. Chiang Kai-shek's forces controlled three-fourths of the country's territory. These forces were made up of a multi-million man army, which the Americans proceeded to arm at a rapid pace. The United States gave the antinational regime other aid as well, providing vast amounts of money and materiel, and political and diplomatic support, all of which was intensified by direct armed intervention in China's internal affairs.

Manchuria, like all of China, was divided into two camps. The area west of Changchun and north of Kirin, as well as the Liaotung Peninsula, where, in accordance with the terms of the Sino-Soviet Treaty of August 14, 1945, Soviet troops were disposed, actually became the base of people's power, led by the CCP. Democratic organs of people's power created by free expression in this territory with a population of 150 millions began to prepare for radical social and economic transformations. The Kuomintang controlled the rest of Manchuria.

The Chinese Revolution commenced a period of gathering strength under conditions of peaceful development. Upon the initiative of the

CCP, a decision was made at a meeting of Communist Party representatives and the Kuomintang, held between August 29 and October 10, 1945, to call a political consultative conference of representatives of all political parties and groups. The conference was to discuss questions concerned with building a democratic state and to prepare for the convocation of a National Congress to form a coalition government.

However, subsequent development of events revealed that the Chiang Kai-shek regime had set other goals. Under cover of slogans promoting creation of a coalition government, and with the support of American imperialism, they proceeded to establish their dictatorship in the country, and began to take action against revolutionary and democratic forces. In turn, the United States tried to use this situation to convert China into an American colony of sorts. The United States flooded the Kuomintang regions with advisors and emissaries who landed in Chinese ports and took direct part in military operations against Chinese revolutionary forces.* [9] American aircraft moved the Kuomintang Army into areas controlled by the CCP.

Given these conditions, the Soviet Union took active diplomatic measures to prevent aggression in China, aggression that Washington was practicing under the guise of aid to the Kuomintang. At the suggestion of the Soviet government, during the Moscow meeting of the ministers of foreign affairs of the USSR, the USA, and Great Britain in December 1945, a decision was made to confirm the policy of nonintervention in the internal affairs of China, to acknowledge the need to stop the civil war in China, and to unite and democratize all of the organs of the national government of the country. [10]

This same meeting also achieved "complete agreement with respect to the desirability of the withdrawal from China of Soviet and American armed forces as quickly as possible commensurate with the fulfillment by them of their obligations and their responsibilities." [11] The Soviet command had presented the Kuomintang authorities with a plan for evacuation of its troops as early as November 1945, a plan which anticipated completion of the evacuation by December 3 of the same year. In accord with this plan, Soviet units withdrew from Yingkow and Hulutao, and from the area to the south of Shenyang. However, the Kuomintang government itself declared that it would "find itself in an extremely difficult situation" in the event of withdrawal of Soviet troops from Manchuria at the appointed time, because it would be unable to organize a civil ad-

---

* American troops in China numbered 98,000 at the beginning of 1947.

ministration by that time.[12] The Soviet government agreed to postpone the withdrawal of its troops from the northeastern provinces.[13]

Some time later the government of Chiang Kai-shek once again asked the Soviet government to postpone withdrawal of troops, playing for time to regroup its own, and the American armed forces, in order to capture the revolutionary base in Manchuria. At the same time, Kuomintang propaganda began to make provocative noises to the effect that the USSR had "seized" northeast China.

The withdrawal of Soviet troops from Manchuria began in March 1946, and ended on May 3 of that year.[14] However, the Kuomintang was unable to use the withdrawal to strengthen its position in Manchuria. Chinese revolutionary troops and the people's democratic administration, having won from the population a high degree of authority, took control of areas vacated by Soviet units, and established revolutionary order in them.

Soviet troops, having smashed the Kwantung Army, dismantled military arsenals and certain other enterprises that had serviced this army, which thus became trophies of the armed forces of the USSR. The Kuomintang militarists had counted on using all of these in the war against the PLA and the liberated regions. But these designs were thwarted.

The Kuomintang clique, infuriated by the failure of its plans, began a slanderous anti-Soviet campaign against the "export of equipment by the Soviet Union." This campaign was readily taken up by imperialist propaganda. However, Chinese patriots understood that the steps taken by the Soviet Army prevented the Kuomintang from using Japanese military industry in Northeast China for purposes detrimental to the national interests of the Chinese people. After formation of the PRC, the Chinese Communists interpreted the question thus:

> . . . if the equipment had not been taken away it would have fallen into the hands of Chiang Kai-shek's army, which then would have used it to manufacture weapons and munitions in order to strengthen itself in its death agony, and the Chinese people would have spilled more blood in the liberation war. The Chinese people are well aware of the fact that the actions taken by the Soviet Army at that time were in the best interests of our people's revolution. Practically speaking, this was a form of assistance, for which we should be extremely grateful.[15]

After the departure of Soviet troops from regions ruled by the Kuomintang administration (South Manchuria), the Chiang Kai-shekists resorted to repression of local democratic organizations, Soviet institutions, the consulates, and the Soviet section of the Chinese Changchun Railroad (CCRR) administration.

The Kuomintang forcibly removed the Soviet administration and Soviet railroad workers from their CCRR jobs on March 20, 1946. They seized warehouses and all railroad property and began to remove stolen goods to Peking. In Mukden, Sungkiang, Szepingkai, Liaoyuan, and other places, homes of Soviet railroad workers were surrounded by barbed wire, and Soviet citizens were not permitted to go beyond the limits of these reservations without the permission of the Kuomintang secret police. Efforts were made to force Soviet citizens to wear special arm bands and name tags on their chests. Soldiers burst into apartments of Soviet citizens, searched, plundered, mocked, and insulted. Many Soviet railroad workers were evicted from their quarters without being permitted to take the most basic necessities. In Mukden, on March 21, Fascist Chiang Kai-shek thugs shot four Soviet citizens, employees of a Soviet foreign trade organization. Kuomintang soldiers and officers bound six Soviet citizens, including the station master, Gorbachev, the division chief, Agapov, and his wife Tselikovskaya, the division engineer, in Liaoyuan station, then paraded them through the streets, to be jeered at and beaten unmercifully. Kuomintang authorities did not reply to the protests of the Soviet part of the CCRR administration. Moreover, General Tung Yang-ch'in, director of Chiang Kai-shek's Northeast Headquarters, published in the press a declaration that he could not "guarantee the safety of Soviet citizens." This was a direct incitement to new violence. The result was that in Changchun alone, after occupation by Kuomintang troops on April 20–21, 1946, 10 Soviet citizens were shot, five brutally tortured, and 11 others reported as missing. The homes and property of Soviet economic organizations and of the CCRR were plundered.

In all, 60 Soviet citizens who had been working for the CCRR were brutally tortured and killed, and over 200 families were robbed during the period of Kuomintang rule. The Kuomintang committed a number of terrorist acts against official representatives of the Soviet government as well.

The Kuomintang pogroms were carried out with the connivance or under the leadership of their American masters. American officers came in "jeeps" and photographed the "excesses" during the provocative outrages and violence perpetrated against Soviet citizens in Mukden, Liaoyuan, Telin, Sungtzatung, and Szepingkai, and later on in Changchun.

Given the above conditions, there was no question of CCRR's normally operating as a joint enterprise. The Soviet government was forced to instruct Soviet citizens employed by the CCRR to depart for home.

The railroad temporarily ceased operations as a joint enterprise. Only a small group of Soviet railroad men, headed by railroad manager Zhuravlev, remained with the CCRR to maintain contact with the people's democratic authorities in Harbin.

Responding to the "Cold War" doctrine advanced by Washington, Chiang Kai-shek feverishly turned over to American imperialists Chinese ports to establish a network of naval and air bases aimed at the Soviet Union. On November 6, 1946 Chiang Kai-shek's government concluded with the United States a so-called treaty of friendship, commerce, and navigation, as well as a number of other agreements strengthening the union between the Kuomintang and imperialist circles in the United States.

Simultaneously, Kuomintang forces attempted to blockade the Dal'-niy-Port Arthur area, a treaty zone for the disposition of Soviet troops. The Chiang Kai-shekists were particularly bitter about the fact that the Soviet government had decisively refused to allow their troops through the port of Dal'niy from South China into Manchuria for the struggle with the revolutionary forces. The Kuomintang government was informed that in accordance with the Sino-Soviet agreement of August 14, 1945, Dal'niy was a commercial port to be used for transporting cargo, not troops. The disembarkation in this port of any troops would have constituted a violation of this agreement.

The Kuomintang press tried to convince the Chinese people that the Soviet Union, and not American imperialism, was China's main enemy; that "the Soviet Union was conducting an imperialistic policy." The Kuomintang government portrayed the demand by the USSR that American troops be withdrawn from China as "interference in the internal affairs of China."

Soviet representatives in China were placed in an intolerable situation. Kuomintang reactionaries staged demonstrations in front of the Soviet Embassy in Peking, forcing the population to scream anti-Soviet slogans, to threaten reprisals against Soviet representatives, and to attack vehicles used by Soviet diplomats.

The Kuomintang reactionaries, in their rabid hatred of the Soviet Union, reached the point of openly advocating a "crusade" against the USSR. They artificially inflamed war hysteria, raising the cry of "Red aggression in China."

At the same time the Kuomintang regime tried to escalate its struggle against the revolutionary forces in China. In March 1947 Chiang Kai-shek's troops undertook a broad offensive against an area under the control of the CCP, Shansi-Kansu-Ninghsia, with its center in Yenan.

Large-scale offensive operations were perfidiously initiated by his forces in Manchuria and other regions. The territories controlled by the CCP and the PLA, particularly the Liaotung Peninsula, the provinces of Hei-lungkiang and Kirin, and the Sinkiang region were subjected to economic blockade.

It was during this difficult period that the revolutionary bases in Man-churia became the main bastions of the Chinese revolution. It was here that the revolution assembled the forces for its army, and it was here that the liberation campaign to the South was launched in 1948–1949, end-ing with the complete smashing of the Kuomintang regime.

4. Help provided by the Soviet Union in strengthening the revolutionary base in Manchuria

The Soviet Union, despite tremendous difficulties associated with postwar restoration of the country, undertook effective measures to strengthen the people's democratic region in Manchuria which had re-sulted from the rout of the Kwantung Army.

People's democratic organs of power, freely elected, were active in the territory of Manchuria controlled by the Communists and by the PLA. The People's Democratic Administrative Commission, the highest executive organ in China's Northeastern Provinces (as the territory was called at that time), was located in Harbin.

This was the seat of the Northeastern Bureau of the CC CCP, which exercised party control in Manchuria. It was allowed considerable auton-omy because the seat of the CC CCP was in Yenan. The independent role of the Northeastern Bureau increased particularly because Yenan was captured by the forces of Chiang Kai-shek in March 1947, and the leadership of the CC CCP, hiding from pursuit, lost its capacity to guide effectively the revolutionary struggle on a country-wide scale. The compo-sition of the Northeastern Bureau of the CC CCP included Kao Kang, Chen Yun, Chang Wen-tien, Lin Piao, Li Fu-chun, P'eng Chen, and others.

The people's democratic regions, from the very first days of their existence, received all manner of support from the Soviet Union. This played an important role in strengthening the United Democratic Army (UDA), as the armed forces of the CCP in Manchuria were called at that time. The UDA was equipped with first-class weapons that had belonged to the Kwantung Army, and had been taken as booty by Soviet troops.

Direct contacts between leading figures in our parties were developed between 1945 and 1949, in order to begin collaboration with the people's democratic authorities in Manchuria. †For example, a delegation from the people's democratic regions in Manchuria, headed by Kao Kang and Liu Shao-ch'i, visited the USSR in 1945, where it met with Soviet leaders.

†A group of representatives of the CPSU, which maintained operational contact with the CCP, and particularly with the Northeastern Bureau of the CC CCP, was in Manchuria from 1945 until the proclamation of the PRC.

The Soviet Union, even during that period, provided a great deal of assistance in training Chinese national cadres, imparting its experience in government and economics to the people's democratic organs of power.

The stationing of Soviet troops in Manchuria was very important to developing and strengthening Manchuria's economy. Many important enterprises were restored and put back in operation with help of Soviet specialists, particularly in regions traversed by the Chinese Changchun Railroad and in the treaty zone of Port Arthur-Dal'niy. Units of the Soviet Army in Manchuria gave their wholehearted cooperation to local authorities in repairing and building paved roads, and in organization of public services and amenities in populated areas. Vocational training for workers and improvement of specialists' qualifications in different fields were organized with their help. Fundamental reconstruction of the naval base in Port Arthur was carried out. Equipped with modern artillery, aircraft, and a navy, this base was converted into both a dependable bastion on the shores of the Yellow Sea and a school for Chinese naval cadres.

The people's democratic regions in the Liaotung Peninsula played an important role in the strengthening of Sino-Soviet collaboration. Liaotung became yet another take-off point for the victorious offensive of the people's democratic forces of China.[16]

The regions of the people's democratic zone in Manchuria, cut off from the central provinces of China, were extremely short of fuel, vehicles, coal, pharmaceuticals, salt, cotton, textiles, shoes, clothing, sugar, and many other goods. The urgent needs of the population, as well as those of the battling PLA, were attended to with the assistance of the Soviet Union.

The first trade talks between Soviet foreign trade organizations and the People's Democratic Administrative Commission for the Northeastern Provinces of China were concluded on December 21, 1946 (the Soviet Union was represented at these talks by M. I. Sladovskiy of the Ministry of Foreign Trade of the USSR, and by M. I. Sulimenko, Deputy Chairman of the All-Union Combine "Eksportkhleb"). A contract was signed under the terms of which deliveries of Soviet goods for the population and for the army would begin, as would deliveries of equipment for outfitting hospitals, dispensaries, schools, and the like. In addition, captured war materials and food requisitioned by the Soviet Army from Japanese interventionists were turned over to the people's democratic organizations in the Northeastern Provinces.

With the capture by Kuomintang troops of the southern part of Manchuria came a sharp deterioration in supply to the Liaotung Peninsula. Soviet organizations immediately began to make deliveries of food grains, vegetable oil, sugar, and canned goods from Vladivostok by sea directly into the port of Dal'niy and in transit through ports in northern Korea. Food delivered to Dal'niy was distributed at fixed prices by the local Chinese People's Democratic Administration with the cooperation of the civilian administration of the Soviet Army. All costs of transporting, storage, and distribution of food were paid for by the Soviet side in order to give free aid to the Chinese population.

A trade delegation from the people's democratic authorities in China's Northeastern Provinces, headed by Kao Kang, a member of the Political Bureau of the CC CCP, arrived in Moscow in the summer of 1949. Resulting from the successful negotiations was an agreement on mutual exchanges of goods for a period of one year.

Under the terms of this agreement the Soviet Union undertook to export to the liberated regions of Northeastern China industrial equipment, trucks, petroleum products, textiles, paper, pharmaceuticals, and other goods. The People's Democratic Administration for the Northeastern Provinces agreed to deliver to the Soviet Union soy beans, vegetable oils, corn, rice, and other goods.[17]

Trade ties between Soviet foreign trade organizations and the People's Democratic Administration for the Northeastern Provinces expanded steadily. This will be seen from the following data on the trade turnover between the northeastern companies (less Liaotung) and Soviet foreign trade organizations between 1947 and 1949 (in millions of rubles).[18]

	1947	1948	1949
Exports from USSR	48	74	100
Imports into USSR	45	77	105
Total trade turnover	93	151	205

Trade unquestionably played an important role in strengthening the people's democratic authority in the Northeastern Provinces, which were becoming the most important base for preparations for the general offensive by the PLA against the Kuomintang regime.

The development of trade and economic ties required that further improvements be made in communications, including the use of the water arteries in the area, the Amur and Sungari rivers.

In April 1947 the Harbin Division of the Soviet organization "Dal'-vneshtrans" (Far Eastern Foreign Trade Transportation Trust) helped prepare landings in Chiamaze, Fukdin, and Seisin, as well as building of additional berths in Harbin's river port, before the navigation season opened on the Sungari River. Traffic along the Sungari River was of exceptional importance to the people's democratic regions of Northeastern China because Chiamaze was one of the most important rear area centers of the PLA. Located there were military schools, central hospitals, and supply bases. In collaboration with Chang Wen-tien (at that time known by his party name, Lo Fu, and a member of the Northeast Bureau of the CC CCP), and guided by party, civilian, and rear area concerns in this center, Soviet foreign trade and transportation organizations were able to provide an uninterrupted flow of needed supplies of materials, fuel, pharmaceuticals, clothing, shoes, and other supplies along the Sungari River during the navigation seasons of 1947 and 1948, the years of the decisive struggle of the people's democratic forces with Kuomintang troops.

Military operations in Manchuria had resulted in the damage or destruction of some 6,000 kilometers of railroad lines. The length of the railroad network was only 10,000 kilometers by the end of 1945. Main rail lines in this region belonged to the Chinese Changchun Railroad (formerly the Chinese Eastern Railroad), which had been built by Russia between 1897 and 1903. Soviet railroad men had begun the restoration and operation of the Chinese Changchun Railroad from the very first day of the entry of the USSR into the war with Japan. For example, the Japanese were driven out of the Manchuria border station on the night of August 8–9, and on August 9 Soviet railroad men brought the first troop train into this station.

Japanese troops, beating a hasty retreat under the decisive blows of the Soviet Army along western and eastern lines of the Chinese Changchun Railroad, wrought great destruction to the entire 1,500-kilometer length of the railroad. All signal installations and communications were destroyed in Mutankiang, Anansi, Hailar, and at Manchuria Station, local cable networks were torn out, railroad bridges were blown up, and the water supplies were destroyed. The Japanese destroyed the roundhouses in many of the large stations (in Hailar, Hengtaohotze, Mutankiang, and in other stations). They dismantled and removed trackage and destroyed structures in 57 stations and sidings. One of the largest locomotive repair works in Manchuria, Manchuria Station, was blown up.

Soviet railroad men and Soviet Army troops opened the east and west lines of the Chinese Changchun Railroad to regular train traffic with the signing by Japan of the unconditional surrender agreement on September 2, 1945. They completed a tremendous volume of construction work in a remarkably short time in order to bring the destroyed trackage and installations up to what could be considered reliable operating condition, and to increase the speed and safety of train movements.

Upon the initiative of Soviet railroad men, the Chinese Changchun Railroad organized courses to train Chinese railroad cadres in the mass vocations. The central courses enrolled 536 men, the line divisions over 900. Soviet specialists supervised the training of 400 students in engineering-construction, transportation, economics, and electrical engineering departments of the Chinese Changchun Railroad Polytechnical Institute, which had opened the very day the Chinese Changchun Railroad began operations. This was of great political and practical importance because Chinese had been used on the railroads as laborers, with all technical positions filled by Japanese.

The entire burden of restoration work and operation of the railroad rested on the shoulders of Soviet railroad men while Chinese national cadres were being trained.

Plants in Siberia and the Far East made repairs on worn-out and damaged locomotives and cars belonging to the Chinese Changchun Railroad. Soviet organizations sent materials (rails, beams, metal, tools, and others) and rolling stock (locomotives, cars, and other items) into the zone of the People's Democratic Administration. Soviet specialists helped make up the cadres of all railroad services. As a result of the brotherly assistance rendered by the Soviet people, the spring of 1947 saw many of the main railroad lines in Northeast China restored, and railroad communication with the USSR opened through the stations in Zabaykal'sk and Grodekovo.

China's railroads encountered many difficulties during the Civil War. The retreating Kuomintang troops, trying to delay the advance of the PLA, inflicted great damage on rail transportation, particularly in the southern part of Northeast China and on the Peking-Mukden Railroad. They destroyed two large bridges over the Sungari River between Harbin and Changchun and between Changchun and Kirin, as well as depots, shops, pumping stations, and permanent rights of way. Railroad communications south of Harbin were paralyzed, and the link between the main centers in the northeast was broken. This made further movements by the PLA of China difficult, particularly those against the large Kuomintang disposition in South Manchuria. Restoration of rail communications became an urgent matter, particularly in the case of railroad bridges over the Sungari River.

In June 1948, at the request of the People's Democratic Administrative Commission for the liberated areas, the government of the USSR sent yet another group of Soviet railroad specialists to China. The group brought along its own equipment, including construction trains, diving stations, cranes, and other machinery.[19]

Already available when Soviet specialists arrived were plans for rebuilding two of the largest destroyed bridges (one on the Harbin-Changchun section, the other on the Kirin-Changchun section). These plans had been drawn up in Harbin by Japanese engineers, who had estimated the time required to complete the work as 18 months.

The Soviet group of specialists and workers, however, rebuilt the "Sungari-II" bridge in a record time of two months. This bridge was on the Harbin-Changchun section, and was particularly important to the planned operations of the PLA. Putting this bridge back in use made it possible for the PLA command to concentrate large forces of troops for the offensive against the largest city in Manchuria, Mukden (which was liberated on November 2), and then to mount an offensive in the direction of Peking. The Soviet specialists proposed, and the Northeast Bureau of the CC CCP approved, organizational measures for the development of restoration work on railroad transportation.

The plan for restoration of the railroads, drafted from data obtained by engineering surveys, and approved by the Northeast Bureau for each railroad line, primarily involved work associated with ensuring successful military operations by the PLA.

To summarize, work done under supervision of Soviet railroad men by December 15, 1948 restored over 15,000 kilometers of the most important rail trackage in Manchuria, 120 large and medium bridges, with a total length of over 9,000 meters, and including huge bridges such as the "Sungari-II" bridge, 987 meters long, the 320-meter-long bridge over the Yinmahe River on the Harbin-Changchun section, and the 440-meter bridge across the Sungari River on the Kirin-Changchun section, as well as 12 large and medium bridges on other sections.

Restoration of the railroads took place under rigorous conditions prevalent in war time. Kuomintang aircraft systematically strafed and bombed areas in which restoration was in progress, particularly along the Kirin-Changchun and Tungliao-Hsin Litun-Ihsien lines. These flights resulted in damage to some 150 locomotives and much rolling stock, and the destruction of the stations in Hsin Litun, Cheng Chiatung, and Tungliao. Victims were claimed from among the Chinese railroad workers and Soviet specialists.

The successful restoration of the main rail lines in Central and South

Manchuria made possible large-scale regrouping and concentration of units of the PLA, aiding the final rout of Kuomintang troops, and completion of Northeast China's liberation, thus providing the conditions needed for a victorious offensive in the south.

Direct rail communication between the Soviet border stations of Otpor* and Grodekovo and the cities of Dal'niy and Port Arthur, interrupted in 1945, was restored on November 25, 1948.

Soviet specialists supervised the training of the PLA's railroad troops; 4,615 specialists in different professions were trained in the summer of 1948 alone.

The result of the unselfish assistance rendered by the Soviet Union in building and restoration of railroads and bridges in Manchuria, and in converting the Chinese Changchun Railroad into a huge industrial and training base ensuring the accumulation of experience and the training of cadres, was to make the northeast revolutionary base the springboard for the tempestuous offensive of the revolutionary forces against the regime of Chiang Kai-shek in 1948–1949. The leadership of the CCP regarded highly the contribution made by the Soviet people in development of the Chinese revolution, seeing in it a clear expression of proletarian solidarity and sincere friendship for the Chinese people. Soong Ch'ing-ling, Deputy Chairman of the PRC, stressed the fact:

> Among the first of the Soviet workers to arrive in China were Soviet engineers. They worked on the complex questions of providing the assistance that made possible the restoration of our railroad network many months sooner than had been planned. They did their job, and did not ask anything in return.[20]

The assistance rendered the Chinese by Soviet doctors had many facets. An epidemic of plague broke out in the liberated provinces at the end of 1947, posing a threat to the densely populated areas of South Manchuria and North China. By request of the people's revolutionary authorities the USSR sent in anti-epidemic teams led by Professor O. V. Baroyan and Professor N. I. Nikolayev. These teams brought with them laboratories, prophylactics, and medicines, and upon arrival attacked the outbreak of plague along a broad front, with the result that by mid-1948 the epidemic was wiped out. As leaders of the People's Democratic Administrative Commission pointed out, the Soviet doctors saved tens of thousands of inhabitants of Northeast China from certain death.

* Now Zabaykal'sk.

Still another plague epidemic broke out in the spring of 1949 and spread quickly over wide areas of the liberated territory of Inner Mongolia, in Chahar Province (around Kalgan and other points). By request of the people's democratic authorities, the Soviet government dispatched special aircraft with an antiplague expedition including doctors, zoologists, and medical workers.

Here is what Soong Ch'ing-ling, an eminent public figure in the CCP, wrote about the unselfish assistance rendered by Soviet medical personnel during the plague epidemic:

> We had insufficient doctors and specialists to cope with this most dangerous epidemic, so we turned to our great neighbor. And in short order the antiplague teams arrived from the USSR. They came, gave help, finished their work, and went home. They harbored no thoughts of securing payment or concessions. They asked for no privilege other than that of helping the Chinese people.[21]

A new epidemic of plague broke out to the northwest of Peking in October 1949. Peking was blockaded, supplies to the city were interrupted, and the city began to encounter economic difficulties. Within twenty-four hours after receiving a request from Mao Tse-tung to provide assistance, several antiplague teams and their equipment (trucks, fumigating installations), including medical personnel and medicines, arrived by air from the USSR. Millions of people were vaccinated. The threat was swiftly eliminated.

As the PLA moved southward, and into the areas in which Lin Piao's army in particular was disposed, the troops were stricken with malaria. Within two days after receiving the request from Lin Piao, the USSR flew in almost a ton of quinine. The quinine helped maintain the army's ability to fight and to carry on successful combat operations against the forces of the Kuomintang.

In August 1949 the CC CCP requested that the Soviet Union send to China a large group of specialists to provide organizational and technical aid in restoring and developing liberated areas. The Soviet Union immediately placed the required number of highly-qualified workers at the disposal of the people's democratic authorities.

The first group of specialists (some 250 in all), upon arriving in China, was assigned as needed and by agreement with the leadership of the CCP. Some developed the structure for running the country, determining the functions of future ministries and departments, and how to operate them, and then participated in organizing the administration and stimulation of the national economy. Others were assigned directly to the largest of the plants to organize restoration work, administration, and the operation of active enterprises.

Soviet technicians and engineers played an important role in the restoration of the shipbuilding yard in Dal'niy. Soviet equipment began to arrive in the yard at the beginning of 1947. By the end of 1947 the yard was employing 254 engineers and technicians, 261 office personnel, and over 2,000 workers. The shipyard underwent extensive reconstruction between 1948 and 1949, and by the end of 1949 was producing at a rate well in excess of the prewar level.

All suggestions made by Soviet specialists for setting up organs of administration and their structures were passed along to the CC CCP, and to organs of the state apparatus then in formative stages. Many ministries and departments were headed by people who had been in the Army or partisan units and were without applicable training or work experience. Guided by a sense of internationalism, our advisers and specialists freely shared their wealth of experience with new Chinese cadres, training them on a day-to-day basis.

The assistance given by Soviet specialists was particularly broad in scope after formation of the PRC.

Reviewing Sino-Soviet relations prior to the victory of the revolution, and during the flowering of those relations, one is struck by the fact that even in the best years there were definite difficulties, attributable to the fact that some cadres of the CCP, particularly those petty bourgeois by birth, were infected with nationalistic and anti-Soviet feelings.

Part of the leadership of the CCP, headed by Mao Tse-tung, overestimated their own strength and underestimated the strength of the enemy. Petty bourgeois notions about the Chinese Revolution, fluctuating from one extreme to the other, were inherent traits of Mao Tse-tung during this period. Our party, and the international Communist movement, recommended that the CCP gather its forces and create, by diplomatic and political struggle, the necessary conditions for equipping and training the PLA for the forthcoming offensive. But it was at precisely this period that Mao Tse-tung developed "revolutionary impatience," indicated by the fact that he had, for many years, been disseminating a story that went something like this:

> Stalin himself is the one who has been delaying the Chinese Revolution. Stalin said it would be impossible to wage a civil war, that we must cooperate with Chiang Kai-shek. Otherwise the Chinese nation would perish. We did not listen then, and the revolution triumphed.

This deliberate slander against the policy of our party was readily seized upon by anti-Communist historians. As a matter of fact, discussion at that time centered on how to use diplomatic and political maneuvers to preserve the strength of the Chinese Revolution, and to prepare for the forthcoming offensive and insure a quick victory.

The leading group in the CCP did not understand, or did not want to understand, that the policy of a united front, not only during the anti-Japanese war but in 1945–1946 as well (when Chiang Kai-shek and his army still had strength plus strong support by American imperialism, and when the strength of the Communist Party was still scattered), was the policy superseding all others which gave the Chinese Revolution the advantage. The combination of a political and diplomatic form of struggle, waged simultaneously with a build-up in military potential, was the only correct road to take at this stage of the Chinese Revolution.

Later, on the eve of victory in 1949, Mao Tse-tung expressed scepticism as to the strength of the Chinese Revolution allied to the USSR, the first country of socialism. Even during the concluding stage of the struggle, when the Revolutionary Army had been successful in advancing into the south, Mao Tse-tung made statements to the effect that the revolution could not succeed any earlier than two years, and was helpless when it came to solving the practical problems involved in the establishment of the people's authority throughout China.

Mao Tse-tung's conception of what China's foreign policy ought to have been during this period is extremely indicative of his true *Weltanschauung*. †His stated opinion was that it would be better for China not to conduct diplomatic relations with the Soviet Union or the United States. Simultaneously, even at this point, he advanced the claim that the national liberation movement throughout Asia, and particularly in Southeast Asia, should come under Chinese control.

Mao Tse-tung evidenced defeatist tendencies which were engendered by fear of Kuomintang forces who captured Yenan in 1947 and forced him to escape to the northern regions of China. †It is known that after the capture of Yenan Mao Tse-tung was roaming the roads of North China, far from the center of the revolutionary struggle, which at that time had moved to Manchuria. Yenan, on the eve of the decisive battle, lost its importance as the headquarters of the CCP and of its armed forces. This role then shifted to Manchuria, which became the main base of the Chinese Revolution.

The political instability of Mao Tse-tung in other instances confirms the petty bourgeois nature of his outlook, which ranged from one extreme (the instigation of revolution in 1945–1946) to the other (doubts in 1948–1949 as to the possibility of quick victory for the Chinese Revolution).

Negative tendencies toward the Soviet Union also appeared within a definite group of the leadership of the Northeast Bureau of the CCP. The nationalist and anti-Soviet sentiments of this group had been so widely disseminated that in 1946–1947 the Bureau was forced to conduct a number of investigations, during which a number of leading figures were charged with serious accusations. Nevertheless, the main leadership of the CCP was reluctant to condemn these workers at that time, keeping them in leadership posts and permitting them to spread anti-Soviet slander.

Portents of the future appeared at that time, particularly when party organs in Manchuria obstructed the work of the Chinese-Soviet Friendship Association. The newspaper *Wen Hui Pao* (Culture), published in Northeast China, had long been printing anti-Soviet propaganda fabricated by its editor, Hsiao Chung-ya, urging "the ejection from China of imperialists of whatever color," including the USSR. The paper was subsidized by the Communists, and it was not until the end of 1948 that the Northeast Bureau of the CC CCP decided to close it.

Only the firm policy of the Soviet Union and the CPSU, supported by other Marxist-Leninist parties and the Chinese internationalists, averted widespread intervention by American imperialism in China, strengthened the revolutionary forces, created in Manchuria a strategic military base, isolated the Chiang Kai-shek regime inside the country, obtained from progressive world society moral and political support for the Chinese Revolution, and ensured the great victory of the fraternal Chinese people in 1949.

Thus historical facts prove that the alliance between the revolutionary forces in China and the USSR, and through it with the world revolutionary movement, was one of the decisive factors in the victory of the Chinese revolution. This brotherly alliance between Chinese workers and world socialism compensated for the relative weakness of the working class in China, helped consolidate internal forces of the Revolution, protecting them against the export of counterrevolution, and created favorable international prerequisites for fulfillment by Chinese revolutionaries of their historical mission.

NOTES

1. *Pravda,* February 21, 1948.
2. *Vneshnyaya politika Sovetskogo Soyuza v period Otechestvennoy voyny. Dokumenty i materialy,* t. III. M., 1946, str. 112 (*Foreign Policy of the Soviet Union in the Period of the Patriotic War. Documents and Materials. Vol. III,* hereinafter referred to as *Foreign Policy of the Soviet Union*) (Moscow, 1947), p. 112.
3. S. M. Shtemenko, *General'nyy shtab v gody voyny,* M., 1968, str. 360 (*The General Staff in the War Years,* hereinafter referred to as *The General Staff*) (Moscow, 1968), p. 360.
4. Mao Tse-tung, *Izbrannyye proizvedeniya (Selected Works),* Vol. 4 (Moscow, 1953), p. 617.
5. *Pravda,* August 11, 1945.
6. *Pravda,* August 17, 1945.
7. *Pravda,* July 21, 1949.
8. *Kuang-Ming Jihpao,* September 3, 1951.
9. *Leninskaya politika SSSR v otnoshenii Kitaya* (*The Leninist Policy of the USSR in Relation to China,* hereinafter referred to as *The Leninist Policy*) (Moscow, 1968), p. 126.
10. *Vneshnyaya politika Sovetskogo Soyuza. 1947 god. Dokumenty i materialy* (*Foreign Policy of the Soviet Union. 1947. Documents and Materials. Part I,* hereinafter referred to as *Foreign Policy of the Soviet Union, 1947*) (Moscow, 1952), p. 375.
11. Ibid., p. 376.
12. *Izvestiya,* November 30, 1945.
13. *Izvestiya,* November 30, 1945.
14. *Vneshnyaya politika Sovetskogo Soyuza. 1946 god. Dokumenty i materialy* (*Foreign Policy of the Soviet Union. 1946. Documents and Materials,* hereinafter referred to as *Foreign Policy of the Soviet Union, 1946*) (Moscow, 1952), p. 112.
15. *Answers to Questions Regarding Socialist Ideological Education,* 5th edition (hereinafter referred to as *Answers to Questions*) Futs'an, Jenmin ch'u pan she (Peking, 1957).
16. *The Leninist Policy,* p. 130–133.
17. *Vneshnyaya politika Sovetskogo Soyuza. 1949. Dokumenty i materialy* (*Foreign Policy of the Soviet Union. 1949. Documents and Materials,* hereinafter referred to as *Foreign Policy of the Soviet Union, 1949*) (Moscow, 1953), p. 124.
18. *The Leninist Policy,* p. 133.
19. Ibid., p. 135.
20. *Narodnyi Kitay (People's China)* (Peking), No. 1, 1950. (In English).
21. Ibid.

CHAPTER TWO

Sino-Soviet Relations in the Years of the Molding of the PRC (1949–1952)

The long years of struggle by the Chinese people for their liberation were crowned by a historical victory. The PRC was proclaimed on October 1, 1949. The Chinese revolution dealt a crushing blow against positions of imperialism in Asia, helped change the balance of power in the world arena in favor of socialism, and gave new impetus to the national liberation movement in the colonial periphery of the capitalist world.

The victory of the Chinese revolution was made possible by an extremely favorable international situation. The defeat of German Fascism and Japanese militarism resulted in the formation and further development of the world socialist system, the offspring of the international proletariat. The Chinese revolution received constantly increasing support from the brotherly states, from the world Communist movement, and particularly from the Soviet Union.

1. First acts in relations between the USSR and the PRC and their significance

The CC CPSU and the Soviet government made every effort, from the very inception of the PRC, to strengthen Sino-Soviet friendship, and to develop collaboration between the USSR and the PRC.

The Soviet Union was the first state to announce recognition of the new People's China and establishment of diplomatic relations between the USSR and the PRC. "The Chinese government and the Chinese people," read the note from the PRC Ministry of Foreign Affairs in connection with the establishment of diplomatic relations, "are experiencing unbounded joy because of the fact that today the Soviet Union became the first friendly power to recognize the People's Republic of China."[1]

The Soviet Union attached great importance not only to the material content of its international assistance to the Chinese people, but also to the creation of a strong basis in international law for Sino-Soviet rela-

64

tions. The Treaty of Friendship, Alliance, and Mutual Assistance between the USSR and the PRC, signed on February 14, 1950, was of extreme importance in strengthening the PRC's international position and developing Sino-Soviet friendship. The treaty embodied the highest principles of complete equality, respect for territorial integrity, state independence, national sovereignty, and noninterference in each other's internal affairs, and was a model for a new type of state relationship inherent between brotherly socialist countries. In his telegram of greetings to Soviet leaders on the occasion of the first anniversary of the signing of the treaty, Mao Tse-tung said:

> The signing of the Treaty of Friendship, Alliance, and Mutual Assistance between China and the USSR not only was of tremendous help in building the new China, it was a strong guarantee in the struggle against aggression and for the preservation of peace and security in the Far East and throughout the world.[2]

Taking into consideration the root changes in the situation in the Far East after formation of the PRC, the Soviet government acceded to the wishes of the Chinese and created a solid legal basis with respect to questions concerning the Chinese Changchun Railroad, Port Arthur, and Dal'niy.

The agreement reached on these questions, signed on February 14, 1950, stipulated that the Soviet government would transfer to the government of the PRC all of its rights in connection with the joint administration of the Chinese Changchun Railroad, together with all railroad property, no later than the end of 1952, and would do so without compensation.

During this same period, the governments agreed that Soviet troops would be withdrawn from the joint naval base at Port Arthur, with all base installations to be transferred to the government of the PRC.

The government of the USSR further agreed that all property it used or rented in Dal'niy would be transferred to the government of the PRC in 1950, under terms that would be determined within three months from the date of the agreement.

Equally important for strengthening friendly ties between the USSR and the PRC was the agreement whereby the Soviet Union granted the government of the PRC a credit in the sum of 300 million American dollars, or 1,200 million rubles.* Soviet deliveries to the PRC were

---

* The total credit was not stipulated in rubles in the agreement. Conversion into rubles was made at a later date, after the establishment of the new rate, four rubles to the dollar, on March 1, 1950.

designed to restore and reconstruct the most important branches of the national economy. It was anticipated that over a five-year period (1950–1954) deliveries from the Soviet Union to China equal to the total credit would include equipment and materials for electric stations, metallurgical and machine building plants, coal mines, rail and road transportation, and for other branches of the Chinese economy.

Recognizing the tremendous destruction to China's national economy resulting from extended military operations on China's territory, the Soviet government advanced China credit on unusually favorable terms. China would pay only one percent for the use of the credit, terms without precedent in world credit practice.

The Soviet Union assumed an obligation to assist the PRC in building 50 large industrial enterprises.

An agreement with respect to the establishment of joint Soviet-Chinese stock companies was signed on March 27, 1950, and included:

(a) the "Sovkitmetall" Company (Chung-Su Chin-shu Kung-sze),* founded to prospect, survey, extract, and process nonferrous and rare metals in Sinkiang province;

(b) the "Sovkitneft'" Company (Chung-Su Hsi-you Kung-sze), founded to prospect, survey, and extract oil, gas, and related petroleum products, and to refine them, in Sinkiang province;

(c) the SKOGA (Chung-Su Min-hang Kung-Sze) Company for the operation of the following air lines: Peking-Shengyang (Mukden)—Changchun—Harbin—Tsitsihar (Lungkiang)—Hilar—Chita; Peking—Taiyuan — Sian — Lanchow — Suchow — Hami — Urumchi — Kuldja —Alma Ata; Peking—Wuchuan (Kalgan)—Ulan Bator—Irkutsk.

Under terms of the agreements, which were to run for 30 years, the joint Soviet-Chinese companies were set up on an equal footing, each side participating equally in the capital of the companies, and in administration of their affairs. Direction of the companies was to be in the hands of a representative of each side in turn.

These companies, in addition to production problems faced during the initial period of restoration of the Chinese economy, agreed to train qualified technical and administrative cadres from among the Chinese.

---

* Even prior to World War II, Soviet geologists, at the request of the Chinese authorities of Sinkiang province, had prospected in this region for deposits of nonferrous metals and oil. These deposits became the bases for the establishment of joint Soviet-Chinese enterprises for the extraction and concentration of a number of nonferrous metals in Burchum, and for the extraction and refining of oil in the Tushantse region. These enterprises operated until 1943. Later on they were laid up by Chiang Kai-shek's authorities. They became the basis for the establishment of the joint Soviet-Chinese stock companies.

This was accomplished by companies establishing technical schools and courses or by sending Chinese citizens to schools in the Soviet Union. The newspaper *Jen Min Jihpao* (People's Daily), on October 13, 1954, wrote:

> Thanks to the use of advanced Soviet experience in economic construction and first-class techniques, success in returning things to normal and in expanding the work of the enterprises administered by these companies was quick in coming. Imperialists very often resort to the export of capital to colonial and semicolonial countries in order to carry out economic aggression against those countries. However, the capital investment of the socialist Soviet Union in the companies mentioned above is an entirely different matter, and is for completely different purposes. These purposes are to use money and equipment to help develop those natural riches we have, and which we cannot develop with our own resources, or to return to normal operation those enterprises we have which we would have difficulty in operating with our own resources, while at the same time helping to create conditions for the economic independence of the people of our country. . . . The Soviet government has helped us put the joint companies in business, has trained cadres, given us the benefit of its experience, and now is giving us our share of participation in the work of these companies. That is, we now have enterprises subordinate to these companies that will wholly become state enterprises of our country. Comparing these facts with the economic aggression of the imperialists with respect to old China, our people really are hard pressed to express their deepest appreciation to the Soviet Union for its sincerely noble help to our country.

A trade agreement establishing the overall legal bases for trade relationships between the USSR and the PRC was signed in Moscow on April 19, 1950. Under the terms of this agreement, the USSR was to export to China gasoline, kerosene, lubricating oils, miscellaneous machinery, tools, equipment, transportation equipment, fuel, cotton, and other raw materials necessary for the restoration and development of the economy of the PRC.

A number of other agreements were concluded between the USSR and China in 1950, including an agreement on post, telegraph, and telephone communications, an agreement on the leasing of Soviet films in China, and an agreement on river navigation and the corresponding rules.

Assessing the value of the treaties and the legal documents signed by our countries during this period, Mao Tse-tung told a session of the government of the PRC that:

> The new Sino-Soviet treaties and agreements have legally strengthened the friendship between the great peoples of China and the Soviet Union,

and have given us a dependable ally. They have simplified our work in
the field of internal construction and have simplified the taking of joint
counteraction against imperialist aggression in the name of preserving
peace throughout the world.[3]

*2. Economic assistance from the Soviet people in the first years of
the molding of the PRC*

The support given the PRC by the Soviet Union was of extreme importance in what for the Chinese people were very difficult years as they
molded the people's power. The situation in the country was extremely
difficult as a result of the long anti-Japanese and civil wars, and because
of open plundering by imperialists. The productive capacity, poor
enough to begin with, had been destroyed and people were experiencing
hunger and poverty. The following data will provide some idea of the
economic situation in the young republic. The PRC in 1950 mined 36
million tons of coal, and produced 877,000 tons of pig iron and 584,000
tons of steel. Industrial production lagged badly behind the maximum
output of 1942–1943. Coal mined was down to 61 percent of that level,
pig iron to 46 percent, and steel down to 63 percent.

The country's agriculture was badly run down. The harvest of food
crops in 1949 was less than 75 percent of prewar figures, and the cotton
crop had been cut almost in half.

The material position of the population was very serious. The price
of one chin (about 400 grams) of *chumisze,* a type of millet, rose by a
factor of 15.3 in Peking, and by a factor of 14 in Tientsin, between
April 1, 1949 and November 1, 1949. In this same period the price of
rice increased by factors of 13.8 and 11.5, respectively, in these cities.
In November 1949, as compared with the end of October, the prices of
foodstuffs rose once again, this time by a factor of between 3 and 4,
while the prices of industrial goods rose by a factor of between 2 and 3.
In 1950 the Central People's Government adopted a budget that showed
an 18.9 percent deficit.

This situation was aggravated in 1951, when the imperialists imposed
a trade embargo on China. In December 1949 the NATO countries and
Japan had created a Coordinating Committee, the purpose of which was
to monitor and observe exports of goods with a "strategic purpose" to
the socialist countries, including the PRC. This committee became the
basis for the establishment of the China Committee, the membership of
which also included representatives of Australia, the Latin American
states, and a number of other countries. The committee periodically published lists of "strategic goods," the export of which to the PRC, and

countries adjacent, was forbidden. These measures deprived China of the possibility of buying materials, machinery, equipment, and other goods the country needed in capitalist markets. Moreover, use of middlemen resulted in additional expenditures of hard currency, which the PRC lacked.

Just as during the years of struggle for liberation, the Soviet people, still not recovered from unprecedented destruction in the Patriotic War, once again extended to China the hand of brotherly assistance and began to render all sorts of help in restoring and developing their economy.

Soviet experts, noted Soong Ch'ing-ling,

> brought to China precious experience in solving practical problems, whatever their magnitude. They brought with them methods based on the highest scientific achievements, and a wealth of experience in working for the good of the people. Many of them participated in the restoration of the economy after the October socialist revolution. All of them have participated in the heroic building of socialism and are participating in the preparations for communism in the USSR. The conditions which we have in China, and which we must overcome, already are familiar to them and have been overcome by them in their own time. They are coping with the task imposed upon them with the greatest of enthusiasm, the task of helping the Chinese people to master this experience for the building of a new China.[4]

Trade with the Soviet Union was of exceptional importance to the PRC. The USSR, in ninth place in China's exports in 1948, rose to third place in 1949, and reached first place by the end of 1950. The role of the Soviet Union in China's imports increased from 1949. The share of the USSR in those imports rose from 4.86 percent in 1949 (fifth place) to 20.4 percent in the first nine months of 1950 (second place).

A series of new agreements between the USSR and the PRC was signed in 1951, indicative of further development in Sino-Soviet collaboration.

An agreement on rail communication, envisaging the direct transportation of passengers, baggage, and freight, was signed on March 14. An agreement on establishing the rate of exchange for the ruble with respect to the Chinese yuan was signed on June 1. Under the terms of this agreement the rate of exchange for the ruble was set directly in terms of the yuan on the basis of the gold content of the ruble and of the official price of gold in Peking, rather than in terms of the American dollar rate of exchange. The agreement with respect to the establishment in Dal'niy of the joint Sino-Soviet ship repair and shipbuilding stock company, "Sovkitsudstroy," was concluded in Peking on July 28, 1951. The company was founded on an equal footing for a period of 25 years.

Simultaneously, both sides exchanged notes in accordance with which the Chinese government undertook to maintain the volume of Soviet orders on the "Dal'dok" Yard for the first three years at the levels of orders actually completed for Soviet organizations between 1949 and 1950.

These agreements not only helped stabilize the economy and finances of People's China, but also served to strengthen China's international position.

A clear example of the close collaboration between the USSR and the PRC was the broad trade turnover between them, a turnover that increased monthly. In 10 months of 1951, the trade turnover between the USSR and the PRC was 77 percent above that for the same months in 1950 (including an increase in imports by the PRC from the USSR as compared with the same period in 1950 of 117 percent, and an increase of 54 percent in exports to the USSR). In September 1951 the USSR's share was 40.7 percent of China's imports and 41.12 percent of its exports. Thanks to the assistance provided by the Soviet Union, the development of the national economy of the PRC in 1951 was accompanied by a further strengthening of planning principles and an improvement in the quality of planning. The government of the PRC, with the assistance of Soviet experts, made a number of decisions and approved a series of documents of great importance to improving and intensifying planning efforts at the center, as well as locally. In July 1951, for the first time in the history of the PRC, a unified annual state plan was drafted for restoration and development of the national economy.

The collaboration with the Soviet Union and its comprehensive aid and support made 1951 a year of further strengthening and growth in the socialist sector of the national economy of the PRC. The high proportion of the socialist sector in industry will be seen from the following breakdown (in percents):

Heavy industry	80
Petroleum	100
Pig iron	98
Coal	72.5
Electric power	76
Machine building	82
Light industry (*by numbers employed*)	33
Cotton industry (*manufactured textiles*)	70

In accordance with the agreement of February 14, 1950 the Soviet Union began large shipments of heavy industrial equipment to the PRC.

In 1951 the value of this equipment was 30.9 million rubles, and in 1952 the figure was 36.6 million rubles.*

Later on shipments of industrial equipment became the main item of Soviet exports to the PRC. Shipments of equipment also included assistance in prospecting and planning efforts, activating enterprises, mastering production of new types of industrial products never before manufactured in China, participation in erection and adjustment of equipment, and training cadres.

A great many qualified Soviet experts participated in development and implementation of the plan for hydraulic engineering construction work on the largest rivers in the PRC and in restoration of the railroads.

The struggle of the Soviet Union to support the PRC against the aggressive plans of the United States took on special meaning and importance in those years. The decisive actions taken by the USSR in the United Nations Organization to mount a broad international campaign against the American occupation of Taiwan are well known.

Assistance provided by the Soviet Union in these difficult years for the Republic was not limited to diplomatic measures and development of comprehensive collaboration in the fields of economics, science, culture, and military construction. There were, as well, direct military actions that cooled the aggressive intentions of the imperialists.

†In 1949–1950 large aviation forces of the Soviet Union, at the request of the government of the PRC, provided air cover for Shanghai, East China's industrial center. Flights by the Americans and by the forces of Chiang Kai-shek were disrupted. They were given a stern lesson by Soviet air aces.

In 1950, also at the request of the government of the PRC, our country transferred crack aviation divisions to Manchuria, which provided dependable air cover against enemy air attacks for the industrial centers in Northeast China. These divisions shot down scores of American aircraft in the air battles that took place.[5]

There was close military collaboration between the USSR and the PRC during the period of military operations in Korea. The Soviet Union provided the People's Army of Korea, and the Chinese volunteers, with an uninterrupted supply of weapons, ammunition, fuel, food, and medicines. Soviet advisors, including eminent military leaders, were present in Korea. Soviet pilots participated in the battles with the aggressors.

* Here and in what follows the figures are given in new rubles.

3. Sino-Soviet relations at the end of the Restoration Period

The Soviet Union engaged in a variety of forms of collaboration with China in the first years of the existence of the PRC. Personal contacts between leaders of the two countries were important for strengthening political ties between them.

Attending the signing of the Treaty of Friendship, Alliance, and Mutual Assistance in Moscow was a delegation to the Soviet Union that included Mao Tse-tung, Chou En-lai, and other prominent state and party leaders of the PRC. Liu Shao-chi (it was he who headed the delegation of the Communist Party of China to the 19th Congress of the Communist Party of the Soviet Union), and Marshal Chu Teh were frequent visitors to the USSR. In turn, leading Soviet figures often made friendly visits to the PRC.

Important to Sino-Soviet relations were Soviet talks with the Chinese government delegation, headed by Chou En-lai, which visited Moscow in September 1952. These talks resulted in the sides agreeing to take steps to have the Soviet Union hand over to the PRC, without indemnity and in full title, its rights concerning joint administration of the Chinese Changchun Railroad. The Ministers of Foreign Affairs of the USSR and of the PRC simultaneously exchanged notes concerning the question of continuation of joint use of the Chinese naval base in Port Arthur. The results of the talks were assessed by the Chinese government as acts of disinterested and brotherly assistance on the part of the Soviet Union.

The entire length of the Chinese Changchun Railroad was restored between 1950 and 1952. The Soviet government handed over to the government of the PRC all rights concerning the administration of the railroad on the date fixed by the agreement, December 31, 1952. Accordingly the main lines of the Chinese Changchun Railroad, those running from Manchuria Station to Pogranichnaya Station (Suifenho) and from Harbin to Dal'niy and Port Arthur, together with railway installations and structures, rolling stock, electric stations and communication lines, as well as other enterprises and institutions servicing the railroad were transferred to the Chinese.

Mao Tse-tung, in his telegram to the head of the Soviet government, J. V. Stalin, evaluated this act as a "tremendous contribution on the part of the Soviet Union to railroad building in China." Chou En-lai, in a speech made on the occasion of the signing of the final protocol concerning the transfer of the Chinese Changchun Railroad, said:

> The Chinese people will never forget this brotherly assistance on the part of the Soviet people. It should be pointed out, in particular, that the sin-

cere and patient giving of their knowledge by our Soviet comrades has enabled the Chinese employees and workers of the Changchun Railroad to absorb the advanced experience of the Soviet Union and has helped us train many cadres for railroad building in the new China.

The newspaper *Jen Min Jihpao,* in its lead article on December 31, 1952, said that in the fact of handing over to China the Changchun Railroad without compensation, and in the agreement to extend the set term for the withdrawal of Soviet troops from Port Arthur, "there is yet greater evidence of the respect the government of the Soviet Union has for the governmental independence and national honor of our country."

And a representative of the PRC told the Soviet-Chinese Commission charged with effecting the transfer of the Chinese Changchun Railroad:

> We sincerely and wholeheartedly thank the Soviet government . . . for its tremendous, unselfish, assistance to our Chinese People's Republic, to our Chinese people. The fact of the transfer of the Chinese Changchun Railroad is yet another tangible piece of evidence of the high regard the Soviet government has for the state sovereignty and national dignity of the Chinese people, as well as of the unlimited faith the Soviet government has with respect to the friendship and alliance between China and the USSR. . . .

When the government of the PRC decided, in 1952, to start production of natural rubber in its own country, the government of the Soviet Union advanced to China a credit in the sum of 8.55 million rubles to finance the cost of developing rubber plantations on Hainan Island and in the coastal regions of the southeastern part of the country.

Trade relations between the USSR and the PRC continued to develop in 1952. The total trade turnover between the USSR and the PRC almost doubled as compared with 1950.[6]

The Soviet Union increased its technical assistance to the PRC substantially. A great deal of assistance was forthcoming in mastering the complex technical equipment provided, as well as in construction of new industrial enterprises. This was in addition to prospecting and planning done in 1952. For the most part the Soviet Union met its obligations to provide technical assistance in 1952; the following large projects began operations: a flax-spinning combine in Harbin; an automobile repair plant in Urumchi; a 25,000-kilowatt electric station in Fursin. The production planned for six automobile repair shops and factories that began operations at the end of 1951 was reached in 1952. Some 1,000 Soviet specialists were at work in the PRC in 1952 (over 400 of these specialists were there under contract for purposes of providing technical assistance, the others in accordance with the terms of the agreement of March 27, 1950).

Po Yi-po, Candidate Member of the Politburo of the CC CCP, in his report to the assembly celebrating the third anniversary of the signing of the Treaty of Friendship, Alliance, and Mutual Assistance between the USSR and the PRC, characterized the work done by the Soviet specialists as follows:

> The help given us by the Soviet specialists is extremely diverse, and every measure that we are undertaking in our economic life is being taken with the help of their advanced technical guidance. It would be impossible to list all the advantages our country has obtained as a result of their help. Were it not for the unselfish help from the Soviet specialists, it would have been very difficult for us to have achieved those tremendous successes in the restoration and reconstruction of the national economy of our country that we have over the past three years, beginning with the healing of the wounds inflicted by the war, and ending with basic improvements in our financial and economic position and in the creation of the different conditions needed to carry out the First Five-Year Plan of construction.[7]

Direct participation of Soviet specialists resulted in the reorganization of the system of higher education, courts, and judicial system, in the creation of new ministries, and in a system of state planning.

The Soviet people helped authorities in the PRC publish over 3,100 Soviet books in the Chinese language in the first three years. These titles included 943 on social sciences and 348 dealing with questions of culture and education.[8] In the fall of 1952 the PRC began to reconstruct all its educational programs and curricula, using as a model Soviet higher institutions of learning. It also embarked on a major program of translating the materials used in the higher institutions of learning in the USSR. The workers assigned in 1952 to the Agricultural Institute of Northeast China, for example, translated into Chinese and distributed to all PRC higher institutions of learning in the field of agriculture Soviet curricula covering 141 disciplines.

Popularization of Soviet experience in different fields of socialist construction was widely organized under the slogan, "Learn from the Soviet Union." One manifestation of this program in the first years after liberation was the mass movement to study the Russian language. In the first two years of its existence, the people's authorities in the PRC opened 12 Russian language institutes, with 5,000 students enrolled.[9] In addition, 57 institutions of higher learning had divisions and courses in the

Russian language in 1952. Russian was taught in all middle schools in Northeast China, in 59 schools in Peking, and in other cities.

Soviet-Chinese cultural ties developed successfully. A clear expression of the friendship between the Soviet and Chinese peoples was Chinese-Soviet Friendship Month (November-December 1952), which took the form of a huge political campaign. Chou En-lai, at the opening of the month, said, "The generous and unselfish assistance on the part of the government of the USSR had made it possible for us to strengthen our defense, to cope with the economic blockade established by the imperialist states, and to insure quick successes in the work of restoring the economy." The Soviet delegation of cultural, scientific, and artistic leaders who visited the PRC for the occasion were warmly received by the Chinese people as they traveled about the country. Soviet artists gave over 80 concerts, attended by 500,000 spectators, during their stay in China. A Red Army ensemble presented the songs and dances of the Soviet Army at 60 concerts viewed by almost one million persons.

Thanks to Soviet assistance, the development of the PRC in 1952 can be characterized by further strengthening of the dictatorship of the people's democracy, and by significant success in state, economic, and cultural construction. In the field of economics, 1952 was primarily a year of completion of the restoration and further development of the most important branches of the national economy, as well as of preparations for widespread economic construction in accordance with the provisions of the First Five-Year Plan.

The gross output of industry increased 24.7 percent in 1952, as compared with 1951, with production by state industry contributing over 60 percent of the total value of the country's production. Agriculture, in addition to completion of the agrarian reform program, saw the beginning of the movement to increase production and to set up cooperative types of peasant labor. The result of land reforms was to distribute 44 million hectares of land to the peasants. On these lands the peasants had been paying rent to the landowners of at least 30 million tons of grain annually.

Great social and economic changes took place in the PRC during the restoration period. Relying on comprehensive economic and political support and assistance of the Soviet Union, and on broad military collaboration reliably guaranteeing the country's national security, the people's government, having inherited ruin and decay, could develop and implement a broad program of social reforms and restoration of the national economy.

The authority of the people's revolutionary dictatorship was strengthened. A socialist sector appeared in the economy. The state seized the basic means of production and the principal economic levers (credit, supplies of raw materials, markets), with the help of which it was able to control the private capitalist sector. Agriculture, commerce, and other fields were reorganized. In 1949 the gross output of state industry was 26.7 percent of the country's industry as a whole. This figure increased to 44.7 percent in 1952. The material well-being of the population improved, and national science and culture developed.

The restoration period proved an important stage in Sino-Soviet relations because the international support and tremendous assistance provided by the Soviet people enabled China to overcome international and domestic difficulties and prepare all conditions needed for successful transition to planned socialist construction.

NOTES

1. *Jen Min Jihpao* (*People's Daily*), October 2, 1949.

2. *Jen Min Jihpao,* February 14, 1951.

3. *Jen Min Jihpao,* April 13, 1950.

4. *Narodnyi Kitay* (*People's China*), Vol. III, No. 9–10, 1951, p. 20.

5. M. S. Kapitsa, *KNR: dva desyatiletiya—dve politiki* (*The People's Republic of China: Two Decades—Two Policies,* hereinafter referred to as Kapitsa) (Moscow, 1969), p. 36.

6. M. I. Sladkovskiy, *Ocherki ekonomicheskikh otnosheniy USSR s Kitayem* (*Essays on the USSR's Economic Relations with China,* hereinafter referred to as *Economic Relations with China*) (Moscow, 1957), p. 310.

7. *Jen Min Jihpao,* February 15, 1953.

8. *Narodnyi Kitay,* No. 22, 1952, p. 27.

9. *Narodnyi Kitay,* Vol. IV. No. 7–8, 1951, p. 19.

CHAPTER THREE

Sino-Soviet Relations in the Years of the First Five-Year Plan (1953–1957)

1. Further expansion in cooperation between the USSR and the PRC, 1953–1957

The genuine successes attained in economic construction and democratic transformation within the country, attributable to the selfless labor of the Chinese people and to the disinterested assistance provided by the Soviet Union, provided the basis for adoption by the CCP in 1953 of the general line of shifting from capitalism to socialism. This line was adopted in 1954 by the National People's Congress, and then strengthened in the Constitution of the PRC.

The successes attained by the PRC in different fields of building a new life rested on the comprehensive experience of our country and on the vast material aid provided by the Soviet people. The political report of the CC CCP to the 8th Congress expressed appreciation to all friends of the Chinese people for their aid and assistance. "The Soviet Union," said the document, "was of tremendous help in the business of socialist construction in our country. The countries of people's democracy in Europe and Asia too were a big help in this regard. The Chinese people never will forget this comradely help provided by the fraternal countries."[1]

The PRC received from the USSR and other fraternal countries everything needed to develop domestic industry, science, and engineering, and was given the opportunity to sell its traditional exports on the markets of those countries. Hence the attempts of the United States and its partners in the aggressive bloc to organize an economic blockade of China were completely unsuccessful, largely because of our government's energetic struggle in the international arena to increase the authority of the young republic, and to break up the plans of the imperialists to isolate the PRC.

The First Five-Year Plan for Development of the National Economy of the PRC was adopted in 1953.

The main objective of the Communist Party's line during the transition period was to transform socialist property into the means of production as the economic base of the state and social system in the PRC. Consequently, the central task during the transition period was to effect the socialist industrialization of the country and a socialist transformation in agriculture, in cottage industry, and in private capitalist industry and trade. It was contemplated that the fulfillment of these tasks would take approximately 15 years.

Initially leading figures in the CCP, and Chinese propaganda as a whole, understood correctly the relationship between efforts of the Chinese people and aid provided by the Soviet Union and other fraternal countries in the matter of socialist construction in the PRC. *Jen Min Jihpao,* in its lead article entitled "We Thank the Soviet Union for Its Great Help," published on September 16, 1953, wrote:

> Chairman Mao Tse-tung, refuting the mistaken concept that the victory of the Chinese Revolution "would have been possible even without international help," has explained that "in the epoch of the existence of imperialism a genuine people's revolution cannot expect to be victorious, regardless of the country, without the different types of help that the international revolutionary forces can provide. . . . This means that we needed help in the past, that we need it today, and that we will need it in the future."

Speaking at the Fourth Session of the People's Political Advisory Council in February 1953, Mao Tse-tung, in listing the three main "historical" tasks, as they were characterized by the press, said:

> . . . we must learn from the Soviet Union. We have to do a tremendous amount of state construction, we are faced with a difficult job, and we do not have the necessary experience. So we will just have to study the advanced experience of the Soviet Union. Everyone must persist in learning from the Soviet Union, be he a Communist party member, or not, old cadre or young cadre, technical worker or doing intellectual work, worker, or peasant. Not only must we study the theories of Marx, Engels, Lenin, and Stalin, but advanced Soviet science and engineering as well. We must set afoot throughout the country a widespread movement to study the experience of the Soviet Union in the interests of building our state.[2]

A great deal of work was done in 1953–1954 to create constitutional bases for the PRC, which now are under particularly furious attack by the leaders of the CCP. The CC CCP requested, and the Soviet side provided, a number of observations which found expression in the draft of the Constitution of the PRC, officially published on June 15, 1954.

Elections to the Chinese National People's Congress ended on August 25, 1954. In all, the country elected 1,226 deputies. The First Session of this Congress took place in Peking between September 15 and 28, 1954, and was one of the most important landmarks on the road to democratization of the country. The Constitution of the PRC was adopted at the First Session, and established the basis for the PRC, the congresses of people's representatives. The result of general elections, these congresses were a step forward compared with previously existing organs of authority, for they expressed completely the will of the people, and were genuinely democratic organs of the people's government. The State Council and local people's committees, as executive organs of authority, were under control of the national and local people's congresses, respectively.

The Constitution of the PRC, adopted unanimously at the First Session of the National People's Congress, was directed at further development of democracy in the country, and, simultaneously, at the creation of a unified, centralized governmental leadership.

The Constitution of the PRC reflects the yearnings of the Chinese people for friendship and cooperation with the Soviet Union. The Constitution states, "Our country already has established ties of indestructible friendship with the Union of Soviet Socialist Republics, and with the countries of the people's democracies. . . ."[3] In the report on the draft constitution Liu Shao-ch'i said, "The path of the Soviet Union is the path corresponding to the law of historical development and along which human society must inevitably walk. It is impossible to avoid this path."[4]

In 1953 the PRC embarked on the First Five-Year Plan for development of the national economy. Aid at this time from the Soviet Union to the PRC was on a still grander scale. The First Five-Year Plan for China was developed with the active participation of Soviet specialists. It insured rapid and planned development of the republic. Actually, the First Five-Year Plan for the PRC, successfully fulfilled by the Chinese people, was, from material, scientific and technical standpoints, based on comprehensive aid from the Soviet Union.

The agreement on provision of aid by the Soviet Union to the PRC to expand in-service electric-power stations and build new ones was signed in Moscow on March 21, 1953.

The Sino-Soviet agreement on assistance to the PRC in building and reconstructing 141 industrial plants was signed on May 15, 1953. This number included 50 enterprises under the terms of the February 14, 1950 agreement, and 91 additional industrial enterprises.[5]

The result of the strengthening and developing of foreign trade ties between the Soviet Union and the PRC was to increase the trade turn-over 25.5 percent in 1953, as compared with 1952. Exports from the USSR to the PRC increased 28.8 percent on a cost basis over the 1952 figure, and USSR imports from the PRC similarly increased 21.9 percent. The share of the PRC in the total volume of the Soviet Union's foreign trade turnover in 1953 was 20 percent, and that of the Soviet Union in the total volume of the PRC's foreign trade turnover was 55.6 percent. In 1953 the Soviet Union continued to provide technical aid to the PRC, and the volume of this aid almost doubled as compared with 1952.

The first years of the Five-Year Plan were primarily important in establishing the foundation of Chinese industry; thus the assistance provided by the USSR in strengthening the leading branches of industry in the PRC played an invaluable role in the country's economy.

In 1954 the CC CPSU took new and important steps to further strengthen Sino-Soviet relations. A Soviet governmental delegation arrived in the PRC on an official visit in the fall of 1954.

Candid talks between the Soviet delegates and the government of the PRC concluded on October 12 with the signing of a number of important documents directed at further strengthening peace in Asia and throughout the world; specifically, joint declarations by the governments of the USSR and the PRC on questions of Sino-Soviet relations and the international situation, and about relations with Japan; a communiqué and agreements on the naval base in Port Arthur, on the question of the mixed Soviet-Chinese stock companies, and on scientific-technical cooperation on the construction of the Lanchow-Urumchi-Alma Ata Railroad; and a joint communiqué by the governments of the USSR, the PRC, and the Mongolian People's Republic on the construction of a railroad from Tsinan to Ulan Bator.

The value placed on results of the talks is attested to by the following statement of Premier Chou En-lai at the Soviet Embassy reception of October 12, 1954: "No one can separate us. Friendly relations such as these will continue to be strengthened and will develop with irresistible force day by day. They will develop unfailingly over the centuries and generations."[6]

The governments of the USSR and of the PRC, in joint political documents, emphasized their complete unity of views with respect to the development of two-way collaboration, and in their estimates of the international situation.

The Standing Committee of the National People's Congress approved the results of these talks on October 16, 1954, after listening to and discussing Chou En-lai's report of the Sino-Soviet talks. Chinese leaders at that time were highly appreciative of the brotherly actions of the Soviet Union.

For example, in connection with the gift to the PRC of machinery and equipment for organizing a large-scale state grain economy, Mao Tse-tung said that the Chinese people "see in this generous assistance of the Soviet people yet another bit of evidence of their deep friendship toward the Chinese people, and of the Soviet people's concern for, and support in, the work of construction the Chinese people are carrying out."[7] Guided by principles of internationalism, friendship, and collaboration with the PRC, and taking into consideration the strengthening of its international position and defensive capability, the Soviet government on its own initiative, decided to withdraw the Soviet military units from the jointly-used Chinese naval base in Port Arthur, and to turn over to the PRC, without compensation, this base together with all newly built installations of military and strategic importance.

In accordance with the agreement of October 12, 1954, also ceded to China were the rights and all of the Soviet shares in the mixed Soviet-Chinese stock companies, "Sovkitneft' " and "Sovkitmetall," the company for the extraction and refining of oil, and the company for the mining of nonferrous and rare metals, and subsequently the Soviet-Chinese Civil Aviation Company (SKOGA).

These mixed companies had played an important role in the restoration of the economy of the PRC. The "Sovkitmetall" Company, for example, had developed 11 mines for the extraction of new ores of nonferrous and rare metals. Soviet specialists, during the period of existence of the company, had trained 5,150 Chinese engineers, technicians, and skilled workers in 73 different specialties, and some 300 persons for administrative and control apparati.

In 1954 the Soviet Union helped the PRC build 169 plants; total technical assistance provided in 1954 almost doubled as compared with 1953. On January 1, 1955 some 800 Soviet specialists were in the PRC just to provide technical assistance. In addition to meeting its obligations under the agreements, Soviet specialists trained Chinese cadres. Specifically, 800 installers and adjusters of electric power equipment were trained, as were some 600 in machinery installation work and over 1,000 skilled workers in different vocations. Soviet advisers in the departments and institutions sent to China under the terms of the Sino-Soviet agreements of March 27, 1950 continued to provide a great deal of assistance in the economic construction of the PRC. Some 500 such advisers were at work in the PRC on January 1, 1955.

The December 1954 Moscow meeting on scientific and technical co-operation in accordance with the agreement of October 12, 1954, concluded that the Soviet Union would freely hand over to the PRC the designs for construction of metallurgical and machine-building plants and electric power stations, together with blueprints for production of machinery and equipment, technological documentation, and the scientific and technical literature involved. The Soviet side gave the PRC extensive drawings and plans of machinery installations for different branches of the national economy.

The Soviet government agreed to assist China in using atomic energy for peaceful purposes. Under the terms of the April 27, 1955 agreement, the Soviet Union engaged in construction of the first Chinese experimental atomic reactor and cyclotron.[8] Apropos of this, a resolution of the State Council of the PRC of January 31, 1955, stated:

> This is a glorious expression of the peaceful foreign policy of the Soviet Union, a new contribution to the strengthening of the great friendship between China and the Soviet Union. The Chinese people and government express their heartfelt appreciation for the sincere and unselfish assistance given by the Soviet Union.[9]

The total volume of foreign trade between the USSR and the PRC was 5.2 percent higher in 1954 than it had been in 1953. Data compiled by the Ministry of Foreign Trade of the PRC revealed that the USSR's share of China's foreign trade in 1954 was 51.8 percent.

An important event in the life of the PRC in 1954 was the opening in Peking of the Exhibition of the Economic and Cultural Achievements of the Soviet Union. Mao Tse-tung wrote the following in the guest book:

> We are proud of the fact that we have so powerful an ally. The might of the Soviet Union is an important condition for the overall rise in the economics and cultures of the countries of the camp of peace and democracy, and an important factor in the struggle for peace throughout the world and for the progress of mankind.

Specialists assigned to the Soviet exhibition in Peking popularized achievements of the USSR; they made frequent visits to plants; they conducted some 1,000 lectures and meetings attended by over 55,000; they regularly showed Soviet films in the exhibit.

In 1954 the USSR and the PRC exchanged numerous delegations representing different strata of the community, as well as artistic groups. Twenty Chinese delegations visited the Soviet Union, including a delegation of journalists headed by the chief editor of the newspaper *Jen Min Jihpao,* Teng T'o.

In 1955 a group of Soviet scientists headed by the Vice President of the Academy of Sciences of the USSR, Bardin, visited China, as did a delegation of medical scientists headed by the Vice President of the Academy of Medical Sciences of the USSR, Krotkov, and a delegation of atomic scientists. This broad exchange of delegations played a major role in strengthening Soviet-Chinese friendship, and contributed to the expansion of working arrangements between divisions of institutions and professional ties between the leading figures in the fields of culture, science, and art in the USSR and in China.

An agreement on cultural cooperation between the USSR and the PRC in fields of science, engineering, education, literature, art, public health, printing and publishing, radio broadcasting and television, cinematography, and sports, was signed in Moscow on July 5, 1956. This agreement summed up the long and fruitful years of cultural cooperation and established the foundation of cultural ties for the future.[10]

Between 1949 and 1958 134 Chinese artistic groups visited the USSR, and 102 Chinese films were shown. During this same period 112 Soviet groups visited China and almost 2 billion [sic] people saw 747 Soviet moving pictures.[11] A broad program of training Chinese national cadres was carried out. In 1956 alone, 1,800 students and postgraduate students were studying in the USSR.

The years 1953–1955 are characterized as years when cooperation between the USSR and the PRC in the international arena was close. The governments of both countries joined in supporting many foreign policy actions.

It was during this period that the PRC gained widespread international recognition as a participant in the political settlement of the military conflict in Korea. On July 21, 1954 the Democratic Republic of Vietnam, the Soviet Union, the PRC, and other countries signed the final declaration of the Geneva Conference on the restoration of peace in Indochina. The joint Soviet-Chinese declaration concerning the relationship to Japan was of particular significance. China, India, and other countries in Asia initiated the historic Bandung Conference, which established the five principles of peaceful coexistence.

And in each instance, alongside the PRC in its struggle to implement socialist principles of foreign policy was the Soviet Union, a dependable guarantor and defender of people's China.

The policy of active cooperation with the USSR and with other countries, and the struggle against imperialistic aggression led to rapid recognition of the PRC by many states, and to expansion of its international ties.

At the same time, cooperation with China was in the interest of the Soviet Union and, accordingly, in that of the entire socialist camp, because the PRC was able to supply our country with valuable raw materials and other goods needed to develop the economy.

Development of the Chinese economy not only failed to create competition with the Soviet Union, but, conversely, led to further extension and expansion of economic cooperation of a mutually advantageous nature.

Thus it was that the restoration period of the First Five-Year Plan established dependable economic bases for friendly cooperation between China and the Soviet Union. The Chinese Communists-internationalists, genuine patriots of their motherland, and the broad masses of Chinese workers understood that the root interests of China and of the Soviet Union coincided, that cooperation with the Soviet Union on the basis of equality and mutual assistance was the high road to overcoming China's economic and cultural backwardness and to transforming the country into a great socialist industrial power as quickly as possible. Emphasized also is the other principal proposition that comprehensive economic and political cooperation between the young PRC, the USSR, and all other socialist countries was of cardinal importance in the creation of favorable foreign policy prerequisites for the building of socialism in China.

The relative weakness of the working class in China was compensated for by strong external support provided by the world proletariat, and in particular by the great authority of the first country of triumphant socialism, the Soviet Union.

At the beginning of the First Five-Year Plan the proletariat comprised some 1 percent of the country's population; the working class made up some 3 percent of the Communist Party in 1949, and was slightly more than 6 or 7 percent in 1953.

The internationalists in the party understood these conditions. On the other hand, the nationalists had no room for maneuvering at the time, for China still was not firmly established; she was in the throes of military, political, and economic confrontation with the great imperialist countries. Consequently the Maoists chose to suppress temporarily their hegemonistic and anti-Soviet ideas. At this time, even they were interested in cooperation with the Soviet Union.

2. Sino-Soviet relations, 1956–1957

The most important landmarks in the development of Sino-Soviet relations, and in the development of the world Communist movement, were the 20th Congress of the CPSU (February 1956) and the 8th Congress of the CCP (September 1956).

In China, from 1956 to 1957, a struggle gradually intensified between two lines, the Marxist-internationalist on one hand, and the petty bourgeois-nationalist on the other. This struggle became complicated as a result of imperialist diversions (events in the Near East, counterrevolution in Hungary, Poland), and was intensified not only in the PRC but in the international Communist movement as a whole.

The present leadership of the CCP is attempting to claim that differences between the CCP, the CPSU, and the other Marxist-Leninist parties actually began after the 20th Congress of the CPSU, when decisions were reached of which the CCP did not, allegedly, agree in principle.[12]

But the historical truth is that Mao Tse-tung and his group simply used the decisions of the 20th Congress for their subsequent attacks on the CPSU, and to advance special conceptions they had nurtured for so long. It is characteristic that leaders of the CCP at the time had lent their firm support to the decisions of the 20th Congress. The Deputy Chairman of the CCP, Chu Teh, told the 20th Congress that:

> . . . the Central Committee of the Communist Party of China is deeply confident that the 20th Congress of the Communist Party of the Soviet Union will contribute even further to the business of building Communism in the Soviet Union and to the business of preserving peace throughout the world, as well as to inspire the Chinese people even further in their struggle to build socialism in their own country and ensure peace in Asia and throughout the world.[13]

The Chinese delegation to the Moscow Conference of Communist and Workers' Parties (1957), led by Mao Tse-tung, signed the declaration, containing the following stipulation:

> The historical decisions of the 20th Congress of the Communist Party of the Soviet Union are of great importance to the Communist Party of the Soviet Union and to Communist construction in the USSR, and have initiated a new stage in the international Communist movement and contributed to its future development on the basis of Marxism-Leninism.[14]

None other than Mao Tse-tung, in opening the 8th Congress of the CCP in September 1956, six months after the 20th Congress of the CPSU, said:

> [At] the recently held 20th Congress of the Communist Party of the Soviet Union many correct political aims were set, and shortcomings in the party

were discussed. One can say with confidence that their [the Soviet Communists'—authors' note] work in the future will expand greatly.[15]

The decisions of the 20th Congress of the CPSU received the following comprehensive, positive evaluation in the political report of the CC CCP to the 8th Congress of the CCP, in which Mao Tse-tung took part:

> The 20th Congress of the Communist Party of the Soviet Union, which was held in February of this year, is a very important political event, one of worldwide importance. The Congress developed a grandiose plan for the Sixth Five-Year Plan, as well as a whole series of very important political aims directed at the further development of socialism, and condemned the cult of personality, which has had serious consequences within the party. It went on to propose further development of peaceful coexistence and international cooperation as making an outstanding contribution to the relaxation of international tensions.[16]

The following appears in the report of changes made to the Party rules at the 8th Congress of the CCP:

> Leninism requires that all of the most important party questions be decided by the appropriate collective, and not by any one individual. The 20th Congress of the Communist Party of the Soviet Union presented persuasive explanations of the extreme importance of unswerving observation of the principle of collective leadership and of the struggle against the cult of personality. These explanations have had a tremendous influence on the Communist Party of the Soviet Union, just as they have on other Communist parties in all countries of the world.[17]

Mao Tse-tung has, in his time, made very definite pronouncements, but now the Maoists are choosing not to remember them.

In April 1956 Mao said:

> The report on the cult of personality is highly beneficial. Some of its negative aspects can in no way be compared with the benefit our parties have derived as a result of this question having been raised at the 20th Congress of the Communist Party of the Soviet Union.

In their directive entitled "Once Again on the Historical Experience of the Dictatorship of the Proletariat" the Chinese leaders, on December 29, 1956, wrote:

> The 20th Congress of the Communist Party of the Soviet Union demonstrated tremendous resoluteness and courage in doing away with the cult of Stalin, in exposing the seriousness of Stalin's errors, and in liquidating

the consequences of Stalin's errors. Throughout the world the Marxists-Leninists, and people sympathetic to Communism, are supporting the efforts of the Communist Party of the Soviet Union directed at correcting the errors, and are desirous of seeing the efforts of our Soviet comrades crowned with complete success.[18]

At the same time, without wishing to renounce procedures and methods associated with violations of the law and flouting of principles of collective leadership, the anti-Soviets in the CCP carefully "protected" the people and the Communists of China against the purifying ideas of the 20th Congress of the CPSU. They speculated on difficulties which arose in the international Communist movement (the Hungarian events, and others) in order to undermine the authority of the CPSU, and represented themselves as the "custodians of the revolutionary traditions." All of this really had for its purpose one goal, that of setting up the CCP as the leader of the international Communist movement, and to portray Mao Tse-tung as the "leader and teacher of all peoples."

In assessing the role of J. V. Stalin, leaders of the CCP took a characteristically nationalistic approach. Having decided during the early stages of the Chinese Revolution to make Mao Tse-tung the torch-bearer of "the Chinese brand of Marxism," they were interested in doing everything possible to compromise Soviet experience, including that gathered by the CPSU. Despite the fact that after the 20th Congress the Peking leaders demagogically attempted to assume the pose of defenders of Stalin, it is known that there were many extremely unfavorable Maoist assessments of the role of J. V. Stalin; there are even more today.

What must be remembered is that in Stalin's lifetime the leadership of the CCP, while more and more exaggerating the importance of the "ideas of Mao Tse-tung," decided against openly propagandizing these ideas beyond China's borders, and against raising their importance to the level of the world Communist movement. Still, the censure of Stalin's mistakes, in the view of the leaders of the CCP, created conditions for the adulation of Mao Tse-tung, to his glorification as the "man of genius," the "leader of the world revolution," and so on.

The activity of our party in strengthening the Leninist principles of collective leadership was very important for the healthy internationalist tendency in the CCP, stirring this faction to act decisively in defending Marxism-Leninism, and the theory and practice of socialism.

By 1956, because of strenuous efforts of Chinese workers and assistance provided by fraternal countries, the PRC completed what can only be described as a genuine advance in the development of economy, science, culture, and in improvement of the material well-being and defense of the country. The volume of industrial production during the years of the people's authority increased by a factor of 5.

The declaration of a socialist course helped intensify the internationalist tendencies of the party and people, and strengthened the healthy forces in the CCP. Great successes in the development of the economy and culture, in improvement in the standard of living for the population, and in increasing the country's international authority all produced confidence that China was on the right road. Using the experience of the brotherly countries, the CCP made its own contribution to solving the problems of the underdeveloped nations' transition to socialism. Favorable conditions were created for calling the next in a series of congresses of the CCP. The 8th Congress, convened in September 1956, confirmed the fact that the party's line would be that of building socialism in close alliance with all countries of the world socialist system.

The 8th Congress of the CCP had a special place in the history of the party. Its main feature was that it was held under the banner of the strengthening and growth of healthy Marxist-Leninist forces in the ranks of the party.

The Congress required that all Communists pay strict attention to the objective possibilities of developing the economic structure, and that the tempo of construction not be overestimated. It concluded that in the struggle between socialism and capitalism in China the question of "Who-Whom?" had been decided, and that the task now was one of improving the material and cultural level of the people and further expanding democracy in the country and in the party.

The theoretical bases of the CCP were clearly defined in the "Basic Provisions of the Program" contained in the new Party Rules adopted by the 8th Congress. This document declared that the

Communist Party of China is guided by Marxism-Leninism in its actions. . . . Marxism-Leninism is not dogma, but a guide to action. It demands of the people in the struggle for the building of socialism and communism that they proceed from the real situation, that they be flexible and creative in using its tenets to solve different practical problems that arise during the struggle, and that they continuously develop its theory. This is why the party, in its actions, is adhering to the principle of a tight combination between the universal truths of Marxism-Leninism and the concrete, practical, revolutionary struggle in China, and is against any dogmatic, or empirical, deviation.[19]

Thus the 8th Congress of the CCP changed the formulation of the ideological and theoretical bases the party had adopted at its 7th Congress. The documents of the 7th Congress had this to say: "The Communist Party of China is guided in all its works by the ideas of Mao Tse-tung, which combine the theory of Marxism-Léninism with the practical aspects of the Chinese Revolution."[20]

The 8th Congress of the CCP pointed to the gradual completion of the socialist transformation of agriculture, industry, and trade, and to the gradual industrialization of the country, as the basic task of the party "during the period of transition from the creation of the People's Republic of China to the building of a socialist society." According to the "Basic Provisions of the Program," "priority development of heavy industry is necessary for industrialization and achievement of a steady rise in the national economy. . . ."[21] The summary report to the Congress criticized deviation from the general line of the party during the transition period, and discussed leaning to the "left" as well as to the right.

In defining its foreign policy line the 8th Congress, in its "Basic Provisions of the Program," pointed to the fact that the CCP

> . . . is embarked on a foreign policy of preservation of peace throughout the world and of peaceful coexistence with countries with different systems. . . . The party is attempting to develop and strengthen friendship with the countries in the camp of peace, democracy, and socialism, led by the Soviet Union, to strengthen the solidarity of proletarian internationalism, to study the experience of the world Communist movement. It supports the struggle of Communists, of the progressive elements, and of the working people of all countries, the purpose of which is to ensure the progress of mankind, and to indoctrinate its members, and the people, in the spirit of internationalism expressed in the slogan "Workers of the World, Unite!"[22]

The summary report to the Congress stated that "without the great international solidarity of the proletariat of all countries, and without the support of international revolutionary forces, the victory of socialism in our country is impossible, and if the victory is won it cannot be strengthened." The slogan, "demonstrate love and modesty in relations with any of the fraternal parties . . . struggle decisively against any manifestations of dangerous tendencies toward great-power chauvinism and bourgeois nationalism"[23] was advanced at the Congress. Pressure of circumstances forced the leaders of the Communist Party to mask their real sentiments and views. Mao Tse-tung, in his opening speech, emphasized the need to intensify the work of mastering Marxist-Leninist theory of socialist construction, called upon the party not to become conceited and to study the experience of the Soviet Union:

> We are faced with an exceptionally difficult task in converting backward agrarian China into an advanced industrial China, and we have very little

experience. So we will have to learn. We will have to learn from the Soviet Union, which is going forward; we will have to learn from all the brotherly parties, and we will have to learn from the peoples of all countries. In no case . . . should we become conceited because of the victory of the revolution and because of certain successes in construction.[24]

Mao Tse-tung was forced to concede that:

If one is talking on the international level, then our victory was won because of the support given by the Soviet Union, the leader of the camp of peace, democracy, and socialism, and because of deep sympathy on the part of the peace-loving peoples throughout the world.[25]

The "Basic Provisions of the Program," contained in the Regulations of the CCP, also stated that:

. . . proceeding from democratic centralism in the party, each party organization must observe strictly the principle of the combination of collective leadership with personal responsibility. *Every member of the party* and every party organization *should be under the control of the party,* exercised from the top down, and from the bottom up. [Italics are the authors'.][26]

The important results derived from the work of the 8th Congress of the CCP can be explained in many ways.

First, by this time socialist construction in China had significant achievements to its credit. The First Five-Year Plan had been completed, and socialist production in town and village had been strengthened. Chinese Communists, on the basis of their own experience, were convinced that China, by taking the Marxist-Leninist road, and using the experience of building socialism in the USSR and other fraternal countries, could overcome centuries of backwardness and make basic improvements in the life of the broad masses of workers.

Second, the domestic and international successes scored by the PRC were inseparably bound up with the tremendous international assistance given China by the Soviet Union and the other socialist countries. Thus internationalism in action showed the Chinese workers that "without the great international solidarity of the workers of all countries, and without the support of the international revolutionary forces," the victory of socialism in China would have been impossible.[27]

Third, under the influence of the CPSU, and of the other Marxist-Leninist parties, the 8th Congress of the CCP turned its attention to the extreme significance of undeviating observance of the principle of collective leadership and the struggle against the cult of personality, and changed the wording of the ideological and theoretical bases of the party, as set forth in the Regulations, emphasizing that "the Communist Party of China is guided by Marxism-Leninism in its actions."[28]

These decisions, however, were in sharp contradiction to the political conceptions of Mao Tse-tung and created a real threat to his absolute rule. Striving to avert further developments of such events, and to regain once again the initiative, Mao and his supporters have in the ensuing years used for their own purposes the national progress and the natural strivings of the Chinese people to bring their country into the ranks of developed socialist states as rapidly as possible.

If the decisions of the 8th Congress of the CCP were to be realized, it was imperative that the shortcomings in party and state construction and in ideological work, evident in preceding years, be eliminated. These decisions became the roadblock to voluntaristic, petty-bourgeois concepts of building socialism, to adventuristic decisions in foreign policy.

The new stage of socialist construction set for the leadership of the PRC its next tasks, the resolution of which was made difficult because the representatives of different tendencies in the CCP took different approaches to the principal decisions arrived at by this Congress.

The very first steps along the road to implementing the decisions of the 8th Congress revealed that an influential wing of the Peking leadership at the very least took a declarative, shallow approach to carrying them out. There were attempts to advance voluntarist aims, such as those laid down by the course "Let a Hundred Flowers Bloom, Let a Hundred Schools of Thought Contend" and "the struggle with the rightists," which, because of their general appeal, were designed to bring to life the nationalistic, anti-Soviet sentiments in the country—that is, to undermine the decisions made by the 8th Congress which were unsatisfactory to the nationalists.

It is no accident that decisions of the 8th Congress of the CCP have come under particularly malicious attack by the nationalists today. What condemnations are being hurled at these decisions by the inspirers of the "cultural revolution"! Nevertheless, it would appear that at that time the nationalistic forces in the CCP were not yet ready for the "main battle." They carefully dissimulated and bided their time in order to destroy all those of a different mind, to throw out Marxist-Leninist theory, to clear the ground for the creation of their own special party, with its own special ideological and organizational base.

3. Political cooperation between the USSR and the PRC, 1956–1957

Cooperation in the field of foreign policy continued to develop between our two countries in 1956 and 1957. The PRC made common cause with the USSR on a number of very important international questions.

On September 14, 1956 the Standing Committee of the National People's Congress passed a resolution which stated that:

> The Soviet proposal [on disarmament—authors] is in the interests of the Chinese people, and of the other peoples in the world. The Standing Committee of the National People's Congress therefore fully supports the proposal contained in the Appeal of the Supreme Soviet of the USSR to the parliaments of all countries throughout the world for disarmament.

The leaders of the PRC and the CCP correctly assessed the 1956 events in Hungary. The joint Soviet-Chinese statement issued on January 18, 1957, signed on the occasion of the arrival in the USSR of a delegation from the PRC headed by Chou En-lai, pointed out that:

> The armed revolt in Hungary was provoked by imperialist aggressive circles and by Hungarian counterrevolutionary elements, who exploited the discontent among the Hungarian toiling masses and the youth with the errors of the previous leadership. They attempted to destroy the socialist system in Hungary, to restore the Fascist dictatorship, and at the same time to cause Europe to become the breeding ground for war. By their conspiracy in Hungary they attempted to open a breach for purposes of carrying out their plan, that of alienating the socialist countries and beating them one at a time.
>
> The rapid rout of the counterrevolutionary forces by the Hungarian people, under the leadership of the Hungarian Socialist Workers' Party and the Workers' and Peasants' Revolutionary Government, with the assistance of the Soviet Union, is a great victory for peace and for socialism.
>
> The Soviet Union, by aiding the Hungarian people to put down the counterrevolutionary revolt, fulfilled its international duty to the workers of Hungary and to the other socialist countries, and this reflects, to the highest degree, the interests of protecting peace throughout the world.[29]

On November 2, 1956 the government of the PRC published a statement concerning the Soviet Union's declaration of October 30, 1956 on the bases for the development and further strengthening of friendship and cooperation between the Soviet Union and the other socialist states. This statement pointed out that "the government of the People's Republic of China is of the opinion that the declaration made by the Soviet Union is correct."[30]

In November-December 1956 a delegation from the National People's Congress, headed by the Deputy Chairman of the Standing Committee of the National People's Congress, P'eng Chen, visited the Soviet Union. The delegation visited Irkutsk, Omsk, Moscow, Leningrad, Tashkent, and Tbilisi. Familiarization with the Soviet Union, and the warm reception given them everywhere, left a great impression on the Chinese representatives.

In January 1957 a governmental delegation from the PRC, headed by the Premier of the State Council and Minister of Foreign Affairs, Chou En-lai, paid a friendly visit to our country. The delegation visited Moscow, Irkutsk, Omsk, and Tashkent, and familiarized itself with a number of industrial plants, collective farms, and institutions of learning. Governmental delegations representing the Soviet Union and the PRC exchanged views on important questions concerning the international situation, including Anglo-Franco-Israeli aggression against Egypt and the counterrevolutionary revolt in Hungary, as well as questions concerned with future friendly cooperation between the PRC and the socialist countries.

In April-May 1957 an official visit of friendship to China was made by the Chairman of the Presidium of the Supreme Soviet of the USSR, K. Ye. Voroshilov. Together with state leaders from the USSR he traveled about the country and visited Peking, Anshan, Shenyang (Mukden), Tientsin, Shanghai, Kienshui, Canton, Yunnan, and Kunming. They stopped at plants and visited agricultural cooperatives, inspected scientific institutions and schools, as well as historical and cultural monuments in China. The Chinese people greeted their Soviet guests warmly. Meetings with workers became grandiose demonstrations of Soviet-Chinese friendship.

The delegation met with Mao Tse-tung, Chu Teh, Liu Shao-ch'i, Soong Ch'ing-ling, Chen Yun, Teng Hsiao-p'ing, P'eng Chen, Ho Lung, and other Chinese leaders. Discussed during the meetings were problems of Soviet-Chinese relations and various questions concerned with the international situation. Mao Tse-tung was invited to visit the Soviet Union.[31]

During the visit of the Soviet delegation to the PRC, Chinese leaders repeatedly stated their high regard for the policy of the Soviet Union with respect to China, and for the internationalist course taken by the CPSU. On April 15, Mao Tse-tung, during his meeting with K. Ye. Voroshilov at the airport in Peking, said:

> The Soviet people have given us, and continue to give us, the greatest support and sympathy for the Chinese revolution and for the work of construction. Permit me to express to you and through you to the Soviet

people, to the Soviet government, and to the Communist Party of the Soviet Union, our heartfelt appreciation.[32]

On May 3, 1957, at a reception in the Embassy of the USSR in Peking, he said:

In these past few days the whole world once again has seen the monolithic unity and solidarity, as well as the close and deep friendship of the peoples of China and of the Soviet Union. This type of solidarity and friendship is a factor that is most favorable to the building of socialism and communism in both our countries, as well as an important component part of the solidarity of the socialist countries, reliably guaranteeing general peace and the progress of mankind. The Chinese people, like the Soviet people, will, in the future, make every effort in the name of uninterrupted strengthening and development of relations of solidarity, friendship, and cooperation between our two countries.[33]

In September-October 1957 a delegation from the Supreme Soviet of the USSR visited China to take part in the celebration of the 8th anniversary of the founding of the PRC.

One of the manifestations of the firm, consistent course followed by our party in the development and cementing of relations between the USSR and the PRC was the establishment on October 29, 1957 in Moscow of the Soviet-Chinese Friendship Association.

The Association's tasks were to participate in the further cultivation of brotherly friendship between our two great peoples, to expand cultural cooperation, to make comprehensive exchanges of experiences in cultural construction with the PRC, to better acquaint Soviet society with the life of the Chinese people and their experience in building socialism, and to acquaint the Chinese people with the life and work of the Soviet people.

The Soviet people celebrated the 40th anniversary of the Great October Socialist Revolution in November 1957. A party and governmental delegation, headed by Mao Tse-tung, came to Moscow for the occasion. The delegation included the Vice Chairman of the Standing Committee of the National People's Congress, Soong Ch'ing-ling, the General Secretary and Member of the Politburo of the CC CCP, Teng Hsiao-p'ing, Vice Premier of the State Council and Minister of Defense, Member of the Political Bureau of the Central Committee of the PRC, P'eng Te-huai, and other important party and state leaders of the PRC.

At the session of the Supreme Soviet, celebrating the 40th anniversary of the Great October Socialist Revolution, Mao Tse-tung noted that in the entire history of relations between states there could never have been any relations like those that had been established between the countries of socialism, in which peoples of these countries share joy and grief, treat each other with mutual respect and confidence, and inspire each other. "Our destiny, our breath, are at one with the Soviet Union, and with the entire socialist camp," said Mao Tse-tung.

This statement was of a hypocritical nature, because even at that time Mao Tse-tung had decided to impose his platform on the socialist countries.

The gradual revision of the decisions of the 8th Congress of the CCP by a definite segment of the party's leadership continued. A nationalistic, anti-Soviet course was activated. Different approaches were used for this purpose, and campaigns to weaken the position of Marxism-Leninism in the PRC were mounted. The events of 1957 tell the story.

Statements by rightist elements were quite widespread in the PRC at that time. The nationalists among leaders of the CCP chose an extremely original tactic to use in the "struggle" with these elements, as has now become clear as a result of the "cultural revolution." The leaders of the CCP took considerable time to unmask the slanderous statements of the rightists. From the beginning of May to the middle of June 1957, the rightists actually were provided with forums for dissemination of propaganda through the press, meetings, and radio. Moreover, leaders of the CCP essentially encouraged the rightists to make statements, which in particular were abetted by the proclaimed slogan of "Let a Hundred Flowers Bloom, Let a Hundred Schools of Thought Contend."

Most important of the rightist attacks were anti-Soviet statements, and there were plenty of opportunities for making them. For instance the newspaper *Heilungkiang Jihpao,* the organ of the Provincial Committee of the CCP, provides abundant quotes from Ch'in Yu-hai calling for the "return of the land seized by the Soviet Union," for a struggle to the last drop of blood against the USSR under the slogan "Revenge." "If, right now, there were a Soviet and an American standing before me," said this maddened anti-Soviet type, "and if I had but one cartridge, I would, without the slightest hesitation, shoot the Soviet." The newspaper *Kang Chiang Jihpao* printed something by a rightist named Chun Yu-wen to the effect that "Vladivostok and Mongolia are Chinese territory." Still, leadership of the CCP continued to follow deliberately its course of temporization, and did not unmask the anti-Soviet fabrications of the rightists.

Due to connivance by Chinese authorities, the rightists attempted to shift from propaganda to direct provocation. In February 1957 a crowd of over 100, carrying anti-Soviet slogans, burst into the courtyard of the hotel in Sian where Soviet specialists were living. In May 1957 anti-Soviet elements intended to arrange a provocation during the visit to Kwangchow (Canton) by the Chairman of the Presidium of the Supreme Soviet of the USSR, K. Ye. Voroshilov.

The rightists showered the pages of the newspapers with anti-Soviet slanders, and published mass circulation collections of articles with vile anti-Soviet statements. These statements were criticized by leaders of the CCP, but only in the most general terms, with no attempt to refute them by widespread use of factual documents. The territorial claims against the USSR advanced by the rightists were in no way repudiated.

This position will be completely understandable if one considers that the nationalists within the CCP in point of fact are repeating the same slanderous anti-Soviet fabrications used by the rightists in 1957. Characteristically, many of those rightists who inveighed against the Soviet Union were subsequently rehabilitated. At the end of 1958 conferences and congresses of the democratic parties elected to their central organs such very active ringleaders among the rightists as Ch'en Min-shu, Hang Shao-hsun, Chang Po-chun, Lo Lung-chi, and others. In addition to rehabilitation, special attention was devoted to the memory of the leader and leading mouthpiece of the rightists, Lung Yun, who died in 1962. The committee appointed to organize his funeral was led by Chen Yi, a member of the Politburo of the CCP, and included other members of the Politburo as well.

The views of the rightists, published in individual collections of articles, were recommended for political indoctrination courses. It means that in 1957 the nationalists, using antisocialist and anti-Soviet statements of bourgeois elements, propagated throughout the strata of Chinese society anti-Soviet slander, simultaneously laying the foundations for the beginning of the destruction of Sino-Soviet relations. Yet the Mao Tse-tung group tried to hide behind the mask of noninvolvement.

At about this time there appeared definite signs of a struggle within the leadership of the CCP; the question of relations with realistic intellectual forces within the CCP still was strong, and the need for cooperation with the Soviet Union still so great, that the leadership was forced to maneuver. Condemnation of the rightists also reflected the struggle of the two lines within the leadership.

In his report to the 4th Session of the National People's Congress, Chou En-lai said:

> Some are turning away from the study of the experience of the Soviet Union, and even feel that the shortcomings and mistakes that have occurred in the work of building in our country too are the results of the

study of the Soviet Union. These are extremely harmful views. . . . If we don't learn from the experience of the Soviet Union in building socialism, perhaps we should learn from the experience of the United States in building capitalism? As a matter of fact, it is precisely because we have seriously studied the advanced experience of the Soviet Union that we have been able to avoid many wrong paths and achieve tremendous successes.[34]

The Chinese trade union newspaper *Kungjen Jihpao,* in a lead article entitled "The Course of Learning from the Soviet Union Is Steadfast," published in August 1957, said:

The rightist elements, disclaiming the successes achieved by the People's Republic of China in all fields, simultaneously try to depict our learning from the Soviet Union as worthless. They say that learning from the Soviet Union is "dogmatism," "blind, mechanical transference of experience from the Soviet Union." . . . The goal of the rightist elements is nothing less than to use the pretext of the "struggle with dogmatism" to inveigh against our learning from the Soviet Union, and, at the same time, to weaken the building of socialism in our country. It is necessary, therefore, to decisively refute the slanderous fabrications of the rightist elements on this question.[35]

Similar statements during the years of the "cultural revolution" were declared "counterrevolutionary," and their authors were subjected to physical and moral punishment.

Against the background of present events in the PRC, it becomes particularly obvious that in the campaigns under the slogan "Let a Hundred Flowers Bloom, Let a Hundred Schools of Thought Contend" the struggle with the rightists reflected petty bourgeois, nationalist views in the CCP. Behind these campaigns was the purpose of sowing doubts about the policies of the CPSU and the Soviet government.

Nevertheless, the great successes achieved by the PRC in socialist construction, directly attributable to the unselfish assistance of the USSR and other fraternal states, continued to act as hindrances to the Maoists in their destructive work in the sphere of Sino-Soviet relations, thus forcing the leadership of the CCP to maneuver.

The political hypocrisy of the Maoists, their subversive attempts to undermine the authority of the CPSU and to prepare the ground for open attacks against the CPSU and the USSR, all were completely exposed during the Moscow Conference of Communist and Workers' Parties in 1957.

The CCP delegation, headed by Mao Tse-tung, was lavish in flattering and in vowing loyalty to the Soviet Union. This entered into the calculations of the Maoists, who were continuing to solicit from our country increases in economic and military assistance.

Prevalent at this conference, however, was a "second background" of activity on the part of the leaders of the CCP. Ideological "incursions" seeping through this background formed a foundation for subsequent attacks on Marxism and replacement of the latter by Mao's special views.

† It is characteristic that the CCP delegation to the conference did not publicize its views, but instead resorted to presenting them in the semi-official "Theses of Opinions on the Question of Peaceful Transition," which were passed unofficially to one of the Soviet colleagues working with the delegation, after the conference ended. Absolutely false is the *Jen Min Jihpao* statement that "in 1957, during the Conference of Representatives of Communist and Workers' Parties, the delegation from the PRC had a pointed discussion with the delegation from the CPSU on the question of the transition from capitalism to socialism,"[36] professing that in the Soviet draft of the declaration no mention was made of the possibility of other than a peaceful road for revolution.

The special position of the leadership of the CCP at the Moscow Conference also was apparent with respect to Mao Tse-tung's position on war. Mao Tse-tung literally said the following at the time:

> Can you conjecture how many people will die in a future war? Possibly as many as one-third of the 2,700 million people on the earth, that is some 900 million people. I feel that even this number is too small if atomic bombs are dropped. This is terribly frightening, of course. But half that number would not be bad. Why? Because it is not we who want this, but they, they who impose war on us. If we fight, then atomic and hydrogen weapons will be used. My personal thought is that mankind all over the world will have the suffering of half, and possibly more than half of all of mankind, perishing. I argued this question with Nehru. He was more pessimistic in this regard than I. I told him that if half of all mankind were destroyed that still would leave half, but in return imperialism would be completely destroyed and only socialism would reign throughout the world, and in half a century or a century the population would increase once again, by even more than half.[37]

The impression was given during this period that this position was the result of honest delusions on the part of Chinese leaders with respect to prospects for the development of peace, and that this position was dictated by motives of approaching, however extreme the means, the triumph of socialism on a worldwide scale. But subsequent events revealed that the ultra-revolutionary aims of the CCP leaders, reflecting nihilistic disdain for the struggle for peace, actually served to mask their true intentions, which were to provoke a military confrontation between the USSR and the USA in order to realize their own great-power, nationalistic aspirations.

† At the 1957 Moscow Conference, the delegation of the CPSU took exception to the inclusion in the text of the Declaration the wording "the socialist camp headed by the Soviet Union." Yet it was the CCP delegation who stubbornly insisted that this wording be adopted and included in the text. And this was done in a situation under which Chinese leaders, as they now confirm, felt that our party was moving along the road of "revisionism." The reasoning behind their action went something like this: the CPSU is the leader, but a leader with a "flaw," so that will have to be changed, and this the CCP and Mao Tse-tung, are capable of doing.

Nevertheless, the Maoists were still not ready for direct attacks against our party, and against the general line of the world Communist movement. With this, as well as sentiments within the CCP, in mind, the nationalistic segment of the leadership continued to maneuver. In May 1958 the 2nd Session of the 8th Congress of the CCP in a special resolution unanimously approved the Declaration and Peace Manifesto of the 1957 Moscow conference, declaring that they "opened a new stage in the contemporary international Communist movement, and, to a tremendous degree, inspired all workers, all forces for peace, democracy, and progress throughout the world."[38]

4. Sino-Soviet economic, scientific, and technical cooperation in the concluding years of the First Five-Year Plan

The Soviet Union, as before, sincerely tried to contribute to the success of the Chinese workers in socialist construction during the years of the Five-Year Plan, despite some acrimonious moments in the relations between our party and some CCP leaders. Our party understood that the assistance given in creating socialist bases in the PRC was primarily for the Chinese people, and not for a group of leaders of the CCP, a group that gradually destroyed the brotherly alliance between the two states.

Aid given by the Soviet Union to the PRC increased in 1956 and 1957. A governmental delegation headed by A. I. Mikoyan visited the PRC in April 1956. The delegation continued the talks with the government of the PRC which had begun earlier in Moscow concerning future development of economic cooperation between the two countries. The signing of important documents resulted from these talks. On April 7,

1956 an agreement was signed, under which the Soviet Union was to give the PRC assistance in the development of certain branches of industry. Anticipated was construction of 55 new industrial plants, in addition to the 156 plants built in accordance with previous agreements. Included were metallurgical, machine-building, and chemical plants, plants for the production of artificial fiber and plastics, plants for the electrical and radio industries, a plant to produce artificial liquid fuel, electric power plants, and scientific research institutes for the aviation industry. The total cost of deliveries of equipment, of design work, and of other types of technical assistance provided by the Soviet Union for construction of these plants would have been some 2.5 billion rubles (in the old prices). The agreement further anticipated expansion of assistance to China in carrying on geological survey work.

In addition, a Soviet-Chinese communiqué concerning the building of a railroad from Lanchow through Urumchi to Aktogay Station on Soviet territory, and the organization of through service on this road was signed.

Also the fact that the Soviet Union continued to provide China with an impressive amount of aid for purposes of strengthening its defensive capability should be pointed out. The defensive potential of the PRC was built primarily with the help of the Soviet Union until leaders of the CCP started severing cooperative ties with the USSR. Thousands of Soviet specialists imparted the experience of our armed forces; all military plants in the PRC were built with USSR assistance, and the Chinese Army was equipped and armed as a result of aid from the Soviet Union.

On August 18, 1956, in Peking, the Soviet Union and the PRC signed an agreement on joint scientific research work in the Amur River basin to determine the basin's natural resources, establish prospects for development of the region's industrial potential, and for survey work leading to the drafting of a plan for the joint use of the waters of the Argun' River, and those of the upper course of the Amur River.

In 1956 the Soviet Union sent a large group of scientists to the PRC. This group helped develop a broad 12-year plan for the development of science in China. The PRC was also assisted in organizing research on the peaceful uses of atomic energy. Eighteen hundred Chinese students and graduate students were studying in the USSR in 1956 alone. The Soviet Red Cross hospitals in Dal'niy, Inin, and Urumchi were turned over to the PRC without indemnity.

A number of other agreements between the USSR and the PRC were concluded in 1956, including the following:

(1) An agreement dated June 15 on cooperation between the USSR,

the Democratic Republic of Vietnam, the PRC, and the Korean People's Democratic Republic in fields of fishing, oceanological and limnological research in the western part of the Pacific Ocean (Mongolia became a party to this agreement on December 15, 1958). The term of the agreement was 10 years. Its purpose was to coordinate research in the region of the Pacific Ocean important for fishing. The joint efforts of the socialist countries resulted in the obtaining of more complete data on the status of the raw materials base, and on the commercial fishing potentials of this region.*

(2) An agreement dated July 3 between the governments of the USSR, the PRC, and the Korean People's Democratic Republic to cooperate in life-saving and assistance to ships and aircraft in distress at sea.**

(3) A protocol dated March 30 on the ceding without indemnity of Russian Church Mission property in China, parcels of land, together with the buildings on them, in different cities and regions of China, printing equipment, and dairy farm property in Peking.

The Soviet Red Cross hospital in Peking, founded in June 1952, was handed over without indemnity to the Chinese government on March 13, 1957. The hospital treated 500,000 outpatients during its existence, while the number of those hospitalized was in excess of 9,300.

The 6th Session of the Soviet-Chinese Commission on Scientific and Technical Cooperation, held in Peking in July 1957, was of particular importance in the development of mutual assistance between the USSR and the PRC. The Soviet Union pledged the PRC a cost-free supply of plans and drawings for building hydroelectric power stations, for metallurgical production, as well as for machine tools and machines for light industry. Other plans and drawings dealt with the production of steel, rubber products, tires, paper and cellulose industry, dyes and medical preparations, seed and planting documents for agricultural crops, and a variety of handbook and informational type documents.

The PRC, in turn, was to give the Soviet Union a cost-free supply of drawings and plans for the production of certain nonferrous metals, for the preparation of raw materials needed in their production, for use of natural stone in the refractory materials industry and in carbon concen-

---

* On May 21, 1965 the Ministry of Foreign Affairs of the People's Republic of China handed the Ambassador of the USSR to Peking a note stating that the "Government of China considers that there no longer is any need to extend the effective term of this agreement and that it will be without force as of June 12, 1966."

** This agreement too was denounced unilaterally by the Chinese authorities in 1966.

tration plants, for grain processing machinery, for sorting tea, and for a description of the technology used in hydraulic packing of worked-out space in coal mines, and other materials.[39]

An agreement on scientific cooperation between the Academies of Sciences of the USSR and of the PRC was signed in Moscow on December 11, 1957. Under its terms joint research and joint expeditions were to be conducted, and work on important problems in science and engineering was to be coordinated.

An agreement on commercial shipping along border and adjacent rivers and lakes was concluded between the USSR and the PRC on December 21, 1957.

Study and use of Soviet experience was particularly important in successes gained by the PRC in socialist construction. The slogan "Learn from the Soviet Union" did not ring hollow during these years. The CC CCP frequently supported the study of the first country of socialism's experiences despite the wishes of the nationalist segment of the leadership. The result was that the PRC and the Chinese people achieved very definite successes in creating the bases for socialism, and in the training of their own cadres. This line was singled out as one of the "crimes" of Liu Shao-ch'i and his adherents during the "cultural revolution."

But in 1956 and 1957 Mao Tse-tung, as well as other Chinese leaders, spoke of the importance of Soviet experience, albeit hypocritically. In his speech "On the Correct Handling of Contradictions among the People," made to an expanded session of a State Council conference on February 27, 1957, Mao Tse-tung emphasized that:

> . . . we must study the good experience of all countries, regardless of whether they are socialist or capitalist. Of this there can be no doubt. However, the most important thing is to learn from the Soviet Union.[40]

In a speech at the jubilee session of the Supreme Soviet of the USSR celebrating the 40th anniversary of October, Mao Tse-tung said:

> It is quite clear that if, after the October Revolution, the proletarian revolutionaries in the different countries ignore, or if they do not give serious study to the experience of the Russian Revolution, if they do not give serious study to the dictatorship of the proletariat and socialist construction in the Soviet Union, and if they do not use this experience analytically and creatively in accordance with the concrete conditions prevailing in their countries, they will not be able to master Leninism, the new stage in the development of Marxism, and they will not be able to solve correctly the problems of revolution and construction in their own countries. In this case they will fall into dogmatic mistakes, or into revisionist mistakes.[41]

On November 6, 1957, during the great public rally in Peking in celebration of the 40th anniversary of the October Revolution, Liu Shao-ch'i, in the name of the CCP, declared:

> The Soviet people today are going forward on the road to building communism. The mighty Soviet Union has become the strongest stronghold of universal peace. Over a period of 40 years the Soviet Union has accumulated a rich experience in revolution and building. As of today there is not a single socialist country with the comprehensive experience possessed by the Soviet Union. This experience is a priceless asset and is the contribution of the Soviet people to the depository of all mankind.

Tung Pi-wu, a member of the Politburo of the CC CCP, and a Vice Chairman of the PRC, in an article entitled "Steadfastly Forward along the Road of the October Revolution," published in November 1957, characterized the relationship between Marxist-Leninist theory and the experience of socialist revolution and construction in the Soviet Union on one hand, and the experience gained by the PRC on the other, in the following way:

> Since revolution and construction in China are taking place under the new international conditions that have prevailed since the end of World War II, China has gained some new experience in the field of policy with respect to the bourgeoisie within the country, in organizing agriculture into cooperatives, in concrete forms of organizing state and public life. Yet all of this experience has been gathered on the basis of the fundamental principles of Marxism-Leninism, and of the basic experience of revolution and construction in the Soviet Union. We consider inadmissible any form of revisionist views that include a departure from the fundamental principles of Marxism-Leninism and that underestimate the basic experience of the Soviet Union since the October Revolution. . . . Soviet experience remains, at least up to this point, the most complete in terms of questions of the proletarian revolution and socialist construction. This comprehensive experience is the most valuable asset in the international Communist movement.[42]

The sober assessment of the social and economic situation in the PRC, and the attentive attitude toward the experience of the Soviet Union, helped to develop among many leading cadres in the PRC a realistic approach to conditions and to basic factors of socialist construction in China for short- and long-term development prospects.

As distinguished from Mao Tse-tung's later theory that "agriculture is the basis of the entire national economy," emphasized at this time in China was that industrialization of the country was the decisive link in creation of the material and technical base of socialism. Mao Tse-tung, in February 1957, following decisions made by the 8th Congress of the CCP, in "On the Correct Handling of Contradictions among the People," declared that "Heavy industry is at the center of economic construction in our country. This we must state with complete certainty."[43] The idea of industrialization permeated all concrete economic activities of the CCP during the first years after the victory of the revolution. In reviewing the tasks of the transition period from capitalism to socialism in China, Vice Premier and Minister Li Fu-chun, in a report on the First Five-Year Plan, said:

> The socialist industrialization of the country is the central task of our government during the transition period, and the central link in socialist industrialization is the priority development of heavy industry. . . . The policy of priority development of heavy industry is the only correct policy that will lead the state to prosperity and power, and our people to a happy life. . . .[44]

Responding to those who were of the opinion that given the concrete conditions prevailing in the PRC, the country did not have to speed industrialization, Li Fu-chun emphasized that "We consider this view to be mistaken."[45]

Characteristically, the Soviet people, imparting to China their wealth of experience, unselfishly shared with the Chinese people their advanced achievements, and, in addition, warned the young republic and its cadres against omissions and mistakes which our country had encountered. This genuine fraternal international assistance gave China concrete material results; it strengthened the authority of our country and of the PRC, and evoked feelings of great love and appreciation among the Chinese workers.

Nevertheless, there were in these same years worrisome moments in the field of concrete intergovernmental relations.

For example, in the course of implementing the plan for cultural cooperation between the USSR and the PRC there was the case in 1956 of Chinese organizations refusing to exchange ideological workers. With no explanation of the reasons for doing so, they refused to send to the USSR a delegation of artistic and museum workers to exchange work experiences.

By the end of 1956 the middle and higher institutions of learning in the PRC departed more and more from extensive reliance on Soviet curricula and textbooks used prior to this time.

The number of articles on the Soviet Union appearing in the Chinese press dropped off sharply. Whereas *Jen Min Jihpao,* the organ of the CC

CCP, printed 173 articles on the Soviet Union in 1955, only 98 appeared in 1956. The publication and dissemination of Soviet literature in the PRC began to decrease. The proportion of Soviet literature in new editions of foreign literature published in the country decreased from 94 percent in 1955 to 89.3 percent in 1956, in terms of titles, and from 92 percent to 88.9 percent in terms of numbers of copies.

In 1957 the CC CCP decided to cease the publication of the newspaper *Druzhba* (in Russian). This newspaper was the organ of the Sino-Soviet Friendship Association and was published in 70,000-copy editions, of which 60,000 copies were sent to the USSR for distribution, some 9,000 copies were distributed in the PRC, and a few more than 1,000 copies were sent to the socialist countries.

Despite the nationalistic activities of the Mao Tse-tung group, of decisive importance in 1956–1957 was the fact that by this time the Chinese people could see the advantages of socialism, and could evaluate the role of international solidarity and unselfish assistance provided by the Soviet people. The genuine leap in the development of economics, science, and the rise in the material well-being of Chinese workers was accomplished during this period on the basis of Leninist principles of socialist economic development, with the international assistance of the fraternal countries. At the same time, there was intensification in the struggle between the two lines in the CCP, between the nationalist and the internationalist, and this surfaced in the field of Sino-Soviet relations.

NOTES

1. *Narodnyi Kitay,* Supplement, No. 19, 1956, p. 49.
2. *Narodnyi Kitay,* No. 4, 1953, p. 7.
3. *Konstitutsiya KNR (Constitution of the People's Republic of China,* hereinafter referred to as *Constitution of the PRC)* (Peking, 1954), p. 9.
4. Liu Shao'ch'i, "The Draft of the Constitution of the People's Republic of China," *Materialy pervoy sessii Vsekitayskogo sobraniya narodnykh predstaviteley (Materials on the First Session of the National People's Congress,* hereinafter referred to as *Materials)* (Moscow, 1954), p. 30.
5. *The Leninist Policy,* p. 166.
6. *Jen Min Jihpao,* October 13, 1954.
7. *Sino-Soviet Relations, 1917–1957,* p. 308.
8. *The Leninist Policy,* p. 167–168.
9. *Sino-Soviet Relations, 1917–1957,* p. 314.
10. Ibid., p. 316–317.
11. Kapitsa, p. 92.
12. "Occurrence and Development of Disagreements between the Leaders of the Communist Party of the Soviet Union and Us," *Jen Min Jihpao* and *Hung-ch'i* (September 1967).
13. *XX s'yezd Kommunisticheskoy partii Sovetskogo Soyuza (20th Congress of the Communist Party of the Soviet Union,* Stenographic report, Vol. I, hereinafter referred to as *CPSU 20th Congress)* (Moscow, 1956), p. 228.
14. *Programmnyye dokumenty bor'by za mir, demokratiyu i sotsializm (Program Documents on the Struggle for Peace, Democracy, and Socialism,* hereinafter referred to as *Program Documents)* (Moscow, 1961), p. 20.
15. *Materialy VIII Vsekitayskogo s'yezda Kommunisticheskoy partii Kitaya (Documents from the 8th All-China Congress of the Communist Party of China,* hereinafter referred to as *Documents)* (Moscow, 1956), p. 5.
16. Ibid., p. 59.
17. Ibid., p. 92.
18. *Jen Min Jihpao,* December 29, 1956.
19. *Documents,* p. 508.
20. Liu Shao-ch'i, *O partii (About the Party)* (Peking, 1951) (in English).
21. *Documents,* p. 508–509.
22. Ibid., p. 510–511.
23. Ibid., p. 76.
24. Ibid., p. 5.
25. Ibid., p. 4.
26. Ibid., p. 512.
27. Ibid., p. 76.
28. Ibid., p. 508.
29. *Izvestiya,* January 19, 1957.
30. *Pravda,* November 2, 1956.

31. *Izvestiya,* May 28, 1957.
32. *Izvestiya,* April 16, 1957.
33. *Izvestiya,* May 4, 1957.
34. *Druzhba (Friendship),* June 28, 1957.
35. *Kungjen Jihpao,* August 31, 1957.
36. *Jen Min Jihpao,* March 31, 1964.
37. *Pravda,* September 22, 1963.
38. *Vtoraya sessiya VIII Vsekitayskogo s'yezda Kommunisticheskoy partii Kitaya (2nd Session of the 8th All-China Congress of the Communist Party of China,* hereinafter referred to as *2nd Session, 8th Congress)* (Moscow, 1958), p. 65.
39. *Izvestiya,* July 18, 1957.
40. Mao Tse-tung, *K voprosu o pravil'nom razreshenii protivorechiy vnutri naroda (On the Correct Handling of Contradictions among the People,* hereinafter referred to as *On the Correct Handling)* (Moscow, 1957), p. 48.
41. *Druzhba,* No. 8, 1957, p. 3.
42. *Druzhba,* No. 9, 1957, p. 4.
43. Mao Tse-tung, p. 46.
44. *Narodnyi Kitay,* Supplement, No. 17, 1955, p. 7.
45. Ibid.

CHAPTER FOUR

Sources of Emerging Nationalistic and Anti-Soviet Tendencies in the Policies of the CCP Leadership

Analyses of Sino-Soviet relations between 1945 and 1957 reveal that they developed along lines involving step-by-step strengthening of friendship and cooperation between our parties and countries.

Preceding chapters have discussed the development of comprehensive economic, political, diplomatic, cultural, and military cooperation between China and the Soviet Union and have pointed out the very great importance of brotherly international assistance from the Soviet Union at all stages of the Chinese Revolution and socialist construction of the PRC.

But by the end of the 1950s great-power chauvinistic forces entered the Chinese political arena and began to play an ever more important part in Sino-Soviet relations. These forces in time completely dominated the leadership of the party and the country, and suppressed the internationalist tendencies in the CCP. This raises the question of how to explain the fact that in recent years a group of leading figures in China, who continue to call themselves Communists, have created a threat to the socialist achievements in the country, have engaged in open declaration of ideological and political struggle against the Communist parties and the socialist states and severed ties with the international proletariat? What happened to bring about the dominance of nationalist, anti-Marxist tendencies now determining the political situation in the country? For it is well known that the CCP has performed great revolutionary services; it led the heroic revolution completed by a great people traveling the dangerous road of a long and bloody liberation struggle.

Thus it is useful to examine both the objective and subjective factors which explain this complicated, historical zigzag in the policy of the leaders of the CCP.

1. The social and historical roots of the petty bourgeois, nationalist views of the leadership of the CCP

The molding of the CCP, the formation of the views of the Chinese Communists, took place under extraordinarily complex conditions. The CCP was born in a semicolonial, semifeudal country, one that was extremely backward from the standpoint of economics, sociology, politics, and culture.

Although the development of the capitalist method of production and goods-money relationships beginning at the end of the nineteenth century hastened the breaking up of feudalism, the main branch of China's economy remained agrarian, thus suffering remnants of feudalism. In 1949 Chinese industry provided but 17 percent of the gross output of the country, with the remainder coming from agriculture (almost 70 percent), home weaving, and the handicraft industry.

The country's underdeveloped social structure matched its backward economy. There were only 2.5 to 3 million industrial workers in China in 1949. Petty bourgeois elements predominated among the urban inhabitants. At least 90 percent of the country's 475 million population were peasants. The bourgeoisie, as a class, were weak and split into two groups, the compradors, primarily prominent entrepreneurs collaborating with foreign imperialists, and nationalists, including primarily the middle and most prosperous stratum of the petty bourgeoisie.

Interwoven into the ideological life of Chinese society were various currents of patriarchal and feudal tendencies, elements of petty bourgeois and bourgeois attitudes, anarchism and Utopian socialism, and, finally, religious beliefs (Buddhism, Confucianism). The militant, Great Han nationalism which for centuries had been instilled by the ruling classes of feudal China was deeply rooted. The centuries of feudalism in China under conditions which isolated her from the rest of the world, and the relatively high level of Chinese culture as compared with the cultures of her neighbors, who often were no more than vassals, acclimated the Chinese to considering their country, institutions, and culture as something exceptional—of "heavenly" origin. The country occupied the leading position in East Asia in ancient times and during the Middle Ages. Its large population, its comparatively high level of civilization, its isolation from other countries, all served to create the illusion that China was the center of the universe. For centuries the ruling clique instilled this notion into the consciousness of the Chinese people. The contradiction between these notions and the real situation in a country which, in modern times, had been transformed into a semicolonial territory led to extreme intensification of national sentiments, and gave rise to the attempt to restore its former grandeur, whatever the cost. The tremendous vitality of this archaic political ideology had long been noted in China. Chinese ethnocentricity had become the highest measure of all values in the consciousness of the ruling circles, as well as in the intellectual strata of Chinese society. Even the majority of the advanced revolutionary intellectuals, to which many present Chinese leaders belong, perceived Marxism and all other progressive foreign revolutionary thought through the prism of traditional Chinese ideology, and primarily in terms of Confucianism.

The victory of the Great October Socialist Revolution in Russia, marking the beginning of the epoch of revolutionary transition from capitalism to socialism on a world scale, had a tremendous effect on China. It pointed to the Chinese people the way to liberation and contributed to the dissemination in the country of Marxist-Leninist doctrine, of the ideas of scientific socialism. As has been elaborated, Marxist circles were formed in the country with the versatile assistance of the Communist International; these were followed by Communist groups which became the basis for the founding of the CCP in 1921.

The transitional period in the formation of the party was effected with relative speed. Contributing were various revolutionary democratic organizations with Marxist groups as their nuclei. Communists became members of these groups, and adherents of anarchism, peasant socialism, and other philosophies joined them. This diversity resulted later in ideological instability among individual groups of Chinese revolutionaries.

The specifics of the social and economic situation and the political life of Chinese society were reflected in the development of Marxist thought in the country, in the formulation of political views by individual leaders of the CCP, and created great difficulties for the revolutionary movement.[1] These difficulties were specifically associated with the weakness of the proletarian stratum of society. The young proletariat, which never had to endure the long class struggle, was a tiny island in a boundless ocean of petty bourgeois elements. The workers' movement in China had in fact just begun in history, and did not have the necessary experience. The majority of the Chinese Communists, in their social origin, were typical petty bourgeois revolutionaries, with all inherent inadequacies and vacillations. "Given the existing situation in China, the workers' movement is hardly a big enough factor to be capable of carrying with it all of the national movement against imperialism," wrote G. Voytinskiy, at that time the Comintern representative in China, in October 1923.

Another source of difficulty was the fact that Marxism was unknown in China prior to 1917. This helped complicate the formation of a genuine revolutionary advance guard in the country. Chinese revolutionary democrats, and many Communists, particularly those among the intelligentsia, considered their primary task the gaining of national, and not social, liberation of China.* Consequently ideas of nationalism prevailed in their consciousness, superseding ideas of the class struggle. What they saw above all else in Marxist-Leninist teachings and in the October Revolution, as Mao Tse-tung himself wrote, was the key to "national rebirth," and the "saving of China."

The weakness of the proletariat, the merging into a single revolutionary torrent the tasks of social, antifeudal, and anti-imperialist revolutions, the complex ideological situation, all had their effect on the formation of Marxist thought in the country and on the political views of individual leaders of the Communist Party. People who designated themselves Marxists and proletarian revolutionaries, and who actually were ready to struggle selflessly for liberation of their motherland, frequently joined the CCP and became its leaders, yet in fact their ties to Marxism and the workers' movement were tenuous. This explains the fact that the leaders of the CCP, treading the correct international path for the most part, and heroically doing battle for the working class, stumbled and made mistakes.

The Plenum of the CC CCP, meeting in November 1927, in a resolution entitled "Immediate Organizational Tasks of the Communist Party of China," noted that:

> One of the basic organizational shortcomings of the Communist Party of China is that virtually all the most active leaders of our party are neither workers nor even poor peasants, but rather are representatives of the petty bourgeois intelligentsia. The Communist Party of China began to take shape as a political movement and as a party at a time when the Chinese proletariat had not yet constituted itself as a class, and when the class movement of the workers and peasants was still in its embryo state. The rise of the national liberation movement, one in which the bourgeoisie initially played a tremendous role, and this is particularly true of the petty bourgeois intelligentsia, determined for a long time to come the growth of class consciousness and of the class struggle of the exploited masses in China. At that time the most radical elements of the petty bourgeoisie rushed to the ranks of our party, occupying the extreme left wing of the front of the national liberation movement. These elements also

* Translator's note: in this latter respect, Chinese Communists faced a situation vastly different from that which confronted the Russian Marxists before the Revolution.

made up the original nucleus of the Communist Party of China. The mass influx of workers and poorest peasants into the party began comparatively late and as a result of the development of the revolutionary class movement of the workers. Consequently, the leadership role in the Communist Party of China has been retained by those who have come from the petty bourgeois strata. Stirred by the wave of revolutionary enthusiasm and the enthusiasm of the first period, with no training in the theoretical schools of Marxism-Leninism, unaware of the experience of the international proletarian movement, not associated with the exploited lower strata of the Chinese people, standing apart from the class struggle of the workers and peasants, many of these revolutionary petty bourgeois elements could not be digested by the Communist Party of China, nor did they become proletarian revolutionaries later on, yet they brought to the Communist Party of China all of the political instability, inconsistency, inability for organization, nonproletarian skills and traditions, prejudices, and illusions of which only petty bourgeois revolutionaries are capable.[2]

An article celebrating the 30th anniversary of the CCP noted that:

The Communist Party of China for a long time was located in villages, separated by its enemies, so that it was extraordinarily easy oftentimes for village and petty bourgeois spontaneity, subjectivism, sectarianism, bureaucratism, as well as adventurism, capitalism, and other tendencies to find their expression in the ranks of the party.[3]

Among other objective factors having a negative effect on the formation of ideology and policies of the leadership of the CCP were the absence in China of democratic traditions of political and economic life, the special role of the army in the course of the revolution, the subsequent activities of the party, and finally the large population of China.

The absence of democratic traditions in the country was aggravated by the fact that the revolution occurred under the conditions that prevailed during a prolonged partisan war, in a situation of isolation from the cultural and political centers in the country. Under those conditions it was inevitable that what occurred during the struggle was a merging of the revolutionary army and the party. Soldiers constituted over 80 percent of the party from the mid-1930's up to 1949. The army's role was both that of an armed force to resist the counterrevolution and also that of an organization that carried on party political work among the population of liberated regions, exercising control over economic activities as well. The army thus served as the direct transmission belt between the party and the masses. It became tradition and habit for CCP cadres to solve all problems concerned with revolution and construction by resorting to the army and to military methods. A style of administration became dominant in the party which substituted army commands for democratic centralism.

The size of the population created the illusion among Chinese leaders that human resources were inexhaustible. This led to a sharp degradation of personal value in China, creating indifference to the destiny and conditions of human existence.

Nevertheless, despite these extraordinary difficulties, there formed within the CCP a nucleus of theoretically trained revolutionary Marxists who had gained some practical experience and who were confirmed adherents of proletarian internationalism.

Two definite lines began to take shape within the CCP, the Marxist-internationalist, the banner of which was the idea of the October Revolution, and the nationalist—the petty bourgeois, with its own ideological concept. A significant effect on the course and outcome of the struggle between these two directions was that activities of the CCP after 1927 occurred under conditions of terror, this being the period of the Chiang Kai-shek coup. The central Kuomintang government and the provincial militaristic cliques, the troops of Western imperialists, and the Japanese occupiers all fought the Communists with the same hatred. The Communists proved to be models of selflessness and heroism in the battles for the liberation of the workers, but the majority of the experienced CCP leaders perished in these battles. First to be bled white were party organizations in proletarian centers.

Thousands of Communists fell at the hands of Kuomintang adherents. Membership of the CCP decreased fivefold in the first six months after Chiang Kai-shek's coup alone, from 50,000 to 10,000. At the beginning of the 1930s repressions against the Communists in Shanghai, as a result of the treachery to which Kang Sheng was a party, caused heavy losses.

At the beginning of 1935 the majority of old party cadres, including many of the most experienced leaders, were physically destroyed, and anything resembling real organization in the cities had been crushed. This was a real tragedy for the CCP.

All party work was in fact concentrated in the military forces under the control of the CCP, in a few support bases far from the political centers of the country and cut off from the main masses of the Chinese proletariat. For a long time party ranks were replenished by the peasantry, by petty bourgeois elements, by defectors from the exploiter classes, and by the intelligentsia. The influx of workers into the party ceased for all practical purposes and the pressure of the petty bourgeois element intensified.

It was during this period that nationalist elements were able to strengthen their position within the leadership of the CCP and within the army, weakened by the losses they had borne. They leaned both on the army and on the petty bourgeois.

It should be noted that under these concrete conditions the nationalists in the CCP were forced to remain in the mainstream of the revolutionary struggle of the Chinese people. The enthusiasm of the masses, the vital need for international support, particularly support from the Soviet Union, dictated to the CCP leadership the only possible road to take, that of the revolutionary struggle. The Maoists, for all their nationalist tendencies, did not believe that the political situation in the international arena, or in China proper, left them any other choice.

Of course it is impossible not to record the dual role of nationalism during the period of the liberation struggle. One side of the coin was progressive, feeding patriotic feelings, rallying the nation to struggle against the foreign invaders, the other the conservative, nationalist side, leading to isolation and confrontation of China with other nations. In such a case nationalism can also develop into chauvinism, and even merge with racism.

This dual role of nationalism is particularly marked in the case of China, with its strong traditions of Great Han chauvinism. Yet at the stage of the anti-imperialist democratic revolution, nationalism, or, more precisely, aspects of nationalism served as the ideological base for rallying and uniting the broadest masses of the Chinese population, and even temporarily put class differentiation into the background. But with the end of the anti-imperialist, democratic stage of the revolution, nationalism exhausted its progressive potential and began to play a completely reactionary role, feeding chauvinistic remnants, interfering with the assertion within the party of the principles of proletarian internationalism and Marxism-Leninism as the only ideological base for the new type of revolution. This gave rise to the most intense struggle between the two lines, nationalism and internationalism, within the CCP and within Chinese society as a whole.

At the beginning of the 1950s the PRC became involved in an active struggle with the vestiges of feudalism; important social transformations were made, the tasks of the bourgeois democratic revolution were concluded, and the prerequisites for the successful building of socialism were created. The broad scope of assistance given China by the Soviet Union, and by other socialist countries, the use within the PRC of the international experience of socialist construction, all of this made it difficult for the nationalists to maneuver and served to strengthen internationalist tendencies in China and in the CCP.

But the situation changed at the end of the 1950s. More and more facts have become known, showing to what extent Mao Tse-tung and his adherents ignored the theory and practice of scientific socialism. In light of the past history of Maoism this change was no accident, although it would be erroneous to consider it the inevitable, fatal result of the preceding development.

Lenin's teachings to the effect that it is necessary, indeed vital, for a Communist party to develop the correct policy, to base itself on the working class, to be able to go among the peasantry without becoming lost among them, when conditions are those found in a peasant, petty bourgeois country, are particularly important. Present events in China show the results of ignoring these instructions, when the party lets itself be overwhelmed by petty bourgeois elements, and when it breaks its international ties with other fraternal parties and countries.

The nationalism and adventurism inherent in petty bourgeois revolutionaries gradually rose to the top in the policy of the CCP leadership.

At one time the CC CCP made quite clear the possibility of the revival of nationalist tendencies in the PRC. In an editorial entitled "Once again on the History of the Experience of the Dictatorship of the Proletariat" *Jen Min Jihpao,* the organ of the CC CCP, pointed out:

> We Chinese must remember in particular that during the Han, Tang, Ming, and Ching dynasties our country too was a great empire, and that despite the fact that over the course of approximately one hundred years, since the second half of the nineteenth century, our country, having become the object of aggression, was transformed into a semicolony, and although our country today still is backward in the economic and cultural senses, when conditions change, the tendency toward great power chauvinism no doubt will become a serious danger if it is not completely prevented. It must also be pointed out that at this time this danger already has begun to appear among certain of our workers.[4]

The tendencies toward great-power chauvinism intensified with the increase of the PRC's economic strength during socialist construction.

The building of socialism requires certain prerequisites: material in the form of developed industry, and social in the form of an industrial proletariat. A country in which these prerequisites are in nascent stages can successfully build socialism only with comprehensive political, material, scientific, and technical assistance of the world socialist system, with the help of its experience, with the support of the world workers' movement. The example of China once again has confirmed the reality of Lenin's instruction to the effect that the task of the Communist Party in an economically backward, historically oppressed country is to make every effort to form and increase a working class, to educate it politically, and, at the same time, to establish ties between the working class in that country with the world working class and "merge into the common struggle with the proletariat of other countries."[5]

The petty bourgeois, hegemonistic views of the Maoists gradually became increasingly dominant within the leadership of the CCP. This has been clearly demonstrated since the beginning of the 1940s.[6]

There has been more than one attempt in the PRC in recent years to present the history of relations between the world Communist movement and the CCP in a false light. Apologists for the cult of Mao, distorting the truth, ascribe to him the sole development of all basic positions on strategy and tactics of the Chinese revolution, and declare that the Comintern and the CPSU "only impeded the Communist Party of China in developing the correct line." It is not only political servility that explains this gross falsification. The Maoist "theoreticians" have as their goal the rewriting of the entire history of the Chinese Revolution and of the CCP along nationalist lines.

Historical literature published in Peking is silent on the international and domestic factors that ensured the victory of the Chinese Revolution and disparages the role of the world Communist movement. What it does with premeditation is distort the picture of the struggle of the nationalist and internationalist tendencies within the CCP, glamorize the political face of the present Chinese leadership, and whitewash the methods used in the internal party struggle. The outstanding feature of these works is the unrestrained exaggeration of the role of Mao Tse-tung at different stages of the Chinese Revolution, and the ignoring of all facts and information that unmask the nationalists who now occupy leading posts in the CCP.

2. Some facts from the history of the development of nationalist tendencies in the CCP early in the 1940s

The period that began in the 1940s has a special place in the history of the CCP and its relations with the international Communist movement. There was the campaign "to rectify the style of work" that unfolded between 1941 and 1945 in Yenan, the center of the liberated region. It was during this "rectification" campaign, or movement, as it was called, that reprisals were taken against the old cadres, concentrating first on those educated in the USSR. In essence, the "cultural revolution" was a copy of the Yenan reprisals against the Communists-internationalists.

During the "rectification" campaign anti-Soviet, nationalist tendencies within the ranks of the CCP developed further, the Mao Tse-tung cult of personality became stronger, and the "theorists" who rejected the applicability of the teachings of Lenin to the conditions of the Chinese revolution put in an appearance. Mao Tse-tung was being called the "Chinese Lenin" openly.

Propaganda published by the CCP, as early as the beginning of the 1940s, widely popularized the thesis that the "ideas of Mao Tse-tung," supposedly an integral system of views, were "a special contribution to the development of Marxism-Leninism."[7] Mao Tse-tung is "a creative Marxist of genius, linking as he has the universal truth of Marxism, mankind's superior ideology, with the concrete practice of the Chinese revolution," pointed out Liu Shao-ch'i at the 7th Congress of the CCP in 1945.[8] And further, "What Comrade Mao Tse-tung has done . . . has been to combine Marxist-Leninist theory with the practice of the Chinese Revolution, with the result that Chinese Communism, the ideas of Mao Tse-tung, were born." Mao Tse-tung, the 7th Congress was told, had changed Marxism from its European form into a Chinese form.[9]

Chinese theoreticians became increasingly persistent in their efforts to advance the hypothesis that the importance of the October Revolution was limited by the context of the imperialist, particularly the European, countries, and that the revolutionary model for the colonial and dependent countries was the Chinese Revolution.

Here is what Wang Ming, a party veteran, and for many years one of the leaders of the CCP, wrote about the campaign of the 1940s in Yenan:

> In his preparations for [the campaign], and in the course of it, Mao Tse-tung repeatedly said that by carrying out this campaign he wanted to achieve three goals: (1) replace Leninism with Mao Tse-tungism; (2) write the history of the Communist Party of China as the history of Mao Tse-tung; (3) raise the personality of Mao Tse-tung above the Central Committee and above the entire party. Why did he have to do this? He answered this himself. It provided him with two possibilities, the first of which was to take over the leadership of the party and thus take into his hands alone all of the authority in the party, and second, once he was sitting at the top of the party leadership no one ever would be able to overthrow him.[10]*

* He wrote this while in exile in Moscow.

The "rectification" campaign consisted of three stages, or periods. The first (from the fall of 1941 to the spring of 1942) consisted of "the study of 22 documents" which were mostly speeches by Mao Tse-tung and his adherents. Its tasks were to demonstrate that Mao Tse-tung was a "great theoretician," and an "initiator of new ideas."

The second period (from the spring of 1942 to the spring of 1943) was devoted to the "ideological testing of the cadres," which simply was a program of savage reprisals against party workers to whom Mao objected. The third period (from March 1943 to the 7th Congress of the CCP in 1945) can be characterized as that of the "campaign to expose the spies" and of the party purge.

As is obvious from the content and character of the first period, its main task was to make CCP members aware of the thesis that the "ideas of Mao Tse-tung" were the party's dominant ideology, and to substitute these "ideas" for Marxist-Leninist teachings. This campaign (more correctly, general purge), in its second and third periods, created within the party, and in the liberated region with its center in Yenan, a situation of psychological terror and conditions for elimination (including physical elimination) of those who did not agree with Mao Tse-tung and his group.

Wang Ming recalls how Mao Tse-tung artificially split the party into two camps, the "dogmatic" and the "empirical." He included all Communists who had studied in the Soviet Union, those who were engaged in ideological and political work, as well as those who by their social origins belonged to the intelligentsia in the so-called "pro-Soviet, dogmatic group. . . ."[11]

Mass reprisals against those who did not support Mao Tse-tung took the form of the "campaign to expose spies," which began in March 1943. "Shock work to trap spies" was organized in Yenan, and this was accompanied by general meetings with threats, demands for confessions of "antiparty activities," and recantations.

Those in authority forced party leaders as well as rank and file Communists to confess their "sins" in writing. The organizers of this "movement" first obtained from the accused various types of slanderous statements against the CPSU and the Soviet Union. Another indispensable part of the "repentance" was unrestrained praise for Mao Tse-tung, and self-flagellation for having supported the views and the institutions of the Comintern. Similar "educational methods" were invoked to undermine the faith of Chinese Communists in genuine Marxism and in proletarian internationalism.

† People who had lived or studied in the USSR were required to

"confess" in the form of slanderous attacks against the Soviet Union and against our party during the 1942–1943 rectification campaign. Any occasion was used to sow distrust of the Comintern and of the CPSU. Instilled in the Communists were notions that the Comintern had given instructions detrimental to the Chinese Revolution; that the Comintern influenced the Chinese studying in the USSR to turn against the CCP; that they became indoctrinated as "foreign lackeys of the comprador type" who should "usurp leadership of the Communist Party of China." Statements made by the "penitents" at the 7th Congress of the CCP (1945) were similar in nature. Thus even then relations with the Soviet Union were guarded, and often frankly hostile.

Thus even at the beginning of the 1940s ideological and organizational conditions had been created for the replacement of Marxism-Leninism by "the Chinese brand of Marxism," clearing the way for the installation of the "ideas of Mao" as the dominant ideology in the Communist Party of China.

The stronger the position of the Maoists in the leadership of the CCP, the more definite became their nationalism. Naturally, the Maoists assumed a cavalier attitude toward their international obligations.

† At the most crucial early period of the Great Patriotic War, the Comintern and the Soviet Union went to the leaders of the CCP with the question of coordination of activities designed to pin down Japanese forces and prevent them from attacking the Soviet Union. On June 27, 1941, the head of a group of Soviet workers in Yenan reported to Moscow that in accordance with his instructions he had raised the question with leaders of the CCP of help to the Soviet Union in event of an attack by Japan on the USSR. Chinese leaders responded that they already had planned a number of measures, and at the final meeting of the sides Chu Teh asked that the Soviet Union be advised that in the event Japan attacked the USSR, the Eighth Route Army would attack the Japanese with all strength available and would be able to provide sufficient support for the Soviet Union. This assurance was confirmed by the leaders of the CCP on July 3, 1941.[12]

Actually, no practical measures were undertaken. In July 1941 it was reported in Yenan that the Japanese would send their mobilized troops to the mainland, and a request was made that effective measures be taken to prevent their concentration along the Peiping-Kalgan and Paotow directions, that is opposite the USSR, and to disrupt normal traffic on the railroads leading to these points. But this request, like all the others, was ignored by the leaders of the CCP.

† As witnesses to these events recall, Mao Tse-tung once again was

asked what actions the CCP could be expected to take if Japan went to war against the USSR. This was on September 3, 1941. The reply came in the form of confused and evasive statements, hedged by endless reservations and containing what were known to be demands the Soviet Union could not meet under the circumstances. When asked directly to say what, with no "ifs" attached, the CCP would do in the event of an attack by Japan on the Soviet Union, Mao unceremoniously broke off the talks on this very important question, charging the Soviet representative with lack of dialectical thinking. All further attempts to agree on coordinated action were blocked.

Highly important to the struggle against Japanese militarists and to successful development of the Chinese revolution was the role of the Comintern in implementing the tactics of the United Front of the CCP and the Kuomintang. These aims corresponded to the general policy of the Comintern, and were directed at development of mass movements within the framework of a united international front for the struggle to defend China, for the countries enslaved by German Fascism, and for defense of the USSR. They were directed at the immediate creation inside the country of a united national front and this required the establishment of contact with all the forces opposed to Fascism. But the Maoists, continuing to vow fidelity to their international duty, actually procrastinated and avoided in every way possible following the advice and requests of the Comintern to intensify the struggle against Japanese imperialists.

There was deep disagreement on the question of the United Front among leaders of the CCP. The internationalists met resistance by the nationalists, who rejected the need for a united front and organization of a nationwide struggle against Japanese aggression together with the Kuomintang. And it was not until reality dictated the unquestioned need to create a united front that Mao Tse-tung began to pretend to be an active adherent of this course. But the present Maoist chroniclers say that the tactic of the United Front was the greatest personal contribution Mao Tse-tung has made to Marxism-Leninism.

The narrow nationalist course set by some CCP leaders had a result that beginning with 1941–1942 the troops of the CCP gradually slowed their activities. Mao Tse-tung justified his tactics by saying that "it is better for us to conserve our strength, to defeat the Kuomintang, to take over power in China, and then, with the help of the USSR, England, and America, liberate China from the Japanese invaders. . . ."

† The passive attitude of the nationalist wing of the CCP to the war with militaristic Japan in a period when interests of the international

proletariat, interests in the common struggle against Fascism, demanded intensification of action against Japan is yet another example of the retreat from internationalism.

Mao Tse-tung spelled out his aim when he said, "Ten percent of our forces to the struggle with Japan, 20 percent to the struggle with the Kuomintang, and 70 percent to the growth of our own forces." In accordance with this stated aim, the Eighth and Fourth Route Armies took no active part in combat operations against the Japanese for several years. The views that were fostered went something like this: why irritate the Japanese and bring down unpleasantness on ourselves. Better that we live like friendly neighbors with the Japanese. We won't bother them, and they won't bother us.

"All units have been ordered not to conduct military operations against Japanese troops and to withdraw when Japanese troops are engaged in offensive operations," reported a Soviet war correspondent who was in Yenan in January 1943. "Should the opportunity present itself, conclude a temporary armistice with them. . . . All areas, every unit of the CCP [the military units under the supervision of the Communist Party of China —*authors*], is trading with the Japanese rear. The headquarters usually do not discuss military operations, but rather talk a great deal about trading operations."[13]

Thus in the 1940s internationalist obligations of the CCP in general, and regarding the Soviet Union in particular, bothered the Maoists as slightly as now they disturb China with respect to meeting its international duty to the people of the socialist countries, particularly to the heroic people of Vietnam.

3. Nationalist manifestations of anti-Sovietism among the leadership of the CCP in 1945–1949

The erroneous tendencies in the political line and practice of the Chinese leaders were already apparent on the eve of victory of the Revolution. One example of this is the idea put forth at the end of the 1940s that China "isolate itself" from the socialist countries, including the Soviet Union. This nationalist approach to assessing the future of the Chinese revolution would have interfered adversely with social changes in China and would have moved the democratic revolution away from development into a social revolution.

Mao Tse-tung persistently advanced the idea that transition to the building of socialism in China was in the far distant future, and that China should spend a considerable period of time in the "new democracy" stage before raising the question of socialism. Characteristic also was that Mao Tse-tung saw substantially "favorable conditions" for this in a long period of isolation for China. He had this stage in mind when he suggested that after the victory of the Chinese Revolution the USSR and other socialist countries take their time in recognizing China. It would be better, he said, if China were first recognized by the big imperialist powers: the United States, Great Britain, France, and others.

This "plan" evolved from a narrow nationalist approach to the Chinese revolution. The nationalists in the CCP even then were secretly nurturing the idea of China as a third force to play on the contradictions between the two social systems. It was not until these "ideas" met with a decisive rebuff at the 2d Plenum of the CC CCP's seventh convocation in March 1949 that Mao rejected them. In his article entitled "On the Democratic Dictatorship of the People" he now appeared as an enthusiastic adherent of alliance with the USSR, and a proponent of the "support one side" line.

Well known also are other zigzags and excursions on the part of the nationalists. For example, on the eve of the disintegration of the Kuomintang, Mao Tse-tung asserted that the CCP should be in no hurry to seize the main industrial centers in China, such as Nanking, Shanghai, and others. He argued that the CCP was in no position to seize the large cities because "it had no cadres," the Communist Party being composed mainly of peasants.

† These and other attitudes caused concern, and patient explanatory work was conducted with leaders of the CCP (by the Comintern). Attempts were made to persuade Mao Tse-tung that it was necessary to pay more attention to the working class in China, to devote more attention to work in the largest of the industrial centers, to see to the purity of the party's ranks, and to spread developmental work among the trade unions.

The process of fouling the CCP and its leadership with alien elements intensified during the Civil War of 1946–1949, when Kuomintang divisions, corps, and whole armies came over to the PLA of China, together with generals and staffs. This was a period of growth for the CCP exclusively because of the addition of these nonproletarian elements, these holders of petty bourgeois and nationalist views, these members of the Kuomintang.

† It should be noted that as early as 1936 the Comintern, addressing the CC CCP, emphasized that:

> We are worried in particular by the decision that the party will accept all those who desire to join, regardless of their social origin, and that the party is not worried about its ranks being penetrated by certain careerists,

as well as your report of your intention to accept into the party the likes of Chang Hsueh-liang [a militarist, a double-dyed reactionary—*authors*]. . . . We also would consider it to be a mistake to resort to indiscriminate acceptance into the ranks of the Red Army students and former officers in other armies. . . . We consider it to be incorrect to permit representatives of the propertied classes to exercise political control in Soviet regions . . ."[14]

Nevertheless, Chinese leaders not only failed to exhibit necessary concern for the purity of the ranks of the CCP as a Marxist-Leninist party, but instead followed a diametrically opposite policy. The masses of the people who had joined the CCP during the Yenan period, and afterward, knew no other course than Maoist "re-education" and "repentance." They then became the additions to the cadres of political organs, editorial boards, and Red Army officers. The "rectification" campaign at the beginning of the 1940s was directed exclusively at those who followed the line of the Comintern, and did not share the views of Mao Tse-tung, but it was, in essence, a campaign of total forgiveness so far as actual antiparty elements were concerned. †The Maoists granted new amnesty to antiparty bourgeois elements on the eve of the 7th Session of the CCP in 1945, stating that "the roots" of the left-deviationist and right-opportunist mistakes "had been eliminated" and that "all comrades who had admitted to mistakes in the past should be welcomed and enlisted to work for the advantage of the party without prejudice of any kind, so long as they remembered their mistakes and set about correcting them." Moreover, the amnesty usually favored people with anti-Soviet leanings who had adopted the "ideas of Mao" without question. This became the original forerunner of the "cultural revolution" which developed within the PRC in the second half of the 1960s.

The international Communist movement and the CPSU hewed to the line of supporting the CCP and providing it with comprehensive assistance during the Chinese Revolution. Genuine internationalists could do no less for the Chinese people who had risen to struggle for their liberation, and for the Chinese Communists who were leading this struggle. Then too, despite the grave shortcomings in its leadership, the CCP was a serious ally of the progressive forces in the struggle against imperialism. As we already have pointed out, the CCP, relying on support of the international forces of the proletariat, the experience of the CPSU, and on the tremendous assistance given by the Soviet Union, was able to play its role as the leader of the national liberation and revolutionary struggle of the Chinese people and bring the revolution to victory.

4. Anti-Soviet aspects in the policies of the leadership of the CCP in the first years of the existence of the PRC

Anti-Sovietism on the part of some CCP leaders during this period seemed an unfortunate exception in the general atmosphere of friendship and cooperation. Nevertheless, this tendency was not random in nature and is worth mentioning in order to establish a more comprehensive analysis of Sino-Soviet relations. Even at the conclusion of the Treaty of Friendship, Alliance, and Mutual Assistance, for example, the leadership of the CCP displayed definite distrust and suspicion in relations with the USSR. Chinese leaders were dissatisfied with the fact that the USSR had extended the PRC a credit of "only" 300 million dollars. They did not want to take into consideration the fact that at that very time the USSR itself was having considerable problems associated with the need to overcome consequences of the war as quickly as possible.

Then, as years passed, the Chinese leaders tried to enlist help from the USSR without considering the latter's capacity to help. Pretensions of nationalist elements in the CCP were so great that in some years they demanded deliveries which would have amounted to as much as 80 percent of the annual production of certain types of machine tools in the USSR.

† Mao Tse-tung, in a meeting with the Soviet Ambassador in October 1951, said, "Not everyone in the country, in fact not all the members of the party, agree with our policy of friendship with the Soviet Union." This, however, was the position of Chinese leaders themselves, and not the feelings of the rank and file of the CCP.

All of these aspects were viewed [in Moscow] as temporary deviations at the time, but in light of subsequent events in the PRC, similar "random occurrences" have acquired an entirely different coloration. They were deliberate steps which led leaders of the CCP to an open political struggle with the CPSU.

Measures were undertaken in 1953 and 1954 to nullify the influences of the Sino-Soviet Friendship Association in propagandizing the idea of internationalism and knowledge of the USSR. There was a clearly observable leaning to the side of propaganda dealing primarily with economic and scientific and technical experience, rather than with the experience of the USSR and the CPSU as a whole. At just about this time the Sino-Soviet Friendship Association for all practical purposes curtailed its activities as an organization with branches all over the country. The conference made personnel changes in the leadership of the Sino-Soviet Friendship Association. Members who were to become active champions of the basic anti-Soviet line in the CCP were appointed to supervisory organs of the association. The number of members of the Central Administration Board of the Sino-Soviet Friendship Association dropped from 197 in 1949 to 60 in 1954.

The first years of the people's power already saw numerous cases of misuse of Soviet specialists. They were barred from production, from concrete work in ministries and departments, without which they were unable to give qualified recommendations based on conditions in corresponding branches of the economy. In some institutions Soviet specialists were burdened with petty current assignments, resulting, naturally, in a paucity of suggestions and recommendations on important questions. Subsequently, this line was transformed in 1958–1959 into an entire campaign of belittling Soviet experience, as will later be discussed.

Great-power chauvinism and adventurism made themselves felt in the first period of the existence of the PRC even in international affairs. At the conference of trade unions of the countries of Asia and the Pacific Ocean held in December 1949 in Peking, the Maoists claimed to occupy the leading position in the Asian revolutionary movement. They asserted that situations in Asian and Pacific countries were quite similar to the situation in China prior to 1949, and that revolutionaries should therefore be guided in their actions under the leadership and experience of Peking. The Chinese representatives proclaimed that "The path selected by the Chinese people for victory over imperialism and its stooges, and for the creation of the PRC, is the path along which the peoples of many of the colonial and semicolonial countries should move in the struggle for the winning of their national independence and of a people's democracy. . . . This is the path, the path of Comrade Mao Tse-tung. . . ." Many delegates refused to accept these concepts and the Maoists had to back off.

In 1950–1951 the Maoists attempted to foist on the Communist parties of Indonesia and India programs which ignored the concrete situation in each of these countries, and which required that they copy the experience of the liberation struggle in China (the formation of peasant armies, the creation of liberated regions). †J. V. Stalin took a decisive stand against this line.

But these were individual cases. The PRC still was an economically backward country needing much assistance from socialist states in order to strengthen its defensive capability and to develop its economy; thus the Maoists were not too openly venturesome.

The nationalist, anti-Soviet tendencies inherent in the Mao Tse-tung environment during early stages of the Chinese revolution became even more pronounced after the death of J. V. Stalin. Mao Tse-tung, in order to "take over" the leadership of the Communist movement, developed a definite strategy and tactics, the reasoning behind which finally was clarified during a later period: use all economic, military, and other help available from the USSR in order to create the material prerequisites for carrying out his course of action; simultaneously use all available means to undermine the authority of the USSR in the world arena and complicate the realization of the plans for building communism in our country. Roadblocks in effecting these plans were the Soviet Union as well as the Chinese people and the Chinese Communists, who were well aware of the importance of the Soviet Union in building socialism in the PRC.

Nationalists among the leadership of the CCP attempted to make it difficult to establish contact between the Chinese workers and the Soviet people arriving in China to help in socialist construction. In May 1954 the State Council adopted and sent to the provinces a special decision categorically forbidding all Chinese, other than workers in foreign sections of corresponding administrative organs, to meet with Soviet citizens who were members of different missions on other than business.

Beginning in 1953 Mao Tse-tung began the gradual elimination of all those who did not share his nationalist, anti-Soviet line. Whatever labels were now used to cover Mao Tse-tung's attack on Wang Ming [alias Chen Shao-yü—*translator*], Kao Kang, P'eng Teh-huai, Chang Wen-t'ien [party name Lo Fu—*translator*], and others, his reprisals against many leading cadres of the CCP had a single purpose, that of eliminating the obstacles in the way of his petty bourgeois, chauvinist course. Documents on the "cultural revolution" indicate that one of the major "crimes" of the CCP leaders aforementioned were their friendly feelings toward the USSR and the other countries of socialism.

It later became known that the struggle between the internationalist Marxist-Leninists and the Maoists—the great-power chauvinists and the nationalists among the Chinese leaders—intensified at the beginning of the 1950s. The alarm was the arrest and death in prison in 1955 of Kao Kang, a member of the Politburo, and a Vice Chairman of the PRC. The various criminal charges brought against him were completely unfounded. Nothing was said about his major "crime," his being a true friend of the USSR, constantly fighting nationalist deviation to uphold the party's internationalist line.

However, Mao at that time was of the opinion that there was much still to be obtained from socialist countries in strengthening the PRC, which remained in need of protection. The central factor was that sentiments within the CC CCP and the party as a whole in favor of friendly relations with the USSR through a flexible and reasonable policy were so strong that Mao and his adherents were forced to consider them. This held even more true after the CCP, now wielding power, had to make decisions in connection with the main tasks of the socialist revolution on political and economic fronts.

It must be emphasized that the leaders of the CCP, as they indulged in their nationalist meanderings, never lost hope of extricating themselves from difficulties through the support of the United States of America. There is additional information indicating that in the 1940s these leaders made a number of attempts to reach mutual understanding with the Americans, but at that time these attempts could not have been successful. Washington at that time still was concerned with the prospects for maintaining American influence in China through the Chiang Kai-shek regime, thus distrusted advances of CCP leaders. Chinese leaders close to Mao tried to avoid the slightest action that could alienate the Americans and the British. They came out against the participation of Japan and India in the trade union conference that the countries of Asia and Oceania held in Peking in 1949, for example, because of the fear that "this would irritate Washington and London." At the end of 1949 the Chinese leaders declared that Soviet specialists should not be sent to Shanghai and Taishan because "big American and British economic interests were concentrated there during this period."

The Korean War erupted in 1950, straining Sino-American relations and for a long time preventing any deal between the CCP nationalists and ruling circles in the United States and, concurrently, forcing CCP leaders to proceed with a policy of expanding cooperation with the USSR.

Mao Tse-tung and his followers also had to consider that there were those in the party as well as among the leadership of party forces maintaining that alliance and friendship with the USSR were one of the most important conditions for a socialist victory.

All these factors, in one way or another, tended to slow development of nationalist anti-Soviet tendencies within the CCP and among its leadership, tendencies which later blossomed so luxuriantly.

Given this situation, the Peking leaders were forced to put aside realization of their great-power nationalist program. They pretended to be friends of the Soviet Union in order to obtain help from the USSR in creating the material-technical base needed to achieve their goals.

This circumstance made it extremely difficult for us to recognize the true nature and the main thrust of Maoist leadership of the CCP in the international Communist movement.

*5. Factors contributing to the rise of nationalist tendencies
in the CCP*

The serious subjective features of the activities of leaders headed by Mao Tse-tung were mixed with objective factors contributing to the birth and development of nationalist, petty bourgeois currents in the CCP. These activities were aggravated by serious gaps and errors in the party line, and by flagrant deviations from Leninist principles of party life.

Soviet specialists who worked in China have drawn the picture of right-opportunist practices in the CCP, a most important aspect of which was its relationship to the working class. They point out that after the victory of the Chinese Revolution leaders of the CCP did nothing radical to create political and economic conditions which would enable the working class to consider itself dominant. Workers continued to lead a wretched, half-starved existence; the working day, in accordance with the labor statute, was 12 hours long. Wages remained identical to those paid under Kuomintang domination.

Leading circles within the CCP, as usual, underestimated the role of the working class in the revolutionary transformation of the country. They considered the workers "immature, illiterate, and politically backward," thus "not actively participating in the revolution."

Despite the fact that the CCP had for many years been supported by the peasantry, which had formed the mass base of the PLA and the source of its material supply, Chinese leaders were also indecisive and fearful of undertaking revolutionary measures, even in the villages.

On the other hand, the Maoists obviously were favorably inclined toward the bourgeoisie. They imposed no taxes on trade, engaged in no decisive struggles with black marketeers. The absence of restrictive measures of any kind, even with respect to the big national bourgeoisie, favored the stirring up of its reactionary activities.

The theory that the "new kulaks" to arise as a result of land reforms would thus be a "revolutionary force" supporting the Communist party and the People's Government was propagated among certain groups of Communists and within ruling circles of the Communist party.

The Chinese leaders, in meetings with representatives of the fraternal parties in 1949, declared that:

> The fact that a new type of rich peasant is appearing in the villages poses absolutely no danger, because this rich peasant has received his wealth from the new authority, and supports it decisively. . . . This new rich peasant is revolutionary minded.

In 1949 Soviet specialists characterizing the situation within the CCP noted:

> The growth of the party attributable to the working class is insignificant. There is no active effort afoot to attract workers into the ranks of the party. Party organizations are quite cluttered up with the landlord-rich peasant and bourgeois elements, and people are being accepted into the party in many regions without grounds.

These impressions gained by Soviet residents are confirmed by the observations of leaders of fraternal parties who visited China in those years. Viewed with alarm was the fact that Mao "was not providing his people, and the working class in particular, with clear, coherent prospects. Consequently, the concentration in his hands of absolute power excites certain apprehensions." There also was talk of the "serious danger of complete restoration of capitalism in the city, as well as in the countryside, because the leaders of the CCP did not understand the terrible danger and were doing nothing to combat it."

The Peking leaders asserted:

> It is impossible to permit any sort of class struggle in private enterprises in new China, and we must give the owners the freedom to act if we are to increase production. The working class in China is illiterate, irresponsible, and thus cannot yet be drawn into the class struggle.

Chinese leaders were unconcerned with strengthening the leading role of the working class in its capacity for organization because they placed primary reliance on the rich peasantry. Their statements in a 1951 meeting with Academician P. F. Yudin are of interest in this regard. In their words there were, within the CCP, sentiments in favor "of considering the rich peasants the main figures in the villages, and from this concluding that it was only by following a course of developing the rich peasant economy of China that the productive forces of villages could be developed," thus "creating the grain and raw materials base for cities and industry. It is necessary, therefore, to support in the villages those Communists whose farms can develop into rich peasant farms and not exclude them from the party. These Communists should serve as the examples for all the peasants."

Analysis of the causes and factors for the gradual increase in petty bourgeois and nationalist tendencies in the actions of CCP leaders emphasize a definite inconsistency in accomplishment of social and economic reforms. Despite a great deal of work along these lines, the private capitalist sector in the national economy of the PRC remained impressive. In 1953 the proportion of private industry in the total volume of the country's industrial production was 32.2 percent. The total number of large private capitalist industrial enterprises registered in the country in 1953 was 18,091,* with 185,940 small ones. The actual number was higher, for there were many unregistered private enterprises in the country. The financial organs of the PRC estimated that there were some 10,000 private capitalist industrial enterprises in Shanghai alone that were unregistered and untaxed. Such enterprises employed 5.4 million people in 1953.

Serious breakdowns in Leninist standards in the life and activities of the CCP interfered with successful accomplishment of socialist construction in the PRC from the first years of the republic's existence. Plenary sessions of the CC CCP were irregular. The Central Committee, elected in 1945 (approximately 40 strong), did not reflect the actual situation of the party in the country, either in numbers or in composition, and was unable fully to cope with the tasks facing it. The CC CCP had virtually no experienced economic and party workers; the military prevailed. Party and administrative authority was concentrated in the hands of leading workers in the provinces, cities, districts, enterprises, and schools. The secretary of a province committee of the CCP was simultaneously the chairman of the province's People's Committee. The director of a large enterprise was simultaneously the secretary of the party committee.

The struggle against corruption, waste, and bureaucracy revealed that the party, particularly the state apparatus, was severely polluted by persons alien to the socialist system and to the working class. A great many spies, grafters, bureaucrats, and plunderers of state property were unmasked in a number of organizations and institutions. Many party and state officials were inattentive to hostile schemes of the class enemy. Instructions issued by the CC CCP on January 1952, in connection with prosecution of the above campaigns, stated that as many as 50 to 60 percent of the total number of workers in many organizations were involved in various types of unlawful activities or immoral acts.

Many flaws in the social and party policy of the CCP which had first appeared during early stages of the Revolution and in the first years of the people's power now had serious effects. Party ranks were overswollen, yet strict class selection for admission to the CCP was lacking,

---

* This category in the PRC included enterprises with 16 or more employees, equipped with machinery, or with 30 or more employees, without machinery.

and the Mao cult of personality was increasingly inflated. All this served to create conditions favorable for the growth of petty bourgeois, nationalist tendencies. Party membership growth was particularly heavy between 1953 and 1957, when 70 percent of all Communists were accepted into the CCP. It is understandable that the increase in the ranks of the CCP, at such tremendous rates and on this vast scale could not help but affect the quality of the party. Commenting on the great shortcomings in acceptance into the party, the newspaper *Szechwan Jihpao* noted that:

> . . . some party members have a low level of consciousness, are unclear as to what the party means, and are readily subject to the influence of bourgeois ideology. Some party members have been infected by bourgeois ideology, have mistaken views, have shortcomings in their work style. They are unable to respond fully to the demands imposed on party members. Even the party members who had become members earlier are not without shortcomings in their views and work styles.[15]

There were very few workers and employees in China on the eve of liberation, no more than 8 million. A rapid increase in the ranks of workers and employees occurred after formation of the PRC, but the proportion of industrial workers remained as before.

It was the social composition of the CCP which lent itself to the development of nationalist tendencies. The party grew with unjustified rapidity, feeding off the petty bourgeois environment. According to May 1953 data, only 450,000 of the 6,100,000 members of the CCP were workers, or only 7.3 percent. Being illegal, organizations of the CCP in major industial centers prior to their liberation from Kuomintang domination were not large. In Shanghai, for example, there were 600,000 industrial workers, yet six months after liberation there were only 6,000 Communists. Because the main peasant mass in China is illiterate, the majority of party members who came from the peasantry also were illiterate, and this presented objective difficulties in carrying on ideological and political indoctrination of party cadres. In 1950, for example, 1 million of the 1.5 million Communists in party organizations in Northeast and North China were illiterate.

One of the most important factors serving to stimulate the growth of nationalist tendencies in the CCP was the consciously fostered Mao cult of personality. Mao Tse-tung's works were published in the PRC in massive editions right after liberation. By October 1951 the Hsin Hua (New China) News Agency alone had published almost 2.4 million copies of these works.[16] A vast campaign to study the works of Mao

Tse-tung was organized in the country, while study of the works of the founders of Marxism-Leninism was completely ignored.* In August 1951, for example, local trade unions presented their plan to the All-China Federation of Trade Unions. This plan called for six or more weeks devoted to the study of Mao Tse-tung's articles. Cadres of workers in state institutions were to devote at least six hours a week to political study, including in particular study of the works of Mao Tse-tung. Students at universities and those studying in the middle schools were to devote 12 to 15 hours a month to studying the works of Mao Tse-tung, in addition to the usual political disciplines.

Publication of Mao Tse-tung's *Selected Works* began in October 1951, in accordance with a decision made by the CC CCP, and gave new impetus to the movement to study the "ideas of Mao Tse-tung." In a report to the 3d Session of the All-China Committee of the People's Political Consultative Council, held in October 1951, Chou En-lai said:

> We must . . . organize the study of the works of Mao Tse-tung on a broad, systematic basis among the active elements of all strata of society, among the soldier heroes, the outstanding workers, members of the democratic parties, all teachers, specialists, and cadre workers, and, through them, provide help for the broad masses of people in their study. The first volume of *Selected Works* of Mao Tse-tung was published during this session of the National Committee. We must assume the responsibility for encouraging the study of Mao Tse-tung's *Selected Works* among all strata of the population.
>
> We must arm ourselves with the ideas of Mao Tse-tung, which combine Marxism-Leninism and the revolutionary experience in China. This is a new task for the democratic united front of the Chinese people.[17]

Chinese propaganda even then stressed the thesis that the "ideas of Mao Tse-tung" were an integral system of views "contributing to the development of Marxism-Leninism." This thesis was advanced for the first time at the 7th Congress of the CCP in 1945.

The thesis of the "ideas of Mao Tse-tung" and their decisive role in the victory of the Chinese revolution was strengthened in speeches by a number of the leaders of the CCP on the occasion of the 30th anniversary of the CCP (July 1951). These speeches abounded with references to Mao as "great," "genius," and the like.

In addition to elements of the Mao Tse-tung cult of personality, there were other circumstances that facilitated the struggle of the nationalists

* Translator's note: this is reminiscent of the campaign to study Stalin's works in Russia in the 1930s.

in the CCP with the ideology of internationalism in the party and the country.

Despite the fact that during the first years after formation of the PRC, Chinese propaganda occasionally spoke of the need to master Marxist-Leninist theory, in practice CCP leaders were little concerned with businesslike and detailed solutions of concrete problems of socialist construction and use of the experience of the fraternal parties.

So long as the CCP followed the road built by the Soviet Union, ignoring Marxist-Leninist theory caused no serious negative consequences. But once the Chinese leaders began to underestimate, and then completely disregard Soviet experience, the lack of proper detailed Marxist-Leninist solutions to problems of socialist construction led to serious mistakes in practical activities of the CCP.

Documents from the "cultural revolution" in China provide the basis for the assertion that a struggle between two lines had in fact developed within the Chinese leadership, after the country's liberation, over the question of the socialist rebuilding of the PRC, and over its foreign policy. The struggle of views on questions of the internal course of the CCP was also reflected in the international policy of the PRC. Chinese leaders in those years tried to introduce their voluntarist views into the party's policies. Despite their pseudorevolutionary cast, their substance was the conserving of capitalist forms of property particularly in the cities, keeping ties with the imperialist world, and maintaining parasitical attitudes in dealing with the USSR, though simultaneously discrediting Soviet experience and disparaging the authority of our country.

Once having strengthened their position within the party and in the country, and having restored the economy, the Maoists took decisive actions to thrust upon the country their great-power, adventurist views. Initially these experiments on the part of the nationalist elements in the CCP were introduced in domestic policy, and following their failure, in the international sphere.

The negative consequences of the policies of the Peking leaders provide striking examples of where the voluntarist method of leadership, and the cult of personality, alien to Marxism-Leninism, lead if they fail to meet the necessary rebuff. The development of events in China at the end of the 1950s and in the 1960s graphically confirms how dangerous the petty bourgeois nationalist course is for the revolutionary movement. These events should serve as a serious warning to all detachments of the world revolutionary movement.

NOTES

1. A. M. Rumyantsev, *Problemy sovremennoy nauki ob obshchestve* (*Problems of Contemporary Social Science*) (Moscow, 1969)—"Maoizm i antimarksistskaya sushchnost' yego 'filosofii' " (Maoism and the Anti-Marxist Nature of Its "Philosophy," *Kommunist,* No. 2, 1969.

2. O. Vladimirov and V. Ryazantsev, *Stranitsy politicheskoy biografii Mao Tze-duna* (*Pages from the Political Biography of Mao Tse-tung,* hereinafter referred to as *Mao Tse-tung*) (Moscow, 1969), pp. 15–16.

3. *Narodnyi Kitay* (*People's China*), Vol. IV, No. 1–2, 1951, p. 12.

4. *Jen Min Jihpao,* December 29, 1956.

5. V. I. Lenin, *Polnoye sobraniye sochinenii* (*Complete Collected Works,* Vol. 39), p. 330.

6. O. Vladimirov and V. Ryazantsev, "On Some Questions of the History of the Communist Party of China," *Kommunist,* No. 9, 1968.

7. Chang Ju-long, *Idei Mao Tze-duna—kitaizirovannyy marksizm* (*The Ideas of Mao Tse-tung—The Sinification of Marxism*) (Yenan, 1944).

8. Liu Shao-ch'i, *About the Party.*

9. Ibid.

10. Wang Ming, *O sobytiyakh v Kitaye* (*On Events in China*) (Moscow, 1969), p. 37–38.

11. Wang Ming, p. 39.

12. O. Vladimirov and V. Ryazantsev, *Mao Tse-tung,* p. 53–54.

13. Ibid., p. 55–56.

14. Ibid., p. 68.

15. *Szechwan Jihpao,* April 16, 1957.

16. *Narodnyi Kitay,* Vol. IV, No. 7–8, 1951, p. 28.

17. Ibid.

CHAPTER FIVE

Soviet-Chinese Relations in the Period
of the Formation of the Special Direction
Taken by the Leadership of the CCP
in Domestic and Foreign Policies (1958–1959)

The years 1958–1959 can be characterized by a further strengthening of the policy of peaceful coexistence, and of an intensification in the
struggle for collective security, carried on by the Soviet Union and other
socialist countries. Our country continued to firmly champion China's
interests in the international arena. The government of the PRC also
took a number of steps in the spirit of an agreed policy of the fraternal
states (proposals for collective peace in the Far East, the establishment
of a nuclear-free zone in Asia, and others).[1]

However, in 1958, and particularly in the succeeding period, elements
of great-power chauvinism and adventurism appeared more and more
frequently in the foreign policy of the PRC. There was interference in
the internal affairs of other countries, advancement of territorial pretensions, a "theory" regarding the usefulness of nuclear war for revolution,
the assertion that the "East Wind" [read Peking—*authors*] would prevail
over the "West Wind." All this caused concern sufficient to make the CC
CPSU use interparty channels for appropriate communications with fraternal parties. These, however, believed that healthy Marxist forces
would be able to withstand such tendencies and that the nationalistic factors would be neutralized in the general stream of socialist construction
in the PRC.

1. Sino-Soviet Cooperation, 1958–1959

True to its international duty, the Soviet Union continued to provide
China with a great deal of assistance in developing its economy, science,
engineering, and culture. A delegation from the PRC headed by the
President of the Academy of Sciences, Kuo Mo-jo, concluded a stay of

over three months in the USSR in January 1958. The delegation met with the State Committee on Science and Technology of the Council of Ministers of the USSR, the Academy of Sciences of the USSR, the State Committee of the Council of Ministers of the USSR for Foreign Economic Ties, the Minister of Higher Education of the USSR, and leading members of scientific research institutes in the Soviet Union to discuss very important questions concerning development of science and engineering, and further expansion in scientific and technical cooperation between the Soviet Union and the PRC. Over 600 renowned scientists and specialists took part in these discussions on the Soviet side.

In the course of the talks the Chinese delegation expressed a desire for the Soviet Union to help China in solving its most important scientific and technical problems included in the prospective plan for development of science and engineering in the PRC to 1967. This help was to include sending Soviet scientists and specialists to China, training and improving qualifications of Chinese scientific and engineering-technical workers in the USSR, and delivering necessary equipment, instruments and materials.

The result of the talks was the conclusion of an agreement between the governments of the USSR and the PRC on January 18, 1958 for joint conducting of most important research in fields of science and engineering, and aid from the Soviet Union to China in this work.

The agreement envisaged joint work over the period 1958–1962 on 112 scientific and technical problems of great importance to the PRC, as well as further strengthening of direct ties between the scientific research institutes in both countries.

Agreements on cooperation in the conduct of scientific and engineering research between the Ministers of Higher Education of the USSR and of the PRC, as well as between the Academies of Agricultural Sciences in these countries, were signed at the same time.[2]

A Treaty of Commerce and Navigation between the USSR and the PRC was signed in April 1958. The high contracting parties agreed to "take all necessary measures to develop and strengthen commercial relations between both states in a spirit of friendly cooperation and mutual assistance, on the basis of equality and mutual benefit."[3]

The Treaty of Commerce and Navigation had an appendix: "On the Legal Status of the Trade Representatives of the USSR in the People's Republic of China and of the Trade Representatives of the People's Republic of China in the USSR," stipulating that Soviet and Chinese trade representatives would perform the following functions: (a) cooperate in the development of commercial and economic relations between both states; (b) represent the interests of their own state in all matters concerned with foreign trade; (c) regulate in the name of their own state the commercial operations with the other state; (d) conduct commerce between the USSR and the PRC.[4]

The June-July session of the Sino-Soviet Commission on Scientific and Technical Cooperation was successful. Measures designed to further strengthen cooperation were discussed in detail and corresponding decisions concluded. These included expansion of direct ties between similar scientific research and planning institutes in the USSR and the PRC.

An agreement between the governments of the USSR and the PRC was signed in Moscow on August 8, 1958, whereby the PRC was to be given technical assistance in building and expanding 47 plants in the metallurgical, chemical, coal, machine-building, and wood-working industries, in the building materials industry, and electric power stations.

Under terms of the agreement, Soviet organizations were to do surveys, research and design work for a number of the plants, hand over projects for individual shops and installations for repeat use, insure delivery from the USSR of technological equipment, instruments, cable parts, and certain special materials for manufacturing the on-site equipment. Soviet organizations were obliged to send the necessary specialists to provide help in installation, adjustment, and starting plants, as well as the training of national cadres to work in such plants.

The agreement also stipulated that the Soviet side would provide the Chinese side licenses to manufacture products, as well as drawings and other technical documentation needed to organize the manufacture of the products.

Payment of costs of Soviet organizations to provide the technical assistance envisaged by the agreement would be made by the Chinese side in the form of deliveries to the USSR of goods under conditions included in the effective Sino-Soviet trade agreement.[5]

The Soviet government, unwavering in its support of the PRC, in September 1958 announced its recognition of the 12-mile zone of territorial waters of China claimed by the PRC government.

A definite watershed in Sino-Soviet relations occurred in 1959. That was the final year that relations, overall, could be said to have still been improving. Beginning in 1960 the leadership of the CCP must assume blame for the rapid curtailment of economic, scientific-technical, and cultural cooperation between the USSR and the PRC, and for exacerbation and general deterioration of Sino-Soviet relations.

Throughout 1959 the leaders of the CCP continued their protestations of faith in Chinese-Soviet friendship, their high regard for the domestic and foreign policies of the CC CPSU and the Soviet government, and their emphasis on the exceptionally great importance of Soviet assistance. Chou En-lai, chief Chinese delegate, speaking from the rostrum at the 21st Congress of the CPSU, declared:

> The convocation of the 21st Congress of the Communist Party of the Soviet Union is a great event in modern political life. The people see in this congress a demonstration of the incomparable might of the Soviet Union, the mightiest bulwark of peace in the world, and they also see a majestic, beautiful future for all of mankind, communism. This makes the peoples of all countries, peoples who have been struggling persistently for peace throughout the world and for the progress of mankind, extremely happy and inspired.[6]

Chou En-lai noted that the CPSU and the Soviet people had been highly successful in strengthening the solidarity of the international Communist movement, and in uniting the forces of peace-loving states and peoples in the struggle to ease international tensions and avert the danger of war.

Chou En-lai presented greetings to the 21st Congress of the CPSU from the CC CCP, signed by the Chairman, Mao Tse-tung. Included, in particular, was the statement that:

> Today the Communist Party of the Soviet Union, on the basis of its great program for the building of communism, has revealed the plan for the development of the national economy for 1959–1965. Accomplishment of this plan will lay down a strong foundation for the transition to communism in the Soviet Union, from the material and spiritual points of view, and will enrich the treasure-house of Marxism-Leninism with valuable experience in the building of communism. At the same time, the accomplishment of this plan will lead to further change in the balance of power in the world, and will contribute even more to the noble work of general peace and progress for mankind.[7]

A new agreement on Soviet aid for the PRC was signed in Moscow on February 7, 1959. This agreement involved assistance in building 78 large plants for metallurgical, chemical, coal, petroleum, machine-building, electrical, radio, and building materials industries, and in building electric power stations.

This agreement included provisions for Soviet organizations to do research and design work based on the latest achievements of science and engineering, to provide equipment, instruments, and certain types of special materials, as well as to send a great many Soviet specialists to provide technical assistance in building the plants, installing and adjusting equipment, and putting the plants in operation. Large groups of Chinese specialists and workers were to be accepted for production and technical training in corresponding plants in the USSR.

As in previous agreements, it was stipulated that the Soviet side would freely turn over to the Chinese side licenses for production of goods in these enterprises, as well as necessary technical documentation for organization of the corresponding manufacture and preparation of complex equipment needed.

The total cost of Soviet equipment, planning work, and other types of technical assistance was some 5 billion rubles (in old rubles). China was to pay for the equipment and for all types of technical assistance provided by the Soviet Union by delivering to the USSR goods in accordance with the Sino-Soviet trade agreement.

The communiqué issued in connection with the signing of the agreement pointed out that:

> The governments of the Soviet Union and the People's Republic of China consider the signing of this agreement to be a new, important link in further strengthening and expanding fruitful, mutually advantageous economic cooperation and brotherly mutual assistance between both socialist states.[8]

Trade talks were held in Moscow at the end of 1958 between governmental delegations of the PRC and the USSR concerning completion of exchanges of goods in 1958, and future development of trade between the two countries. The parties agreed to additional deliveries of Soviet goods in the fourth quarter of 1958, as a result of which the scope of the original protocol of April 23, 1958 was expanded so that trade between the USSR and the PRC was increased by 600 million rubles. The sides agreed that when the trade talks for 1958 were concluded they would make preparations for a long-term trade agreement.[9]

Talks on 1959 trade exchanges between the USSR and the PRC were also concluded successfully. Conforming to common goals and tasks, the sides agreed to expand Sino-Soviet trade considerably.

There was a considerable increase in the flow of goods from the USSR to the PRC, particularly in the form of turbo-generator installations, diesel-generators, power transformers, locomobile electric power stations, and small hydroelectric power stations for use in the agricultural regions of the country. These deliveries were in addition to the equipment deliveries made under the terms of prior agreements. Deliveries from the USSR to the PRC of powerful drilling rigs, transportation equipment, bearings, and many other Soviet commodities needed for the national economy of the PRC also increased as compared with 1958.

Plans called for the delivery to the Soviet Union in 1959 by the PRC of tin, tungsten, molybdenum, raw silk, wool, tea, citrus, and other goods, as had been the case previously.

Chinese leaders, at the April 1959 session of the National People's Congress, commented on the great importance of Sino-Soviet economic cooperation. In his report to the session the Premier of the State Council of the PRC, Chou En-lai, said:

> The countries of the socialist camp, led by the great Soviet Union, have provided us with all kinds of help in the matter of socialist construction in our country. The 166 large enterprises built with the help of the Soviet Union during the years of the First Five-Year Plan played a tremendous part in the development of economic construction in our country. The rich experience accumulated by the Soviet Union during the years of its existence too is for us an important basis for the development and accomplishment of plans for economic construction. From this rostrum, I, in the name of the government and of the people of our country, want to express my deep appreciation to the governments and peoples of the Soviet Union and of the other socialist countries. . . . Strengthening solidarity with the Soviet Union, and with all the socialist countries, is the basic course of our country."[10]

Talks between government delegates of the USSR and of the PRC on concluding a consular treaty took place in Peking between June 16 and 23, 1959. The talks culminated in the signing of a treaty that called for regulation of rights and duties of consuls, as well as of other questions connected with consular service.

The PRC celebrated its 10th anniversary in 1959. Summarizing PRC progress, Chinese leaders could not help but recognize the tremendous part the broad development of interstate relations with the Soviet Union had played in the construction of the PRC. In an article entitled *The Great Decade,* Chou En-lai wrote:

> Marking the 10th anniversary of the founding of the People's Republic of China, the people of our country express particular appreciation to the Soviet Union, which helped our country in the building of 166 enterprises during the First Five-Year Plan, and once again has concluded, last year, and this year, agreements to help our country build 125 enterprises. The Soviet Union in these past ten years in addition has sent to work in China over 10,800 specialists in the fields of economics, culture, and education.[11]

The assistance of the Soviet Union would have created the necessary prerequisites for successful socialist construction in the PRC, had not the Chinese nationalists, with their special attitudes and views, interfered with this progressive process.

By the beginning of 1958 the PRC had experienced a tremendous upsurge in all phases of political and economic life. At this time the tasks of the restoration period had been accomplished, and the First Five-Year Plan for the development of the national economy had been considerably overfulfilled.

China, with the help of the USSR, had built 135 plants, including 12 for the coal industry, 29 electric power plants, 1 for the petroleum industry, 17 for ferrous and non-ferrous metallurgy, 7 for the chemical industry, 26 metal processing plants, 1 textile mill, 1 paper mill, and 2 plants for the food industry.

Forty-five of the 135 were to have been built and put into service during the five-year period. In fact, 68 plants were built and put into service, 56 of them completely, 12 partially. The plants in full use included 5 in the coal industry, 15 electric power plants, 6 in the metallurgical industry, 7 in metal-working, and 6 for other industries. Five electric power plants were in partial service, as were 3 metallurgical plants and 4 chemical plants.

Over 900 objects in excess of those planned were built during the First Five-Year Plan in the PRC.[12] But it was plants built with the help of the USSR which provided the basis for modern industry in China and made it possible to then effect the entire program of industrialization in the PRC. Not only did these plants enable the PRC to create a whole series of completely new branches of industry, such as aluminum, tools, mining equipment, synthetic rubber, automobile, tractor, aviation, electrical, radio, defense, and the like; they also increased by 1959 the productive capacity for the most important types of industrial products, which, when compared with 1954, showed the following increases:

pig iron	340 percent
steel	300 percent
rolled products	410 percent
copper	146 percent
tin	177 percent
tungsten concentrate	111 percent
molybdenum concentrate	175 percent
coal	28 percent
oil refining	120 percent
electric power production	150 percent
steam boilers	38 to 40 percent
metal cutting machinery	77 percent
turbogenerators	1480 percent
synthetic ammonia	250 percent
sulfuric acid	25 percent
concentrated nitric acid	940 percent

The 1957 production of steel, as compared with 1952, the last year of the restoration period, had increased 296 percent, pig iron by 208 percent, electric power production by 166 percent, oil by 335 percent, coal by 96 percent, metal-cutting machinery by 104 percent, grain by 20 percent, and cotton by 26 percent.[13]

Tremendous successes were achieved in the socialist transformation of agriculture. By the end of 1957, 98 percent of peasant households were included in agricultural cooperatives, with 96 percent of them combined into higher type cooperatives. Some 90 percent of handicrafters were put into cooperatives.

Socialist transformation in the field of private industry and trade, for all practical purposes, had been completed. At this time, only 0.1 percent of gross industrial production in the country was accounted for by untransformed private industrial enterprises, and private trade (primarily small shopkeepers) accounted for but 3 percent of the total volume of retail commodity trade.[14]

The exceptionally high rates of development of the national economy achieved in 1957 were not only maintained, but in fact increased significantly. In the first four months of 1958 gross industrial production increased 26 percent over the comparable 1957 period, with a growth in April of 42 percent. Irrigation construction and the movement to expand reforestation proceeded on vast scales.

2. Revision of the decisions of the 8th Congress of the CCP. The "Three Red Banners" Policy

The successes of the PRC in political and economic fields were good grounds for further development of socialist construction. But at precisely this time the struggle within the leadership of the CCP worsened. Whereas during the earlier stages the nationalist elements had masked their views and had been forced to act in accordance with historical tasks of the revolutionary movement in China, now with great victories already achieved by the Chinese people, with the help of the USSR and other brotherly countries during the restoration period and during the First Five-Year Plan, the nationalists in the CCP decided to seek openly realization of their great-power, nationalist views.

The Second Five-Year Plan, as contemplated by the 8th Congress of the CCP, was discarded. In 1958 the course of the 8th Congress was reviewed and replaced by the so-called course of the "three red banners —the general line of the great leap forward and the people's communes." Plans which in 1956 were expected to be completed in the course of three and more Five-Year Plans now were to be carried out in a few years, according to the Chinese leaders. It was decided to increase gross industrial production 6.5 times during the 1958–1962 Five-Year Plan period (the annual growth rate was to be an average 45 percent) and to increase gross agricultural production 2.5 times (annual growth rate 20 percent).[15]

These plans were drafted without an economic basis and without regard for the country's real potential. People's communes established in villages were to insure the "leap to communism" in three to six years.

The adventurist policy of the "three red banners" attracted those party cadres who did not immediately grasp its disastrous consequences. Nevertheless, the policy signified a complete break with the line adopted in 1953 and confirmed in 1956 by the 8th Congress of the CCP. †And the leaders of the CCP ignored the friendly advice of the Marxist-Leninist parties, all of which were concerned about the Chinese experiments and warned of their terrible consequences.

The policy of the "three red banners" was an attempt to artificially force the pace of economic development, to outstrip all other countries and, bypassing the necessary stages in the building of a socialist society, to "leap" to communism, all at the expense of tremendous pressure on China's labor force.

Although the leaders of the CCP advertised their policy as a model for the development of other countries, the theory and practice of the "leap to communism" was contrary to objective reality in China and the world, to science, and to the experience of the socialist countries and the international Communist movement. It was clear that the voluntary goals were unattainable; it was impossible to leap over definite stages of socialist construction; slogans could not replace equipment; and subjective factors could not be omnipotent in material production or social relations. It should be pointed out that Mao Tse-tung in particular had suggested the thesis of the need to adopt maximum rates of socialist construction for many years. As was established at the 2d Session of the 8th Congress of the CCP, this thesis had been the basis for a "long struggle" within the party. In a report of July 1955 entitled "The Question of Cooperatives in Agriculture," Mao Tse-tung set forth the task of accelerating the rates of socialist transformation, and in December 1955, in a foreword to the brochure "Socialist Progress in Chinese Villages," he raised the question of the need to increase rates of economic construction. Mao Tse-tung explained that:

> Now the question turns on the fact that in many areas we still are hampered by right-leaning conservative views, because of which efforts in

these areas have not had time to catch up to the objective situation. Now the question turns on the fact that there are many who feel that what can be done under corresponding conditions is unattainable. That is why constant criticism of the actions of the existing right-leaning conservative attitudes is absolutely necessary.

The capabilities that developed as a result of the successful overfulfillment of the First Five-Year Plan actually opened up before the leaders of the CCP the prospects for a definite increase in rates of socialist construction. But CCP leaders, still unsatisfied, decided not simply to increase the rates, but to "make the leap" that would, as swiftly as possible, transform China into a mighty, thriving power. This idea was expressed in Mao Tse-tung's slogans "struggle stubbornly for three years and achieve changes in the basic make-up of the majority of the regions of the country," and "a few years of persistent work, ten thousand years of happiness."

The "great leap forward" course on the "accelerated march to communism" was indubitably the result of the appearance of nationalist, hegemonistic aspirations on the part of Chinese leaders, and of their attempt to put a base under great-power pretensions to a leading position in the socialist commonwealth and the world liberation movement. The leaders of the CCP no longer limited themselves to the boundaries of China, but, instead, intensified the thrust of their adventurist course of the "great leap forward" on other socialist countries and the world Communist movement.

The policy of the "great leap forward" was a serious breach of the principles of the Declaration of the Moscow Conference on 1957, which had stated:

. . . [the] processes of socialist revolution and socialist construction are based on a number of laws inherent in all countries embarking on the road to socialism.[16]

One such general law was the "balanced development of the national economy, directed at building socialism and communism, at raising the standard of living of the workers."[17] Consigning to oblivion the immutable truths of Marxism-Leninism, the Chinese leaders proclaimed a leap in the development of the economy, ignored the natural proportionality inherent in a planned, socialist economy, and completely ignored the interests of raising the living standards of the workers. The declaration spoke of the need to create the economic and technical bases of socialism, once the working class seized power. In attempting to ensure the success of the "great leap forward," by such primitive technical means as "small-scale metallurgy," for example, the Chinese leaders rejected even this provision of the declaration.

Ministries, departments, and organizations lower on the administrative scale, urged by appeals for ever-increasing rates of progress, confronted daily new plans and obligations which were virtually impossible to accomplish. Given the general fever created by rates established by leaders of the CCP, it is no wonder that their sense of reality disappeared to be replaced by obvious self-delusion.

The following data serve to illustrate how impetuous, and primarily how unjustified, were the increases in plans for development of the national economy of the PRC. In accordance with proposals for the Second Five-Year Plan, adopted in 1956, planned steel production at the end of the Five-Year Plan period, by 1962, was to be between 10.5 and 12 million tons. The report to the 2d Session of the 8th Congress of the CCP in May 1958 stated that in the first year of the Second Five-Year Plan, that is in 1958, steel smelting would exceed 7.1 million tons. Finally, in August 1958, at the meeting of the Politburo of the CC CCP, it was decided to raise steel production in 1958 to 10 million tons,[18] that is, to fulfill the Five-Year Plan for steel in one year! The All-China Conference on Questions of Local Metallurgy, meeting in mid-1958, decided to use local labor to build 200 medium and small converter steel furnaces with a total annual capacity of 10 million tons of steel in one year.[19]

Similar unjustified indices were set for other branches of industry as well. In 1957 the PRC produced 631,000 tons of chemical fertilizer. The Second Five-Year Plan called for an increase in production to between 3 and 3.2 million tons by 1962. But in 1958 this figure was discarded and the task was set to surpass United States production of chemical fertilizers by 1962. According to Chinese estimates United States production by that time should have been 35.8 million tons.[20]

Totally incredible expectations were advanced for increases in crop yields. The project "Basic Provisions for the Development of Agriculture in the People's Republic of China 1956–1967," which had been reviewed in October 1957, called for an average annual harvest of grains in the most heavily cultivated regions in the country of 800 chins per mu (as opposed to 400 chins in 1955) by 1967.

The Second Five-Year Plan called for a 1962 production of some 500 billion chins of grain, some 48 million tons of cotton, and an increase to 250 million pigs. But by 1959 grain production was fixed at 1,050 billion chins, cotton at 100 million tons, and pigs at 1 billion head.

In 1958 Mao Tse-tung, during a visit to an experimental commune in a village, announced, "The people's communes are good." This was sufficient to begin the unjustified break-up of production relationships in the countryside.

In August 1958 the leaders of the CCP proclaimed "the beginning of a new era in the development of China, the era of the founding of the people's communes." This idea was the result of the same voluntarist strivings, to "omit, despite everything, the long period involved, even of relatively rapid development, to leap immediately to the realm of might and prosperity." Here, in the creation of the people's communes, is the concentrated embodiment of all phenomena which are a manifest break with reality, a breach of laws of social development, and a departure from reliance in the struggle for communism on the united forces of all socialist countries. Writings of Chinese authors on the role of the people's communes not only lack a clearly defined position concerning the dependence of the successful solution of this problem on cooperation with the socialist countries, but also imply that China will reach communism before the others. As to the accomplishment of communism in China stressed in the decision of the CC CCP of August 29, 1958, "On the Creation of the People's Communes," it was no longer something in the far distant future. Here the primary revelation is the fully revealed fact that the nationalist view had begun to prevail in the policy of the leadership of the CCP. Since that time these leaders have moved even further away from basic positions with respect to the socialist camp and have, in the process, placed themselves in opposition to the CPSU and to the entire international Communist movement.

The 8th Plenary Session of the CC CCP convened in August 1959. A group of Central Committee members protested against the "great leap" policy, classifying it as a petty bourgeois fantasy which cost the Chinese people dearly. The Maoists attacked these leading comrades with malicious criticism and curses. The communiqué issued by the 8th Plenary Session of the CCP stated that these cadres "are slandering the 'great leap forward' movement and the movement to create people's communes, calling these movements 'petty bourgeois fantasy movements'." Among those disagreeing with the Maoist line were P'eng Teh-huai, a member of the Politburo of the CC CCP, and Chang Wen-t'ien, a candidate member of the Politburo, as well as many leaders of provincial committees of the party, ministries, and departments.

The 8th Plenary Session was forced to recognize that figures for national economic summaries for 1958 were questionable, and announced accurate figures. The grain harvest was found to have been 250 million tons, instead of 375 million, cotton 2.1 million tons instead of 3.35 million, and steel 8 million tons instead of 11 million.

The 8th Plenary Session could not ignore the obvious failures of the "great leap." This realization was expressed in reductions made in the 1959 plan, and in a different approach to the people's communes. It was recommended "to phase in gradually the principles of administration and cost accounting: distribution according to labor, more pay for more work." In other words it was proposed to turn once again to the previously existing socialist principles of distribution. The desirability of having production brigades, rather than people's communes, as basic units was recognized. These brigades were to be approximately equal in size to the earlier production cooperatives.

But the overall political direction of the decisions of the 8th Plenary Session remained the same. These decisions, as had been the case in decisions of the 6th Plenary Session, extolled the policy of the "great leap forward," and the party and the people were called upon:

> Under the leadership of the Central Committee of the party and of Comrade Mao Tse-tung . . . to overcome the right-opportunist attitudes among some of the unstable elements . . . and to struggle for fulfillment of the Second Five-Year Plan two years ahead of time (by 1958–1959).[21]

Despite the fact that Mao Tse-tung and his adherents had been successful in suppressing and discrediting their enemies, there was no unified opinion among the leaders of the CCP concerning the country's future development, so grounds for a new intensification of disagreements remained. There was debate over the question of methods and means to transform China into a mighty world power, and the tempos for construction of a socialist society. One direction, which was approved by different people at different stages, was that of resorting to rational methods of developing the national economy, taking into consideration the experience of other socialist countries. Another, approved by Mao Tse-tung, categorically rejected international experience in the building of socialism, and pressed for voluntarist methods of forcing rates of economic construction. The development of events after the failure of the "great leap" policy saw those adherents of Mao Tse-tung's nationalist course who had come out against P'eng Teh-huai gradually begin to disagree with Mao on ways and means to achieve great-power goals.

Mao Tse-tung's authority within the party and among the people began to decrease, as did faith in his infallibility. The response was to adopt a course which resulted in further restrictions on party and state democracy, in militarization of society, in strengthening the role of the army, in arousing nationalist passions, and in an even greater exaggeration of the cult of Mao.

The widespread movement developed by the CCP against "blind faith" in foreign experience, which in fact was converted into a campaign to discredit the experience of socialist construction in the USSR, contributed somewhat to the spread of the irrational approach to solving the variety of tasks of economic and cultural construction and to developing science and technology.

Critical attitudes toward using Soviet experience intensified at Mao's initiative. Justification for the new approach was the need to struggle against "the mechanical copying" of foreign experience, against "ignoring the concrete conditions and peculiarities of the situation within the PRC."

The Chinese leaders initially undermined faith in Soviet experience by advancing the thesis of "independence" and by adopting a critical attitude toward recommendations made by Soviet specialists. †Chou En-lai, at the 1st All-China conference of capital construction workers held at the end of February and beginning of March 1956, sharply condemned Chinese workers for their noncritical response to proposals made by Soviet specialists and for ignoring experience and conditions in China in putting these proposals into practice. The proposition with respect to creative use of foreign experience, in itself correct, gradually acquired its own misshapen forms, accompanied by the ignoring of requirements of science and technology as well as accumulation of experience.

Mao's group consciously used the movement against "blind faith" to intensify nationalist feelings. The theme of elevating Chinese science, engineering, and industry to a higher world level, over the best of the foreign examples, occupied an increasingly more prominent place in Chinese propaganda.

The struggle against "blind faith" was directly reflected in the use of Soviet experience. Cases of criticism and direct disregard for recommendations made by Soviet specialists became more and more frequent, the quality of Soviet equipment became suspect, signs of underestimation of the value of Soviet assistance appeared, and attitudes developed which were to evolve into the theory of "stand on two legs," in discrediting the experience of the USSR.

The chauvinistic intoxication of the period of the "great leap," and the disappointment of the people that followed upon failure of the policy, were used adroitly by Maoists to further encourage anti-Soviet, nationalist sentiments. A new wave of attacks against Soviet experience occurred. Writing on the use of our country's experience, the journal *Hsüeh-hsi* (*Study*) made the flat statement that, given conditions in China, "there is no great need to use the old method of the Soviet Union in industrialization." The article continued that so far as the mechanization of agriculture was concerned, there really was no reason to go to mechanization immediately after the completion of cooperatives in agriculture because the country had little arable land, and a great deal of manpower.

The slogans "struggle with blind faith in the establishment of technical norms and rules in foreign experience," "struggle with conservatism," and the like, advanced in 1958 by leaders of the CCP, were essentially directed against the use of Soviet experience, against Soviet specialists, and at the refusal to comply with strict fulfillment of norms and requirements of technological blueprints.

The immediate result was a negative effect on the status of technological discipline and on the quality of work in plants. The threat of breakdowns of most important types of equipment was posed. Chinese construction organizations tolerated numerous deviations from specifications contained in Soviet designs, arbitrarily changed materials called for in the plans, and departed unwarrantedly from standards adopted for planning in the USSR.

Serious accidents, often fatal, became frequent as a result of ignoring the recommendations of Soviet specialists, and of grossly violating Soviet specifications. Examples of such cases are the accidents which occurred at the Hsinan and Hsin Fu hydroelectric stations.

Soviet specialists decisively inveighed against these "innovations," which brought with them disorganization in production after so much effort by Chinese workers and Soviet specialists. They recommended to leaders of industrial plants that no unjustified departures from any technological process established and verified in practice take place, and that prohibition of breakdowns in managerial structures of plants be instituted.

Soviet specialists did not limit themselves simply to oral recommendations. In addition, they wrote special letters to plant leaders and to corresponding ministries.

Soviet specialist A. S. Pestovskiy, who worked on installing power equipment in the PRC in 1958–1959, addressed a conference of power engineers in February 1959 on the serious departures from the requirements of engineering standards. He said:

> For example the Chinese comrades decided to simplify power installations at the cost of reducing their dependability, by refusing to follow individual electrical engineering rules. They began to permit the installation of equipment under conditions that violated safety rules. They rejected technical norms, rules, when machinery was in operation. They arbitrarily overloaded equipment, violated the rules for water levels in boilers, and the like. Yet these violations were justified as part of the struggle with dogmatism, conservatism, and mysticism with respect to technology. These departures from norms and rules placed us, the Soviet specialists working in the People's Republic of China, in difficult working conditions.

Soviet specialist N. P. Zgonnik, in his September 28, 1959 letter to the Deputy Minister of the First Machine Industry, Wang Tao-hang, pointed out that:

> As a result of familiarity with the production by the Chuchow and Fushun insulator plants it has been established that the tests of hanging insulators required by the All-Union State Standard* are not being made and they are not being impregnation tested. All insulators produced must meet the technical standards of the USSR, particularly for porosity, in order to be satisfactory for use on high-tension transmission lines. Workers in these plants cannot show me a single insulator that does not have open pores. The people at the Chuchow plant tried to make me believe that this was of no particular importance.

Individual Soviet specialists were not the only ones to appeal to Chinese authorities; appeals were directed at official levels as well. On June 7, 1958 the Minister of the First Machine Industry, Chao Er-lu, was handed a note from the Soviet Embassy to the PRC telling him of gross violations of technological discipline in a number of defense plants.

On January 5, 1959, the Chief of Administration for Work with Foreign Specialists of the State Council of the PRC, Yang Fang-shi, was handed a note concerning violations of technology and unwarranted abolition of technical services in the Fularki heavy machine-building plant, the Harbin electrical machine-building plant, and the Anshan Metallurgical Combine.

There were many such letters and statements. These appeals were in no way meant to interfere in the internal affairs of the PRC, but were predicated on concern for effective utilization of costly Soviet equipment

---

* Translator's note: the All-Union State Standard, or GOST, is a Soviet Union specification.

in Chinese plants and for the rich engineering and technical experience of the Soviet Union. This concern was raised because as a result of ignoring recommendations of Soviet specialists acting precisely in accordance with agreements and contracts, national property was being destroyed, and human casualties were mounting. Chinese authorities created the impression that Soviet people, working in the PRC at the invitation of the Chinese government, were also responsible for the adventurist enthusiasm of the "great leap."

The CPSU did not agree with the "innovations" and the "experiments" of Chinese leaders, which were part of the "great leap" and the people's communes. †However, considering this an internal affair of China, the CC CPSU limited itself to strictly confidential presentations.

Chinese leaders took other actions. In fact, they already had publicized their ideological divergences from the CPSU and other brotherly parties, and had juxtaposed their course to that of the CC CPSU in the area of Communist construction. From these positions, they centered fire on the domestic policy of our party, raising doubts as to its correctness. CCP leaders began to disseminate the "theory" of the existence of three types of socialist countries: first, those countries proceeding to communism at accelerated tempos; second, those "stuck," as it were, at the socialist stage; and third, those turning backward from socialism, to capitalist restoration. They included China in the first category, the Soviet Union in the second, and Yugoslavia in the third.

More and more discernible in the internal ideological work of the CCP was the violation of the principle of a combination of internationalism with nationalism in favor of only nationalism. This was displayed in replacement of Marxist-Leninist propaganda by the "ideas of Mao Tse-tung," regarding in silence activities of the CPSU and achievements of the other fraternal parties and countries, and in an increase in chauvinist tendencies and attitudes. The exaltation of the cult of Mao Tse-tung was raised to a new stage.

The attitude toward the publication and dissemination of Soviet literature in the PRC changed yearly. The percentage of Soviet literature republished decreased from 94 percent to 89.3 percent in 1956 as compared with 1955 in number of titles, and from 92 percent to 88.9 percent in the number of copies. At the same time the rate of increase in publication of books from capitalist countries was much higher than that of Soviet books. The number of copies of published books from capitalist countries almost doubled, while the number of copies of Soviet books increased only 42.7 percent.

While still interested in developing economic cooperation with the

Soviet Union, Chinese leaders even then were attempting to impede spiritual intercourse between the people of the two countries, seeing in it danger for antisocialist views and aims—cultivated in China. In 1958, for example, Chinese organizations, alleging a need to "economize," greatly reduced the plan for cultural cooperation. †In mid-April 1958 the Chairman of the Commission for Cultural Relations with Foreign Countries, Ch'en Chun-ching, during a visit to Moscow, made an official request that Chinese organizations be permitted to withdraw from many of the projects included in the plan (under the pretext of "the heavy work load" and "financial difficulties"). The object was to discontinue the exchange of creative workers. Trips by representatives of Soviet radio and television to the PRC to gather materials preparatory to a series of broadcasts celebrating the tenth anniversary of the PRC, and of Chinese radio workers to the USSR to exchange experience and familiarize themselves with the practical work of Soviet radio and television, were eliminated.

3. The special foreign policy course of the leadership of the CCP, and its influence on Sino-Soviet relations

Encountering internal difficulties, the nationalists in the CCP transferred the center of gravity of their adventurist course to the international arena. This approach took the line of developing a slanderous campaign against socialist countries and Communist parties, becoming engaged in military provocations so as to aggravate the international situation, and expounding ultrarevolutionary slogans designed to create the impression that Chinese leaders were the staunchest and most consistent revolutionaries.

All of this was directed toward definite goals. There was, on the one hand, diversion of party and people from domestic difficulties, suppression of internal discontent, creation of a situation marked by nationalist psychosis and war hysteria, and, on the other, the accomplishment of hegemonistic designs.

Beginning in 1958, the foreign policy of the PRC increasingly deviates from policies of other socialist countries, manifesting tendencies contrary to efforts of the USSR, and those of the entire socialist camp, to liquidate the "cold war" and other expressions of international tensions.

This course did not immediately prevail. It followed a bitter struggle by the Maoists with those forces among the leadership of the CCP who supported socialist principles in the foreign policy of the PRC or who, at the very least, had taken realistic positions. A sharp struggle continued in China between contending forces over the question of socialist development of the country and its foreign policy orientation. This circumstance explains the fact that at this time the PRC continued to line up (with other socialist countries) on international problems. For example, on April 13, 1958, the government of the PRC announced that it fully supported the decision of the Soviet government, on March 31, 1958, first to cease testing any types of nuclear weapons, and the proposals on this issue by the Soviet government to governments of the USA and Great Britain.

The statement pointed out that:

> ... this action on the part of the Soviet government is a persuasive indication that the Soviet government consistently stands for positions that will protect peace. It fully manifests the deep concern of the Soviet people for the tranquility and happiness of the peoples of all countries all over the world, as well as having served to strengthen to a tremendous degree the confidence of all peace-loving states and peoples in the struggle for peace. There is no question that this is a tremendous contribution to the preservation of peace throughout the world and in ensuring the happiness of mankind. The Chinese people warmly greet this great peaceful action by the Soviet Union.[22]

Overall, however, negative tendencies were increasingly apparent in the foreign policy of the PRC. They manifested themselves in a transition from flexible tactics to attempts at a direct offensive and frontal attacks against capitalism, and to an implacable course even in those cases which involved questions which either did not deal with principles, or were of a secondary nature. Chinese leaders manifested tendencies to instigate development of international events, to accelerate the world revolutionary process by artificially stirring up the struggle against imperialism. They overestimated the capability of the PRC to resolve international problems, and lost their sense of sobriety and reality in evaluating the international situation and balance of power in the world arena. Great-power tendencies, the attempt to assign themselves a special role in international affairs, began to dominate the foreign policy of the PRC.

It is characteristic that the leaders of the CCP embarked on the new "rigid course" at precisely the same time that the Soviet Union had undertaken wide-ranging measures to realize the Leninist course of peaceful coexistence of two social systems.

Following their new course, the Maoists in 1958 engaged in a number of actions in the Formosa Strait region leading to serious complication of the international situation. At the end of August 1958 they shelled the offshore islands of the Kinmen (Quemoy) and Matsu groups, declaring that this was in the context of "punitive measures in response to provocations on the part of the Chiang Kai-shek gang." But the latter had not ceased their provocations since they had been banished to Taiwan in 1949. It is known also that Chiang Kai-shek was unable to undertake serious military operations against mainland China, lacking the sanction and support of the United States. Actions undertaken on the initiative of the Mao group in effect dovetailed with the plans of militant circles in the United States attempting to block the course of the Soviet Union aimed at relaxing international tensions. The Mao group counted on these completely uncalled-for actions to strain Soviet-American relations and, by using the machinery of the treaty between the USSR and the PRC, to expand the conflict into an armed clash in the Far East.

The USA responded to the shelling of the offshore islands by concentrating heavy military forces in the Taiwan area, declaring flatly that if the PRC attacked Taiwan it would assist its ally Chiang Kai-shek in every way possible. Thus a situation involving a direct threat of war was created in the Far East in September-October 1958. All these actions were undertaken by the PRC without consultation with the Soviet Union despite direct obligations imposed by the Sino-Soviet treaty. †Chinese leaders had not informed the head of the Soviet government, who was in Peking at the beginning of August 1958, of their plans at the very moment when the decision to shell Quemoy and Matsu had already been made, and when active preparations already had been carried out. Moreover, the Peking leaders began direct double-dealing. On the eve of events occurring in the Taiwan Straits, they signed a communiqué on the Soviet-Chinese meeting in which it was stated that the parties saw eye to eye "on questions of the joint struggle for a peaceful solution of international problems and the preservation of peace throughout the world."[23]

Despite the openly unfriendly position of the Chinese leaders, the Soviet Union, finding the safety of the PRC threatened by the United States as a result of China's adventurist policy, decisively stepped in on China's side to frustrate attempts of aggressive imperialist circles to take advantage of actions of the Chinese leaders. The appeal made by the head of the Soviet government on September 7, 1958 to the President of the United States to be prudent and to take no steps leading to fatal consequences played a decisive role in averting the dangerous development of events.[24]

At present, Chinese leaders blasphemously assert that support given by the Soviet Union to the PRC during the Taiwan Strait events in the fall of 1958 "was of no great importance." Assertions like these not only are at direct variance with the facts, they once again expose the hypocrisy of the Chinese leaders. Mao Tse-tung, in a letter addressed to the Soviet side and dated October 15, 1958, wrote:

> . . . you have, with complete clarity and definiteness, made the positive statement to us that in the event of an attack upon China the Soviet Union will resolutely fulfill its revolutionary duty with respect to China. We are deeply touched by your unlimited devotion to the principles of Marxism-Leninism and of internationalism. I wish to express to you, in the name of all the comrades of the Communist Party of China, our sincere appreciation.

Persuaded of the failure of their adventure, the Chinese leaders retreated. As a result of this crude venture, the international stature of China deteriorated, the more so because Chinese propaganda gave very confused explanations of events. They initially said that liberation of Taiwan was not involved; what they had in mind simply was the liberation of the offshore islands. Then came the statement that the PRC could always wait for a better time to proceed with the liberation of Taiwan and the offshore islands. Intensive shelling and blockade of the offshore islands was changed to shelling every second day on even dates, and, so far as the United States was concerned, the policy was limited to one of issuing "serious warnings." Bourgeois and particularly American propaganda used all of this to discredit the foreign policy of the socialist countries. Regarding Asian nations, the events in the Taiwan Strait merely served to intensify their alarm as to consequences of the "new course" in foreign policy of the PRC.

As help from the Soviet Union restored and developed the Chinese economy and strengthened the position of the PRC in the international arena, leaders of the CCP began to intensify their anti-Soviet activities, to belittle the role and importance of friendship with the USSR, and to look for ways to exacerbate Sino-Soviet relations.

Even at that time there were clear-cut differences in the approaches taken by the CCP and the CPSU to issues that arose between the two countries.

The Soviet Union, in relations with the PRC, has always tried to avoid the slightest grounds for estrangement and distrust, consistently striving for resolution of even the slightest misunderstanding in a spirit of candor and brotherly mutual understanding. Conversely, the Chinese leaders have constantly sought the slightest pretext to exacerbate Sino-Soviet relations; they have juggled and distorted the facts, and have not hesitated to initiate direct provocations.

Disregarding considerations of prestige, Soviet leaders repeatedly took the initiative in establishing direct contacts at the highest level by visiting the PRC during the period when CCP nationalists began to complicate, artificially, issues calculated to destroy friendship between China and the Soviet Union.

It was Soviet initiative which led to the meeting in Peking at the end of July and beginning of August 1958 between leaders of the USSR and the PRC. During the meeting the Soviet Union spelled out its position, and all details including special questions were explained in depth to PRC leaders.

The communiqué on the Soviet-Chinese meeting announced the "complete unity of views on current and important problems of contemporary international positions, questions of future strengthening of relations of friendship, alliance, and mutual assistance between the Union of Soviet Socialist Republics and the People's Republic of China."

But later on Chinese leaders again dragged out specific questions in order to exacerbate Sino-Soviet relations. Subsequent events have made it eminently clear that the "creation" of these issues from the outset was a premeditated action by the Maoists, who looked for ways to attack the Soviet Union, and thus to worsen Sino-Soviet relations.

Leaders of the CCP used the border dispute between the PRC and India in the fall of 1959 to exacerbate Sino-Soviet relations. Prior to 1959 the PRC had established friendly relations with India. Governments of both countries had initiated the famous five principles of peaceful coexistence and had called the Bandung Conference of the countries of Asia and Africa. But in the spring of 1959 relations between the PRC and India grew complicated, a factor of interest to reactionary circles in the United States and India, and to nationalists among the leaders of the CCP. All of these, at first glance different political forces, were scheming the achievement of a serious collision in Asia because of the "Indochinese conflict," one in which the USSR and the United States would become involved, and one that would exacerbate Sino-Soviet relations.

Goals of imperialist forces in the United States and Great Britain were to slander the foreign policy course of the socialist countries, and to undermine the faith the Third World placed in that policy. CCP leaders, following narrow nationalist interests, were unconcerned with the harmful consequences their adventurist actions in the international arena would have on the world revolutionary movement.

The border dispute between the PRC and India intensified in the fall of 1959. Border skirmishes occurred at the end of August, and again in October, with loss of Indian lives. The PRC published a statement to the effect that "India has made incursions into Chinese territory with a total area of some 130,000 square kilometers." Although the Chinese-Indian border, which is over 2,000 kilometers long, has never been defined, the statement by Chinese leaders made it clear that they were claiming vast stretches of territory.

The border dispute between the PRC and India resulted in serious damage to peace and socialism. It placed the Indian progressive forces, and particularly the Indian Communist Party, in a precarious position. †Repeated appeals by leaders of the Indian Communist Party to the CC CCP failed to change the position of Chinese leaders.

Peking leaders attempted to imply that the affair was one of the causes of present Soviet-Chinese differences, because the Soviet Union had failed to support the PRC's position in the Chinese-Indian border conflict. This assertion is slander. In point of fact, the Soviet Union, from the very beginning, took the only possible and correct position with respect to the Chinese-Indian dispute, and what must be particularly emphasized is that the Chinese side, despite obligations imposed by the treaty between the USSR and the PRC, failed to enter into timely consultations with the Soviet government. The USSR's position was that it should contribute to the peaceful settlement of the conflict, and block the grounds of reactionary forces for using the conflict to undermine Chinese-Indian relations, thus to compromise a socialist country by charging it with aggression. †The Soviet side resorted to diplomatic and other channels in order to give timely notification of its position to the government of the PRC, and to warn of the possible negative consequences of this incident.

Then, on September 10, 1959, TASS published a statement to the effect that the Soviet Union was preoccupied with the Chinese-Indian border conflict and expressed the hope that it would be settled as quickly as possible:

> Soviet ruling circles have expressed confidence that the government of the People's Republic of China and the government of the Republic of India will not permit this incident to allow the forces that want to aggravate, not relax, the international situation to further their aims, for these are the forces that are attempting to prevent the current relaxation of tensions in relations between states. These Soviet circles are expressing confidence in the fact that both governments will settle the misunderstanding that has arisen by taking into consideration their mutual interests in the spirit of traditional friendship between the peoples of China and India. This also will further strengthen the forces speaking for peace and international cooperation.[25]

The TASS statement pointed out to the PRC government paths to the solution of the dispute, but leaders of the CCP not only failed to evaluate properly the position of the USSR, but tried to distort it as well. On September 13, 1959 the Chinese leaders replied with a rebuff, stating that:

> ... the TASS declaration revealed to all the world the divergence of views of China and the Soviet Union with respect to the incident on the Chinese-Indian border, about which the Indian bourgeoisie, and American and English imperialism, literally rejoice and are exultant.

After the TASS statement of September 10, 1959 the imperialist camp not only did not rejoice, as Chinese leaders had hoped, but it openly expressed disappointment. Presumably, then, it would have been satisfied had the Soviet Union been drawn into this conflict, for direct action on the part of the Soviet Union to provide unilateral and direct support to the PRC in the Chinese-Indian dispute would have undoubtedly implicated the United States of America, Great Britain, and other imperialist powers. All signs pointed to the plans of the USA ruling clique to intervene actively in the conflict which arose between China and India. The position of the Soviet Union prevented a dangerous hotbed of war, and interference on the part of imperialist forces thus became impossible. Despite all these obvious circumstances, the Chinese leaders continued to distort the position of the Soviet Union in the Chinese-Indian border conflict.

The Soviet Union, because it believed the 10th anniversary of the establishment of the PRC to be of primary political significance, sent a delegation representing the highest levels of party and government to China.

†During its stay in Peking the Soviet delegation initiated a frank exchange of views with Chinese leaders, the purpose of which was to improve Sino-Soviet relations. Mao Tse-tung, however, ignored this initiative.

It should be noted that Chinese leaders, stealthily undermining Soviet-Chinese friendship, had made statements which in no way expressed their views, for purpose of camouflage. One of the main strategic goals of some CCP leaders was, and still is, to provoke a conflict between the USA and the USSR, and, in the name of their great-power goals, to exhaust these states in internecine warfare. Their purpose in 1958–1959 was "to sit on the mountain and watch the two tigers struggle." The Maoists, therefore, watched the normalization of Soviet-American relations with irritation.

4. *Summary of Sino-Soviet cooperation, 1949–1959*

The year 1959 was a definite watershed, after which Sino-Soviet economic, scientific-technical, and cultural cooperation, through no fault of the Soviet Union, quickly ceased; thus some summary data on this cooperation are of interest.

In all, over 250 large industrial plants, shops, and objects, all with modern equipment, were built in the PRC with the assistance of the Soviet Union. Included were such plants as the Anshan and Yunnan metallurgical combines, the Changchun automobile plant, the complex of plants in Loyuan (tractor, bearing, and mining equipment), the electrical machine-building, turbine, and boiler plants in Harbin, the synthetic rubber plant and oil refinery in Lanchow, the nitrogen fertilizer plants in Kirin and T'aiyuan, the shale processing plants in Fushun, the heavy machine-building plant in Fularki, a whole string of powerful electric power stations, and other special projects.

Whole branches of industry were created in the PRC with the help of the Soviet Union; aviation, automobile and tractor building, radio and electronics, various branches of chemical production. Large capacity plants in metallurgy, electric power, and other branches of industry were opened. Soviet scientific and technical help to the PRC was highly important in nuclear physics. The first experimental atomic reactor and cyclotron were built in China with the cooperation of the USSR.[26]

The products produced in plants built with technical assistance from the Soviet Union comprise the following in total volume of production in the PRC in 1960: pig iron, 30 percent; steel almost 40 percent; rolled products over 50 percent; trucks, 80 percent; tractors over 90 percent; synthetic ammonia, 30 percent; production of electric power, 25 percent; production of steam and water turbines, 55 percent; generators almost 20 percent; aluminum, 25 percent; and heavy machine-building over 10 percent.

Over 8,500 highly qualified Soviet specialists (not counting military) were sent to the PRC between 1950 and 1960. Some 1,500 Soviet specialists went to China during that same period to assist in science, higher education, public health, and culture.

Soviet teaching specialists sent to the PRC played an exceptional part in training skilled Chinese workers. Between 1948 and 1960, 615 highly qualified Soviet teachers went to the PRC. They played a decisive role in the creation of a modern system of higher and middle special education and they trained a large group of Chinese specialists for national economy and teaching. In all, 1,269 Soviet specialists in higher schools and people's education were sent to China between 1949 and 1960. They worked with authorities in the Ministry of Education as well as in institutions of higher learning.

The Soviet Union, as part of its scientific and technical cooperation program, accepted some 2,000 Chinese specialists and about 1,000 Chinese scientists to acquaint them with scientific and technical achievements and production experience of the Soviet Union. The Soviet Union gave the PRC great numbers of scientific, technical, and other documents vitally needed to develop China's national economy. Of the total number of technical documents given by the Soviet Union to all socialist countries, some 50 percent went to the PRC. China designed 159 objects, and mastered production of over 300 new important types of products with Soviet documents provided by the Soviet Union up to July 1, 1957.

The PRC, in turn, as of January 1, 1961, had given the Soviet Union some 1,500 sets of scientific and technical documents of different kinds.

NUMBER OF SOVIET CIVILIAN SPECIALISTS
WHO WORKED IN THE PRC 1949–1960

Years	Economic Assistance	Science, Culture and Public Health	Scientific and Scientific-Technical Cooperation	Total Number of Specialists
April 1949	174	60	—	234
January 1950	183	65	—	248
January 1951	168	71	—	239
January 1952	410	89	—	499
January 1953	609	144	—	753
January 1954	728	156	—	884
January 1955	1245	278	—	1523
January 1956	1738	377	—	2115
January 1957	2236	403	38*	2677
January 1958	1170	230	152*	1552
January 1959	1116	142	230*	1488

* Number of Soviet specialists who went to China for short periods of time under the scientific and technical cooperation program during the year.

Beginning in 1949, 66 higher institutions of learning in China and 85 higher institutions of learning in the Soviet Union systematically exchanged scientific data and papers. Soviet and Chinese higher institutes of learning worked together on 124 scientific research subjects.

The work of Soviet specialists in the PRC provides a glorious page in the history of fraternal relations of the Soviet people and the CPSU with the people of China. Their selfless assistance earned them great authority and love among Chinese workers, engineers, and technicians. "The specialists from the Soviet Union, and from the countries of people's democracy, working in our country," said the Premier of the State Council of the PRC, Chou En-lai, in his report to the 8th Congress of the CCP, "have made an outstanding contribution to our socialist construction."[27]

The government of the Soviet Union also organized the training of Chinese scientific and technical cadres and of qualified workers in plants, in higher institutions of learning, and in planning and scientific organizations in the USSR. Over 8,000 Chinese citizens were given production and technical training in the Soviet Union between 1951 and 1962. Over 11,000 Chinese students of all levels studied in schools in the Soviet Union over the same period. Over 900 workers in different institutions of the Chinese Academy of Sciences were given scientific training and the opportunity to study research methods in the Academy of Sciences of the USSR. And over 1,500 Chinese engineers, technicians, and scientists came to the Soviet Union to acquaint themselves with scientific and technical achievements and to gain production experience, all as part of the scientific and technical cooperation program.[28]

Virtually all technical personnel, from director and chief engineer to shop and section chiefs, as well as other workers participating directly in plant construction, were trained by the Soviet Union for each industrial object. This training encompassed construction operations, equipment installation, preparation of individual production sections of the enterprise, and initiation of operations.[29]

The USSR gave China 24,000 sets of virtually cost-free scientific and technical documents over a period of slightly more than ten years. Foreign experts are of the opinion that if the PRC had had to go out into the world market to acquire these documents the cost would have been many billions of dollars. Included among these documents were plans for 1,400 large plants. According to Chinese data, between 1952 and 1957, of the 51,000 machine tools built in the PRC, 43,500, or 85 percent, were produced using drawings obtained from the USSR. Today there is not a single branch of industry in the PRC that is not producing goods from drawings, specifications, and technological documents developed and checked in the Soviet Union and given to China.[30]

The quantity of scientific and technical literature the Soviet Union placed at the disposal of China was highly important to reconstruction and development of the national economy of the PRC, and to subsequent planned socialist construction. Even during the years of the restoration period, reference libraries of the Academy of Sciences of the

USSR in Moscow and Leningrad regularly sent to Peking 43 periodicals and 142 serial and multivolume publications, as well as monographs on all branches of science. The PRC received 32,000 copies of books and journals published by the Academy of Sciences of the USSR, the republic academies of sciences, and other scientific institutions in the Soviet Union in 1951 alone.

Some 5,000 Soviet book titles were freely turned over to the PRC in 1952. Many of these books were included in the plans of Chinese publishing houses for translation and publication in Chinese. In this same year, 756 Soviet books with a press run of 8.6 million copies were published in Chinese. Bear in mind that 78 percent of all books republished in the PRC in 1952 were Soviet books, and that between October 1, 1949 and the end of 1952 the PRC published 3,414 Soviet book titles. In addition, the Soviet Union sent some 3 million copies of Soviet books in Chinese to the PRC in 1951 and 1952. The publication of Soviet literature in the PRC reached even greater proportions in subsequent years. In the period 1949 through 1955, 3,000 Soviet scientific and technical books, with a total press run of over 20 million copies, were published in the PRC.[31]

Associations between Soviet and Chinese libraries of their respective academies of sciences underwent further development. The reference libraries of the Academy of Sciences of the USSR, for example, sent the Chinese Academy of Sciences some 70,000 volumes of different varieties of scientific literature in 1956 alone.[32]

The Soviet government, in the interests of economic construction and the strengthening of the PRC's defensive capacities, extended to its government several long-term credits on favorable terms. In all, from 1950 to 1961, the Soviet Union extended to the PRC on favorable terms 11 long-term credits totalling some 2 billion foreign exchange rubles.

From the very first days of the proclamation of the PRC, the Soviet Union, in addition to economic and scientific and technical aid, cooperated to create China's own military industry, and handed over to the PRC technological documentation on production of modern types of military equipment. At the same time the Soviet Union relinquished large quantities of military equipment and material for direct outfitting of the PLA of China.

Trade with the USSR was of vital importance to the PRC. The role of this capacious and stable market for Chinese goods in the Soviet Union is difficult to overestimate, particularly in light of the economic blockade and embargo on trade with the PRC imposed by the United States and many other capitalist countries.

The Soviet Union became the main buyer of Chinese goods, from the first years of the People's Republic. In 1959 the USSR took 28.7 percent of the exports from the PRC, and the mean during the years of the First Five-Year Plan was 59.4 percent. The Soviet Union became practically the sole source of modern production equipment for the PRC.

One must bear in mind, too, that the PRC, as a developing country, found it very difficult to break into world markets, considering the assortment and quality of its goods, and, as well, was unable to meet the competition of even some of the developing countries, let alone that of economically sophisticated capitalist nations. Only close economic ties with the USSR and socialist countries enabled China to export in significant quantities agricultural* and industrial raw materials, as well as other goods, at advantageous prices. Moreover, the Soviet Union often bought or actively helped the PRC market many Chinese products which had no value in world markets.

Cultural cooperation with the Soviet Union was of great practical importance for socialist construction in China. Acquaintance with the cultural life of the Soviet people, who had traveled the long road of the struggle for socialism, with their science, literature, and art, intensified the effect of the Marxist-Leninist outlook on Chinese workers, and on the mastery of socialist ideas by the builders of the new China. Further, it gave vital examples which helped to discover new avenues to progress and which could be used to develop the spiritual life of the multimillioned mass of that extremely backward country, only yesterday semifeudal and semicolonial.

The best works of Soviet literature, those devoted to the heroic deeds of our people during the years of the revolution, the Civil War, and the Great Patriotic War, inspired millions of Chinese workers in the revolutionary and national liberation struggle. In 1950 the writer Yao Yuanfang, in an article entitled "Soviet Literature during the War Became Our Invisible Military Force," stressed:

> We were inspired and mobilized by the feeling of Soviet writers' incomparable anger against the enemy, and their flaming patriotism, both of which permeated every line and every word of their works. We also studied and imitated the great heroes, whose examples were recreated in artistic creative works. . . . The works of Soviet writers, thanks to their vitality and tremendous influence, were converted into an invisible military force in the triumphant war of our People's Liberation Army against the robber bands of Chiang Kai-shek.[33]

* Unprocessed and processed agricultural raw materials and products of subsidiary peasant enterprises made up 90.7 percent of the total exports of the PRC in 1950, and 71.6 percent in 1957.

Many works by Soviet writers, including *The Volokolamsk Highway,* by A. Bek, *Days and Nights,* by K. Simonov, *Front,* by A. Korneychuk, and others, were included on the list of "required reading" for Chinese party and army regulars.[34]

Soviet literature was a fruitful influence on the spiritual life of Chinese society after the formation of the PRC as well. Fiction written by Soviet writers depicting the processes of revolutionary transformations in our country with such tremendous generalizing force became unique textbooks for Chinese builders of socialism who performed similar tasks in their country. The famous literary critic, Tsao Ching-hua, for example, in an article entitled, "Soviet Literature and Its Chinese Readers," in 1954 wrote that M. Sholokhov's *Virgin Soil Upturned* had become a standard text for those participating in completion of agrarian reform in China, for in it they sought answers to many questions. Tsao Ching-hua cited the statement made by a participant in agrarian reform to the effect that "Wherever we were during this intensive struggle, we tried to use every free minute to study this book in detail."[35]

Until the time when nationalists in the CCP began openly to follow their course of severing cultural ties between the PRC and the USSR, the publication of works of classical Russian and Soviet fiction had increased year by year in the PRC. The total press run of such works had exceeded 42 million copies in only six years after the founding of the PRC.[36]

Publication of translated literature occurred on a grand scale in the Soviet Union and in the PRC. The Soviet Union published 671 pieces of Chinese fiction with a total press run of 32,733,000 copies between 1949 and 1958. Ninety books by Chinese authors, with a total press run of 4 million copies, were published in 1958 alone. China translated and published over 13,000 books by Soviet authors in eight years. The circulation was some 230 million copies.

The publication of Chinese literature assumed grand proportions in the Soviet Union. Some 43 million copies of 976 books by Chinese authors, which had been translated into Russian and into 50 other languages of the people of the USSR, were printed between 1946 and 1960. The works of Lu Hsün, Mao Tun, Lao She, Chao Su-li, and other writers were published for mass circulation, as were anthologies of Chinese poetry and the best examples of classical literature.

The Soviet Union, proceeding from the principles of socialist internationalism, sent some 2,000 experienced specialists in the fields of culture and education to work for long periods of time in the PRC in over a little more than ten years (1949–1960). This was requested by the government of the PRC and their number was 20 percent of all Soviet specialists sent to China.

Soviet specialists in the PRC trained some 17,000 teachers, mainly in branches of new techniques, between 1949 and 1960. If one adds to this those trained for the PRC in the Soviet Union (some 1,700), the total number becomes some 19,000, or approximately one-fourth of all teachers in Chinese higher institutions of learning, who, in 1959, numbered 85,000.[37] Over 11,000 students and graduate students from the PRC studied in institutions of higher learning in the Soviet Union between 1951 and 1962.[38] The Soviet government absorbed 50 percent of the cost of their education.

Close ties existed between the USSR and the PRC in the field of cinematographic art. China showed some 750 Soviet films, viewed by approximately 1.9 billion people between 1949 and 1959. The Soviet Union screened over 100 Chinese films in the same period. Over a ten-year period 112 Soviet performing groups visited the PRC and 134 Chinese artistic groups visited the USSR.

Famous Soviet artistic groups visited the PRC between 1949 and 1959. These included the State National Dance Ensemble of the USSR under the directorship of I. Moiseyev, the K. S. Stanislavskiy and V. I. Nemirovich-Danchenko Moscow State Musical Theatre, the "Berezka" State Choreographic Ensemble, the State Dance Ensemble of the Ukrainian SSR, a touring group from the Soviet circus, the Kurmangaza Kazakh State Folk Orchestra, a ballet troupe from the Novosibirsk Theatre of Opera and Ballet, the State Symphony Orchestra of the USSR, the Azerbaijan SSR Song and Dance Ensemble, a ballet troupe from the State Academic Bol'shoy Theatre of the USSR, and many other groups.

Regardless of the field in which our country developed cooperation with the PRC, its intent remained always the same: that of doing everything possible to strengthen both socialism in China and Sino-Soviet friendship.

NOTES

1. Kapitsa, pp. 158–160.
2. *Izvestiya,* January 19, 1958.
3. *Vedomosti Verkhovnogo Soveta USSR (Record of the Supreme Soviet of the USSR,* hereinafter referred to as *The Supreme Soviet)*, No. 17, 1958, p. 688.
4. Ibid., p. 692.
5. *Izvestiya,* August 12, 1958.
6. *Pravda,* January 29, 1959.
7. Ibid.
8. *Pravda,* February 8, 1959.
9. *Pravda,* February 27, 1959.
10. *Pravda,* April 19, 1959.
11. *Jen Min Jihpao,* October 2, 1959.
12. *Jen Min Jihpao,* April 14, 1959.
13. *Jen Min Jihpao,* April 7, 1958.
14. *Jen Min Jihpao,* April 12, 1958.
15. M. A. Suslov, *O'borbe KPSS, za splochennost' mezhdunarodnogo kommunisticheskogo dvizheniya (The Struggle of the Communist Party of the Soviet Union for the Solidarity of the International Communist Movement,* hereinafter referred to as *The Struggle of the CPSU)* (Moscow, 1964), p. 92–94.
16. *Program Documents,* p. 12.
17. Ibid., p. 13.
18. *Druzhba,* No. 39, 1958, p. 30.
19. *Druzhba,* No. 29, 1958, p. 3.
20. *Druzhba,* No. 28, 1958, p. 1.
21. *Jen Min Jihpao,* August 27, 1959.
22. *Izvestiya,* April 15, 1958.
23. *Izvestiya,* August 5, 1958.
24. *Izvestiya,* September 9, 1958.
25. *Pravda,* September 10, 1959.
26. *The Leninist Policy,* p. 202.
27. Ibid., p. 203–204.
28. Ibid., p. 204.
29. Chiang Yan-ching, "Technical Assistance from the Soviet Union Is the Pledge of Our Success," *Vneshnyaya torgovlya (Foreign Trade)*, No. 10, 1959, p. 22.
30. *The Leninist Policy,* p. 204.
31. *Za prochnyy mir, za narodnuyu demokratiyu! (For a Durable Peace, for a People's Democracy!)*, November 25, 1955.
32. *Druzhba,* November 9, 1956.
33. *Wen Yi Pao* (Peking), 1950.

34. *Hsinhua Yue-kan* (Peking), 1950.

35. *Literaturnaya gazeta,* December 9, 1954.

36. N. T. Fedorenko, *Kitayskaya literatura* (*Chinese Literature*), p. 453.

37. *Razvitiye obrazovaniya za 10 let posle provozglasheniya KNR* (*The Development of Education in the 10 Years after the Proclamation of the People's Republic of China,* hereinafter referred to as *The Development of Education*) (Peking, 1959), p. 5.

38. *Pravda,* April 3, 1964.

CHAPTER SIX

The Leadership of the CCP Turns from the Policy of Sino-Soviet Friendship to the Development of an Open Struggle against the CPSU and the Soviet Union

The year 1960 was a watershed in the development of Sino-Soviet relations. It marked the beginning of a new period in the course of which nationalist forces in the PRC came to dominate the leadership of the CCP. The implementation of this course led to a basic reorientation of foreign policy of the PRC, to withdrawal of the CCP from a position of proletarian internationalism, to Peking leaders' severing ties of friendship and cooperation with the Soviet Union and with other socialist countries, and to unfolding an open policy of struggle with them.

The break with Leninist principles of a socialist state's foreign policy made by leaders of the CCP was part and parcel of the internal processes involved in the development of the PRC. It was the direct consequence of the intensification of antisocialist tendencies in China, the implantation within the Communist party of anti-Marxist, anti-Leninist views, the deviation of Peking leaders from the path of socialist construction.

In turn, the internal situation in China during that period was determined by aggravation of the class struggle occasioned by the fact that huge failures in economic construction engendered by the fatal, voluntarist course of the "great leap forward" and the establishment of people's communes weakened the position of socialism in the country, and opened up to the antisocialist forces the opportunity for counterattack.

1. The internal situation in the PRC at the beginning of the 1960s

The situation which evolved in the PRC at the beginning of the 1960s was characterized by a sharp deterioration in the economic situation. The failure of attempts of CCP leaders to overcome China's economic

168

backwardness as swiftly as possible by use of voluntarist methods, and, simultaneously, to create internal prerequisites for realization of their nationalist, avant-garde aspirations, was all too evident.

The country's economy was completely disorganized. The level of industrial and agricultural production had fallen sharply. By 1962 gross industrial production had almost halved as compared with 1959. Steel production had fallen 46 percent, electric power generation 13 percent, pig iron 48 percent, iron ore by a factor of 3, coke by a factor of 3.5, cement by 40 percent, power equipment by a factor of 4, machine tools by a factor of 3.2, and cotton cloth by a factor of 2. Edible vegetable oil production fell by 30 percent, and that of sugar by 12 percent. The grain harvest fell one-third.

Leaders of the CCP were forced to take extraordinary measures to prevent any further drop in production. This led the 9th Plenary Session of the CC CCP, held in January 1961, to reduce the scale of capital construction and to "regulate the rates of development." This meant the mass closing of plants built primarily in the years of the "great leap forward," as well as complete liquidation of the backyard blast furnaces and, beginning in mid-1961, the cessation of capital construction in industry and transportation, including those areas in which construction was nearing completion. Industry, in addition to requirements imposed on it for production of consumer goods, now was faced with the task of giving preferential treatment to agriculture, even though this meant ceasing production of primary products by plants which previously had produced for other sectors of the economy.

Reality forced CCP leaders to abandon the idea of "communization ahead of schedule." The communes that had been set up in cities were discontinued, and those in agricultural areas were reorganized into conventional agricultural production cooperatives called brigades. Free meals, the introduction of which had been unwarranted, were canceled, personal plots were returned to the peasants, and there was a definite restoration of the principle of material incentive.

Such principles as "achieve a high level in production, keep to a low level in life," "firmly put into practice a rational system of low wages," were taken as the basis for economic development. Chinese propaganda, in an effort to justify the freeze in the standard of living of the population, advanced the slogan, "Do Not Fear Suffering, Do Not Fear Death." Villages and plants that had coped with difficulties by relying solely on their own resources, without state aid, were publicized as models to be imitated. Communes, plants, whole cities and provinces were patterned for a natural economy.

Expenditures on social and cultural measures were cut drastically. Beginning in 1959, housing and communal construction, and construction of schools and higher institutions of learning, ceased. The number of students enrolled in higher institutions of learning dropped from 695,000 in 1960 to 250,000 in 1964. The number of students enrolled in the middle schools dropped by 2.7 million, and by 8-10 million in the elementary schools.

Unprecedented difficulties in supplying the populace with food and industrial goods arose as a consequence of the failure of the "great leap forward." Many goods were rationed, and this was followed by a sharp reduction in grain, fats, and sugar norms. In 1962 and subsequent years, the monthly adult ration was 150-200 grams of meat and 100-150 grams of vegetable oil. The annual ration of cotton cloth was 2 to 3 meters per man.

The extraordinary measures introduced by CCP leaders to overcome consequences of the "great leap forward" did have some results. The economy was stabilized somewhat by the end of 1962. Nevertheless, curtailment of heavy industry, an increase in military expenditures, and the course designed to develop a natural economy were hardly the means for providing any substantial forward progress.

Needless to say, many difficulties of economic development in the PRC resulted from objective causes. One need only recall that the PRC with its vast population accounted for only 4 percent of the world's industrial production. The people's power inherited from prerevolutionary China primitive agriculture, backward industry, and poverty and devastation in the country. The difficulties normally unavoidable under such conditions were compounded by mistakes of Mao Tse-tung and his followers, by rejection of brotherly cooperation with the countries of socialism, and by ignoring laws of economic development.

What should be particularly pointed out is that Chinese leaders, while correcting their most grievous failures and mistakes, failed to tell their own people the truth. They continued to assert that the course of the "Three Red Banners" was the only correct, "triumphant" course.

One thing emerging from the "cultural revolution" was that during those years the adventurist policy of the Maoists concerning questions of internal development of the PRC, where the role assigned the Chinese people was that of a "piece of blank paper," met with censure within party ranks, including leaders of the CCP. But the position of nationalist elements was dominant, so the struggle of opinions among authorities in the CCP took the form of a compromise. There was the assertion, on one hand, that the "Three Red Banners" course was not in error, and, on the other, the line that previous policy would be "regulated," that is, reviewed.

It was no accident that Mao Tse-tung, who during the "great leap" years brought the country to severe crisis and the people to starvation, left it to Liu Shao-ch'i, Teng Hsiao-p'ing, and other members of the CC CCP to save the situation while he "concentrated on theoretical work." This was in 1958, when Mao Tse-tung relinquished his chairmanship of the PRC. After the country recovered from the "experiments," Mao hastened to liquidate witnesses of his failures during the "cultural revolution."

Failures of domestic policy, and chronic economic difficulties, intensifying the violations of law and of domestic bases of social life, led to increasing discontent in all strata of Chinese society, including party and state apparati.

As early as August 1959, at the 8th Plenary Session of the CC CCP, a group of Central Committee members protested against the "Great Leap Forward" policy, classifying it as a petty bourgeois fantasy, costly to the Chinese people. Among those disagreeing with the line of the Maoists were P'eng Teh-huai, a member of the Politburo of the CC CCP, Chang Wen-tien (Lo Fu), a Candidate Member of the Politburo, and many of the leaders of the provincial committees of the party, ministries, and departments.

The discontent with nationalist policy in the CCP was even more evident at the beginning of the 1960s. Doubts as to the correctness of the "special course" they were following seized a great many government and party activists and the intelligentsia. For example, Wang Hsiao-ch'uan, director of the propaganda section of the Kweichow Provincial Committee of the CCP, openly said the "black days" that China was experiencing were the result "of certain mistaken leadership ideas," that the "great leap" had failed, that the general line was in error, and that the people's communes were a "bitter lesson." Chou Yang, then deputy director of the propaganda department of the CC CCP, in meetings with writers, called the "great leap" policy rash. Teng T'o, then Secretary of the Peking City Committee of the CCP, wrote in the newspaper *Paiching Wan Pao* on November 26, 1961 of the "braggarts who make a lot of noise, but little sense." It was his opinion that the braggarts think that "they can do anything they choose. What they do in fact is break their heads on the facts and finally collapse." The Chinese reader correctly perceived these words as criticism addressed to those leaders of the CCP who had promised the people the achievement of "a thousand years of happiness in three years."

The famous Chinese economist and Director of the Institute of Economics of the Academy of Sciences of the PRC, Sun Ye-fang, in 1961 appealed for establishment of cost accounting. Objecting to neglect of the principles of material incentive, he considered it necessary to make widespread use of the goods-money relationship in the interests of building socialism. The former rector of the Higher Party School, member of the CC CCP, Yang Hsian-chen, declared the policy of the "great leap forward" a product of "subjectivism and voluntarism." Some representatives of the CCP leadership shared these sentiments.

There can be no question of the fact that adherents of the special course knew of these attitudes, but during this period they still had not decided to openly repress opposition elements. It apparently was assumed that "stabilization" of the economy would lead to normalization of the situation and create more favorable conditions for attacking the opposition.

In 1960 Peking leaders, attempting to justify their pretensions as the advance guard of the world Communist movement, started to promote the propaganda of the "ideas of Mao Tse-tung" on an even grander scale as the "pinnacle of theoretical thought of the modern epoch." A corresponding "justification" was advanced for this thesis. One Chinese article, for example put it this way:

> The fact that modern China has become the birthplace of the ideas of Mao Tse-tung is no accident. There are deep historical and social reasons for this. It is the equal of Germany's having become the birthplace of Marxism in the forties of the nineteenth century, and of Russia becoming the birthplace of Leninism in the twentieth century.[1]

The propaganda of the "ideas of Mao Tse-tung" began increasingly to ring with the thesis that these ideas were applicable not only to China, but were universal in nature. The Peking "theorists" in essence threw out their earlier definition to the effect that "the ideas of Mao Tse-tung" were "an amalgam of the universal truths of Marxism-Leninism with concrete Chinese reality."[2] If CCP leaders earlier had spoken of the "ideas of Mao Tse-tung" as the "taking of Marxism from its European form and recasting it into a form" of "Chinese Communism," now this formula was clearly inadequate. The national clothing in which leaders of the CCP had attempted to robe Marxism in the past, at this stage had become too tight for the "ideas of Mao Tse-tung."

Propaganda of nationalist, great-power ideas was given more emphasis in the political and indoctrinational work being done among the Chinese people. The press in the PRC intensified its "development" of the theme of the exclusiveness of China, of its particularly outstanding role in world history. Chinese newspapers and journals carried numerous articles on the greatness of ancient China, cited the thoughts of the ancient philosophers on how particularly stable were all things Chinese, and how the Chinese unswervingly "converted strangers to their images and likeness." The thesis was advanced that "the economy and culture of the epoch of feudalism in our state, the backbone of which was the Han nation, from the Chin and Han dynasties to the initial period of the Ching dynasty (that is, from the second century B.C. to the seventeenth century A.D.), always was in the very foremost position in the world," and that its boundaries extended for a distance that encompassed the territories of many modern states (all the way to the northern part of the Black Sea and Iran).[3] *Jen Min Jihpao,* in chauvinistic self-delusion, wrote that:

> When many Western peoples that now are famous as cultured nations still were hunting wild animals in the woods, our people already had created a brilliant, ancient culture.[4]

Overtones of racism began openly to creep into the Chinese press with attempts to play off one race against another. *Kungmin Jihpao,* in an article entitled "Criticism of World History Which Does Not Have World Character," asserted for example that "prior to the fifteenth century the pepoles of Asia, that is the yellow race, occupied the leading place in world history. After the fifteenth century this situation underwent a gradual change-over to the European peoples, that is to the white race."[5] The authors of the article predicted that there would be a revival of the former "leading" position of the yellow race.

2. Deviation of the leadership of the CCP from Leninist principles of a socialist foreign policy

Hopes of nationalist elements to effect their ambitious great-power plans on the basis of internal development of China, by transforming it into the foremost power in the world from results of the "leap" method, were dashed with the failure of the "Three Red Banners" policy. Thus they finally recognized the possibility of achieving the victory of socialism by peaceful economic competition with capitalism.

Whereas during the establishment of the people's communes the Maoists had asserted that communism could be built within a stipulated number of years ("three years of persistent work, a thousand years of happiness"), now they veered to the other extreme and moved achievement of this goal into the indefinite future.

> "The final victory of socialism," they now asserted in Peking, "cannot be achieved in the lifetimes of one, or even of two, generations. It will be possible to achieve it completely in from 5 to 10 generations, or perhaps after an even longer period of time."[6]

But this did not mean that Chinese leaders rejected their nationalist, hegemonistic yearnings. Having lost the battle on the economic front, they began to look for new ways to achieve the old goal. Leaders of the CCP transferred the focus of their efforts to foreign policy, believing that war would "give a push" to the world revolution, and that by drawing the USSR and the United States into a mutually destructive military confrontation they could create on the ruins a "new, shining civilization" in which China, because of its overwhelming population, would assume ultimate dominance.

Peking announced that "it is stupid to talk" about building communism "when imperialism exists and is relatively strong in the main regions of the world." Chinese leaders attacked the peaceful coexistence policy of socialist countries, and proceeded to aggravate international tensions. At the same time they tried to steer their course so as to keep to a minimum losses China might suffer, and, so far as possible, to remain aloof from the very danger they created.

The discrepancy between slogans of the Peking leaders and concrete practice in their foreign policy became increasingly evident. Paying lip service to the requirement for struggling with imperialism on the principle of "point against point," these leaders, in fact, strove to regularize relations between the PRC and the capitalist states (including the United States), to the detriment of cooperation between China and the countries of socialism.

Deviation of CCP leaders from Leninist foreign policy principles led to activities of the CCP in the international arena which depended primarily on the use of blackmail and bribery, every conceivable type of provocation, direct interference in internal affairs of others including the socialist countries, ideological differences with fraternal parties, and splitting tactics in the socialist commonwealth and the world Communist movement.

The accelerated international activities of the PRC have been associated to a considerable degree with attempts of nationalists in the CCP to distract attention of the Chinese people from the catastrophic failure of the "Three Red Banners" course, and to establish their control over all facets of life under the slogan of intensification of the struggle with imperialism and with "contemporary revisionism."

The essence of the foreign policy of the PRC during this period was as follows:

—With respect to the socialist camp, to isolate the Soviet Union, to bind as many socialist countries as possible to their goal, and then use the economic and political might of the socialist commonwealth to achieve great-power, nationalist goals.

—In the field of relations with forces of national liberation movements, to alienate these forces from the Soviet Union, and from other socialist states, from the international working class, to hammer together a bloc of Afro-Asian countries and, in the final analysis, to achieve hegemony in countries once on the colonial periphery of imperialism.

—With respect to the Communist movement, to isolate the CPSU, to undermine its authority among fraternal parties, to strengthen the Chinese ideological and political platform as the general line of the international Communist movement, while, at the same time, converting this movement into the weapon of Peking's great-power strategy.

China's foreign policy course was directed at disrupting the policy of peaceful coexistence, of aggravating international tensions, and of accelerating the "decisive military clash with imperialism."

This particular foreign policy course led directly to a deterioration in Sino-Soviet relations. †Ignoring the articles of the Treaty of Friendship, Alliance, and Mutual Assistance of February 14, 1950, the purpose of which was to prevent the rebirth of Japanese militarism, the government of the PRC began to develop its policy of relations with Japan, not only without cooperation of the Soviet Union, but actually to counterbalance it. †A joint statement by a Chinese delegation and a delegation from the Socialist Party of Japan, published in January 1962, included the fact that the corresponding articles of the Sino-Soviet Treaty "naturally will lose their force" simultaneously with the signing of a bilateral Sino-Japanese Treaty of Friendship and Mutual Non-Aggression. The leaders of the CCP in making such a declaration, having a direct effect on Sino-Soviet relations, did not deign to engage in necessary consultation with the Soviet government.

The deviation of Peking leaders from the generally agreed line of the socialist countries in the international arena was revealed with particular clarity in the fall of 1962, during the crisis in the Caribbean. At that time, when the serious danger of invasion by American troops was hanging over Cuba, and when the world appeared to be on the verge of thermonuclear war, Chinese leaders openly attempted to provoke a large-scale international conflict.

During the first stage of this crisis, from October 23 to 28, 1962, when the international situation was extremely tense, and it was particularly necessary to maintain a united front against the aggressive actions of American imperialism, the CCP leaders did not deem it necessary to undertake active measures to support Cuba, as was being done by the USSR and other countries. At the time when it was not sufficiently clear how events would develop, the Chinese leaders adopted a wait-and-see attitude; thus no matter which way the affair ended they would be able to have the last word.

After October 28, 1962, when tensions eased and it was evident that a turning point had been reached in resolving the crisis, the PRC suddenly began a noisy campaign "to signal decisive support for the struggle of the Cuban people to defend their independence, sovereignty, and dignity," and Chinese propaganda unequivocally emphasized that the position of the USSR was detrimental to Cuba. At the same time Chinese leaders, demonstrating their disagreement with settling the crisis by peaceful talks, and nudging the USSR and Cuba to unleash a military conflict, attempted to use events in the Caribbean to prove the "righteousness" of their special views and to discredit the policy of peaceful coexistence. Chinese representatives spread anti-Soviet fabrications with respect to the Caribbean crisis within international democratic organizations and in various international conferences.

The real purpose of the Maoists in connection with the Caribbean crisis was to provoke an armed clash between the USSR and the United States and then to warm their hands at this military fire. The bourgeois press made some interesting statements in this connection. The *New York Times,* on November 7, 1962, wrote that "Peking has long been ready to fight to the last American and to the last Russian."

The Chinese leaders made no businesslike, concrete suggestions to protect Cuban interests and avert war during the period of dangerous events in the Caribbean. Moreover, China not only did nothing to settle the Caribbean crisis, but it took the opportunity, during those terrible days, to commence military operations along India's border, and created yet another source of international tension. These actions show the intentions of the Chinese leaders with obvious clarity. Using the fact that world attention was focused on the acute international conflict, Peking leaders attempted to realize their nationalist plans.

In October 1962 Chinese troops, pleading self-defense, intruded for a distance of 100 kilometers into regions controlled by India. Taking advantage of the evolving situation, Indian reaction launched an attack on democratic rights and the freedom of the workers. Progressive forces were subjected to repressions. The Communist Party of India was in a particularly precarious position. It became the chief target of fierce assaults of reaction. Pogroms of democratic organizations began, and Communists were arrested.

The United States and Great Britain immediately began to send India weapons, and ordered special missions sent to India, all the result of the aggravation of the Sino-Indian conflict, which threatened to spread from a local into an international one. Warnings against this development of events were issued by the Soviet side. *Pravda,* on October 25 and November 5, 1962 published articles containing appeals for the warring countries to cease military operations unconditionally and to begin bilateral talks. But CCP leaders not only refused to listen to those appeals, they attempted to distort the position of the USSR. The Soviet Union was charged with having deviated from proletarian internationalism in the Sino-Indian dispute.

Meanwhile bourgeois propaganda began to raise the cry of the "aggressiveness of international Communism." Speaking in Glasgow on November 16, British Minister of Foreign Affairs Alec Douglas-Home said that "if anyone, at any time, had believed that weakness and neutrality could be protection, there can be no doubt that the experience of India should rid him of that delusion." The imperialists, abetted by Indian reaction, forced India into the embrace of the West, and the leaders of China, through their bellicose and irresponsible adventurist actions, encouraged this in every way possible.

It was only the failure of attempts to negotiate with India from a position of strength, and the prospects of a long, protracted war in which the United States, Great Britain, and their allies in the aggressive bloc would participate, that somewhat deterred Chinese leaders. A cease-fire, and withdrawal of Chinese troops to the line occupied prior to the outbreak of the conflict, was announced on November 21.

The position of the Chinese leaders in the conflict with India resulted in heavy moral and political losses for the PRC and for the entire socialist camp, helping to destroy the faith of young national states of Asia and Africa in socialist policy. Many of these states expressed their sympathies with India in one way or another at the time of the exacerbation of the Sino-Indian border conflict. Over 60 countries around the world condemned China's actions.

The Chinese leaders, following their adventurist course in the inter-

national arena, made national liberation movements their blue chip in
the game, to advance further their own ends. The leaders of the CCP
assumed it would be easy for them to spread their pseudorevolutionary
theory in developing countries, to recruit supporters, and to use the anti-
imperialist enthusiasm of oppressed peoples for advancing their own
great-power ambitions.

One detects a definite plan for use of the national liberation movement in the struggle for realization of their nationalist aspirations in
theoretical discourses of the Peking leaders. Chinese leaders use the
experience of the revolutionary struggle in China (first seize power in
the villages, then surround the cities and seize them) in their global
formula for world revolution, which is first to gain victory for the revolution in underdeveloped countries ("the world village"), cut off imperialism from Asia, Africa, and Latin America, and then destroy it once
and for all. It goes without saying that China, and Mao Tse-tung as its
"leader," thus is arrogating to itself the starring role in the entire world
revolutionary process.

The policy of the Chinese leaders concerning the national liberation
movement assumed a clearly defined anti-Soviet slant. Peking propaganda attempted to belittle the role of the Soviet Union in the international arena, to weaken the solidarity between our country and the
nations leading the national liberation struggle against imperialism. Consciously denigrating the importance of the Great October Socialist Revolution in developing the national liberation struggle in colonies and
dependent countries, CCP leaders strenuously promoted the paramount
importance of the "ideas" of Mao Tse-tung for the fate of national liberation movements. A history textbook published in 1961 by the Hofei
Pedagogical Institute said:

> The ideas of Mao Tse-tung are a new development of Marxism-Leninism
> under the conditions of revolution in colonies and semicolonies. The ideas
> of Mao Tse-tung are the sole truth responsible for the liberation of the
> Chinese people and are the sole truth with the help of which the peoples
> of colonial and semicolonial countries can liberate themselves. Hence the
> ideas of Mao Tse-tung are of exceptional importance not only for China,
> but are of universal importance for the world Communist movement and
> for the national liberation movement of the peoples of Asia, Africa, and
> Latin America.

Historically, Marxist-Leninist parties considered the downfall of the
system of colonial servitude under the impact of national liberation
movements second in historical importance to the formation of the world

system of socialism. Revising this assessment, Chinese leaders began to characterize the national liberation movement as the basic factor in the struggle with imperialism, downgrading the role of world socialist co-operation and the revolutionary movement of the working classes in capitalist countries. The theoretical organ of the CC CCP, *Hung-ch'i,* flatly stated that "the rise of the national liberation movement, and the death of the colonial system, are the main content of our epoch."[7]

Peking propaganda to Asia, Africa, and Latin America began openly to speak of China separately from the socialist camp, as a result of which treatment of the "community of spirit" of the PRC with developing countries acquired essentially an ambiguous, or more precisely, a racial ring: China was arrayed not only against the imperialist powers, but against the socialist commonwealth as well. Openly nationalist movements were increasingly apparent in the propaganda and practical policies of Peking in Asia, Africa, and Latin America. In speaking of the East, for example, Chinese leaders began to regard it as purely a geographic concept, not distinguishing the classical difference between the working masses of this region and those of the exploiter clique. As a result Chinese leaders pushed the slogans "People of Asia, Africa, and Latin America, Unite!," and the "East Wind Will Prevail over the West Wind," which objectively were in conflict with the slogan of proletarian solidarity, "Workers of the World, Unite!"

The fallacy and ambiguity of these slogans were clearly confirmed by statements of a prominent member of Japan's Liberal-Democratic Party, Kenzo Matsumura, who visited the PRC in September 1962. His speech at a reception in Peking in the presence of Chou En-lai and other Chinese leaders was published in the China press, and included the following:

> I consider this visit to be significant. This visit will help us, step by step, to settle relations between our two countries into the type of relations that should exist between peoples with the same color of skin, and the same system of written language. Premier Chou En-lai and Vice Premier Chen Yi have met with us many times, and we have discussed the fact that the East will always remain the East, and that Asians should change world history. We should join together and we should strengthen the bond between our peoples who have the same color of skin and the same system of written language.

Matsumura, in this speech, revealed what Chinese leaders themselves did not think possible to say openly.

CCP leaders, publicizing in every way possible their "vanguard role" in the struggle against colonialism, in fact did nothing to solve the practical problems of this struggle. It is significant that in 1960–1961 the government of the PRC failed to support actions of the Soviet Union and other socialist countries aimed at liquidation of the colonial system.

3. Direct attacks of the Maoists on the ideological position of the CPSU and other Marxist-Leninist parties

The departure of CCP leaders from socialist principles of domestic and foreign policy was accompanied by intensification of their attack on the ideological position of the Marxist-Leninist parties and by more active attempts to impose on the world Communist movement the antiscientific views and conceptions of Maoism.

Under these conditions the CC CPSU took steps to keep leaders of the CCP from eventually engaging in an open ideological struggle with the fraternal parties. True to the principles of proletarian internationalism, the CC CPSU persistently tried to discuss with CCP leaders all questions at issue, and to do so in comradely fashion, and remained unswerving in expressing a firm belief that joint solutions favoring the common effort of the two sides were possible.

On February 6, 1960 the CC CPSU proposed a meeting at a high party level to the CC CCP in order to discuss all questions at issue.

On April 5, 1960 the CC CPSU and the Soviet government extended an official invitation to a party-governmental delegation, headed by Mao Tse-tung, to pay a friendly visit to the Soviet Union in hopes of improving Sino-Soviet relations.

However, the friendly position of the CC CPSU met with anything but a positive response from CCP leaders. Moreover, they initiated actions hostile to the CPSU and to the other Marxist-Leninist parties.

At the end of April 1960 the Chinese press published three articles celebrating the 90th anniversary of the birth of V. I. Lenin (these articles later were combined into a booklet entitled *Long Live Leninism*). These articles subjected to criticism the most important theoretical propositions approved by the Communist and Workers' Parties in the Moscow Declaration of 1957 and signed by CCP leaders.

Long Live Leninism gave a distorted view of the modern era and insisted that imperialism is the force exclusively determining world development. The authors attempted to prove that the world socialist system, the revolutionary workers' and national liberation movement, the anti-imperialist, peace-loving forces are in no position to impose their will on imperialism. The deepening decay of the imperialist system and the downfall of colonial empires were characterized as isolated events so far as the gigantic successes of world socialism were concerned. This position contradicted the conclusion of the 1957 Moscow Declaration that world development in the modern era will be determined by the struggle, course, and results of competition between two opposing social systems, socialism and capitalism; that the growing and increasingly stronger world socialist system has ever more influence on the international situation in the interests of peace, progress, and the freedom of peoples.[8]

The role of the world socialist system was downgraded by Chinese leaders in order to justify their conclusion on other fundamental questions as well.

One of the central ideas contained in the booklet was the impossibility of preventing a world war until such time as socialism was victorious on a worldwide scale. The booklet was permeated with skepticism about the capabilities of world revolutionary forces. Moreover, for all practical purposes, the booklet expressed the thought that the new world war would end with positive results for the people. It includes the statement that:

> The victorious people will, very quickly, create on the ruins of imperialism a civilization a thousand times higher than that known during the capitalist system, and will build its genuinely beautiful future.[9]

What they actually were proposing was the desirability of a world war.

Long Live Leninism was an open declaration by Chinese leaders to the enemy, imperialism, that there existed disagreements within the international Communist movement on basic questions of strategy and tactics.

In the interests of the preservation of unity the CC CPSU did not raise the question of the content of *Long Live Leninism,* or of other similar published statements by Chinese leaders, prior to June 1960. It believed the disagreements that had arisen should be discussed during meetings between leaders of both parties. This is why the Soviet press refrained from indulging in polemics.

†A second invitation to visit the Soviet Union was extended to Mao Tse-tung early in 1960. Once again there was a chance for constructive meetings and talks between Chinese and Soviet leaders. But again Mao Tse-tung refused to use the opportunity, evinced no interest in contacts, and expressed no desire to personally acquaint himself with the life of our country. Future events were to show that this position was assumed deliberately.

In response to the constructive proposal of the CPSU, CCP leaders took a new, completely unacceptable step from the standpoint of relations between fraternal parties. This step could only be assessed as an open split. At the beginning of June 1960, during the Peking session of the General Council of the World Federation of Trade Unions, Chinese leaders expounded their views on a number of important questions of principle, advancing positions that were in conflict with Marxism-Leninism, before a large group of fraternal party representatives.

These actions not only failed to gain support among Communists attending the session, they were decisively rebuffed. The CCP leaders then took another splitting step, this time criticizing the views of the CPSU and other fraternal parties in meetings of the General Council of the World Federation of Trade Unions, as well as before a number of commissions which included many members of non-Communist parties, as well as nonparty trade unionists. These actions in essence were an open appeal to the World Federation of Trade Unions to take up the struggle against views of the CPSU and other Communist parties on the most important problems of contemporary world development.

At this time CCP leaders took active steps to get the Albanian leaders to join them in their splitting tactics. They initially attempted to create the impression that at all times they strove to prevent the deepening of the disagreement between the Albanian Party of Labor and the CPSU and to assist in normalization of Soviet-Albanian relations. In fact, however, the real position of CCP leaders was diametrically opposite. The Mao Tse-tung group gave unqualified support to Albanian leaders at all stages of the disagreement between the leaders of the Albanian Party of Labor and the other parties. Behind all their efforts was the goal of exacerbating rather than regularizing relations between the Albanian leaders and the CPSU and other parties. At a time when all Marxist-Leninist parties were making their assessment of the anti-Soviet line of Albanian leaders on a point of principle, the CCP leaders took every opportunity to emphasize their approval of that course. Talks were held on June 4, 1960 in Peking between Chinese leaders and members of the Albanian delegation who happened to be in China at the time. During the talks, CCP leaders distorted the position of the CPSU on basic contemporary problems, asserting that it was "deviating" from the 1957 Moscow Declaration. Statements of CCP leaders with respect to the CPSU and the Soviet Union were so hostile that even the Albanian representatives regarded these talks as "dirty business," directed at provoking a conflict between Albanian Party of Labor and the CPSU.

At the beginning of June 1960 the CC CPSU suggested use of the convocation of the 3d Congress of the Rumanian Workers' Party in

Bucharest for representatives of fraternal parties to exchange views on then current questions of the contemporary international situation.

On June 21, 1960 the CC CPSU sent the fraternal parties a confidential memorandum in which the bankruptcy of the theoretical positions of the Chinese leaders was convincingly set forth in its entirety, and, in comradely fashion, simultaneously pointed out how obviously mistaken they were and the possible harmful consequences.

The memorandum analyzed what had occurred during the session of the General Council of the World Federation of Trade Unions in Peking, and contained a fundamental criticism of the mistaken positions taken by leaders of the CCP on a number of international questions. This memorandum was in response to the attack by the Chinese leaders, who had openly and unilaterally criticized the CPSU; the Soviet Union expressed its hope that the CCP would consider the interests of the entire socialist camp, and of the international Communist movement, inseparable from the interests of building socialism in the PRC.

Candid discussions were held between the Chinese delegation to the 3d Congress of the Rumanian Workers' Party, headed by a member of the Politburo of the CC CCP, P'eng Chen, and the CC CPSU on the eve of the Bucharest meeting. The purpose of these discussions was to review the questions at issue, to once again point out to the Chinese leaders their mistaken views and actions, and to effect the appearance of a spirit of unity in Bucharest. The Chinese delegation, following orders from Peking, refused to accept the interpretation of the CC CPSU and continued to defend their views, the same views the leaders of the CCP had advanced at the session of the World Federation of Trade Unions in Peking.

Two events took place in Bucharest between June 24 and 26, 1960 in accordance with prior arrangements with the CCP. One was a meeting of fraternal parties of the socialist countries, the other a meeting of the 51 fraternal parties of the socialist and capitalist countries.

Representatives of fraternal parties of the socialist countries took note of the fact that the entire course of world development, the successes in the socialist camp, the international workers' and national liberation movements, the growing struggle for peace, the continuing weakening of the forces of imperialism, confirmed completely the correctness of the conclusions of the Declaration and Peace Manifesto adopted at the Moscow meeting of Communist and Workers' Parties in 1957. Participants of the Bucharest meeting were unanimous in their declaration that fundamental positions taken in the Declaration and Peace Manifesto retained their full force.

The participants in the meeting, with the exception of the Albanian representatives, showed that they were men of high principle and used concrete facts to point out that Chinese leaders had deviated from the principles of the declaration and had attempted to substitute left sectarian views for the ideology of scientific socialism.

The unity and solidarity of the fraternal parties further manifested itself in the joint meeting of Communist party representatives of socialist and capitalist countries. The participants were unanimous in acknowledging that the position and actions of the Chinese leaders were detrimental to the struggle of the revolutionary forces; they were sharply critical of the CCP leaders for their factional methods, and condemned both the behavior of Chinese representatives at the session of the General Council of the World Federation of Trade Unions in Peking and also the dissemination abroad by representatives of the PRC of anti-Soviet materials. Deep concern was expressed over attempts by Peking's leaders to convert representatives of the fraternal countries visiting China to the spirit of their factionist views.

When it became clear to Chinese leaders that their unseemly methods had been unmasked, they assumed an injured pose and began to maintain that the meeting was run by "undemocratic methods." This maneuver was decisively rebuffed.

The question of adoption of a common communiqué was raised by a number of the parties during the concluding stages of the meeting. After lengthy procrastination, the delegation from the CC CCP signed the communiqué "for the sake of unity," although it was no secret that the delegation believed it had to do so or be exposed as factionists and splitters.

The communiqué, signed by representatives of Communist parties from all socialist countries, declared that the Communist and Workers' Parties would, in the future, strengthen the solidarity of the countries of the world socialist system, and would protect, like the apple of their eye, their unity in the struggle for peace and security of all peoples, for the triumph of the great cause of Marxism-Leninism.[10]

The fraternal parties at the Bucharest conference declared unanimously that CCP leaders should consider the criticism leveled at them and draw from it the necessary conclusion in order to ensure unity on root questions of strategy and tactics of the world Communist movement. It was decided to establish a draft committee to prepare the documents for the international conference planned for the fall of 1960.

The results of the Bucharest conference were discussed at plenary sessions of many central committees of Communist parties which had taken part in it, and also were reviewed at the plenum of the CC CPSU held in July. The results of the conference were approved unanimously. The resolution adopted by the plenum emphasized that the:

> . . . successful solutions of the problems facing the Communist and workers' parties requires the continuation of the struggle against revisionism, dogmatism, and sectarianism, which are contradictory to the creative nature of Marxism-Leninism, and which interfere with the mobilization of all the forces in the socialist camp, of the revolutionary workers' and liberation movement in the struggle for peace and socialism and against imperialism.[11]

The Bucharest conference paved the way to overcoming disagreements which had arisen between leaders of the CCP and the world Communist movement. Nevertheless, Chinese leaders did everything possible to block this approach. On June 26, 1960, the last day of the conference, the delegation from the PRC sent a letter to all Communist parties of socialist countries, purposely distorting the nature of the meeting. The letter asserted that the CPSU's delegation had "violated the principles of consultation" in pushing its suggestion for the adoption of the communiqué. This assertion is at variance with the facts because actually the suggestion for adoption by the conference of an agreed document was advanced by delegations from a great many fraternal parties. These parties were correct in emphasizing the urgent need to adopt this document, one which declared support for the Moscow Declaration of 1957, and the readiness of all parties to observe unswervingly its principles—a document that would demonstrate to the world the solidarity of the fraternal parties. The adoption of the communiqué was desirable for yet another reason—to stop bourgeois propaganda's clamoring about disagreements between fraternal parties after the PRC publication of *Long Live Leninism*.

Chinese leaders did not limit themselves to distribution of this letter. They openly attacked the position of participants in the Bucharest conference in lead articles in the newspaper *Jen Min Jihpao* on June 29 and August 13, 1960. Their criticism was unfounded.

The CC CPSU, in August 1960, gave the CCP a convincing answer apropos of the Bucharest meeting. Still, CCP leaders continued stubbornly to hold their mistaken views. Despite the fact that the Bucharest conference considered Chinese propaganda, including *Long Live Leninism,* anti-Marxist, CCP leaders continued to disseminate it abroad over the heads of central committees of fraternal parties.

Chinese leaders attempted to foist their anti-Soviet views on the Soviet people as well. To this end they made use, in particular, of the Chinese journal *Druzhba (Friendship)*, published in Russian and distributed in the Soviet Union. The journal treated Soviet readers to the spirit of Maoist ideas, contradicting the line of the CC CPSU and other Marxist-Leninist parties. Leaders of the CCP also used the Chinese embassy in Moscow to circulate propaganda materials in the Soviet Union.

These actions on the part of the Chinese had nothing in common with the spirit of friendship and cooperation between the PRC and the USSR. The Soviet government therefore was forced to take steps to protect its people from the flow of hostile propaganda, and from involving them unnecessarily in discussions of questions under consideration by the Central Committees of the Communist Parties of China and the USSR. After repeated warnings to the Chinese side by Soviet organizations, there was no alternative but to suggest the cessation of publication of *Druzhba* (in Russian), and, proceeding from the principle of equity, that of the Soviet journal *Sovetsko-kitayskaya druzhba (Soviet-Chinese Friendship)* (in Chinese), as well. In July 1960 the Chinese were informed that materials published in *Druzhba* ran contrary to documents of the international Communist movement, and that such measures contradicted not only the fundamental principles on which intergovernmental and interparty relations between both countries were built, but also aims that the Chinese publishers of the journal themselves had set as bases for their activities.

Another step along the path to deterioration of Sino-Soviet relations taken by leaders of the CCP was a letter from its Central Committee to that of the CPSU on September 10, 1960. This letter contained a further attack on the ideological position of the CPSU and that of other Marxist-Leninist parties. It also contained a number of slanderous accusations against the CPSU. Our party was accused of views alien to it, of actions it never had taken, and of other faults.

The CC CCP, demagogically asserting that a temporary majority cannot transform a mistake into a truth, or a temporary minority a truth into a mistake, flatly stated that henceforth they would ignore the opinion of the fraternal parties and of the whole international Communist movement.

The persistent efforts of the CC CPSU finally succeeded in September 1960. The CC CCP accepted a proposal to hold talks; the meeting took place in Moscow between September 17 and 22, 1960.

But again Maoist leaders remained faithful to their previous line. Leading Peking figures did not make the trip to Moscow. The delegation was headed by Teng Hsiao-p'ing, General Secretary of the CC CCP. He was accompanied by ardent propagandists of the particular views of the CCP.

Holding to the framework of the letter of September 10, 1960, and piling one far-fetched pretension atop the other on the CC CPSU, the Chinese delegation strove to avoid discussion of main problems of the international situation, strategy and tactics of the revolutionary struggle, advancing instead a mass of secondary questions, some of which had long since been decided.

Talks continued for five days, but because of Chinese intransigence without positive results. Moreover, the meeting quite obviously demonstrated that the Chinese leaders intended to expand the circle of their disagreements with the CPSU and the other fraternal parties, to exacerbate the situation in the world Communist movement.

Some time later the CCP delegation returned to Moscow, and between October 1 and 20, participated in work of the drafting committee preparing the project for the statement of the Communist and Workers' Parties conference.

This committee comprised representatives of Communist parties from all main areas of the world, socialist countries, developed capitalist countries, and countries struggling for national independence. Thus it was possible for the committee to discuss all aspects of the questions of principle facing the international Communist movement as well as Communist and Workers' Parties in individual countries and regions. The CC CPSU prepared a project for the statement of the Communist and Workers' Parties conference as the basis for the committee's work, which was unanimously adopted.

The Chinese delegation hailed the fact that the CC CPSU had drafted the project for the document and declared "90 percent agreement with it," and further expressed confidence that despite "certain dissimilar views" the Marxist-Leninist parties would be able to find common language.

The draft of the statement was expanded and enriched during creative discussions, while retaining all fundamental positions of principle. Still, the Chinese delegation, supported by representatives of the Albanian Party of Labor, pressed its stubborn struggle against inclusion in the draft of a number of most important theses pertaining to the theory and tactics of the contemporary world Communist movement. It inveighed with particular bitterness against banning fractioning and group activities in the ranks of the Communist movement and against criticism of the cult of personality. It objected as well to the proposal, advanced by the fraternal parties, that the international importance of the 20th and 21st Congresses of the CPSU be emphasized in the statement. Only the unanimous condemnation of their obstructionist position caused representatives of the Communist Party of China to cease their importunities.

The conduct of the Chinese delegation at sessions of the drafting committee revealed that CCP leaders intended to convert the Moscow conference into an arena for a sharp struggle with the CPSU and other fraternal parties.

On the eve of the conference, November 5, 1960, the CC CPSU replied to the September 10, 1960 letter of the CC CCP. This reply contained convincing proof of the theoretical inconsistency of the Chinese leaders, unmasked their splitting activities, and revealed the anti-Soviet nature of the CCP policy.

In this letter our party once again demonstrated a sincere effort to overcome disagreements. The CC CPSU said it would be a serious mistake, one fraught with serious consequences for the entire Communist movement, to wait for the "verdict of history" to determine who was right. Our party held firmly to the view that one ought not leave to history the decision of a dispute on such vital questions as theory and policy, strategy and tactics, of the Communist movement. The task of Communists is to help people make history and to direct social development along the path to communism. Their duty to the workers of the world is to reach agreement on the fundamental basis of Marxism-Leninism as quickly and decisively as possible, and to achieve consistent implementation of the general line by all fraternal parties in the interests of the great cause of victory over world imperialism.

The letter from the CC CPSU was sent to the fraternal parties which had received the September 10, 1960 letter from the CC CCP. It played an important role in preparations for the Moscow conference by drafting for it Marxist-Leninist positions on contemporary problems.

The Moscow Conference of Communist and Workers' Parties which convened in November 1960 was an important stage in the struggle of the world Communist movement for unity and solidarity on the fundamental basis of Marxism-Leninism. The mistaken views and divisive methods of the leaders of the CCP became subject to severe criticism.

It was the delegation of the CCP which forced discussion on the conference. As a matter of fact, the Chinese delegate's first speech, rendering null and void what delegates of sister countries had agreed to in drafting committee, again raised all areas of disagreement between CCP leaders and the world Communist movement. Revising the 1957 Declaration, the delegate of the CCP particularly expressed disagreement with its thesis on the decisive role played by the international working class and the world system of socialism in the world revolutionary process. Throughout speeches of the Chinese delegation ran a theme directed at undermining the very bases of the general line of the international Communist movement and principles of Marxism-Leninism.

The divisive strategy of the Chinese delegation and the anti-Leninist positions of the Peking leaders met with a determined rebuff from an overwhelming majority of Marxist-Leninist parties at the conference. Representatives of many fraternal parties spoke to the issue that the mistaken and adventurist schemes of CCP leadership completely ignored the new historical situation evolving throughout the world as a result of root changes in the balance of power after World War II. The conference condemned the factional activities of the CCP, as well as attempts to justify these activities on "theoretical" grounds. Stressed was the fact that the splitting policy of the Chinese leaders resulted in special damage being done to parties operating under illegal conditions.

The Marxist-Leninist parties decisively condemned the slanderous campaign of the leaders of the CCP aimed at the CPSU, and were unanimous in confirming the high evaluation given the activities of our party. Attempts by the Chinese delegation to oppose, defame, and slander the CPSU to the other parties were a total failure. The delegates of the fraternal parties stated flatly that work of the CPSU was inseparable from the Communist movement, that the party of Lenin was the center of the world Communist movement. The attempt by the Chinese delegates to undermine the authority of the CPSU was construed not only as an insult to it but to the whole of the international Communist movement as well. Finding themselves under criticism, Chinese leaders accused the CPSU and other parties of an organized campaign, and even of an "attack" against the CCP. This was simply one more fiction. In fact, fraternal parties displayed exceptional patience and self-restraint in dealing with the delegation of the CCP throughout the discussions.

At that time the threat of complete isolation forced the Chinese delegation to alter its tactics and to cease temporarily its efforts to force mistaken conceptions on the international Communist movement. Faced with unanimous condemnation of their anti-Leninist views and the disruptive actions of their leaders, CCP representatives were forced to sign a statement actually rejecting the alien views of Chinese leaders, and condemning their factional activities.

The opposing ideological-political lines were clearly detectable at the conference. One was the line of the international Communist movement, supported by the overwhelming majority of the parties. This was the line of creative Marxism-Leninism, the line of unity and solidarity of the international Communist movement, based on principle. The other line was the nationalist line of leaders of the CCP, the line of deviation from the general course of the international Communist movement and of intensification of sectarian tendencies, supported openly only by the delegation of the Albanian Party of Labor.

The mistaken anti-Leninist line of the Chinese and Albanian delegations went down to total defeat. The Chinese propaganda version of the alleged victory of the Chinese line at the 1960 conference is a gross falsification.

The CC CPSU and the Soviet government took steps to improve Sino-Soviet relations immediately after the Moscow conference. The delegation of the CCP, headed by Liu Shao-ch'i, which had taken part in the conference, was invited to tour the USSR. In talks with members of the delegation, Soviet leaders emphasized the immutability of the course of the CC CPSU and the Soviet government for solidarity with the CCP and the PRC, and for the strengthening and development of Sino-Soviet interparty and interstate relations.

Chinese leaders, in statements published at that time, declared their devotion to Sino-Soviet friendship, and hypocritically expressed their delight in the foreign and domestic achievements of the Soviet Union. Mao Tse-tung and other Chinese leaders, in congratulations extended on the occasion of the 43d anniversary of the Great October Revolution, wrote:

> The great Soviet people, under the leadership of the glorious Communist Party of the Soviet Union, have achieved tremendous successes in the successful accomplishment of the 7-Year Plan for the development of the building of communism, as well as in the struggle for the peaceful co-existence of states with different social systems, and for the preservation of peace throughout the world. The Chinese people rejoice with all their hearts in these tremendous successes of the fraternal Soviet people. The Chinese people in the future will go forward hand in hand with the Soviet people in the common cause of building socialism and communism, in the struggle against the aggression of imperialism, and in preserving peace throughout the world. . . . The great friendship and solidarity between the peoples of China and the Soviet Union . . . express the highest interests of the peoples of China and of the Soviet Union, the highest interests of people throughout the world."[12]

The newspaper *Jen Min Jihpao,* assessing the overall results of the visit to the Soviet Union by the Chinese party-government delegation, wrote that "this visit by Chairman Liu Shao-ch'i unquestionably has even further strengthened and developed the great friendship and solidarity of the peoples of China and the Soviet Union, and has written a golden page in the history of Sino-Soviet friendship."[13]

The 9th Plenary Session of the CC CCP met in January 1961 and reviewed the results of the Moscow Conference of Communist and Workers' Parties. The session heard and discussed a report on this issue presented by Teng Hsiao-p'ing, and adopted the following resolution:

> The plenary session warmly hails the tremendous results achieved by the conference of representatives of the Communist and workers' parties and approves completely of the statement and of the appeal to people throughout the world unanimously adopted at this meeting. The Communist Party of China will resolutely strive for the realization of the common tasks set forth in the documents of the meeting. The plenary session calls upon all members of the party and on people in all countries to hold high the great Marxist-Leninist banner of the Moscow Declaration of 1957 and of the Moscow Statement of 1960, to strengthen solidarity with the Soviet Union in international affairs, to strengthen the solidarity of the entire socialist camp and the solidarity of the international Communist movement, to strengthen the solidarity of the working class all over the world and the solidarity of all peace-loving and freedom-loving peoples, to struggle for new victories in the cause of peace throughout the world and for the progress of mankind.[14]

These assessments indicate that in that period the nationalist elements still had far from complete control of the situation among CCP leaders. Given a situation that had seen failure of the "great leap forward," and conspicuous lack of success by the PRC in the international arena, they were forced to reckon with opposition to their anti-Soviet, divisive course within ranks of the party and the country, to mask their course temporarily, and to engage in various maneuvers while awaiting the proper time to take the offensive. Subsequent events reveal that after the nationalist group had strengthened its position it pursued its struggle against socialist cooperation and against the world Communist movement with renewed vigor.

4. 22nd Congress of the CPSU and the intensification by CCP leaders of the ideological struggle against the fraternal parties

The congresses of the CPSU have importance and influence on the world Communist movement far beyond the confines of our party. They profoundly affect direction and content of ideological and theoretical work of all fraternal parties holding positions of creative Marxism-Leninism.

Recognizing this, the CCP leaders' most important goal became the discrediting of the CPSU 22nd Congress.

Leaders of the CCP tried to represent the 22nd Congress as merely an ordinary event. As distinguished from delegations representing other fraternal parties, the Chinese delegation was headed by the party's Vice Chairman, Chou En-lai, rather than by its Chairman, Mao Tse-tung. The delegation included Kang Sheng, an alternate member of the Politburo and an active adherent of the line directed at straining Sino-Soviet relations.

Leaders of the CCP deliberately assigned a special role to the so-called Albanian question in their attempts to disorganize the work of the congress. Ignoring elementary traditions of hospitality, the CCP representative in his greeting speech stated that provisions of the Summary Report of the CC CPSU containing criticism of splitting actions of Albanian Party of Labor leaders were "impossible to consider as a serious, Marxist-Leninist approach"; as a matter of fact he arrogantly lectured the congress, calling upon those present to support the CCP viewpoint.[15]

Thus Chinese leaders took a most unusual step in relations between Marxist-Leninist parties, by using the podium of the congress to inveigh against the report of the Central Committee of the party who invited them, once again revealing to all the world the disagreements between the CCP and the CPSU (at the same time hypocritically complaining that "open, unilateral censure of any fraternal party is not conducive to solidarity, not conducive to a solution of the problem"). Their action served to announce the claim of Chinese leaders to the role "of orthodox followers" of Marxism-Leninism, "the Superior Force" strengthening the unity of the socialist camp and of all fraternal parties. The speech by the head of the delegation representing the CCP at the CPSU 22nd Congress countered both the provisions of the 1960 Moscow Statement concerning inadmissibility of any actions tending to undermine the unity of the international Communist movement, and also the assertions of the Chinese leaders themselves to the effect that the Chinese people would not tolerate "any dealings and opinions unfavorable to solidarity between our parties and countries."

Despite the unfriendly speech of the head of the delegation from the CCP, and despite the overall contrary position of the Chinese leaders with respect to the 22nd Congress, the CC CPSU exercised a high level of self-restraint and did not permit the congress to be turned into an arena for interparty disputes. Without conceding questions of principle, the CC CPSU firmly and consistently held its course of achieving solidarity between the CCP, our party, and other Marxist-Leninist parties. This was convincingly demonstrated by talks between Soviet leaders and the Chinese delegation, during which the views of our party on current questions were elucidated, and readiness to attempt to overcome disagreements between the sides was emphasized. Disregarding everything, the Chinese leaders continued on their course.

The delegation from the CCP upon return to Peking was rewarded with a pompous reception, attended by Mao Tse-tung, arranged to show that the CCP leadership was in complete agreement with actions of the Chinese delegation at the CPSU 22nd Congress; that it would not lay down its arms but would continue the struggle with our party and with any other fraternal parties who rejected its mistaken views and nationalist pretensions.

While the CPSU 22nd Congress was in session, and immediately afterward, a widespread anti-Soviet campaign took place in the PRC. Chou En-lai, upon return, presented a long report in which he characterized the CPSU 22nd Congress as "revisionist," and launched a series of flagrant attacks against our party. Secretaries of party organizations made special reports on Sino-Soviet relations during November-December 1961. These reports were made at both closed and open meetings. They attempted to place blame for PRC difficulties between 1958 and 1960 on the Soviet Union. Stories concocted for dissemination stated that Chinese factories had been shut down because of shortages of spare parts and equipment which the Soviet Union "refused" to sell to the PRC, that the USSR "had demanded" of China immediate reimbursement of all loans and credits, for which China had to pay in foodstuffs, that the Soviet Union "did not want" to give assistance in the form of foodstuffs, and that the Soviet people "were not concerned" with their international obligations to the workers of other countries.

Behind the demagogic slogan of "the people will figure out who is right and who is wrong," CCP leaders threw wide the doors for penetration of bourgeois propaganda into China. Simultaneously, all objective information on Soviet life disappeared from the Chinese press.

In China, bulletins *Ts'an K'ao Shou-Ts'e* (*Reference Handbook*) and *Ts'an K'ao T'sai-Liao* (*Reference Materials*), considered secret, were used to disseminate the slanderous fabrications of bourgeois propaganda about the USSR. The circulation of the first of these bulletins reached 100,000 copies in Peking alone by the end of 1961. The journal, in the guise of providing readers with an "unbiased" account of "comments from abroad," reprinted slanderous articles from the bourgeois press about the Soviet people and the CPSU. Articles from *Ts'an K'ao Shou-Ts'e* were even recommended as "texts" for the party education network.

5. Efforts of the CPSU to overcome the ideological differences between the leadership of the CCP, our party, and other Marxist-Leninist parties

Early in 1962 our party took a new important step in an effort to halt the exacerbation of Sino-Soviet relations. The CC CPSU, on February 22, wrote a letter to the CC CCP expressing concern over the turn relations between the two parties were taking. The CC CPSU proceeded from the assumption that root interests of the cause of socialism and Communism demanded that our two parties rise above differences and reach agreement on all questions of principle. Given the situation, most important was to devote attention to anything that would assist in normalization of Sino-Soviet relations, while simultaneously avoiding overemphasizing the issues. The CC CPSU called for a display of good will in regulation of future disagreements, curtailment of unnecessary disputes over divergent issues, and cessation of publicized statements that not only failed to smooth out divergences, but in fact widened them. Carrying disagreements into relations between governments of the socialist countries, into their economic, political, military, and cultural cooperation, was particularly unacceptable. The CC CPSU confirmed proposals advanced earlier by the Soviet side directed at development of Soviet-Chinese contacts along all basic lines, and expressed its readiness to resolve disagreements in comradely fashion rather than let them accumulate to the point of aggravation.

The CC CPSU letter provided Chinese leaders with an opportunity to bring disagreements between the CCP and the international Communist movement into the framework of comradely discussions, and to create conditions for normalization and successful development of Sino-Soviet relations.

But the CC CCP in its reply of April 7, 1962 failed to accept the proposals made by the CC CPSU, and in fact again seized upon the notorious "Albanian question" and tried to use it for divisive and anti-Soviet purposes.

Albanian leaders, from the outset of their break with the CPSU and other sister parties, were both mouthpiece and champion for the splitting policy of Mao Tse-tung and his group. Their numerous statements and press reports abounded in harsh attacks against the CPSU and the Soviet government. Statements of Albanian leaders in defense of the "purity of Marxism-Leninism," and all their "arguments substantiating the independence" of their views on current, basic questions, were carbon copies of Peking.

The creation of the anti-Soviet alliance between Chinese and Albanian leaders and their joining into a single opportunist bloc directed against the CPSU was one of the first results of the divisive course of Peking leaders in the socialist camp and the world Communist movement. There can be no question that the splitters would have hesitated to range themselves so clearly and openly against the CPSU and the entire world Communist movement if they had not received the patronage and complete support of Peking. This support was material, as well as ideological, from the start. Even the first anti-Soviet statement by the splitters on the 1960 meeting of the Communist and Workers' Parties was paid for generously by Chinese leaders. This pay-off, disguised in false slogans of "international fraternal help," was subsequently used regularly.

For some time after the 1960 meeting Chinese leaders pretended objectivity, and "appealed to the CPSU and the Albanian Party of Labor to initiate a rapprochement" in the interests of unity. This was sheer hypocrisy. Actually, CCP leaders systematically urged the Albanians to widen the breach. The CC CCP did not appeal to leaders of the Albanian Party of Labor to seek improved relations with the CPSU or with other fraternal parties; quite the contrary. Chinese leaders did everything possible to encourage development of an anti-Soviet campaign in Albania. It is no accident that the bourgeois press wrote that Tirana was "Peking's mouthpiece," after the first statements of Albanian Party of Labor leaders attacking the CPSU and the Soviet Union.

The Maoists, at this point, still thought it impossible to openly declare their hostility toward the CPSU. They required, therefore, other organizations to slander our party. The feverish creation, by Peking, within the ranks of the world Communist movement of all sorts of splinter groups was a deliberate move. The more strident and scandalous the anti-CPSU abuse, the more filthy and cynical their anti-Soviet lies, the more support these groups found in Peking.

Leaders of the splinter groups were rewarded with the title of "great," and were called "solid Marxist-Leninists" in the Chinese press and in official statements. In each instance, Peking sent high-flown salutes, overblown with sanctimonious epithets and puerile flattery. The splitters, in turn, swore "always to be faithful" and "eternally grateful" to Mao Tse-tung for his "concern" and "support."

The leaders of the Communist Party of China, in a letter to the CC CPSU of April 7, 1962, urged it to take the initiative "to get together" with the Albanians. At the same time Chinese leaders made it clear that they desired to be present at this meeting to arbitrate Soviet-Albanian relations.

On May 31, 1962 the CC CPSU sent a new letter to the CC CCP. This letter contained a suitable rebuff to the unscrupulous maneuvers of the Chinese leadership. The CC CPSU once again emphasized the need to stop the process of backsliding into a new round of sharp debate and mutual recriminations, the need to rise above outstanding disagreements, and the need to strengthen the united front of the struggle against imperialism. The CC CCP had declared its readiness to take a new step along the road to overcoming outstanding disagreements and strengthening the unity of the two parties. Guided by these considerations, the CC CPSU had not taken up all questions raised in the Chinese letter of April 7, 1962, despite the fact that our party held other views on some of them. The CC CPSU did not feel it imperative to respond to all unfounded accusations by Peking, directly or indirectly. But it was emphasized that should the need arise in the future, the CC CPSU was prepared to make a detailed statement of its views on all questions raised by the CC CCP letter.

The CC CPSU did not limit itself to appeals for unity and solidarity. It stated that it was necessary to repulse jointly and publicly the more malicious attacks of hostile propaganda, and to take more effective measures in exchanging foreign policy information and coordinating actions by fraternal parties in international organizations. All of this was dictated by the sincere efforts of our party to end disagreements and misunderstandings, and by a desire to restore unity between the two Communist parties.

The new initiative of the CC CPSU posed a dilemma for Chinese party leaders: either proceed to normalization of relations with the CPSU, or hold to the old positions. And once again those leaders showed neither the courage nor the desire to choose the right road.

The 10th Plenary Session of the CC CCP, held at the end of September 1962, set the task of intensifying the class struggle internally, as well as on an international scale; the latter primarily aimed at intensification of the anti-Soviet campaign.

6. *New attacks by the Chinese leadership on the* *Marxist-Leninist parties*

The press in the PRC opened a virulent attack on the ideological positions of the CPSU, and on the whole of the world Communist and workers' movement, at the end of 1962. Occasions for this purpose were the congresses of the fraternal parties held at the time: the 8th Congress of the Bulgarian Communist Party, the 8th Congress of the Hungarian Socialist Workers' Party, the 10th Congress of the Italian Communist Party, and the 12th Congress of the Communist Party of Czechoslovakia.

Initially, official Chinese propaganda attempted to minimize the calling of these congresses. The press limited itself to laconic reports of the opening and closing of the congresses, to listing agendas and decisions. Summary reports on the congresses of the fraternal parties were not published, even in condensations.

At first the Chinese press was trying to hide from its own public the fact that the congresses of the fraternal parties subjected to severe criticism the splitting line of the leaders of the CCP. News was slanted to make it appear that these congresses were launching unilateral attacks against the Albanian Party of Labor, and that CCP leaders were its defenders against the danger of splitting. At the congresses of the Bulgarian Communist Party and Hungarian Socialist Workers' Party, the head of the Chinese delegation continued to repeat the formula that any critical statements directed at the Albanian Party of Labor "are in no way serious Marxist-Leninist approaches," and that the CCP, for its part, was devoting all its efforts to the cause of unity in the ranks of the international Communist movement.[16]

Chinese leaders, when hopes of hushing up the real course of events were unrealized, finally threw off the mask of "protectors" of the Albanian Party of Labor and openly rushed to attack the CPSU and the other Marxist-Leninist parties. This attack was launched by an editorial in *Jen Min Jihpao* on December 15, 1962, entitled "Workers of All Countries Unite, Oppose Our Common Enemy!"

Jen Min Jihpao, in initiating attacks against the CPSU and other fraternal parties, continued its hackneyed version of "self-defense" advanced by the leaders of the CCP. Under the circumstances, continued the article, "we have no alternative but to make the necessary reply" when "some . . . make public to the whole world their slanders and attacks against China." The CCP leadership, highlighting the question of "who was the first to begin," made a conscious effort to conceal the real reasons for their struggle against the CPSU and other fraternal parties.

It deliberately attempted to avoid discussion of the substance of questions raised at congresses of fraternal parties. The Maoists advanced the thesis that "an adverse current, opposed to Marxism-Leninism, opposed to the Communist Party of China," had appeared in the ranks of the international Communist movement. This thesis helped give the disagreements between the CCP and the international Communist movement the appearance of a split within the international Communist and workers' movement itself, simultaneously placing all parties who criticized the CCP leadership among the ranks of those composing the "adverse current," and proclaiming them to be the "common enemy of the workers of the world." Leaders of the CCP deliberately kept the true disposition of forces within the world Communist movement, and the unanimous condemnation of their splitting activities by practically all parties, from their people.

The December 15, 1962 article in *Jen Min Jihpao* attempted to "summarize" the congresses of the four fraternal parties. But the "summary" did not cite the importance of the congresses, and, in fact, tended to belittle the activities of the fraternal parties while defending the special course of the Chinese leaders. Almost 70 of the fraternal parties represented at the 12th Congress of the Communist Party of Czechoslovakia were falsely accused of being part of the "adverse current" in the world Communist movement simply because they had criticized the special course taken by CCP leaders and had unmasked their splitting activities.

The Chinese press, at the end of December 1962 and at the beginning of 1963, published a series of articles amounting to nothing less than gross, slanderous attacks against our party and against the other Marxist-Leninist parties, amounting to a public revision of the fundamental theses of the Declaration and the Statement of the Moscow Congresses of Communist and Workers' Parties held in 1957 and 1960.[17]

The Chinese press continually advanced arguments to prove its contention that it was possible to restore capitalist relations in the countries of victorious socialism. CCP leaders thus systematically prepared "theoretical" positions from which they could launch critical attacks against the socialist countries, and against those fraternal parties taking exception to their special views. The fact that imperialist propaganda utilized these positions on a massive scale for anti-Communist purposes is sufficient to show the nature of the writings of the Peking "theoreticians."

Thus the community of tasks of Chinese and imperialist propaganda machines in developing an ideological attack against the position of socialism, fabricating and disseminating anti-Soviet lies, was completely revealed. This community of tasks can be illustrated by the fact that as a result of activation of the disruptive ideological activities of Peking, representatives of the United States Information Agency in the countries of Southeast Asia began to cut back local personnel. Those discharged declared that the Americans treated them like "masters with a dog that was no longer able to bark louder than all the others." "They fired us," they said, "because we could not abuse the Soviet Union as loudly and as nastily as the Chinese leaders."

The obvious nature of the CCP leaders' splitting policy can be judged from its evaluation in capitalist countries. The US State Department in March 1962 sent NATO members a document on Sino-Soviet disagreements which pointed out:

> ... the Chinese are interpreting the interests of the Communist movement in terms of how best they apply to China. . . . A military alliance with the USSR makes sense to the Chinese only if it will help them to achieve their nationalist goals. . . . The Chinese will be no more inclined to put the interests of unity above their own interests as time goes on than they are at present.

The ideological conditioning of the Chinese population in the spirit of the divisive, anti-Soviet course of the CCP leaders was even further developed. Dignitaries of the CCP spoke to huge meetings at the end of December 1962 and the beginning of 1963. There was a joint meeting of delegates to the Peking trade union conference, the conference of the Peking Branch of the All-China Federation of Women, and the conference of people's committees of three Peking regions. This meeting, held on December 30, 1962, heard a bitter diatribe against our party.

Party and political training was subordinated to the task of indoctrinating the Chinese population in a spirit of anti-Sovietism. The exercises conducted within the system of party education were based on slanderous materials, depicting the Soviet people as "wholly and completely bourgeois," "grown fat and flabby," and as "having committed to oblivion the principles of proletarian internationalism."

The Peking splitters developed disruptive activities among representatives of fraternal parties working in Chinese organizations (radio, publishing, schools, and the like), among foreign students, and among members of foreign delegations visiting the People's Republic of China. The pro-rector of Peking University, in a December 30, 1962 speech to foreign specialists at the university, launched slanderous attacks against the policy of the Soviet Union, and attempted to persuade his listeners that the CPSU showed fear in the struggle with imperialism. Anti-Soviet materials purchased in capitalist countries, as well as similar materials printed in Peking, were made available to the foreign teachers at the university.

7. Frustration by Peking of CC CPSU proposals to cease open polemics

The CC CPSU, in light of the splitting activities by Peking leaders, attempted to halt public polemics. Our party, even under these conditions, continued its endeavors to turn the CCP to the path of solidarity and unity with the international Communist movement, and to the path of normalization and strengthening Sino-Soviet relations. †The Soviet side in a January 3, 1963 meeting between the CC CPSU and the Chinese Ambassador, Pan Zi-li, once again emphasized the fact that the CPSU was trying to restore the once friendly state of Sino-Soviet relations by all possible means.

Pravda, on January 7, 1963, published an appeal from the CC CPSU to strengthen the unity of the Communist movement for the triumph of peace and socialism. *Pravda* emphasized that disagreements between individual Communist parties on specific questions do not have deep roots in the social system of the socialist countries; they are without objective foundations, but rather are primarily subjective. "Consequently," wrote *Pravda,* "all the conditions exist for successfully overcoming these differences. One must proceed from the higher aims and interests of the Communist movement and seek ways of drawing closer together, ways of cooperation and unity."[18]

The chief delegate of the CC CPSU at the 6th Congress of the Socialist Unity Party of Germany on January 16, 1963 declared that "the Central Committee of our party is of the opinion that it now would be useful to discontinue polemics between Communist parties and criticism of other parties within our own parties. . . ."[19] This proposal, supported by many Marxist-Leninist parties, could have served as a starting point for gradual resumption of normal relations between the CCP, the CPSU, and other fraternal parties.

But the speech of the CCP representative to this same congress on January 18, 1963 demonstrated disinterest in halting public polemics. The head of the delegation of the CCP stuck to its old positions and repeated attacks against the CPSU on questions causing disagreement, including assessment of the Caribbean crisis, the Sino-Indian border conflict, and others. The Chinese representative's speech confirmed that leaders of the CCP wanted to manipulate events so as to guard themselves against criticism, at the same time continuing their splitting activities and their earlier hit-and-run attacks against the CPSU and other Marxist-Leninist parties.

Chinese leaders reinforced their negative reaction to the proposal for discontinuing public polemics in an editorial appearing in *Jen Min Jihpao* on January 27, 1963. This editorial was the first direct slanderous attack against the leadership of our party to appear in the official Chinese press, and it rejected the proposal of the CC CPSU supported by fraternal parties.

The CPSU has never questioned the utility of discussions among Communists and like-minded persons. Without comparison of different opinions and points of view there can be no successful development of the revolutionary movement. But there are no disagreements, no resentments of behavior of a particular party which justify methods of struggle detrimental to the interests of the international Communist movement. The more broadly a party understands goals and tasks of the international working class, the more energy should be expended to settle disagreements quietly, no matter how serious, thus avoiding interference with positive work and preventing disorganization of revolutionary activities of the international working class.

At the same time, the CPSU holds firmly to the view that unity of the international Communist movement cannot be achieved by concessions and compromises on questions of principle. Only a consistent and flexible execution of the general line, based on principles of Marxism-Leninism, of proletarian internationalism, can ensure genuine solidarity.

The correctness of theoretical positions of the Communist parties is verifiable through their practical activities. The CPSU is a firm believer in the admonitions of V. I. Lenin, who taught that disagreements between political parties "usually can be resolved not only by controversy over principles, but by the development of political life itself, and it probably is more correct to say not so much by the former as by the latter."[20]

The CC CPSU adopted these principles as a point of departure for a letter to CCP leaders of February 21, 1963, again proposing that public polemics be discontinued.

Open, increasingly aggravating polemics are shaking the unity of fraternal parties and are seriously damaging our common interests. Disputes which have arisen within the ranks of the international Communist movement obstruct the successful struggle against imperialism, weaken the effort of the socialist countries in the international arena, and adversely affect the activities of fraternal parties, particularly those in the capitalist countries in which the internal political situations are complex.[21]

Chinese leaders responded to this letter saying they definitely favored its proposal concerning discontinuance of public polemics. At the same time, they expressed indifference over consequences the development of such polemics could have within the international Communist movement, and, in fact, asserted these consequences were not very important. CCP leaders considered halting polemics a temporary phenomenon, a type of "truce." While declaring their supposedly positive attitude toward the Soviet proposal, CCP leaders were, in fact, preparing a new round of attacks against the CPSU and other Marxist-Leninist parties.

Five days after the Soviet appeal for cessation of polemics, *Jen Min Jihpao* printed a filthy anti-Soviet article from the Albanian newspaper *Zeri i Popullit*. This was followed by a long series of controversial articles, this time written by the Chinese, attacking the general line of the Marxist-Leninist parties.

The CC CCP replied to the Soviet Central Committee letter on March 9, 1963. It spewed forth another segment of anti-Marxist, splitting ideas. Chinese leaders hypocritically declared their desire to discontinue public polemics. But this declaration was designed purely and simply to delude the CPSU and other fraternal parties. This is indicated by the fact that the Chinese leaders stubbornly pressed for publication of secret correspondence between the CCP and the CPSU, an event which could only lead to continuation of public polemics. Nevertheless, because of the CC CCP's insistence, the February 21 letter of the CC CPSU and the subsequent Chinese response of March 9 were published in China and the USSR on March 14, 1963.[22]

CCP leaders, in insisting on publication of the letters, counted on a propaganda victory. Actually, the letter from the CC CPSU had not been written for publication, so did not contain detailed explanations of positions held by our party on questions in dispute. But the Chinese letter had been written for publication and its content was such as to pervert the line of the CPSU and to present their own position in glamorized form. However, Communists all over the world were able very readily to distinguish the true from the false.

The press and radio in the PRC continued to attack the Marxist-Leninist parties on an ever-increasing scale, even after March 9, 1963.

Slanderous materials produced by the CCP were disseminated abroad in almost all main languages of the world. These materials were advertised as the "highest truth" of Marxism-Leninism.

The promotion of such materials became one of the most important tasks of PRC ambassadors and branches of the Hsinhua Agency abroad. These activities evoked indignation from Communist parties and in progressive society.

Chinese embassies in developing countries actively engaged in spreading propaganda. Bookstores in Ceylon, India, and Indonesia, and in a number of other countries, were flooded with literature containing vicious attacks against the CPSU and the other Marxist-Leninist parties, through the help of Chinese representatives.

In Europe, too, the CCP intensified its divisive propaganda. In Italy, for example, Maoists used the Italy-China Association, which published a magazine of the same title, to spread criticism of the political line of the Italian Communist Party, and propaganda promoting anti-Marxist views of a group of CCP leaders.

A special organization was established within the government of the PRC to publish and distribute Chinese splitting literature in foreign languages. Special display cases were set up in many Chinese cities which foreigners tended to frequent (in hotels, stations, airports). These contained articles in various languages and bore such inscriptions under them as "Help Yourself," "Free," and the like. Similar displays were set up at the international fair in Kweichow (Canton) which is designed to attract representatives of capitalist commercial firms.

8. The Sino-Soviet meeting of July 1963

The CC CPSU in its letter of February 21, 1963 took the initiative in arranging a bilateral meeting between high level representatives of the CPSU and the CCP, during which "it would be possible to take up, point by point, all the major questions of interest to both parties." "Our parties," emphasized the CC CPSU, "are duty bound to find a way out of the existing situation and courageously and resolutely sweep away that which obstructs our friendship."

In their response of March 9, Chinese leaders formally agreed to the meeting, but at the same time deliberately attempted to interfere with successful preparation for the meeting through subsequent intensification of anti-Soviet attacks.

In their letter, CCP leaders had already departed from the previous formulation, whereby differences between the CPSU and the CCP "can be depicted, figuratively at least, as the relationship between one finger and the other nine," that is, that there are differences on particular, individual questions, but both parties are essentially one. They stated: "We ought to face the fact that at present there are serious differences in the international Communist movement on a series of important questions of principle." The CCP letter particularly emphasized the thesis that "if we cannot finish our discussions in one session, several should be held."[23] All the above indicates that Chinese leaders had no intention of obtaining the maximum in results from the forthcoming meeting, and in fact were preparing in advance the ground for failure.

On March 30, 1963 the CC CPSU sent another letter to the CC CCP. This letter contained a concrete suggestion for a bilateral meeting, proposing it begin on May 15, 1963. It further presented views on the questions that should be discussed. The CC CPSU emphasized that it was proposing this meeting "not in order to aggravate the dispute but in order to reach a mutual understanding on major problems that have arisen in the international Communist movement."[24]

It further expressed its resolve to firmly and consistently uphold the platform of the world Communist movement, the general line of which found expression in the declaration and statement of the Moscow conferences of the Marxist-Leninist parties. In complete accordance with these program documents, the CC CPSU set forth its views on major questions of the day and on strategy and tactics of the international Communist movement. It appealed to the CC CCP to overcome existing differences by indulging in a comradely exchange of views, and by seeking ways to strengthen the unity of all fraternal parties and Sino-Soviet friendship and cooperation.

But CCP leaders continued to drag out the date for the organization of the meeting. It was not until May 9, 1963, more than a month after receipt of the CC CPSU letter, that Chou En-lai advised the Soviet Ambassador that the CC CCP had decided to send a delegation to Moscow for the meeting. Chinese leaders had thus failed to support the initiative of the CC CPSU for a top echelon bilateral meeting. They also suggested that the date for the meeting be set back to between June 11 and 20, clearly attempting to play for time to continue splitting actions.

After a further exchange of views the meeting was set for July 5, 1963. Before the meeting took place, on June 14, 1963, CCP leaders published a document with the pretentious title of "A Proposed General Line for the International Communist Movement" (the so-called 25 points). This document extended even further their previous positions on current questions of principle. Hypocritically referring to the verity of the Declaration of 1957 and the Statement of 1960, these leaders nonetheless made it clear that they were not satisfied with the strategic line derived from international meetings of Communist parties and raised the question of replacing this line with their own mistaken platform. Never in the history of the international Communist movement had there been a case of such unparalleled presumption by one party as the arbitrary formulation of a "general line" for the entire movement, startlingly clear evidence of the hegemonic pretensions of the Maoists.

The question of need to formulate a general line for the Communist movement in and of itself was an indication of digression by CCP leaders from the Declaration of 1957 and the Statement of 1960. The Communist movement already had its general line, one developed by collective efforts of all Communist parties.

During the meeting CCP representatives attempted to prove that they had the right to formulate their special "general line" for the international Communist movement, saying it could do so because the CC CPSU, in its letter of March 30, 1963, allegedly had first set down "its" general line.

However, Chinese nationalists completely exposed themselves by such statements. Anyone who reads the CC CPSU letter of March 30, 1963 with care and without bias will note the fact that the CPSU made no attempt whatsoever to propose anything resembling its own general line; instead it set forth, almost verbatim, the provisions of the 1957 Declaration and the 1960 Statement on root questions of modern world development. Articles written and published by CCP leaders at the end of 1962 and early in 1963 had so confused the major question of principles of world development and had so arbitrarily interpreted documents from international Communist forums that the CC CPSU considered it desirable to remind them of basic provisions of the Declaration and Statement. Therefore the CCP leaders in formulating their special course opposing the series of basic questions contained in the CC CPSU's letters simply established their platform in opposition to the general line of the international Communist movement itself.

The CC CCP letter of June 14, 1963 left no doubt that the Chinese leaders were holding stubbornly to the course of shaking the unity of the world Communist movement, and of further exacerbating Sino-Soviet interparty and intergovernmental relations. Recognizing the gravity of this, the CC CPSU felt it necessary to call the attention of its June plenary session to the splitting tactics of CCP leaders. On June 21, the CC CPSU plenum adopted a resolution "On the Forthcoming Meeting of Representatives of the Central Committee of the Communist

Party of the Soviet Union with Representatives of the Central Committee of the Communist Party of China," unanimously approving the political actions of the Presidium of the CC CPSU in its interrelations with the CC CCP.[25]

The plenum instructed the Presidium that during its forthcoming meeting with CC CCP representatives it hold firmly to the line adopted by our party at the 20th, 21st, and 22nd CPSU congresses and at the Moscow conferences of the Communist parties, to explain and defend the CPSU position on basic questions of principle concerning the world Communist and workers' movement, and also on problems of Communist construction in the USSR.

The CC CCP letter of June 14, 1963 clearly was designed to worsen an already unfavorable situation for holding the Sino-Soviet meeting. Recognizing this, the CC CPSU deemed its immediate publication undesirable because "that would lead to a further exacerbation of polemics, would not correspond to understandings already arrived at, but would in fact contradict the views of the fraternal parties with respect to this question."[26]

However, Chinese propaganda portrayed the CC CPSU's concern for unity as the intention to "hide" from Communists and the Soviet people views of Chinese leaders. Mistaking the self-restraint of the CC CPSU for weakness, Mao Tse-tung and his clique, completely disregarding standards of friendly relations between socialist countries, began the unlawful distribution of the CC CCP letter of June 14, 1963, printed for mass circulation in the Russian language, in Moscow and other Soviet cities. Embassy staffers delivered the text to different institutions in Moscow, and in other cities mailed it out and distributed it to private apartments.

The Ministry of Foreign Affairs of the USSR, in an effort to avoid a further exacerbation of relations, on June 17, 1963 made verbal representations to the Ambassador of the PRC, insisting that the Chinese Embassy cease actions clearly incompatible with the status and functions of diplomatic representatives. The Chinese did not draw the proper conclusions, however. On June 24, 1963 the USSR Ministry of Foreign Affairs once again advised the Ambassador of the PRC that such actions on the part of Embassy personnel, and other Chinese citizens residing in the USSR, could only be considered a violation of Soviet sovereignty and a gross disregard for USSR rules and orders established for diplomatic representatives and foreign citizens. Despite all these warnings the distribution of anti-Soviet literature continued and in fact became more widespread. Matters reached the point where Chinese crews aboard the Moscow-Peking train tossed the Russian text of the letter out car windows in railroad stations. The letter was broadcast over the radio when the train stopped. When Soviet people politely pointed out to Chinese citizens the unacceptability of such action, the latter replied that "they would not ask anyone's permission on that score."

Such were the circumstances leading to the note sent by the USSR Ministry of Foreign Affairs to the PRC Ambassador on June 27, 1963, demanding immediate cessation of the unprecedented practice of illegal distribution of the CCP letter. The note further declared *persona non grata* three embassy employees and two other Chinese citizens most brazenly engaged in activities contradictory to generally accepted relations between socialist states and countries in general, who had, by their actions, grossly violated Soviet sovereignty.

Instead of drawing the obvious conclusion from these warnings and taking steps favorable to the conduct of a Sino-Soviet meeting, CCP leaders proceeded further to exacerbate relations. Chinese citizens expelled from the USSR for distributing anti-Soviet literature were given a grand welcome in Peking on June 30, 1963. People who had violated Sino-Soviet friendship were greeted in Peking almost as if they were national heroes.

That same day the Hsinhua Agency published a statement by a representative of the PRC Ministry of Foreign Affairs regarding the June 27 note of the Soviet Ministry of Foreign Affairs to the Chinese Embassy in Moscow, deliberately distorting the facts and attempting to defend the illegal actions of Chinese citizens. The representative of the PRC Ministry of Foreign Affairs falsely asserted that Soviet organizations and personnel in China were supposedly engaging in similar activities.

The Soviet press on July 4, 1963 published a communiqué "At the Ministry of Foreign Affairs of the USSR," which convincingly refuted the conjecture of the representative of the Ministry of Foreign Affairs of the PRC.[27]

CCP leaders, putting pressure to bear as the date for the bilateral meeting approached, issued a statement on July 1, 1963 in which they attempted again to display falsely the motives impelling the CC CPSU to call undesirable the publication of the CC CCP's June 14, 1963 letter.

The CC CPSU decisively rejected this calumny in its statement of July 4, 1963.[28] Since the Chinese leaders showed no interest in stopping the polemics, and, in fact, continued widespread distribution of their letter of June 14, 1963, the CC CPSU decided in due course to print an answer to this letter in the interest of properly illuminating disputed questions as well as defending Marxism-Leninism.

On July 4 the CC CPSU listed the composition of delegates from our party to the bilateral talks and pointed out that the Soviet delegation would attempt to reach the best mutual understanding on major questions of present world development and to create a favorable atmosphere for preparation and convocation of the International Conference of Communist and Workers' Parties. The meeting began in Moscow on July 5, 1963.

While the meeting was in progress, the Chinese took a series of steps designed to complicate the talks. A mass rally was organized in Peking on July 7, two days after the meeting began. Officials, in speeches to the crowd, supported the provocations of Chinese Embassy staffers in Moscow and Chinese graduate students expelled from the USSR for illegal distribution of anti-Soviet materials. Igniting a hostile attitude toward the USSR, Chinese officials continually attempted to prove their right to violate the sovereignty of our state and the established norms of international relations.

The CC CPSU on July 9 issued a new statement, pointing out the danger of such actions on the part of Chinese leaders to the cause of strengthening Sino-Soviet friendship. The statement also emphasized the fact that:

> ... despite these unfriendly actions, the Communist Party of the Soviet Union will in the future do everything it possibly can not to deepen disagreements that already exist, and in fact will do everything it possibly can to surmount the difficulties arising in the relations between the Communist Party of China and the Communist Party of the Soviet Union, and with the other Marxist-Leninist parties.

The Chinese leaders continued to put new obstacles in the path of the normalization of Sino-Soviet relations. In a statement made on July 10, 1963, the CC CCP unconditionally approved the behavior of the Chinese citizens who had been expelled from the USSR for the distribution of anti-Soviet literature, and in effect tried to confer upon themselves the right to interfere in the internal affairs of the Soviet Union. Following this, on July 13, *Jen Min Jihpao* published an editorial that slanderously attacked the CPSU and distorted the true reasons for the exacerbation of Sino-Soviet relations.

The avowedly unfriendly actions on the part of CCP leaders, their persistent attempts to distort the position of our party, prompted the CC CPSU to publish the CC CCP's letter of June 14, 1963, and to give it the warranted assessment. This was done on July 14, 1963, simultaneously releasing an Open Letter to party organizations and to all Communists in the Soviet Union.[29]

The open letter provided a true picture of Sino-Soviet relations and pointed out just who was responsible for difficulties within the world Communist movement. At the same time, this document was a sincere attempt to normalize Sino-Soviet relations, and to strengthen the solidarity of all revolutionary forces. The open letter stated:

> [The CC CPSU] declares to the party, to all of the Soviet people, with all sincerity that we have done and will continue to do everything within our power to strengthen unity with the Communist Party of China, to unite the world Communist movement under the bannner of Lenin, to unite the countries of the world system of socialism, to actively assist all people struggling against colonialism, to strengthen the cause of peace and the victory of the great ideals of Communism all over the earth.

This letter met with complete and unanimous approval by Marxist-Leninist parties of the world.

Strategic designs of the anti-Soviet elements in the CCP envisaged an escalation of the political struggle against the Soviet Union. Prospects of reaching any sort of understanding between the CCP and the CPSU therefore were feared by the Maoists. Peking leaders continued to provoke disagreements in order to wreck normalization of Sino-Soviet relations. Nevertheless, despite the tense situation under which the Sino-Soviet meeting was conducted, the CC CPSU did everything possible to see that the meeting served to overcome disagreements between the two parties.

However, CCP leaders came to the meeting with different intentions. The Chinese delegation, following instructions from Peking, used the July talks to exacerbate further the disagreements, to expand the circle of disputable problems, to create new obstacles along the road to an improvement in Sino-Soviet relations. CCP representatives subjected domestic and foreign policies of our party, as well as the party program, to rude and unfounded attacks.

The Soviet delegation brought to the talks concrete proposals, the purpose of which was to eliminate differences and to develop cooperation between the USSR and the PRC in all areas. They proposed that the question of expanding trade, scientific and technical cooperation, and other forms of economic ties between the two countries be explored, expressed the opinion that prospects for long-term economic development and cooperation be discussed since conclusion of a long-term agreement would be in the interests of both countries, and suggested that information on questions of trade and foreign exchange policies in world markets be exchanged.

The Chinese delegation failed to respond to any of these proposals.

On July 20, 1963, upon insistence of the CCP, talks were broken off without yielding positive results of any kind. The joint communiqué on the meeting said:

> During the meeting both sides set forth their views and positions on a great many important questions of principle concerning contemporary world development, the international Communist movement, and Sino-Soviet relations.
>
> At the suggestion of the delegation of the Communist Party of China it was agreed that the delegations discontinue their efforts at this time; the meeting would be continued at a later date. The place and the time for continuation of a meeting will be by agreement upon further consultations between the Central Committee of the Communist Party of the Soviet Union and the Central Committee of the Communist Party of China.[30]

The CC CPSU believed it imperative to avoid any further exacerbation of Sino-Soviet relations during this break in the talks. To this end, the Soviet side once again proposed to halt publication of articles, statements, and materials, as well as translations of communications containing mutual criticism and at the same time to do everything possible to improve the atmosphere for the resumption of the bilateral meeting and preparations for the international conference of representatives of Communist and Workers' Parties.

9. Aggravation of Sino-Soviet interstate relations

As they began their attacks against the ideological position of the CPSU, CCP leaders carried ideological differences with our party into Sino-Soviet intergovernmental relations more and more frequently. They began to curtail cooperation with the USSR in all main directions using the slogan "rely on own efforts" to attempt to deny to the Chinese people the cleansing ideas of the CPSU.

In 1960 Chinese organizations for political reasons failed to inaugurate many plants built and readied with Soviet assistance.

†Beginning in the second half of 1960, conditions in the PRC rendered it impossible to make a systematic study of its scientific and technical achievements and of its experience in economic construction. †The staff of the Counsellor of the Soviet Embassy for economic

questions was refused subscriptions to 20 industrial, agricultural, and scientific and technical journals, as well as to 209 titles of periodical publications on science and engineering, economics and finance. All had been withdrawn from sale. Members of the staffs of Soviet institutes in Peking for all practical purposes were deprived of using Chinese public libraries.

In 1960, the Chinese by their provocative actions forced Soviet realization of the need to withdraw Soviet specialists from the PRC. The decision was reached under pressure of circumstances all artificially created by the Maoists.

The first groups of Soviet specialists had been sent to China upon request of the CC CCP in August 1949. The number of Soviet specialists increased as Soviet-Chinese cooperation expanded, and by August 1960 over 1,600 people were working in the PRC. During the period of the "great leap," which was accompanied by a sharp intensification of conceit and nationalist arrogance, a scornful attitude toward Soviet experience became increasingly apparent in China. Facts indicating that the Chinese did not trust Soviet specialists appeared more and more frequently.

Specific incidents occurred where neither plant directors, ministry and department heads, nor CCP leaders paid attention to well-founded recommendations of Soviet specialists. This position was none other than a calculated attempt to discredit Soviet technical experience, and to cast doubt on Soviet purposes for such assistance.

The question of the Soviet specialists took on strictly political overtones. Soviet specialists, themselves, were looked upon suspiciously; they were shadowed; their personal belongings were searched; correspondence addressed to them was inspected.

Moreover, beginning in the spring of 1960, Chinese organizations attempted ideological brainwashing of Soviet specialists in an effort to turn them against the policies of our party. The Soviet side repeatedly drew attention to these facts and persistently requested that normal working conditions be provided for our specialists. However, Chinese authorities continued their past policies.

Subsequent events confirmed the fact that Chinese leaders, well on the road to anti-Sovietism, needed "arguments" and "pretexts" to incite within the party and among the people hostile feelings to the USSR. The tremendous losses inflicted on the national interests of the Chinese people and on the economy of the PRC through wrecking fraternal cooperation between the USSR and China were the least of their worries.

Provocations of the Maoists made further stay of Soviet specialists in China impossible. On July 16, 1960, the Ministry of Foreign Affairs of the PRC received a note stating that our specialists sent to work in China were being recalled. In arriving at this decision the Soviet government considered the fact that during the years of people's authority in the PRC their national cadres had increased with a large number of them trained in higher institutions of learning and plants in the USSR. Actually, Soviet leaders beginning in 1958 and in succeeding years repeatedly raised the question of substantially reducing the number of Soviet specialists, who could be replaced successfully by young Chinese cadres educated in the USSR. As events were to show, the CCP deliberately turned down these proposals.

Chinese leaders formally opposed the recall of Soviet specialists, but in fact did nothing constructive to settle problems. The fact that the reply to the Soviet note recalling the specialists was not received by the Soviet Embassy in the PRC until July 31 is indicative. The response from the PRC Ministry of Foreign Affairs was written with one purpose, that of misleading public opinion within the country, as well as abroad, thus establishing China as the "injured" party. All norms of international relations notwithstanding, Chinese authorities officially spoke of their "rights," to carry on further political work among the Soviet people, the content of which was clearly anti-Soviet in nature.

The assertion by Chinese leaders that the recall of Soviet specialists allegedly served the purpose of causing failures in the economy of the PRC and forcing review of the plan for the development of the country's national economy was totally groundless. It is known that the plan for industry in the PRC for the second quarter of 1960 was fulfilled by less than 90 percent overall. Consequently, the failure to meet plans occurred long before the Soviet specialists were recalled. The failure was the direct consequence of the "three red banners" policy.*

The Soviet Union repeatedly expressed readiness to return Soviet specialists to the PRC provided normal working conditions were created. This was communicated in particular to the Chinese delegation which came to Moscow in November 1960 in connection with the meeting of Communist and Workers' Parties, to the CC CCP delegation at the CPSU 22nd Congress in October 1961, to the CCP delegation at the July 1963 meeting, and in a CC CPSU letter of November 29, 1963 to the CC CCP. Chinese leaders failed to take advantage of any such proposals.

* Translator's note: the People's Communes, the General Line, and the Great Leap Forward.

In 1960 the Chinese side for the first time in 11 years failed to meet its obligations under the protocol on mutual deliveries of commodities by a large sum (310 million rubles), and there were many commodities for which no contracts of any description were drawn. Chinese foreign trade organizations filled not a single contractual obligation in 1960. They failed also to meet the minimum schedule for commodity shipments submitted to our trade representative by the PRC Ministry of Foreign Trade. The result was that Sino-Soviet trade turnover decreased 19 percent as compared with 1959; USSR exports fell 14 percent, imports 23 percent. The Chinese side took the initiative in deferring indefinitely the conclusion of a long-term trade agreement between the USSR and the PRC.

†Beginning in the third quarter of 1960, representatives of Soviet supply organizations were forbidden entrance to plants equipped with our machinery, causing difficulties in installation of Soviet equipment. In August 1960 Chinese organizations refused to allow Soviet acceptance and inspection personnel to visit plants producing commodities for our country, with the result that there was a sharp deterioration in the quality of such commodities. All such actions disrupted the manner in which trade relations had been carried on for so many years between the USSR and the PRC, a practice originally established at the behest of the Chinese.

The Chinese government, in a statement of October 31, 1960, demanded that there be a sharp curtailment in all previously concluded agreements and protocols on economic, scientific, and technical cooperation between the two sides. The Chinese side refused to meet its 1960 obligations for commodity deliveries to the Soviet Union as part of a review of the plan for the national economy, supposedly caused "by serious natural calamities and recall of Soviet specialists from the People's Republic of China."

The Soviet government rejected Chinese accusations as far-fetched and unfounded. The statement made by the Ministry of Foreign Trade of the USSR on December 17, 1960 contained an extensive reply to questions raised, and pointed out the need to build trade and economic relations between the USSR and the PRC on the basis of friendship and fraternal cooperation.

Chinese leaders used the next year, 1961, for a series of further steps to curtail Sino-Soviet economic, scientific and technical, and cultural cooperation. Talks on economic, scientific, and technical cooperation continuing from February to June 1961 concluded with the signing of an agreement on June 19. The Chinese representatives, completely disregarding the interests of their own people, refused further assistance from the Soviet Union in construction of 89 industrial plants and 35 other projects worth 1.1 billion rubles. The only obligations undertaken by the Soviet Union for the period 1961–1967 involved providing the PRC with technical assistance in building 66 projects of importance for development of civilian and particularly military industry. Agreement also was reached on Soviet technical assistance in the building of new projects (a gas pipeline, a semiconductor plant, and others). The result was a fivefold reduction in deliveries of complete sets of equipment from the USSR to the PRC in 1961, as compared with 1960.[31]

During the talks held between February and June 1961, Chinese representatives decided it was pointless to base curtailment in economic cooperation with the USSR "on recall of Soviet specialists," apparently aware of the absurdity of this explanation. In arguing their proposals, they pointed out the following reasons:

> First, thanks to the help given China by the Soviet Union, there have been built the preliminary bases for a modern industry and technology, so future construction and planning of most projects will rely on our own efforts because we want to ease the strain on the USSR with respect to aid to China. But we still will have to turn to the USSR for help in the furture on those projects we cannot plan, build, and equip by ourselves.
>
> Second, the Central Committee of the Communist Party of China, and the Chinese government, have recognized the need to concentrate our efforts on the construction of the most important projects, cutting back on the total number of capital construction projects, and on projects of no urgency, in order to better accord with the principles of the building of socialism in the People's Republic of China, "better, more, faster, cheaper." Scales of construction in the future also will be large and the rates of production high.
>
> Third, as a result of the natural calamities that have been experienced in agriculture over the last two years we have been in definite difficulties with our balance of payments, so we hope that by cutting back on the number of projects being built with the assistance of the Soviet Union we will be able to create conditions that will be more favorable for cooperation between our countries.[32]

This explanation appeared quite plausible and furthermore did not preclude future development of Sino-Soviet economic ties. The Soviet government could not refute arguments advanced by PRC leaders, who, in fact, were in a difficult position. The communiqué issued pointed out efforts of both sides to continue mutual cooperation. This was done on Soviet initiative. The communiqué stated that:

> Both sides presented summaries of the work that has been done over the last several years and are of the opinion that economic and scientific and

technical cooperation between the USSR and People's Republic of China, based on the principles of proletarian internationalism, equality of rights, and fraternal mutual assistance has been fruitful.[33]

But within two months of the signing of the June agreement, on August 15, the Chinese government announced a new cutback in deliveries of equipment from the USSR, attributed as previously to difficulties encountered by the PRC. The CC CPSU and the Soviet government once again demonstrated their understanding and bowed to Chinese wishes by deferring deliveries of complete sets of equipment to the PRC despite the fact that a good part (worth tens of millions of rubles) of the equipment was already in production or had been ordered in third countries, and was useless to the national economy of the Soviet Union.

Even this was not the end; at the beginning of December 1961 the Chinese announced total refusal to import complete sets of equipment from the USSR in 1962–1963. Thus, in less than six months, the PRC government unilaterally changed three times conditions of agreements and contracts, disregarding losses to Soviet plants filling Chinese orders.

It was quite apparent that the major reason for action on the part of the PRC government was not economic difficulties but political considerations stemming from the general line followed by CCP leaders to exacerbate Sino-Soviet relations. This was the only way to conceal the real reasons for the decision on the part of the Chinese government to lay up for two years all industrial plants under construction with the technical assistance of the Soviet Union, regardless of the state of completion and of how much equipment had been delivered.

Just what was behind the purpose of this anti-Soviet "operation" in the CCP was revealed later. "Tours" of Chinese, and even foreigners, were organized to the uncompleted construction sites in order to prove that the Soviet Union had "betrayed" China, that it had tried by "economic pressure" to influence the ideological position of the CCP. Organizers of these provocations were aware of the fact that it would be difficult for them to be caught in a lie because all questions of Sino-Soviet economic cooperation were handled through secret intergovernmental channels. Using such dirty tactics Peking leaders fabricated the myth that the Soviet Union was responsible for the lamentable state of the economy of the PRC, and for the famine and disaster which befell the Chinese people.

The agreement of June 19, 1961 envisaged the possibility of Soviet engineering and technical workers being sent to China. Despite the tremendous need of many Chinese organizations for technical assistance, and despite repeated statements of Chinese representatives concerning "losses" supposedly suffered by China as a result of the recall of Soviet specialists, the government of the PRC forwarded only two such requests in all of 1961; one for four specialists to assist in the installation of the equipment in the Sanmenhsia hydroelectric plant, and one for seven specialists to instruct in the piloting of aircraft used in agriculture. Both requests were granted.

There was a sharp cutback in Soviet-Chinese scientific and technical cooperation as well in 1960–1961, and this too must be blamed on the Chinese leaders. It is known that scientific and technical cooperation between the USSR and the PRC, which had undergone intensive development in preceding years, actually amounted to cost-free assistance by the Soviet Union. Here is manifested the genuinely internationalistic relationship between the Soviet Union and the PRC, which was just starting along the road to industrial development.

However, in October 1960, the Chinese unexpectedly suggested that earlier effective Sino-Soviet agreements on scientific and technical cooperation be reviewed, and that all obligations under earlier agreements be canceled. The result was, in June 1961, that two agreements replacing the seven already in effect were signed: the intergovernmental agreement of June 19, 1961 and the agreement between the academies of sciences of the two countries of June 21, 1961.

The review precipitated a sharp cutback in obligations undertaken by the parties; this was done upon insistence of Chinese authorities.

The Chinese evinced interest in obtaining from the USSR secret data on different aspects of the latest technologies, primarily defense. At the same time, Chinese organizations evaded exchange of experience with the USSR in those areas of science and technology in which they had advanced. They refused, for example, to engage in joint tests of Soviet models of equipment, apparatus, instruments, and materials under tropical conditions, to acquaint Soviet specialists with their experience in cultivation of chlorella algae under field conditions, or to continue work of the joint paleontological expedition in China.

Foreign trade was not exempt from the same Chinese line. The protocol signed on April 7, 1961 set the volume of exchanges for 1961 at 789 million rubles, that is, a reduction of 47 percent in the turnover that actually had taken place in 1960. This included a reduction of 63 percent in exports and 33 percent in imports. Even this level was not reached. In November 1961 the Ministry of Foreign Trade of the PRC announced that the Chinese side was unable to meet its obligations for deliveries in

1961 of certain commodities included in the protocol. Overall, the PRC failed to meet commodity deliveries to the Soviet Union by 43 million rubles.

The question of debt owed the Soviet Union by the PRC as a result of 1960 trading operations, and attributable to the "great natural calamities that had befallen agriculture in the People's Republic of China," also was discussed during Soviet-Chinese trade talks.[34] This debt amounted to 288 million rubles. The Soviet Union, proceeding from principles of proletarian internationalism and in the interest of Soviet-Chinese friendship, was quite understanding and agreed to the PRC request for a five-year extension of payments without extra interest charges.

The Chinese side, as noted in the communiqué:

> . . . accepted with appreciation the proposal of the Soviet Union concerning the delivery to the People's Republic of China of 500,000 tons of sugar on credit prior to the end of August of this year, to be repaid during the period 1964–1967 without extra interest charges.

Recognizing the difficult food situation in the PRC, the Soviet side released the Chinese from deliveries of food products in 1961 remaining due from 1960, and also refused purchase in the PRC of virtually all food products that had been traditional items of Chinese export to the USSR prior to 1961. Our country also provided the PRC with aid in the form of 300,000 tons of grain and flour on credit in that country's difficult spring and summer months. The Soviet Union agreed to buy from the PRC 1,000 tons of silver and to pay for it in convertible currency.

The trend toward curtailment in cultural cooperation with the USSR by the Chinese side became particularly noticeable in the second half of 1960. Chinese purchases of Soviet motion pictures fell. Chinese organizations in 1960 rejected 19 films suggested by the Soviet side, including "Ballad for a Soldier," "Lullaby," and others. Characteristic changes occurred as well in the field of book exchanges. Chinese orders for Soviet literature fell by 65 percent in the third quarter of 1960, and orders for political literature virtually ceased. Propaganda and publicity about Soviet books diminished. Even such books as *The Biography of V. I. Lenin* were withdrawn from sale.

At the beginning of 1961 the Soviet side persisted in its efforts to end this curtailment of cultural ties between the PRC and the USSR. A rather broad plan for Sino-Soviet cultural cooperation was signed

February 4, 1961. It envisaged exchanges of tours by artistic groups and soloists, the organization of motion picture film festivals and demonstrations, exchange of radio and television transmissions, Soviet and Chinese music weeks, and creative meetings of writers, musicians, cinematographers, and other cultural leaders. One specific result of this plan was the Exhibit of the Achievements of the Soviet Union in the Study of Space, which opened in China.[35] On June 21, 1961, the Academies of Science of the USSR and China signed a new five-year agreement on scientific cooperation to expand joint research in the most important branches of knowledge.

Nevertheless, the scope of cultural cooperation between China and the USSR in 1961 dropped to the lowest level since the inception of the PRC. By Chinese initiative sections on cooperation in the fields of printing and publishing, public health and journalism, and on direct contacts between Soviet and Chinese cultural institutes were excluded from plans for cultural ties. Curtailment of cooperation in such fields as cinema, radio, television, higher education, and education in general was particularly drastic.

Gradually Peking severed cultural ties with our country. One example was the severance of Sino-Soviet cooperation in radio broadcasting and television. Under the agreement of May 25, 1961 because of urgent Chinese requests the number of Soviet half-hour broadcasts carried by Chinese radio dropped from 7 to 3 a week. After October 1961 the Chinese side, violating the agreement, unilaterally removed them from its programs.

The unfriendly position of the Chinese leaders was even more obvious by their attitudes toward such worldwide historical events as man's first flight in space, accomplished by the USSR on April 12, 1961. Attempting to belittle the importance of this outstanding Soviet achievement, CCP leaders did not even bother to congratulate the CC CPSU or the Soviet government on the flight made by Yu. A. Gagarin.

After 1960, when Chinese leaders openly embarked on their anti-Soviet course, they persistently shied away from high level contacts along party and state lines. In 1961, under pretext of economic difficulties, they postponed the visit to the PRC by the Chairman of the Presidium of the Supreme Soviet of the USSR, despite his having been officially invited by the Chairman of the PRC in December 1960. Yet these same difficulties did not prevent trips to the PRC in 1961 by the King of Nepal, the Queen of Belgium, Britain's Field Marshal Montgomery, and statesmen from other countries.

The curtailment of economic and cultural cooperation with the

USSR reflected the general line of the Maoists in loosening China's ties with all socialist countries. In 1961, as compared with 1959, there was a sharp drop in trade between the PRC and the European socialist countries with the exception of Albania. Reduction in total volume of the PRC's foreign trade from 14 billion yuan in 1959 to 8 billion in 1961 was due almost entirely to reduction in trade with socialist countries. Chinese leaders even began to refuse equipment manufactured in socialist countries on orders placed by the PRC, despite the fact that in many cases deliveries were to have been made on credit. The PRC totally halted exchanges of information on economic questions and the like with socialist states.

The sharp reversal in the policy of economic cooperation between the PRC and socialist countries had negative effects on these countries, particularly China, and definitely damaged the interests of the world socialist system. Chinese leaders failed to consider this, however, and ignored the line of strengthening comprehensive cooperation between socialist countries as established in the 1960 Statement of the meeting of fraternal parties.

Peking leaders, while curtailing economic cooperation with socialist countries, expanded foreign trade ties between the PRC and the capitalist world. Chinese organizations began buying goods and equipment in capitalist Europe that could have been acquired with greater advantage in socialist countries. The PRC purchased aircraft, tractors, vehicles, and other items in England in 1960–1961; trade with Japan, the Federal Republic of Germany, and Italy also increased significantly in those years.

10. CCP leadership aims to create tensions along the border with the Soviet Union

The fact that neighborly relations were not strained by mutual territorial claims and border disputes did much to enhance such relations between the Soviet Union and the PRC. In the Treaty of Friendship, Alliance, and Mutual Assistance, signed four and a half months after the founding of the PRC, the two countries solemnly agreed to build their relations on the basis of "mutual respect for state sovereignty and territorial integrity."

The Sino-Soviet border was a border of friendship and neighborliness for the first ten years of the PRC's existence. People in border areas enjoyed extensive communications, carried on lively trade, engaged in cultural exchanges, and by joint efforts resolved economic problems, helped each other, and fought natural calamities together. Soviet authorities allowed the Chinese people to hay, gather firewood, fish, and engage in other domestic activities on many parts of Soviet territory. The border guards of both states developed comradely relationships. Any border questions were resolved in an atmosphere of mutual understanding and fairness.

The leaders of the CCP and the PRC never mentioned territorial questions in dispute between China and the Soviet Union, and never left any doubt as to the legality of the Sino-Soviet border. Quite the contrary. CCP leaders repeatedly emphasized the fact that after the October Revolution the Soviet state built its relations with China on the basis of equality and respect for the sovereign rights of the Chinese people. Mao Tse-tung, at the 7th Congress of the Communist Party of China in 1945, said that "the Soviet Union was the first to reject unequal treaties and to conclude new equal treaties with China." Mao Tse-tung made identical statements on December 16, 1949 during his visit to Moscow.[36]

The Sino-Soviet border as it exists today evolved over many generations and follows the natural border that divides the territories of the Soviet Union and China. It came about as a result of a whole series of treaties, which, as we know, are still in force today. In the early 1950s at Chinese request the Soviet Union handed over to the PRC complete sets of topographic maps showing the boundary line. Having familiarized themselves with the maps, the Chinese authorities made no comments with respect to the boundary line shown, and this line was observed in practice.

Not until 1957 were there any statements regarding the existence of unresolved territorial and boundary questions between China and the Soviet Union. These questions were raised in speeches made by bourgeois right-wing elements coming into the open in the struggle against the Communist party. The fact that CCP leaders, while rebuffing excursions of the right-wingers, allowed their pretensions to territorial claims against the USSR to go unanswered should be pointed out. As later events were to show, this was done deliberately.

Once nationalists within the CCP publicized their struggle with the Soviet Union they began to aggravate artificially the situation along the Sino-Soviet border, advancing territorial claims against the USSR, and using this for purposes of inflaming nationalist, anti-Soviet feelings in the PRC.

In the summer of 1960 the PRC provoked a border incident in the vicinity of Buz-Aygyr, where Chinese cattle breeders, deliberately violating the state boundary of the USSR, intruded deep into Soviet territory. Despite demands of Soviet border guards, the Chinese citizens refused to return to China, even after winter had set in. Soviet authorities naturally had to supply Chinese peasants who had crossed the border with needed supplies. The border guards asked them why, now that they had nothing to feed their cattle, they did not return to China. The chairman of the people's commune, who was among the Chinese peasants, stated that they had crossed the frontier on direct orders from the Chinese administration, and that they were now afraid to return without its permission.[37]

Violations of the Sino-Soviet border by the PRC became systematic in subsequent years. Several thousand such instances were recorded in 1961–1962. Only restraint on the part of Soviet border guards prevented major incidents.

The Maoists attempted to put a corresponding "theoretical base" under territorial claims against the Soviet Union and other neighboring countries. This took the form of openly nationalistic distortions of world history. It is no accident that nationalism became the banner of social sciences in China at this time. Commonly known historical facts were revised from a nationalist bias; roles of historical figures were reassessed; imperial conquerors were glorified. The following statement was made in October 1961 at a scientific conference on the occasion of the 50th anniversary of the Chinese bourgeois revolution of 1911: "It is impossible to brand as aggressors those who have merely striven for expansion, and to call those who had fallen into decay and perished the objects of aggression, and express sympathy for them." Justifying Chinese expansion in the past, one of the speakers asserted that:

> At that time expanding nationalities and states experienced a period of regular progress while expansion was going on, while nationalities and states falling into decay and death experienced a period of atrophy. Atrophication is not deserving of respect.

Mingshui Tuan-ch'i, a Peking journal, carried an article entitled "The Historical Ties of Sinkiang with China" in its February 1962 issue. This article had the temerity to state that the "Western Region" of China went well beyond the limits of what was the territory of Sinkiang, and that:

> ... according to reliable materials now available, the Western Region at the time was broken up first into 36, and later on into some 50 principalities encompassing what is now Sinkiang, Kashmir, the northern border

region of Afghanistan, Kokand, the Kazakh Republic, Northwestern Khorezm, the northern shores of the Black Sea (belonging to the Soviet Union), and what is now Iran."[38]

Chinese historians, from their chauvinistic positions, unanimously extolled the activities of Genghis Khan, ascribing to him a progressive role in the history of China,[39] as well as in the histories of "40 other states." The predatory expeditions of Genghis Khan and his successors were depicted almost as a boon to those peoples enslaved by his troops. The journal *Li Shih Yen-chiu,* in an article celebrating the 800th anniversary of the birth of Genghis Khan, asserted that because of his campaigns conquered peoples had "opened to them a large world in which they could live and act. The people saw higher culture that could be learned."[40]

These assessments are in basic contradiction to the conclusions of Marxist-Leninist science. B. Shirendyb, president of the Academy of Sciences of the Mongolian People's Republic, writes that:

Marxist scholars consider the wars of Genghis Khan and his successors against other countries and peoples to be predatory, plunderous, reactionary wars. Any attempt to revise the Marxist assessment of the campaigns of conquest carried on by the different invaders and conquerors —by the khans and *noyons* [feudal lords—authors]—means complete retreat from the fundamental bases of historical materialism, and simply adds grist to the mill of the aggressors, imperialists, revanchists, and chauvinists, of all these invaders of others' territories.[41]

CCP leaders attempted to use events associated with the 1962 mass movement of inhabitants of Sinkiang into the USSR to exacerbate Sino-Soviet relations. This exodus was no accident. It was the result of serious mistakes by CCP leaders in domestic policy, of the grave material situation of the population, and of bends in nationality policy.[42] Yet leaders of the CCP tried to attribute the consequences of their actions to the USSR. Chinese officials gave contradictory explanations for causes of the incident. The PRC Vice Minister of Foreign Affairs initially called it an "accident," but subsequent notes issued declared that the incident was caused by "disruptive activities of Soviet authorities."

The indigenous population of Sinkiang was not the only victim of the antisocialist, nationalistic policy of PRC leaders. Others included numerous groups from Russia and the USSR (the Kazakhs, Uighurs, Russians, and others). By decrees of the Presidium of the Supreme Soviet of the USSR of November 10, 1945 and January 20, 1946, some 120,000 such persons received Soviet citizenship and foreign residential permits. †At the same time a great many of these people, for a variety of reasons, did not receive similar papers, although under Soviet law they remained citizens of the USSR.

Relations between the Chinese authorities and Soviet citizens in Sinkiang on the whole were friendly in the first years after the formation of the PRC. But a drastic change occurred with development of anti-Soviet attitudes in Chinese policies. Soviet citizens who were permanent residents of Sinkiang found their rights infringed upon in matters of property, law, and other questions; they were dismissed en masse from state institutions and plants, and were increasingly persecuted. Employees of Chinese institutions subjected Soviet citizens to openly rude and arbitrary treatment, refusing to comply with even their simple requests. At the beginning of 1962 local authorities in Sinkiang almost stopped issuance of exit visas for the USSR to Soviet citizens wishing to return.

All this encouraged a mass exodus of desperate inhabitants from Sinkiang. In the period from April 22 to the beginning of June 1962 some 67,000 people illegally crossed into the Soviet Union.

The Chinese side tried to blame Soviet authorities, claiming that "they had accepted border violators." The Soviet government sent the PRC government a memorandum on the subject on April 29, 1962, rejecting the unfounded accusations and pointing out the fact that the border crossing had been effected from the Chinese side, under the eyes of those Chinese authorities who should have taken timely and appropriate measures to prevent it.

Despite the facts, Chinese leaders continued leveling preposterous accusations against the Soviet Union. A memorandum written by the PRC Ministry of Foreign Affairs on August 30, 1962 stated definitively that the Soviet side supposedly "had prepared and organized the mass crossing," and that Sinkiang supposedly was under threat "of serious subversive activities on the part of the Soviet Union."

The Soviet government, on September 19, 1962, sent a note to the PRC Ministry of Foreign Affairs setting forth its position concerning the mass crossing of Sinkiang inhabitants, and replying to the slanderous accusations of the Chinese against our state. The PRC government did not reply to the Soviet note for some time, until the July 18, 1963 bilateral Sino-Soviet meeting. Then it responded with a statement asserting that workers in Soviet institutions in Sinkiang supposedly had engaged in "subversive activities against the People's Republic of China." The statement attempted to place responsibility for the crossing on the Soviet Union, as well as responsibility for the bloody events in the city of Kuldja (Ining) during spring 1962, in which Chinese authorities had organized the lethal battle with those inhabitants not of Han nationality. The Chinese repeated the demand that all refugees be forcibly returned, and confirmed the PRC refusal to send representatives to do explanatory work among the refugees.

The provocative fabrications by the Chinese were glaringly exposed in the Soviet government's note of October 31, 1963. The Soviet government once again emphasized its readiness to resolve all questions in a spirit of friendship and mutual cooperation, including the question of the Sinkiang exodus.

As a result, Chinese authorities were forced to reckon with attempts of Soviet citizens and those of Russian birth to return to the Soviet Union. †In September 1962 the PRC Ministry of Foreign Affairs requested that the Soviet government permit those persons seeking to leave for the USSR to do so under a simplified procedure. This request was honored and Soviet authorities temporarily permitted Soviet citizens and members of their families to enter the USSR from China without visas. Over 46,000 persons entered the USSR from Sinkiang between October 15, 1962 and May 1, 1963. Again the artificiality of the Chinese version of Soviet complicity in "getting the inhabitants of Sinkiang to cross over to the USSR" was confirmed.

Nevertheless, the Chinese side engaged in a series of provocative actions against those working in Soviet consulates in Sinkiang, including forcible detention and searching of diplomats. Local societies of Soviet citizens were disbanded and their leaders arrested on false.accusations of "antigovernmental activities" and violation of Chinese laws.

The government of the USSR, faced with these conditions, decided to close the Soviet consulate general in Urumchi and the consulate in Kuldja. This was followed by the closing of the USSR's trade representative office in Urumchi, upon urgent request of the Chinese, and the recall of Soviet foreign trade workers from border points of Khorgos and Turugart.

Provocations similar to those in Sinkiang were repeated elsewhere in the PRC. Chinese authorities in Harbin, in September 1962, sealed all premises and objects belonging to the local Soviet citizens' society, and members of its board and employees in the city and in outlying districts were arrested. They were subjected to abusive interrogations, including physical force resulting in the death of two men. Absurd accusations of "illegal activities" were leveled at Soviet citizens. The USSR consulate general in Harbin was blockaded by police.

As expected, attempts of the Chinese authorities to create in Harbin the situation needed to "prove" the thesis of subversive activities on the part of Soviet citizens came to naught. Promises of Chinese authorities to present "facts" confirming accusations against Soviet citizens and institutions remained unfulfilled as these "facts" actually were nonexistent.

Faced with the evolving situation, in September 1962 the Soviet government decided to close the consulates general of the USSR in Harbin and Shanghai, and then the offices of the trade representatives of the USSR in Dal'nyy, Shanghai, and Kwangchow (Canton), and the "Sovfrakht"* agencies in Chinese railroad stations in Manchouli (Lupin) and Tsinan.

Development of the anti-Soviet course by CCP leaders resulted in even further deterioration of conditions under which the Soviet Embassy in the PRC was forced to operate. Chinese leaders refused meetings with Soviet representatives, even when important missions of the CC CPSU and the government of the USSR were involved. The level at which staff of the Embassy of the USSR was received in the Ministry of Foreign Affairs of the PRC fell; direct communications between the Embassy and Chinese social organizations were restricted, and trips by Soviet diplomats around the country were reduced to a minimum (60 such trips were made in 1960, 23 in 1961, and 15 in 1962). Occasionally the PRC Ministry of Foreign Affairs refused to permit Embassy personnel to accompany Soviet delegations on trips in China. Chinese authorities took unfriendly approaches when called upon to resolve questions of providing services for the Embassy. The work of Soviet correspondents in the PRC was strictly regulated and placed under careful control.

Nevertheless, attitudes toward the PRC's Embassy in Moscow remained friendly as always. At no time was the Ambassador of the PRC shunned by the head of the Soviet government or some other leader upon requesting a meeting. The Chinese Embassy in Moscow had broad opportunities for contact with Soviet workers, for making trips around the country, and for visiting plants, collective farms, state farms, and schools.

11. The anti-Soviet campaign in the PRC in connection with the Nuclear Test Ban Treaty

Chinese leaders opened a new anti-Soviet campaign immediately after the breaking off of the Sino-Soviet meeting in July 1963. This time the pretext for attacks on the CPSU and other Marxist-Leninist parties was

---

* Translator's note: "Sovfrakht" is the All-Union Association for the Chartering of Foreign Tonnage.

the treaty banning nuclear tests in three media,* signed in Moscow on August 5, 1963 by the governments of the USSR, the USA, and the United Kingdom. The Chinese side published official statements on the Moscow treaty three times (July 31, August 15, and September 1, 1963); their attitude toward the treaty was negative. They refused to be a party to it, and pounced on it with unprecedented attacks against the Soviet Union and the CPSU.

Chinese leaders, in governmental declarations, monstrously asserted that they blamed the Soviet Union for supposedly conducting a policy of "uniting with the forces of war for the struggle against the forces of peace," "with imperialism for the struggle against socialism," "with the United States for the struggle against China," and "with reaction in different countries for the struggle against people all over the world." All such unbridled slander was snatched up voraciously by the Chinese press. *Jen Min Jihpao* alone published over 500 anti-Soviet pieces in the summer of 1963.

Many important questions of the time, dealing with war and peace, peaceful coexistence of states with different social systems, and others, were broached in Peking's statements regarding the Moscow treaty. However, neither the official documents published by the government of the PRC, nor the widespread propaganda campaign in the Chinese press based on these documents, resembled a statesmanlike discussion of these problems. They were statements by people whose purpose was to discredit the CPSU and the Soviet Union, to deepen the split in the world Communist movement, and to impair the unity of the anti-imperialist forces. The Maoists, understanding the vulnerability of their ideological positions, deliberately tried to reduce discussion of contemporary questions of principle to the level of noisy squabbles and unsubstantiated accusations.

Peking leaders in their attacks on the Moscow treaty deliberately ignored the fact that the conclusion of this treaty was the first, albeit limited, real success in the long struggle of the people, of Communists throughout the world, against the danger of nuclear war. This success did not blunt the vigilance of workers to the intrigues of imperialism, as Chinese propaganda asserted; quite the contrary, it gave new impetus to the struggle for peace, and strengthened faith in the possibility of forcing the imperialists to compromise. Peoples of the world saw the practical significance of the treaty as ending the threat of polluting the air with

* Translator's note: the reference is to the Test Ban Treaty of August 5, 1963, prohibiting nuclear weapon tests or other explosions in the atmosphere, in outer space, or under water.

radioactive substances (strontium 90, cesium 137, and others), thus diminishing the danger to health for present and future generations.

Attempts by the Chinese to represent the conclusion of the Moscow treaty as a weakening of the defensive capability of the socialist commonwealth were completely unfounded. The treaty imposes identical obligations on all parties, so no signatory receives unilateral military advantage.

The negative attitude of the Maoists to the treaty is explained primarily by their efforts, at whatever costs, to possess nuclear weapons for realization of great-power goals. A statement by Peking leaders on September 1, 1963 frankly proclaimed that despite economic difficulties, China was ready to build its own nuclear weapons even if it took 100 years.

Evident in statements by the government of the PRC concerning the Moscow treaty was that the Chinese government, ignoring its duty as an ally and abusing the confidential nature of relations between socialist countries, had embarked on the road to divulging secret documents and information affecting defensive capabilities of socialist commonwealth countries. In this connection the Soviet government was forced to state that:

> ... after actions such as these on the part of the government of the People's Republic of China, there is scarcely anyone who will believe in the sincerity of its assertions or who will trust it with information of defensive value. It is clear that the Soviet government is drawing its own conclusions on that score.[43]

Statements by Chinese leaders also revealed their striving to use the Moscow treaty to distort and discredit the policy of the Soviet Union, to wreck the Leninist policy of peaceful coexistence conducted by our country and by the other socialist states.

In attacking the Moscow treaty, the Chinese had come out against not only the Soviet Union and the CPSU, but also against the position of the overwhelming majority of socialist countries, and against the entire world community. The collective opinion of socialist countries on banning nuclear tests was expressed in the decision of the August 1963 conference of first secretaries of the central committees of the Communist and Workers' Parties and heads of governments of states party to the Warsaw Pact:

> The achievement of agreement on the question of banning nuclear testing is the result of the consistent, peace-loving foreign policy course of the Soviet Union and of all socialist countries, of the success of the Lenin policy of peaceful coexistence of states with different social structures.

> The Conference believes that this treaty will lend itself to the relaxation of international tensions, and will be a positive factor in the struggle of peoples for peace and against the threat of a new world war.[44]

The fraternal Marxist-Leninist parties on all continents of the world approved the agreement. They regarded it as the serious result of the consistent conduct of the course of the international Communist movement to strengthen the forces of peace and progress. Concurrent with this statement, Communist and Workers' Parties condemned decisively the position of Peking leaders with respect to the Moscow treaty.

The slanderous anti-Soviet attacks by the Chinese leadership demanded a decisive rebuff. In August and September 1963 the Soviet government published statements in which it exposed the anti-Soviet trend in the position of CCP leaders with respect to the Moscow treaty, and pointed out that this position damaged the cause of peace and socialism.[45]

The CC CPSU and the Soviet government, scoring the hit-and-run anti-Soviet attacks by the Chinese leadership, at the same time demonstrated self-restraint and good will toward the normalization of Sino-Soviet relations. The Soviet government's statements of September 21-22, 1963 once again expressed readiness to take any avenue to overcome disagreements, and appealed to PRC leaders to halt their polemics.

The Soviet government emphasized that it was inadmissible to shift ideological disagreements between parties to relations between socialist states, and to use such disagreements to foster chauvinism, thus sowing distrust and discord between peoples:

> There is no justification, nor can there be any, for the fact that the leaders of the People's Republic of China, rather than engaging in comradely discussions of disagreements that arise in the course of such discussions as is proper among Communists and like-minded persons, have embarked on the road of hostile attacks and slanderous assaults against our party[46]

Still anti-Soviet members of the CCP continued to move down this slippery road. Their attempts to undermine the moral and political unity of the Soviet people, to sow distrust in their party and in its leadership among workers in the Soviet Union, became even more brazen and open. They used Chinese propaganda about the Moscow treaty for these purposes. The Maoists resorted to direct provocations in order to distribute such propaganda in the USSR. Proof of this behavior is the events at the Soviet border station of Naushki on September 7, 1963 when Chinese citizens, on the train from Peking, had confiscated by Soviet customs officials anti-Soviet literature forbidden in the USSR. Chinese passengers responded by engaging in hooliganistic tactics; they prevented the train from leaving on time, committed excesses in the station, insulted Soviet official representatives, and even attempted violence.

The Ministry of Foreign Affairs of the USSR the same day reported this unprecedented event to the Embassy of the PRC in Moscow, lodging a protest in connection with the provocative conduct of the Chinese citizens. The Ministry of Foreign Affairs simultaneously pointed out that it expected the Chinese side to take immediate steps to prevent such lawlessness as was demonstrated by Chinese citizens at Naushki.

Despite demands of Soviet authorities, the Chinese train brigade as well as passengers who were citizens of the PRC continued obstructing departure of the train; they set red signals and used a stop crane. As a result, over 100 passengers, citizens of the Soviet Union as well as other countries, were sent to Moscow on an extra train after a delay of four and one-half hours.

The Chinese citizens refused to proceed to Moscow and instead continued their outrages in Naushki station, engaging in hooligan activities and provocative acts against Soviet personnel on duty. They interfered with activities of the railroad administration, the traffic control point, and the customs, blocked entrances to service areas, delayed officers of the border service, as well as other duty personnel, and grossly violated social order.

Actions such as those in Naushki are criminal offenses under Soviet law. However, guided by the desire to avoid straining relations between our countries, the Soviet government limited itself to expelling persons involved from the territory of the Soviet Union.[47]

One would assume that Peking would take steps to avoid repetition of such incidents, which could only lead to the exacerbation of Sino-Soviet relations. The Maoists, however, dramatized the incident at Naushki station to intensify further the usual anti-Soviet hysteria in China. Upon their return to the PRC, those responsible for the outrages in Naushki station were greeted by noisy meetings organized in their honor, at which these rowdies were characterized as martyrs, victims in the struggle for the "purity of Marxism-Leninism!"

12. Anti-Soviet attacks by the Chinese press under the pretext of replying to the Open Letter of the CC CPSU of July 14, 1963

The leadership of the CCP embarked on a new attack against the CPSU and the Soviet Union, beginning in September 1963. *Jen Min Jihpao* and

Hung-ch'i published a series of scurrilous anti-Soviet articles advertised as "replies" to the Open Letter of the CC CPSU of July 14, 1963.

These articles, for the first time since the inception of disagreements with the CPSU, contained the Chinese leaders' actual thoughts on all subjects earlier referred to allegorically; they openly wrote of the entire foreign and domestic policy of the CPSU and the Soviet state with shameless, crude, and slanderous evaluations. Adopting for their arsenal the line and methods of the Trotskyites, the Maoists attempted to set the Soviet people and Soviet Communists against the leadership of our party and country. The Peking press and radio appealed to the Soviet people to struggle against the CC CPSU and the Soviet Government. Chinese propaganda, in the licentiousness of its attacks, became one with the anti-Soviet, anti-Communist fabrications of reactionary imperialist circles.

Chinese leaders, having rejected the declaration and statement written collectively by the Communist and Workers' Parties and signed by their own delegations, set an opposition "platform" thus to negate decisive actions of the world socialist system on the course of social development, to look with scorn on the struggle of the working class in capitalist countries, to counterpose the national liberation movement to the world system of socialism and the international workers' movement, to embark upon a program of adventurism in foreign policy, to keep the "Cold War" going, to retain the cult of personality condemned by the Communist movement, and to justify the splitting struggle going on in the Communist movement.

Peking leaders tried to strengthen their anti-Soviet course at the Fourth Session of the National People's Congress, which took place between November 17 and December 3, 1963. The session was held behind closed doors. But even the scanty reports published in the Chinese press confirmed that from beginning to end the session had an openly anti-Soviet direction. Chinese leaders used the tribunal of the supreme organ of authority in the PRC for unbridled slandering of the Soviet Union. They attempted to shift the blame for the economic difficulties which had been created in the PRC to the "Soviet authorities," thus "substantiating" and "justifying" their so-called "rely on own efforts" course, the line of rejection of cooperation with the Soviet Union of intensification of splitting, disruptive activities in the socialist camp.

The course of the Chinese leadership, aimed at severing cooperation with the Soviet Union, was officially sanctioned by the supreme legislative body of the PRC in the main political result of the session.

13. Attempts of the CC CPSU to halt further exacerbation of Sino-Soviet relations

The anti-Soviet course of CCP leaders took on an increasingly dangerous aspect, eventually encompassing all spheres of relations between the two countries, with serious negative consequences to the world Communist movement and the socialist community. Decisive measures were immediately needed at least to slow further development of this course. Our party, without hesitation, took such measures.

The Soviet side, on October 25, 1963, once again proposed that open polemics be discontinued. This was followed by a unilateral decision on the part of the Soviet press to cease publication of materials written to expose the chauvinist course of the CCP.

Chinese leaders completely ignored our party's discontinuance of open polemics, cynically labeling it a "trick" and a "snare." The Chinese press not only kept proposals of the CC CPSU from readers but continued publishing anti-Soviet materials. *Jen Min Jihpao* alone carried over 200 such articles in November and December 1963.

Despite the unprecedented scope and persistence of the anti-Soviet campaign in the PRC, the CC CPSU on November 29, 1963 sent a letter to the CC CPSU once again proposing that open polemics be discontinued, and that the two sides develop and carry out together measures to eliminate disagreements and to normalize relations. Of particular concern to the CC CPSU was that ideological disagreements had been carried over into interstate relations and had appeared in the sphere of concrete policy, impairing friendship and solidarity among peoples of the socialist commonwealth, weakening the anti-imperialist front, and distracting the strength and attention of fraternal parties from solutions to urgent tasks of socialist construction.

The CC CPSU was of the opinion that it was necessary to focus the main goal of Sino-Soviet relations, that of developing cooperation in the interests of friendship between the Soviet Union and China, between all the socialist countries and fraternal Marxist-Leninist parties, and agreeing on actions in different types of international organizations directed at common goals of defending peace and struggling against imperialism. †To those ends, the CC CPSU proposed early development of plans for trade exchanges between the PRC and the Soviet Union, an increase in exports to China of Soviet goods of interest, and of imports from China by the USSR. Also proposed was agreement on expanding Soviet technical assistance to the PRC in construction of industrial plants under terms favorable to both countries.

In connection with the drafting of the scheduled Five-Year Plan for 1966–1970 in the Soviet Union, and of the Third Five-Year Plan in China, the CC CPSU proposed that the possibility of developing trade and other ties between the USSR and the PRC be discussed, and that corresponding measures be considered in plans for the national economies of both countries. The letter expressed a desire to expand Sino-Soviet scientific and technical cooperation and cultural ties as well.

Of special importance was the CC CPSU proposal to hold friendly consultations toward delineation of boundary lines along certain sections, thus to eliminate causes of concern along the Sino-Soviet border.

The letter pointed out the need to create conditions favorable to improvement in relations with respect to the party line as well, to avoid anything that could aggravate difficulties that had arisen in the world Communist movement. Our party was aware that overcoming disagreements was a complicated business, one requiring serious efforts and much time. But it was important to go forward in this direction, step by step, to show Leninist concern for strengthening unity of the world Communist movement on a principled Marxist base, permitting no actions to undermine unity, rebuffing splitters and factionists.

The leadership of the CCP did not respond to the CC CPSU letter for three months (the reply was not made until February 29, 1964), but all its actions indicated no intentions of entertaining proposals concerning normalization of Sino-Soviet relations. The Chinese press continued daily filling its pages with materials openly anti-Soviet in content.

14. Attacks by the leadership of the CCP against the CPSU in connection with preparation of the conference of fraternal parties

The leaders of the CCP, by intensifying their splitting activities, made calling an international meeting of Communist and Workers' Parties an increasingly imperative task of the world Communist movement.

A number of fraternal parties (Indonesia, New Zealand, Democratic Republic of Vietnam, Sweden, Great Britain) had proposed calling an international meeting at the end of 1961 and beginning of 1962. The CCP, in its letter to the CPSU of April 7, 1962, had supported calling a meeting, but at that time made abundantly clear its desire to introduce into discussion "the problem of Soviet-Albanian relations." Clearly, Chinese leaders had planned on using this question to prevent the international forum of Communists from becoming a factor in strengthening the unity of socialist collaboration and the world Communist movement, and to convert it into an arena for exacerbation of disagreements.

The CC CPSU, in its reply of May 31, 1962, expressed disagreement that the main topic of discussions ought to be the problem of Soviet-Albanian relations. It emphasized that preparations for the meeting, as experience had shown, first required a detailed analysis of new conditions of international life, and agreement in a spirit of collective decisions, on fundamental aspects of current tactics of the new Communist movement.

As to the creation of an atmosphere favorable to holding the meeting, the CC CPSU stated that first for discussion obviously should be discontinuance of direct and indirect attacks against fraternal parties, and observance of principles of proletarian internationalism in relations between parties, for these were in the interests of solidarity and unity.

The CC CPSU, in a new letter to the CC CCP dated February 21, 1963,[48] once again stated that the CPSU as well as many other fraternal parties were calling for the meeting because there were sufficiently serious grounds for doing so. The meeting, it was felt, ought to review general problems of the struggle against imperialism and against imperialist aggression, future development of people's liberation movements, solidarity and all-round development of the world socialist commonwealth, and means to strengthen unity of the Communist movement. The CC CPSU also suggested a bilateral meeting of representatives of the CPSU and the CCP.

The CC CCP response dated March 9, 1963[49] noted that it favored calling a meeting of fraternal parties, and repeated its proposals set forth in the letter of April 7, 1962. It further stated agreement with the proposal of the CPSU for a meeting of representatives of the two parties.

Many fraternal parties associated the question of an international meeting with a favorable outcome of the Sino-Soviet meeting. But the already referred to meeting held in Moscow between July 5 and 20, 1963 failed to develop positive results through the fault of CCP leaders. Because CCP leaders had so rudely rejected Soviet proposals, and were intensifying splitting activities and the campaign of anti-Sovietism, the CC CPSU was faced with the need to resume publication of materials explaining those party positions so maliciously distorted by Chinese leaders.

The CC CPSU, attaching exceptional importance to this issue, decided to detail the situation created as a result of the splitting activities of the Maoist leadership, since these activities tremendously damaged the unity of fraternal parties and the revolutionary and national liberation struggle of the people. The plenum CC CPSU convened in February 1964 heard and discussed a report by M. A. Suslov "On the Struggle of the Communist Party of the Soviet Union for the Solidarity of the International Communist Movement," and adopted a resolution on this question.[50]

This plenum stated that the CCP leaders had not discontinued open polemics, and had in fact intensified the campaign against the general line of the Communist movement. The Maoists, hypocritically mouthing loyalty to Marxism-Leninism, and talking profusely about the struggle with alleged revisionism, actually attacked fundamental theoretical and political lines currently guiding the world Communist movement.

The resolution of the CC CPSU plenum noted that Chinese leaders, deviating from the strategy and tactics of the Leninist line of the world Communist movement, had proclaimed their separate course, one that merged petty bourgeois adventurism and great-power chauvinism. What occurred, essentially, was that CCP leaders had adapted Trotskyite methods of waging the struggle against Marxist-Leninist parties, by encouraging factionalism.

Materials from the February plenary session were not published immediately. Evincing concern for the solidarity of the Communist movement, the CC CPSU advised fraternal parties that publication of materials would not take place until a reply to the appeal for an immediate discontinuance of open polemics was received from the CC CCP.

As expected, Peking rejected the appeal to discontinue open polemics and embarked on an even more flagrant campaign of anti-Soviet propaganda, activating its splitting activities worldwide.

A new proposal was advanced at the end of March. This dealt with addressing an appeal to a number of parties, including the CCP, to immediately cease open polemics. The CC CPSU, in the interest of unity, agreed to this proposal. But Peking once again took a negative position. On March 31 the CC CCP released its next splitting article.

Our party refrained from criticizing the CCP leadership for some time after the plenum. And it was only after all proposals for discontinuance of open polemics were rejected, only after a new wave of malicious attacks by Peking leaders against the CPSU and the world Communist movement, that the Central Committee of our party, having exhausted all means for diverting discussion into interparty channels, published materials from the February plenum session of the CC CPSU on April 3, 1964.

The CC CCP replied to CC CPSU's letter of November 29, 1963 on February 29, 1964. The Chinese leadership remained silent on the program of constructive measures designed to normalize and develop Sino-Soviet relations, as advanced by the CC CPSU.

In striving to postpone calling the international meeting of fraternal parties, the Chinese leaders formulated a whole series of conditions in their letter. In particular, they proposed the organization of innumerable bilateral and multilateral meetings of representatives of the CCP, the CPSU, and other parties in order "to reach through consultations a general agreement" on the cessation of open polemics, to do "a great deal of preparatory work," and to overcome other "difficulties and obstacles." It was proposed that the bilateral Sino-Soviet meeting be held between October 10 and 25, 1964.

The CC CPSU replied to the letter of February 29, 1964 on March 7, 1964. In order to prevent further delay in calling the international meeting of fraternal parties, it proposed that talks between representatives of the CPSU and the CCP be held in Peking in May rather than October 1964, that the preparatory meeting be held in June-July of 1964, and that the international meeting of the Marxist-Leninist parties be held in the fall.

The CC CPSU also noted lack of grounds for the CC CCP proposal that the preparatory meeting consist of representatives of 17 parties only. In the opinion of the Soviet Central Committee it was desirable to have representatives from all those parties that had representatives on the drafting committee of the 1960 Moscow meeting: Albania, Bulgaria, Hungary, Vietnam, the German Democratic Republic, China, Korea, Cuba, Mongolia, Poland, Rumania, the USSR, Czechoslovakia, France, Italy, the Federal Republic of Germany, Great Britain, Finland, Argentina, Brazil, Syria, India, Indonesia, the United States of America, Japan, and Australia. The CC CPSU letter stated that this would provide representation from the main regions of the revolutionary movement, and reminded that at the time this representation had the approval of all fraternal parties, thus resulting in the successful conduct of the 1960 conference, and in production of its documents.

But, predictably, the CC CCP opposed these constructive proposals relative to convening the international conference of fraternal parties. The Chinese leaders in the May 7, 1964 letter dealt with the question of the preparatory meeting by saying that it would "depend on the results of the talks between the representatives of the Chinese and Soviet parties." In turn, the talks themselves, they said:

> . . . would be impossible in May, and in fact October of this year is too soon. We feel it would be more desirable to hold the talks between the representatives of the Chinese and Soviet parties in the first half of next year, say in May. If, by that time, either of the parties, the Chinese or

the Soviet, considers that the time still is not ripe, they can be postponed even further.[51]

In their letter, the CCP leaders once again confirmed their line of continuing polemics, and, as well, their shameless, slanderous campaign against our party and other Marxist-Leninist parties. They stated plans to give unilateral publicity to the secret correspondence between the CCP and the CPSU; this they did on May 8, 1964. It was an act of grossest violation by the Maoists of generally accepted norms of relations among Communist parties.

The CC CPSU, on June 15, 1964, replied to the May 7, 1964 letter, once again asserting that the meeting should not be postponed, and that concrete dates for the meeting, as well as agenda and composition, should be agreed to in the course of further consultations with fraternal parties.

The CC CPSU reiterated its readiness to resume Soviet-Chinese conversations.

On July 28, 1964, CCP leaders rejected the CC CPSU proposals. They categorically demanded that representatives of pro-Peking splitter groups be invited to the meeting of fraternal parties.[52]

The CC CPSU, on July 30, 1964, addressed a letter to all fraternal parties taking into consideration the clearly expressed will of the absolute majority, and expressing the view that the time for preparatory work on calling the international meeting had come; it proposed that a drafting committee consisting of 26 Communist parties meet in Moscow in December 1964. The CC CPSU emphasized the fact that the goal of the meeting should be to strengthen unity of the world Communist movement; that it meet not simply to condemn or excommunicate anyone from the Communist movement and the socialist camp, nor to paste abusive labels or level irresponsible charges against each other.

The CC CPSU proposals met with widespread support among ranks of the world Communist movement. Peking leaders, however, paid no attention. The CC CCP, on August 30, 1964, rejected all proposals for calling an international meeting, and categorically refused to participate in the work of the drafting committee, as uncompromisingly as in their letter of July 28, 1964.

15. The leadership of the CCP stirs up further
anti-Sovietism in the PRC

The Maoists, rejecting the constructive program of normalization of Sino-Soviet relations advanced by our party, continued to expand and deepen their anti-Soviet activities. The so-called replies to the CC

CPSU's open letter of July 14, 1963, containing malicious, slanderous lies about our party and country, were initiated in September 1963, on the basis of mass political indoctrination work in the country. These materials were even studied in the middle schools. A letter sent to the Soviet Embassy by Chinese students contained the following:

> Whereas our political lecturers in the past said that the Soviet Union was our older brother, that we should follow the example of the USSR in all things, that we should learn from its experience, and so on, now those lessons have taken a directly opposite direction. The former friend and teacher now is abused in the vilest of terms. What once had been called help is now called exploitation.

The anti-Soviet campaign intensified even further with the May 1964 publication in the Chinese press of correspondence between the central committees of the CCP and the CPSU. Reports claiming that the USSR intended to sever diplomatic relations with the PRC—and even declare war—were read to workers and employees.

French tourists visiting the PRC in the summer of 1964 related the following:

> The villages we visited had radio facilities and the villagers heard reports directed against the USSR from morning to night. One sometimes saw newspapers containing nothing except materials directed against the Soviet Union. Generally speaking, the Chinese publish a great deal of literature against the Soviet Union and provide it to all tourists. Anti-Soviet literature even is placed in the lavatories.

The Maoists, through deception, intimidation, and direct repression were able to include all new state, party, and social organizations in the anti-Soviet campaign. Grossly slanderous attacks against our party and country were heard in February 1964 at the regional party conference of the Ninghsia Hui Autonomous Region, and in March at a session of the National People's Congress of the Sinkiang Uighur Autonomous Region.

The 9th All-Chinese Congress of the Communist Youth Union met in Peking in June 1964, and it too attacked the CPSU and the Soviet Union.

Anti-Soviet propaganda had the greatest coverage in the Chinese press. The newspaper *Jen Min Jihpao* itself printed some 500 different anti-Soviet pieces in the period between February 16 and July 24, 1964.[53]

The CCP leaders never abandoned hopes of organizing anti-Soviet propaganda in Soviet territory and, with this goal in mind, systematically engaged in activities that purely and simply interfered in the internal affairs of our country. Despite repeated verbal and official protests of the Ministry of Foreign Affairs of the USSR, the PRC Embassy in Moscow continued efforts to distribute the information bulletin published by the Embassy in Russian, propagandizing views hostile to our country, to Soviet institutions, social organizations, and individuals.

Anti-Soviet literature continued to enter our country illegally from the PRC. Over 11,000 copies of such materials were sent to private addresses in the USSR from China during a few months in 1964, and some of the addressees were even school children.

Peking radio was active in spreading propaganda containing an anti-Soviet slant. Its daily broadcasts to the USSR were filled with libelous attacks against the CPSU and against the Soviet government. Peking propagandists, in efforts to disseminate malicious lies about the Soviet Union as widely as possible, grossly violated international agreements and rules for the use of radio frequencies for special purposes assigned to aviation, the merchant marine, and radiotelephone and radiotelegraph communications. Peking went so far as to use distress frequencies for anti-Soviet broadcasts, resulting in serious damage to conditions under which the Soviet aviation and merchant marine, as well as those of other countries, had to operate.

On February 22, 1964 the Ministry of Foreign Affairs of the USSR handed the PRC Embassy in Moscow a note protesting illegal actions of the Chinese side. This protest was ignored. Subversive activities of Chinese radio stations against the Soviet Union broadened in scale.

Not the least of reasons for the Maoists' intensifying anti-Soviet propaganda was to divert the attention of the Chinese people from domestic burdens, to intimidate them, and to make it impossible to discover real reasons for the difficulties China experienced as a result of Peking's fallacious domestic and foreign policies.

The PRC economic situation remained precarious in 1964. Budgetary allocations for development of the national economy were about at the 1957 level. Production in the most important branches of industry was at 45 to 75 percent of 1959–1960 indices. The Mao Tse-tung group proclaimed a course supposedly advantageous to agricultural development, but even in this field achievements were negligible. Production of grain, cotton, and animal products, curtailed during the "great leap forward," did not compare even to earlier levels.

The Chinese population was in very serious straits. A comparison between consumption by the urban population of basic food products and of cotton cloth in 1957 and the norm of supplies of these goods per capita in 1963 will provide the overall idea. Bear in mind, however, that 1957 data are for the country's urban population in general whereas figures for 1963 are available for Peking only, a city where the food situation was better than in other areas:

Commodities	Consumption per capita, 1957	Norms for supply per capita, 1963
Meat	8.7 kg	4.0 kg
Vegetable oil	4.7 kg	1.8 kg
Sugar	1.5 kg	1.2 kg
Cotton cloth	7.2 kg	2.6 meters

Economic difficulties resulted in deep dissatisfaction with the policies of the Chinese leaders. This was strikingly confirmed in letters from Chinese citizens occasionally slipping through Chinese censorship and finding their way into the Soviet Union.

Leading representatives of Chinese society were well aware that the anti-Soviet policy was an inseparable component of the overall anti-people's course of leadership of the CCP. †Student unrest occurred in Peking University in April 1964, caused by distribution of slanderous anti-Soviet pamphlets in Chinese. The students wrote "Honorable Chinese cannot believe this!" on the covers of these diatribes. Student dormitories were searched; all "suspect" students were followed; many of them were arrested.

16. PRC provocations along the Sino-Soviet boundary

Violations of the Sino-Soviet border by the PRC became increasingly frequent in 1963–1964. There were over 4,000 such violations in 1963 alone, and the number of Chinese civilians and military personnel involved was in excess of 100,000.

Chinese provocateurs usually refused the legal demands of Soviet border guards that they leave Soviet territory. Authorities of the PRC not only failed to prevent incidents, they encouraged local inhabitants to violate the border, to seize individual sections of Soviet territory, and to refuse meeting with Soviet border representatives to discuss conflicts.

Border violations by Chinese citizens were carried out with the approbation of PRC authorities. The following will make this eminently clear. This directive, issued by the People's Committee of Heilungkiang province and found on one violator detained in 1963, said in part:

Soviet border guards often make claims to our fishermen fishing on the islands in dispute in the Amur and Ussuri rivers to force them to leave these islands. We propose to continue fishing on the islands in dispute and advise that Soviet border guards be told that the islands belong to China, that they and not we, are in border violation. . . . In no case are our fishermen to leave these islands. We are assuming, that the Soviet side, recognizing the friendly relations between our states, will take no forcible measures to dislodge our fishermen from the islands.[54]

Chinese military and civilian personnel became clearly hostile to Soviet border guards. On May 3, 1964, for example, 40 Chinese violators drove two tractors across the state boundary at the village of Bakhta and began to plough up sections of Soviet territory. When our border guards demanded that they leave, the violators responded with hooliganistic tactics. They pushed the border guards, and drove their tractors at them. On June 13, a group of 60 Chinese, in 26 boats and cutters, entered USSR waters along the Amur river. When a Soviet cutter with a border detachment appeared, violators began to brandish poles and oars, threatening the crew of the cutter and the border detachment, and tried to push the border guards into the water.

Chinese authorities artificially inflamed the situation by concentrating military units and numerous detachments of the so-called labor army (numbering more than 100,000 men) in border regions, and by initiating construction of large militarized state farms, essentially military settlements, in these areas. †"Regular detachments" of the people's volunteer militia were organized in border regions at the beginning of 1964, and assigned to guard the frontier. They also were used in maintaining "extraordinary conditions" in populated points adjacent to the border.

Local inhabitants of border regions were split into groups led by community security workers. A strip of territory 200 kilometers wide adjacent to the border was declared a "forbidden zone." All persons suspected of being Soviet sympathizers, or who had relatives in the Soviet Union, were moved out of this zone deep into China.

Flagrant anti-Soviet agitation was unleashed among the population of border regions; slander about Soviet war preparations against the PRC and our "illegal seizures" of Chinese territory was disseminated. The theme was persistently stressed that the border with the USSR was China's "advanced line of defense."

The Soviet government firmly held that there were no territorial problems between the USSR and China, that the Sino-Soviet border had a solid basis in treaties, and that any review was totally inadmissible. In addition, the government of the USSR repeatedly attempted to consult on questions of delineating the Sino-Soviet border along individual sections in order to preclude any grounds for misunderstanding. †The first such proposals were made in 1960. The Chinese side stubbornly refused to consider such proposals.

PRC leaders agreed to the Soviet proposal for a meeting on the border question in November 1963. However, the response itself clearly indicated that the Chinese side intended to go beyond the purposes for which the meeting was intended and to use it for aggravating border questions, rather than regularizing them. The PRC Ministry of Foreign Affairs' note of November 19, 1963 emphasized that there were "many questions requiring discussion" involving the whole extent of the Sino-Soviet border. The Chinese side refused to agree to newspaper publication of a joint communiqué concerning the forthcoming meeting, falling back on "difficulties in agreement as to its text."

Also worthy of attention is that on the eve of the meeting Chinese leaders launched a furious attack against the Soviet message of December 31, 1963 to the heads of governments (states) all over the world dealing with the peaceful settlement of territorial and border disputes, a message that met with widespread international acclaim and support. This statement continued as a target of attack by Chinese propaganda, even after Sino-Soviet consultations on the border questions had begun.

The Sino-Soviet meeting convened in Peking on February 25, 1964. The Soviet delegation was headed by a plenipotentiary with rank of deputy minister, P. I. Zyryanov. The Chinese delegation was headed by the vice minister of foreign affairs of the PRC, Chen Yuong-chuan.[55]

The Soviet delegation introduced constructive proposals that would have enabled the sides to clarify promptly the line of the Sino-Soviet border along certain sections in dispute. Successful settlement of this question would have made an important contribution to maintaining friendly relations between our peoples and states.

However, Chinese leaders continued to press their territorial claims. *Jen Min Jihpao,* on March 8, 1963, published an article which cited as "unequal" the concluded treaties between China and Russia, establishing the present line of the Sino-Soviet border. Mao Tse-tung, in a meeting with a Japanese delegation on July 10, 1964, said:

> Approximately 100 years ago the territory to the east of Baykal became Russian territory, and since that time Vladivostok, Khabarovsk, Kamchatka, and other places have been Soviet territory. We still have not balanced that account.

The official Chinese representative threatened "to think about other ways to settle the territorial question," and declared their intention to "restore historical rights."

The Sino-Soviet border talks were broken off on August 22, 1964. †It was agreed in principle that they be continued in Moscow on October 15, 1964, but despite repeated reminders by the Soviet side, the PRC government for many years has refused to resume the talks.

17. Sino-Soviet economic, scientific and technical, and cultural cooperation in 1962–1964

The result of CCP policies was to reduce to a minimum Sino-Soviet business connections of all kinds by the end of 1962. The scope of economic cooperation between our countries in 1962 was approximately 5 percent of what it had been in 1959. Deliveries to China of Soviet machinery, materials, technical equipment, and documentation decreased to 41–42 million rubles, as against 428 million rubles in 1960; that is, by a factor of more than ten. Deliveries of sets of machinery totaled 7.8 to 8 million rubles as against 336.5 million rubles in 1959, a reduction by a factor of approximately 40.

At the beginning of 1964 the Soviet Union proposed to the PRC to discuss clarification of the volume and kind of machinery the Chinese side wanted from the USSR in addition to that anticipated by the agreement of May 13, 1962. The Chinese side refused to consult, claiming "difficulties in drafting the plan for the national economy of the PRC." These difficulties did not, however, prevent it from expanding economic ties with capitalist countries, who provided China with machinery, including that for oil refineries and chemical plants, which China had, for two years, put off importing from the USSR. In 1963 the PRC concluded contracts for delivery of machinery for chemical plants with firms in England, Denmark, Italy, Holland, and France.

Intentionally loosening economic ties with the Soviet Union, the CCP leadership continued its slanderous campaign against our country, doing everything it could to downgrade the importance of Soviet aid. In a letter to the CC CPSU of February 29, 1964, they attempted to reduce Soviet-Chinese economic collaboration to trade alone, supposedly carried on under conditions unfavorable to the PRC.

The Maoists did not hesitate to use outright fraud in efforts to discredit Sino-Soviet economic cooperation. In April 1964, for example, they showed representatives of the diplomatic corps a Soviet lathe dismantled in a Yunnan plant, claiming that the machine had been delivered in unsatisfactory condition and could not be used for its intended job. When a representative of the Soviet foreign economic organization in Peking expressed a desire to visit the plant and make an on-site investigation, Chinese authorities, knowing they would be exposed, refused permission. In May 1964 the PRC Minister of Foreign Affairs, in an interview with Norwegian, Dutch, and West German correspondents for bourgeois newspapers, slanderously stated that our country "had robbed" China, "selling machinery and equipment at twice the world prices."

The Chinese side continued to curtail scientific and technical co-operation with the Soviet Union. In 1963 the Soviet side proposed inclusion in the project of a protocol for the next session of the Sino-Soviet commission on scientific and technical cooperation covering 172 items on which technical documentation would be transferred to the PRC. Chinese representatives rejected most of them; only 51 items remained in the protocol. In January 1964 the Chinese side, once again without motivation, removed from consideration 80 percent of its applications, despite the fact that half of them already had been approved by Soviet organizations.

The severing of scientific and technical ties with the Soviet Union resulted in serious setbacks to development of science and technology in the PRC. But Peking leaders appeared unmoved by this consideration, consciously sacrificing the interests of scientific and technical progress in China to their anti-Soviet aims.

Sino-Soviet trade in 1962 was 18 percent below that recorded for 1961. The PRC reduced its purchases of Soviet petroleum products by more than one million tons, those of machinery and equipment by 73 million rubles, and reduced its deliveries to the USSR of tin by 2,500 tons, tungsten concentrate by 5,300 tons, cotton by 3,100 tons, and reduced its deliveries of many other commodities as well. The volume of trade between the USSR and PRC in 1963 fell by 20 percent as compared with 1962.

Talks on Sino-Soviet trade for 1964 took place in Peking in the spring of that year. The situation was a difficult one, created artificially by the Chinese side. PRC representatives refused to sell the Soviet Union goods which had for years been traditional Chinese exports to the USSR. At the same time, the Chinese tried to foist off on the Soviet delegation goods in which the Soviet Union had no interest, and which could not be sold in other countries.

As noted previously, our country, recognizing the difficult economic situation in the PRC, refrained from food purchases since 1961. However, the Chinese representatives at the 1964 trade talks were adamant in trying to obtain agreement from the Soviet Union to take food exports. Nor did they hesitate to exert obvious pressure and blackmail, asserting that the refusal of the USSR to make such purchases meant the Soviets would bear responsibility for trade reduction between our countries. They even threatened to wreck the talks. The provocative nature of such actions soon became open. Peking propaganda spread the fabrication, at home and abroad, that the PRC supposedly would export "hundreds of thousands of tons of meat products" to the USSR, whereas in fact, a little over 40,000 tons of meat products, including canned goods, were exported from the PRC to the Soviet Union in 1964.

In 1964 the Chinese, in addition, curtailed purchases in the USSR of many commodities traditionally exported to China. Obviously, this resulted in a further reduction in trade between the USSR and the PRC. The volume of Sino-Soviet trade in 1964 was 25 percent below the 1963 volume. This resulted in further reduction of the USSR's share in the foreign trade of the PRC to about 15 percent, as compared with 23 percent in 1963.

From 1962 to 1964 the Soviet Union repeatedly expressed its readiness to revive coordination in actions of our two countries in capitalist markets, but Peking showed no enthusiasm. Nor did the government of the PRC show any interest in the Soviet initiative concerning regularization of exchange of experience in economic construction. The government, in particular, rejected a proposal that an exhibit of Soviet economic achievements be opened in the PRC on the occasion of the 45th anniversary of the October Revolution, and that a similar Chinese exhibit be opened in the Soviet Union on the occasion of the 15th anniversary of the founding of the PRC.

Cultural cooperation between the USSR and the PRC shaped up similarly. Its 1962 scope was approximately 30 percent below the 1961 level. The Chinese side consistently belittled the political significance of Soviet measures. During the 1962 talks, for example, the Chinese side refused to accept the Soviet proposal that a display of political placards honoring V. I. Lenin be organized in the PRC and stubbornly insisted on replacing it with a toy display.

Ties among social organizations were severed on Peking's initiative. The enemies of Sino-Soviet friendship strove with particular tenacity to interfere with intercourse between youth of the two countries. Eighteen Chinese youth delegations visited the USSR in 1958–1959, and 15 Soviet youth delegations visited China in return, but in 1962 there was but one Chinese delegation to the USSR and not a single Soviet delegation was invited to China.

CCP leaders began to draw widely on prominent PRC cultural figures in carrying out their nationalist anti-Soviet course. They demanded that writers and artists, painters, and musicians "intensify the struggle against Soviet revisionism." Workers in China's literature and art were given the task of "taking an active part in the class struggle inside and outside the country,"[56] at the second, expanded session of the All-China Committee of the Federation of Literary and Art Workers. Realization of these plans led to further curtailment in cultural relations between the PRC and the USSR.

The Soviet side, during the February 1963 talks in Peking, suggested a project for a new annual plan to double, approximately, cultural cooperation envisaged under the Chinese project. Our suggestion was not adopted. The plan for cultural cooperation in 1963 included 14 projects, as opposed to 50 in the 1962 plan. The exchange of cultural representatives was reduced by three-fourths.

By 1963 Chinese organizations unilaterally severed ties between Soviet and Chinese cultural institutions, libraries, and schools. All measures planned in this field such as those in education, for example, were reduced to an exchange of children's literature (and then only stories).

Beginning in the fall of 1963, Chinese students and graduates in the Soviet Union, on instructions from Peking, organized political discussions during lectures on social disciplines. When they were rebuffed for this practice, Peking instructed them not to attend lectures and to refuse to take examinations in Marxism-Leninism and other social sciences.

On May 13, 1964, the PRC Embassy in Moscow made an official statement to the Ministry of Foreign Affairs of the USSR slandering educational programs of the Soviet higher institutions of learning, as well as Soviet teachers, and raising the optional nature of the requirement that Chinese students attend classes and take examinations in social and political disciplines. The Chinese side grossly violated the Sino-Soviet agreement of August 9, 1952, in accordance with which "all rules established for students and graduate students in the corresponding institutions of learning in the USSR" applied to Chinese students.

Chinese organizations refused to participate in scientific conferences, symposiums, and meetings held in the Soviet Union. The Academy of Sciences of the USSR, in 1963, sent Chinese scientists 23 invitations to conferences and meetings, only eight of which were accepted. The remainder were refused with pleas of "press of current work." The Chinese side, meanwhile, stubbornly refused to invite Soviet scientists to similar undertakings in the PRC.

Even at that time Chinese leaders brazenly attempted the use of cultural relations to undermine the moral and political unity of the

Soviet people, and to thrust upon visiting leaders in culture and arts from our country anti-Marxist views, and malicious, slanderous lies about the foreign and domestic politics of the CPSU. In 1962, for example, during a visit to Yunnan by a delegation from the Ukrainian branch of the Soviet-Chinese Friendship Association, leaders of the Sino-Soviet Friendship Association tried to force members of the Soviet delegation to condemn our country's foreign policy. Needless to say, in all such cases the Maoist provocateurs received deserved rebuffs from all Soviet representatives. Nevertheless, such actions could not help having detrimental effects on development of Sino-Soviet cultural cooperation.

Visits to the PRC by Soviet groups and cultural figures took place in the face of an unbridled anti-Soviet campaign. Provocations occurring in November-December 1963 at the Peking exhibit of the Soviet photographic display "The Seven-Year Plan in Action" were baldly aggressive. Malicious anti-Soviet persons wrote grossly slanderous things in the guest book, including comparing our country to Hitler's Germany.

The Chinese press, printing unpardonably libelous attacks against the Soviet Union, perverted completely the nature of cultural relations between our countries, spread false documents alleging that statements made by Chinese artistic groups, and visits of Chinese cultural workers to the USSR, supposedly resulted in a demonstration of the "warm love of the Soviet people for Chairman Mao Tse-tung."

As a matter of fact, tours by Chinese artists in the USSR often were used by Maoists for anti-Soviet propaganda and provocations. Take, for example, the 1963 stay of the People's Liberation Army Ensemble: The numerous "supervisors" of the ensemble who accompanied it on trips in the USSR, representatives of the Chinese Embassy, and correspondents of the Hsinhua Agency all tried to organize anti-Soviet meetings during intermissions and scattered slanderous literature defaming our party and country in theatres and hotels wherever they appeared.

At the same time Chinese authorities took steps to hamper real contact between Soviet representatives and the population of the PRC. The following incident is typical. In 1964 the Red Army Song and Dance Ensemble was placed under surveillance; walkie-talkies even were used to send orders like "Group of seven Russians gathered in the corridor outside Room No. 5. Find out what they are saying." "A group of dancers has finished rehearsal ahead of time and has left. Follow it!" "Station One, attention! The Russians are leaving. Get the spectators out of the entrance!"

Members of the ensemble were deprived of mixing with spectators during their stay in the PRC, even in the concert halls. Chinese representatives accompanying the ensemble, resorting to physical force, rudely and unceremoniously pushed Soviet artists into the wings when they desired to hold friendly meeting with their audiences.

18. Peking leaders intensify anti-Soviet activities in the international arena

The struggle against our party and country in the international arena was the most important component of the anti-Soviet course established by the CCP.

Dissident groups formed by Peking in various countries actively engaged in spreading anti-Soviet propaganda abroad. The Maoists, in forming these groups, did not hesitate to use slander, bribery, and blackmail where unstable elements were concerned. They willingly added to the ranks "of the fighters against modern revisionism" any political adventurers so long as they reviled the CPSU and other Marxist-Leninist parties. This is why pro-Chinese groups included Trotskyites, anarchists, political adventurers, and morally decadent persons who collaborated with the police and imperialist intelligence. The Maoists even made contact with White Guard Russian émigrés in their efforts to find allies in the struggle against the USSR. In fact, the Chinese representatives established close ties with Ukrainian nationalists in Canada and purchased a large stock of anti-Soviet literature from them. The White Guard rabble, sensing spiritual brotherhood with Maoists in their anti-Soviet feelings, extended their filthy hands to them. For instance, the émigré paper *Vil'ne slovo,* published in Canada, made an appeal "to side actively with Maoist China against Communist Moscow," and called upon Ukrainian nationalists to unite with the Maoists for "the joint struggle against the common enemy."

The same complete coincidence of ideological positions was noted between Maoists and Trotskyites of the "Fourth International," who even wrote an open letter to the CC CCP, stating flatly:

> The Fourth International, which from the day of its founding has carried on . . . a struggle with the ideas which you now oppose, is on your side. . . . The International Secretariat of the International welcomes this discussion you have started throughout the Communist movement. It calls upon you to develop it.[57]

The PRC's foreign policy course, so detrimental to the Soviet Union, became very apparent in the splitting tactics of the Maoists in developing countries, and in particular in 1964 efforts by Peking to prevent the USSR from participating in the Second Afro-Asian Conference.

The Maoist leadership of the CCP had long before established a course, the purpose of which was to wreck relations between the Soviet Union and the "Third World" countries. In December 1961, at the executive committee session of the Organization for the Solidarity of the Peoples of Asia and Africa, the Chinese representative declared that "only the anti-imperialist people's oganizations of Asia, Africa, and Latin America, and not organizations from other regions" could take the initiative in calling a conference on solidarity and make preparations for it. He demanded that no Soviet delegates attend the conference.

The Chinese delegation to the preparatory meeting of the Conference of Asian and African Journalists in Djakarta in 1962 came out against full and equal participation in the conference by the Soviet Union's Central Asiatic Republics' representatives. The Maoists took a similar position at other international conferences, in particular at the Ninth World Conference on the Prohibition of Nuclear and Hydrogen Weapons (Hiroshima, August 1963), and at the executive committee session of the Organization of Afro-Asian Solidarity (Nicosia, September 1963). PRC representatives voted against the acceptance of Uzbekistan at the fourth Session of the Organization of Economic Cooperation of the Countries of Asia and Africa (Karachi, December 1963). The head of the Chinese delegation to the Afro-Asian Solidarity Conference in Moshi (1963), in a meeting with Soviet representatives, openly stated that:

> "We regret that you came here at all, and to think you were needed here is an insult to the solidarity movement of the Afro-Asian countries. . . . Do as you please, but we will be against you."

Chinese delegates indoctrinated representatives of Afro-Asian nations with the notion that since Russians, Czechs, and Poles were white, "they could not be relied upon," that they "will always make arrangements with the Americans, who are white," and that peoples of Asia and Africa have special interests and should form their own separate unions.[58]

CCP leaders, striving to attract to their side representatives of developing countries in international democratic organizations, conducted unprincipled deals on a vast scale. A participant in the Sixth Session of the Afro-Asian Solidarity Council (Algiers, March 1964) said that the Chinese delegation had offered him a large sum of money if he would vote with them. When he inquired as to the question on which he was to "share" the Chinese viewpoint, he was given the reply: "You don't have to know that, just vote along with us."[59]

The representatives of 22 Afro-Asian states discussed preparations for a second conference of Afro-Asian heads of states and governments in Djakarta in April 1964. The Indian and Ceylonese delegates proposed that the USSR, invariably of tremendous help to the Afro-Asian peoples, definitely participate in the conference. This initiative was categorically rejected by the Chinese delegation. It threatened to leave Djakarta if India and Ceylon did not withdraw their proposal.

In its efforts to "excommunicate" the Soviet Union from "Third World" states, the Chinese leadership resorted to the absurd assertion that the USSR is not an Asian country. The Soviet government, in its statement of May 5, 1964, reminded Peking leaders that the Soviet Union accounts for about 40 percent of Asia's territory, and that the Asian part of the Soviet Union is almost twice as big as the territory of all China; moreover, the Asian part of the USSR could absorb such large countries of Asia—all together—as China, India, Indonesia, Pakistan, Burma, and Japan within its boundaries.[60]

But it was not that Chinese nationalists were weak in geography; the Maoists denied the obvious simply to estrange the Soviet Union and the Afro-Asian countries. CCP nationalists, following their line of separating states and peoples serving the cause of peace and national independence, now advanced their racist criterion continually, imparting to it a decisive role in determining the community of political interests and the possibilities of joint action in the international arena. The Maoists, under the pretext of racial harmony, promoted the concept that people of different colors could not understand each other and act together, even if they held common goals and enemies. They moreover gradually indoctrinated suspicion of many socialist peoples merely because they were white.

Peking leaders also tried to undermine economic relations between the USSR and the countries of Asia, Africa, and Latin America, and to distort and discredit the nature of Soviet assistance to these countries, saying that it "was detrimental to their economic and political interests."[61]

All facts pointed to the conclusion that the position of the Chinese leaders on the participation of the USSR in the second Afro-Asian conference simply was an expression of their general anti-Soviet course in the international arena.

At the same time it was Chinese leaders who, by their actions with respect to the countries of the Third World, showed themselves unprincipled politicians ready to bargain with extremely reactionary forces simply to achieve their great-power, chauvinistic goals. For example, Peking, while advancing slogans of liberation for enslaved peoples, steadfastly maintained trade relations with the Republic of South Africa, that most repulsive example of a colonial and racist regime. Trade between the two increased by a factor of ten in the period 1961 through 1963.[62]

19. Condemnation of the CCP's splitting course by the Communist and Workers' Parties

The turn taken by CCP leaders in the period 1960–1964 from a policy of Sino-Soviet friendship to open struggle against the CPSU and the Soviet Union was accompanied by a basic reorientation in the entire foreign policy of the PRC. Each day of this reorientation deepened the split between the PRC and the revolutionary forces, drawing it closer to pro-imperialist forces in the international arena.

The splitting course of Peking leaders caused increasing indignation in the countries of the socialist commonwealth, in the ranks of the international Communist movement, among fighters for national liberation, and in all corners of progressive society throughout the world.

This course, hostile to the cause of peace and socialism, was unconditionally condemned in decisions and in documents of Communist parties in socialist countries. The Central Committee of the Czechoslovakian Communist Party, in a statement made on July 21, 1963, asserted that actions of CCP leaders concerning the world socialist system cannot be termed anything other than splitting and adventuristic.

The plenary session of the Central Committee of the Mongolian People's Revolutionary Party, in a decree adopted on December 22, 1963, stated that in recent years CCP leaders had openly attacked the general line of the world Communist movement developed jointly by the Marxist-Leninist parties and set forth in the 1957 Declaration and 1960 Statement. They dispatched a letter to the CC CCP on June 12, 1964 emphasizing that the splitting, wrecking tactics of Chinese leaders posed a tremendous threat to the unity of socialist collaboration and to the world Communist movement, drawing attention and strength of Communists and the working class, away from the struggle against imperialism.

The Central Committee of the Socialist Unity Party of Germany, in a statement of April 23, 1964, noted that agitation of the Chinese population in a slanderous, anti-Soviet spirit was the grossest contradiction of proletarian internationalism.

The plenary session of the Central Committee of the Bulgarian Communist Party on March 21, 1964 pointed out that Mao Tse-tung and his group had carried ideological differences into interstate relations with socialist countries.

Severe, relentless criticism was leveled against CCP policies by the June 1964 Fourth Congress of the Polish United Workers' Party. Other Communist parties also vigorously condemned the withdrawal of CCP leaders from positions of Marxism-Leninism and proletarian internationalism. The Political Bureau of the French Communist Party, reviewing the situation in July 1963, concluded that theoretical views of CCP leaders together with their practical activities completely contradicted the general line of the world Communist movement. But CCP leaders paid no attention to the voice of those who, guided by the interests of peace and socialism, protested against their splitting, wrecking course. The Maoists, further subordinating party and country to their authority, continued their previous course.

NOTES

1. *Shantung Ta Hsüeh Hsüeh Pao,* No. 1, 1960.
2. *Sinkiang Hung-chi,* No. 6, 1960.
3. *Mingshui Tuan-ch'i,* No. 2, 1962.
4. *Jen Min Jihpao,* August 8, 1961.
5. *Kungmin Jihpao,* February 4, 1961.
6. *Jen Min Jihpao,* July 14, 1964.
7. *Hung-chi,* No. 1, 1962.
8. *Program Documents,* p. 5–6.
9. *Hung-chi,* No. 8, 1960.
10. *Pravda,* June 28, 1960.
11. *Pravda,* July 17, 1960.
12. *Pravda,* November 7,1960.
13. *Jen Min Jihpao,* December 10, 1960.
14. *Pravda,* January 22, 1961.
15. *Pravda,* October 20, 1961.
16. *Jen Min Jihpao,* November 10 and 23, 1962.
17. *Jen Min Jihpao,* December 31, 1962, January 27, February 27, March 8 and 9, 1963 and other issues.
18. *Pravda,* January 7, 1963.
19. *Pravda,* January 17, 1963.
20. *Lenin,* Vol. 11, p. 133.
21. *Pravda,* March 14, 1963.
22. *Pravda,* March 14, 1963.

23. *Pravda*, March 14, 1963.
24. *Pravda*, April 3, 1963.
25. *Pravda*, June 22, 1963.
26. *Pravda*, June 19, 1963.
27. *Izvestiya*, July 4, 1963.
28. *Pravda*, July 4, 1963.
29. *Pravda*, July 14, 1963.
30. *Pravda*, July 22, 1963.
31. *The Leninist Policy*, p. 197.
32. *Za splochennost' mezhdunarodnogo kommunisticheskogo dvizheniya. Dokumenty i materialy* (*For Solidarity in the International Communist Movement, Documents and Materials*, hereinafter referred to as *For Solidarity*), pp. 208–209.
33. *Pravda*, June 23, 1961.
34. *Pravda*, April 9, 1961.
35. *Pravda*, February 5, 1961.
36. *Pravda*, March 30, 1969.
37. *The Leninist Policy*, p. 186.
38. *Mingshui Tuan-ch'i*, No. 2, 1962.
39. *Jen Min Jihpao*, August 10, 1961.
40. *Li Shih Yen-chiu* (*Historical Research*), No. 4, 1964.
41. *Maoizm glazami kommunistov* (*Maoism through the Eyes of Communists*, hereinafter referred to as *Maoism*) (Moscow, 1969), p. 90.
42. T. Rakhimov, *Natsionalizm i shovinizm—osnova politiki gruppy Mao Tszeduna* (*Nationalism and Chauvinism—the Basis of the Mao Tse-tung Group*, hereinafter referred to as *Nationalism and Chauvinism*) (Moscow, 1968).
43. *Pravda*, August 21, 1963.
44. *Pravda*, August 4, 1963.
45. *Pravda*, August 4 and 21, September 21–22, 1963.
46. *Pravda*, September 22, 1963.
47. *Pravda*, September 1, 1963.
48. *Pravda*, March 14, 1963.
49. Ibid.
50. *Pravda*, April 3, 1964.
51. *Jen Min Jihpao*, May 8, 1964.
52. *Jen Min Jihpao*, July 29, 1964.
53. *Pravda*, July 29, 1964.
54. *Pravda*, September 22, 1963.
55. *Pravda*, March 30, 1969.
56. *Wen Hui Pao*, No. 6, 1963.
57. *Pravda*, July 14, 1963.
58. *For Solidarity*, pp. 198–199.
59. M. S. Kapitsa. *Leveye zdravogo smysla* (*O neshney politike gruppy Mao*) (*To the Left of Common Sense* [*The Foreign Policy of the Mao Group*], hereinafter referred to as *To the Left*) (Moscow, 1968), p. 99.
60. *Pravda*, May 5, 1964.
61. *Jen Min Jihpao*, October 22, 1963.
62. *Maoism*, p. 160.

CHAPTER SEVEN

Soviet-Chinese Relations on the Eve of the "Cultural Revolution"

A comparatively short period, that from October 1964 to August 1966, holds a particular place in the history of Sino-Soviet relations.

At this time the Chinese situation was characterized as one of sharp aggravation of antagonisms which, after long development in darkness, blossomed in the fall of 1966 as the so-called "cultural revolution." The basis of the political crisis encompassing the entire sphere of Chinese society was the growing contradiction between the antisocialist course of Chinese foreign and domestic policies and the development of the PRC along the socialist path. Maoists and their cohorts could not engage in open battle with their antagonists. Moreover, as time went on, they were forced to reckon with the opposition and occasionally even retreated to await a propitious time for decisive counterattack. The struggle of the various forces within the Chinese leadership left its imprint on the PRC's internal situation and led to peculiar circumlocutions in domestic and foreign policies.

Overall, however, the greatest influence on development of Sino-Soviet relations came to be the nationalist clique in the CCP. Chinese Communists living under conditions flagrantly violating socialist democracy and completely negating Leninist norms of party life could not successfully withstand the intense pressure of the Maoist leadership, which even resorted to physical violence against those of different persuasion. The Maoists were successful in continuing and strengthening the course leading to open political struggle against the Soviet Union, an important condition for the "cultural revolution." Anti-Sovietism became the most cogent aspect of its political program.

So far as it concerned the USSR, the period under discussion is notable for increased activity in the struggle of our party to return the PRC to the path of friendship and cooperation with all socialist countries in the spirit of proletarian internationalism. The CC CPSU based its decisions on Leninist consistency and the principled approach inherent in its organization, guided by cardinal interests of the Soviet and Chinese peoples and the interests of world Communist and national liberation movements.

1. Sino-Soviet talks of November 1964

A number of new steps were taken after the CC CPSU October plenary session, all designed to create a situation favorable to normalization of relations between the CPSU and the CCP, and between the Soviet Union and the PRC.* The CC CPSU proceeded from the position that when ideological disagreements arise, it is necessary to strive for unity in practical actions, first by developing ties along interstate lines in the struggle with imperialism. The CPSU, supported by other Marxist-Leninist parties, unilaterally ceased press criticism of the Chinese leadership, thus opening prospects for resumption of direct contacts between the Central Committees of the CPSU and the CCP.

However, as before, this failed to suit CCP leaders, who tried pressuring the CPSU to deviate from positions of principle, and from the general line of the world Communist movement. Pertinent is the fact that on the very day the Chinese Central Committee received information on the CC CPSU October plenary session decisions, the PRC exploded its first atomic bomb. Thus Peking appeared to be informing the Soviet Union that its relations with the Soviet Union would be based on a position of strength.

The atomic bomb tests in the PRC were used to inflame further nationalist fever among the Chinese population. Whereas not too long before, Peking propaganda had consistently tried to justify the thesis that the nuclear weapon was nothing but a "paper tiger," now it began to boast of the sharply increased might of China and her corresponding influence on the course of world events.

CCP leaders dampened somewhat their more vulgar anti-Soviet attacks in the first days after the CC CPSU October plenary session, but this was done for tactical considerations. Chinese propaganda briefly refrained from naming the CPSU and the USSR in its attacks, preferring instead to use such terms as "modern revisionists," "one of the great powers," and the like. But the Chinese population, drilled by Maoists, was quite well aware of the real targets of these provocative labels. For

---

* Translator's note: these steps included the removal of N. S. Khrushchev from the party and government leadership.

all practical purposes Chinese leaders did not for a minute cease their anti-Soviet activities.

The Chinese population, at meetings held in the second half of October, was told that the new Soviet leadership "is, as before, revisionist," that "the changes in evidence are essentially no changes at all." Anti-Soviet literature, briefly put away during the celebration of the 15th anniversary of the founding of the PRC, once again appeared in hotels, airports, stations, and other public places. Chinese foreign trade organizations continued wholesale sales of anti-Soviet literature published in the PRC to foreign bourgeois firms at the Kwangchow (Canton) export goods fair.

The Chinese periodical press never ceased publication of anti-Soviet materials. Some examples follow:

On October 16 *Jen Min Jihpao* carried an item on the October plenary session of the CC CPSU, and, at the same time, an article calling for "a decisive struggle with modern revisionism," for "a fight to the death."

On October 17 *Jen Min Jihpao* printed a telegram of greetings from Chinese to Soviet leaders, while another Chinese newspaper, *Ta Kung Pao* (published in Hong Kong), printed a slanderous article repeating Maoist attacks on the Moscow test ban treaty as "a treaty of fraud."

On October 19 *Jen Min Jihpao* reported the publication in foreign languages of a new series of so-called replies to the open letter of the CC CPSU of July 14, 1963, as well as of an anti-Soviet collection, *Greetings to the Fighting Friendship of China and Albania!* On this same day *Jen Min Jihpao* printed an article by the secretary of the Kweichow Provincial Committee of the Communist Party of China that was replete with crude, slanderous attacks against the Soviet Union and the other socialist countries. On October 19 the newspaper *Tsan Kao Shou-tse* wrote that the Chinese atom bomb explosion "is indicative of the defeat of the attempts of imperialism and revisionism, including those of the Soviet Union, to isolate China."

On October 20 *Jen Min Jihpao,* among its reports from Japan, printed that nuclear tests in the PRC "mean a final failure of the conspiracy of the three powers, the United States, England, and the USSR, to dominate the world by their reliance on a monopoly of nuclear weapons," that these tests in China were conducted "in the name of peace and to protect its sovereignty against the threat posed by the USA and the great power mania of the Soviet Union."

The anti-Soviet activities of Chinese diplomats abroad continued.

PRC representatives in Prague, Luxembourg, and Geneva distributed literature inimical to our country and, as before, anti-Soviet publications were sent from Peking to the Federal Republic of Germany, France, and other countries.

Newspapers and journals published abroad by pro-Peking groups continued to pursue their anti-Soviet propaganda purposes. The journal *Renaissance* (its first issue was published in November 1964) was published in Greece with Chinese money and carried articles containing malicious anti-Soviet attacks. The pro-Peking newspaper *People* conducted an active anti-Soviet campaign in Burma. Radio broadcasts from the PRC, beamed to carry anti-Soviet contents in many foreign languages, were especially aimed at the African countries.

PRC representatives at sessions attended by authorities of the World Federation of Trade Unions and the International Democratic Federation of Women, held soon after the CC CPSU October plenary session, transparently masked their slanderous anti-Soviet attacks in decrying "the foreign policy course of one state, whose leadership policies were bankrupt," "the capitulatory line of one great country," and the conclusion of the Moscow nuclear test ban treaty as "a great fraud," with which powers already possessing nuclear weapons want "to ensure their monopoly and bind the hands and feet of all countries and peoples struggling for peace."

Despite the unseemly maneuvers of Peking, the CC CPSU and the Soviet government invited a party-government delegation from the PRC to the celebration of the 47th anniversary of the Great October Socialist Revolution in order to utilize contacts at high levels to seek ways to normalize Sino-Soviet relations.

The Chinese delegation, headed by Chou En-lai, arrived in Moscow on November 5. That same day Chinese newspapers pictured the explosion of the PRC's atomic bomb, as if to remind the Soviet Union that PRC leaders intended dealing with them from a position of strength.

The plans of the Chinese arriving in the USSR can be judged as well by the nature of events occurring in China on the 47th anniversary of the October Revolution. On November 6 there appeared only slightly disguised attacks against domestic and foreign policies of the CPSU during celebrations in Peking. *Jen Min Jihpao's* editorial on November 7 blatantly encouraged the Soviet people to turn against CPSU leadership, against the Soviet State, and against the revolutionary traditions of the workers in our country.

The editorial contained special views of CCP leaders on problems of contemporary world development, and openly declared that strengthening the solidarity of the socialist camp and the international Communist movement was necessary to effect the so-called general line of the international Communist movement (the "25 points") set forth in the CC CCP's letter of June 14, 1963. The authors tried to show that CCP leaders bore no personal responsibility for deterioration in Sino-Soviet relations.

The behavior of the Chinese delegation in Moscow completely betrayed the objectives of its true program: the use of direct and crude pressure to force the CPSU to desert its positions based on principles; the creation of a pool of "facts" to blame the CPSU for "unfriendly" relations with the CCP; the parroting of such slogans as "bankruptcy of modern revisionism" and "victories of the ideas of Mao Tse-tung" to brainwash leaders of other fraternal parties and countries arriving in Moscow; the sowing of discord in the socialist community and in the world Communist movement.

†The Chinese side had the insolence to demand that our party change policies solidly based on historical documents, resolutions, and congresses, to those of Mao Tse-tung, using the "25 points" as a theoretical base. Insisting that a review of CPSU policy was an unalterable condition for normalization of Sino-Soviet relations,* CCP leaders not only desired to subordinate our party to their influence, they also wanted to establish their supremacy in the socialist community and the world Communist movement.

It was only natural that these efforts came to naught, because the political line of the 20th, 21st, and 22nd congresses and our party program expresses the will of the entire party, and of all Soviet people. The position of the CPSU regarding Sino-Soviet relations always has been clear-cut and coherent; in the interests of the cause, both parties in their relationships should proceed from premises which unite and do not separate them. The crux of the problem is how to normalize a situation when there are disagreements. So far as debatable questions of principle are concerned, conditions must be created for businesslike discussions, and this requires time and practice. Open polemics therefore should cease, and the question of the joint steps to be taken by both parties in strengthening the anti-imperialist front should be discussed. An exchange of views on Sino-Soviet interstate ties should also take place.

CCP leaders, as before, refused to accept the proposal that open

* Translator's note: the Chinese, no doubt, misread the removal of Khrushchev ten days earlier as an "admission" by the Soviet leadership of the erroneousness of their policy.

polemics cease. They asserted, moreover, that if the CPSU continued following its program, Peking would not stop its political struggle with our party. The CPSU proposal to keep polemics within the scope of comradely discussion was also categorically rejected.

The CC CPSU, in proposing cessation of public polemics, was not doing so because our party had no definitive opinions in dispute with CCP leaders. The errors and fallacies of the Chinese course were all too obvious. The CC CPSU merely believed that conditions created by open polemics, and particularly the forms in which such polemics were carried on by the Chinese, hampered normalization of the situation and caused serious damage to the world Communist movement.

The Soviet position on the convening of a drafting committee to prepare documents for the forthcoming international conference of Communist and Workers' Parties was detailed by the CC CPSU in meetings with Chinese representatives. †It was emphasized that the planned date for convening the committee was tentative, and that the CC CPSU was ready to discuss with the CCP and other fraternal parties the question of dates for convening the committee, its composition, and the forms and methods of its work. The Soviet Central Committee proposed that the committee do its work in several stages. Initially there would be an exchange of views on the nature of documents to be presented to the conference, on methods that would apply for consultations, and on other questions connected with preparations for the future conference. The representatives of the parties then could depart, counsel with their respective leaderships, and once again assemble and agree on future actions.

But these proposals failed to suit Chinese leaders. The CCP representatives tried to darken the atmosphere of the meeting by any provocation. They supported traditional positions of the CC CCP directed at wrecking the work of the drafting committee, and emphasized Chinese determination not to participate, under any circumstances, in collective activities of fraternal parties to strengthen the unity of the world Communist movement.

The CCP delegation also refused to consider concrete measures for solidifying the anti-imperialist front. They responded only by obscure declarations to the proposal for counsel on ways and methods to fight imperialism and the nature of war, given the current international situation. Also clearly observed was an effort by CCP leaders to prejudice the policy of peaceful coexistence and to aggravate the international situation, particularly in relations between the USSR and the USA.

The Chinese side showed no desire to discuss the problem of Sino-

Soviet interstate relations and advanced no positive proposals aimed at normalizing those relations.

†The Soviet side undertook a new initiative, proposing a high-level conference between representatives of the CPSU and the CCP, as soon as Chinese leaders were ready, in order to discuss a number of questions and to restore confidence between our parties and countries and to strengthen their unity. The Soviet side expressed agreement for such a meeting either open or closed at Chinese discretion, in Moscow or Peking. CCP leaders also rejected this proposal.

The Chinese delegation, prior to departure from Moscow, once again demonstrated its lack of interest in normalizing relations with the Soviet Union and its plans to continue the attack against the CPSU and other fraternal parties. On insistence of the Chinese delegation, a paragraph stating that the two sides had agreed to maintain party-to-party contacts in the interests of strengthening solidarity of the Communist movement on the basis of Marxism-Leninism and proletarian internationalism was deleted from the press release on the meetings. Moreover, the phrase stating that meetings had taken place in "a frank and comradely atmosphere" was omitted from the agreed text when the release was published in the Chinese press.

Upon its return to Peking on November 14, 1964, the Chinese delegation was feted by a magnificent gathering attended by all party and government figures in China, and headed by Mao Tse-tung. This gathering was designed to demonstrate the complete solidarity between the Chinese leadership and Mao Tse-tung with those actions of their delegation which had wrecked constructive talks and had blocked the process of normalization begun upon Soviet initiative.

The remaining faint signs of an unstable "truce" virtually disappeared after the delegation's return from Moscow. The Chinese leaders reversed their hypocritical "peace-loving" gestures and soon resumed their position of openly hostile relations with the CPSU and with the Soviet Union.

On November 21, 1964 the journal *Hung-ch'i* published an editorial equal in its anti-Soviet intensity and vitriolic attacks to any of the earlier violent Chinese diatribes on our party and country. The editorial contained an ultimatum: the CPSU was to categorically reject its general line and adopt the ideological platform and political course of Mao Tse-tung and his group. This was the only way, in the editorial's opinion, that Sino-Soviet relations could be normalized. *Hung-ch'i* took particular aim at the basic tenets of the CPSU program and the foreign and domestic policies of our state.

The editorial abounded in attacks not only against the CPSU and its leaders, but all the Soviet people. CCP leaders made monstrous statements concerning the "degeneration of Soviet society and culture" and the "rampaging of capitalistic forces in the USSR," and accused our state of "complicity with American imperialism."

A series of new, open attacks against our party followed the *Hung-ch'i* editorial. *Jen Min Jihpao,* on November 26, 1964, published the CC CCP's greetings to the 9th Congress of the Communist Party of Japan and interspersed them with slanderous anti-Soviet remarks and statements. In addition, on that same day, anti-Soviet harangues were given at the opening of the All-Chinese review of amateur performances of national minorities; the next day the performance was repeated at a huge rally in Peking celebrating the 20th anniversary of the liberation of Albania. The PRC minister of foreign affairs, speaking in Djakarta on November 27, concocted provocative fabrications about domestic conditions in the USSR, saying that "hundreds of Soviet citizens enter the PRC every day in search of food."

The Maoists, in efforts to create the impression that Peking's anti-Soviet course was gaining wide support in other countries, resorted to their favorite method. They inspired anti-Soviet speeches by adherents abroad, and represented these malignancies as the voice of the "world community."

CCP leaders once again used the tribunal of the highest organ of state authority in the PRC, the session of the National People's Congress which convened in Peking on December 20, 1964, to unleash anti-Soviet propaganda. Chou En-lai delivered the report on activities of the PRC governor. He repeated the hackneyed, provocative phrases of the Maoists concerning the "sudden and perfidious breaking of hundreds of agreements and contracts by the Soviet side," distorted the issues of recall of Soviet specialists and curtailment of equipment deliveries from the USSR, slanderously accused our country of "wrecking activities" in Sinkiang, and hinted at the "restoration of capitalism" in the USSR. The speaker rehashed the perfidious thesis that difficulties in relations between the PRC and the USSR were the fault of the Soviet Union. Speeches by other Chinese leaders at the session of the National People's Congress also contained anti-Soviet attacks.

Beginning in the second half of November 1964, PRC representatives renewed attacks against the Soviet Union in international democratic organizations with new bitterness. Chinese delegations made anti-Soviet statements to the Executive Committee and the Eighth Congress of the International Students' Union in Sofia, to the Conference of

Solidarity with the Vietnamese People in Hanoi, to the Presidium of the World Peace Council in Berlin, to the 47th session of the Executive Bureau of the World Federation of Trade Unions, to the meetings of the International Preparatory Committee of the Ninth World Festival of Youth and Students, and to the economic seminar of Asian and African countries. Disregarding concrete tasks of the struggle against imperialism and colonialism, they concentrated the fire of their criticism exclusively on the Soviet Union. Peking leaders labeled our country "Enemy Number One," attacked Soviet foreign policy, and spread lies to the effect that the USSR was trying to push international organizations into renouncing the struggle with imperialism, and also convert them into an obedient weapon of the "revisionist" course in the international arena.

At the end of 1964 the Soviet side suggested changing the date for convening the drafting commission on preparations for the international conference from December 15, 1964 to March 1, 1965. This would give time to prepare for the meeting of the drafting commission, and to hold additional consultations on this particular question. The Soviet side expressed readiness to continue consultations with the CCP and other fraternal parties, and to seek mutually acceptable solutions to questions concerned with preparations. Naturally, this meant that the CCP in turn would have to contribute constructively to preparations for the international conference. Once again, however, Chinese leaders adamantly refused to participate in the work of the drafting commission, regardless of dates set, and regardless of how it would be convened.

2. CCP leaders frustrate the attempts of the CC CPSU and the Soviet government to normalize state-to-state relations between the USSR and the PRC

The CC CPSU and the Soviet government, after the November meeting in Moscow, and despite hostile statements by Chinese leaders, undertook concete actions to normalize Sino-Soviet relations. The Soviet side attempted to restore confidential exchanges of foreign policy information with the PRC. Materials of this nature were passed to the Chinese leadership repeatedly between November 1964 and January 1965. The Chairman of the Council of Ministers of the USSR in his message of December 28, 1964 supported the PRC's proposal for a summit conference to discuss the question of banning and completely destroying nuclear weapons advanced in Chou En-lai's letter of December 17, 1964.

The Soviet side reacted with identical good will to the request of the PRC government for a United Nations discussion of the problem of restoring to China its legal rights in that organization. Representatives of the USSR took an active part in countering the efforts of hostile forces to bring up the so-called Tibetan question at the 19th Session of the General Assembly.

Soviet organizations initiated an effort to resume an active exchange of delegations with the PRC in order to draw up plans for cultural co-operation and for the friendship associations that had been cut down by the Chinese. Delegations of workers in Soviet cultural and educational institutions, writers, and artistic leaders in the Soviet-Chinese Friendship Association went to China after the October Plenary Session of the CC CPSU.

On December 23, 1964 the Embassy of the USSR in Peking informed the Chinese Committee for Cultural Relations with Foreign Countries of measures necessary to fulfill completely the plan for cultural cooperation in 1964. At the beginning of February 1965 the Soviet organizations concerned presented their projects for the 1965 cooperation plans to the Chinese Committee for Cultural Relations with Foreign Countries and to the Sino-Soviet Friendship Association. The plans envisaged a substantial increase in these exchanges.

On December 18, 1964 it was proposed that the Chinese hold the scheduled 14th session of the Soviet-Chinese Committee on Scientific and Technical Cooperation in December 1964–January 1965. On January 29, 1965 the Soviet State Committee for the Coordination of Scientific Research Work handed the PRC Embassy in Moscow a memorandum containing concrete proposals for materials to be taken up at the 14th Session and for discharging outstanding obligations from the 13th Session. These positive steps by the Soviet side met with no support in China.

Liu Hsiao, Vice Minister of Foreign Affairs of the PRC, in reply to the Soviet Ambassador's expression of views concerning USSR participation in the planned 2nd Afro-Asian Conference, stated that the PRC "did not agree to Soviet participation" in the conference. The PRC Ministry of Foreign Affairs officially confirmed this view on January 14, 1965. Propaganda against the USSR's participation in the conference and attempts to discredit the foreign policy course of the Soviet Union were among primary purposes of the trip made by Minister of Foreign Affairs of the PRC, Chen Yi, to Afro-Asian countries in November–December 1964.

Chinese leaders, in mid-January 1965, issued a statement whose purpose was to drive a wedge into Soviet-Japanese relations and in this way to improve relations between the PRC and Japan. Chen Yi, in a meeting with a member of the Japanese Diet on January 17, 1965, emphasized the fact that China had repeatedly recommended to the Soviet Union that the Kurile Islands, including those in the north, be returned to Japan, and that this view still held. As a result of the Chen Yi interview, which had raised the question of the USSR's territorial integrity and border inviolability, and which contained other statements inimical to the Soviet Union, the USSR Ministry of Foreign Affairs, on January 29, 1965, demanded further elucidation. The Chinese declined comment.

Chinese leaders, at the end of November 1964, once again began to "heat up" the border question and to propagandize their territorial claims against the USSR. On November 28, Lu Ting-yi, PRC Vice Premier, in reviewing the autonomy of national minorities, spoke of "the attempts of imperialism" to separate the northeast, Inner Mongolia, Sinkiang, Tibet, and Taiwan from China, emphasizing that these regions "are in the vanguard of the struggle against imperialism, the Chiang Kai-shek band, the reactionaries, and modern revisionism." On December 6, at the celebration in honor of the tenth anniversary of the Kyzyl-Su Kirghiz autonomous district (province of Sinkiang), the Chairman of the Nationalities Affairs Commission of the National People's Congress called for "crushing of the diversionary and disruptive tactics of the imperialists, reactionaries, and modern revisionists." On December 28, as reported in the Chinese press, the Chairman of the People's Committee of the Sinkiang Uighur Autonomous Region familiarized deputies to the National People's Congress with the "details of the struggle of all nationalities in Sinkiang against the diversionary and disruptive tactics from abroad," including "those from the north." In mid-January 1965 the book *Letters from China* (written in English) by Anna Louise Strong was placed on sale in the PRC. This book contained, among other things, a statement made by Chen Yi at a meeting with foreign delegations on August 19, 1964, in which he dealt with the possibility of the USSR's "seizing Sinkiang, the northeast (Manchuria), and occupying Peking." On January 17, 1965, this same Chen Yi once again said that "the Soviet Union had taken almost 1.5 million square kilometers of territory from China," demonstrating the return of the CCP leadership to the position of Mao Tse-tung in the famous interview with Japanese socialists on July 10, 1964.

3. New constructive steps by the Soviet side

In early February 1965 A. N. Kosygin, member of the Politburo of the CC CPSU and Chairman of the Council of Ministers of the USSR, headed a delegation visiting the Democratic Republic of Vietnam and the Korean People's Democratic Republic.* The CC CPSU decided to utilize the Soviet delegation's stopover in Peking for a new initiative to normalize Sino-Soviet relations and to maintain its contacts with Chinese leaders.

The Soviet delegation met and talked with the leaders of the CCP and the PRC including Mao Tse-tung, during two stops in Peking's airport. The first of these meetings established that Chinese leaders had no constructive positions on which to base joint discussions. The situation in Indochina as a result of intensification of American aggression was reviewed. The Soviet side pointed out that US provocations in Southeast Asia posed a serious threat to world peace and emphasized the need to coordinate efforts of socialist countries for the Vietnamese cause.

Chinese leaders, recognizing the important contribution of the Soviet Union in the Vietnamese struggle against American aggression, nevertheless failed to promote any constructive proposals for helping the Vietnamese people. Moreover, statements were issued in China that the Vietnamese could "cope" with the aggressors without help of any sort, and that victims of American bombing raids over cities and villages in the Democratic Republic of Vietnam could be ignored. *Jen Min Jihpao,* in an editorial published March 22, 1965, cynically wrote that "the more bombs the United States drops, the stronger will be the fighting will of the Vietnamese people." The Soviet delegation rejected any such position, declaring that socialist countries ought to do everything possible to defend the fraternal Vietnamese people against imperialistic American aggression.

The Chinese leaders rejected the Soviet idea of a joint declaration by the Democratic Republic of Vietnam, the PRC, the USSR, the Korean People's Democratic Republic, and other socialist countries, exposing US violation of the Geneva accords of 1964, guaranteeing the independence and safety of the Democratic Republic of Vietnam, and calling for withdrawal of all foreign troops from Indochina. They attributed their rejection to the existence of disagreements between the CCP and the CPSU both on ideological issues and on the question of the cessation of open polemics.

The Chinese leaders stubbornly emphasized that they planned an uncompromising struggle against the ideological positions of the CPSU and

* Translator's note: Kosygin's visit to Hanoi coincided with the first bombing of that city by the US Air Force.

the other Marxist-Leninist parties. They stubbornly declared that they were categorically opposed to the cessation of open polemics.

The Soviet side spelled out our party's position in detail. The CPSU was unopposed to comradely discussion of debatable questions, but it was opposed to engaging in openly hostile polemics because so doing damaged the world Communist movement and particularly the fraternal parties in capitalist countries. But, ignoring the interests of the international Communist movement, CCP leaders proposed continuation of polemics, defending the form and methods used by the Chinese side.

The Soviet side explained to Chinese leaders that the meeting of fraternal parties planned for March 1965 for the preparation of the international conference would be consultative in nature, opening auspicious possibilities for CCP representatives to participate in it. CCP leaders flatly refused to attend a consultative meeting, whatever its form, and in general opposed the calling of an international conference of Communist and workers' parties at any time in the near future. They asserted that a conference of this type was infeasible not only for four or five years, as had been stated officially in the letter from the CC CCP to the CC CPSU, but that eight to ten years might elapse before such a conference could be held.

The Chinese once again rejected the CC CPSU proposal to hold a bilateral meeting by high level representatives of our parties to discuss all questions in dispute. They said the time was not yet ripe for such consultations.

The Soviet delegation even went so far as to propose an exchange of views on problems concerned with development of interstate relations between the USSR and the PRC, but the Chinese leaders also evaded this issue.

The CC CPSU continued its efforts to conciliate Sino-Soviet relations after the meeting in Peking in February 1965. It was suggested that friendship delegations be exchanged in 1965 in honor of the celebration of the 15th anniversary of the signing of the Treaty of Friendship, Alliance, and Mutual Assistance between the USSR and the PRC. Our country attached great importance to celebration of this date. The Soviet side repeatedly took the initiative in maintaining contacts with Chinese leaders. On March 20 the Soviet government extended an invitation to the PRC Minister of Foreign Affairs to stop in the Soviet Union en route to Kabul. At the end of March, in Bucharest, the Soviet delegation attending the funeral of the First Secretary of the Rumanian Workers' Party, Gheorghe Gheorghiu-Dej, suggested to the Chinese delegation, headed by Chou En-lai, that it take advantage of the occasion to exchange views on questions of Sino-Soviet relations.

But all these efforts failed to elicit a positive response from the Chinese leadership.

4. Peking leaders provoke further strain in Sino-Soviet relations

The constructive program of our party, directed at normalizing Sino-Soviet relations, placed those among the Chinese leadership who stubbornly and consciously opposed the program in a difficult position. This group resorted to new anti-Soviet actions in an effort to justify and strengthen its course. These tactics became all too apparent in the anti-Soviet provocation organized by Maoists and carried out by Chinese students in Moscow on March 4, 1965.

Chinese students, on instructions from Peking, used the demonstration by Soviet citizens and representatives of other countries against American aggression in Vietnam at the US Embassy for their provocative acts. Chinese students mingled with demonstrators, screamed anti-Soviet slogans, blaming our party for refusing to help the Democratic Republic of Vietnam, and accusing it of "collusion" with imperialism. They engaged in hooliganistic tactics against Soviet police, and incited Soviet people to speak out against the policy of the CPSU and the Soviet government. The demonstrators properly rebuffed the provocateurs. The instigators of these shameful actions then fabricated lies to the effect that Chinese students in Moscow had been "assaulted" and had become objects of "bloody reprisals."

The Maoists organized a new anti-Soviet campaign around the March 4 events. A massive demonstration by Chinese citizens carrying anti-Soviet slogans was organized in front of the Embassy of the USSR in Peking on March 6, 1965. During these outrages there were cries of "Go home!" and numerous "letters of protest" and other written threats against the Soviet government and the CPSU were tossed onto the Embassy grounds.

Then the Chinese press was unleashed. Between March 5 and 20 it published 25 reports by Hsinhua, the official press agency, of "bloody reprisals against Chinese students in Moscow."

Meetings were held in Chinese institutions and organizations for the purpose of reading anti-Soviet tracts and calling for a "relentless struggle" against the CPSU. Mass meetings organized in Peking and other cities in the PRC on March 19 were used for these same purposes.

The consultative meeting of representatives of 19 fraternal parties was selected by anti-Soviet activists in the CCP as an occasion for new attacks against the CPSU and the Soviet Union. In the article entitled "On the March Meeting in Moscow," published in *Jen Min Jihpao* on March 23, 1965, CCP leaders insolently demanded that the CPSU publicly repudiate decisions of the 20th, 21st, and 22nd congresses, its program, reject the policy of peaceful coexistence, and further promise "never to make the same mistakes again." They qualified their disputes with the CPSU and the international Communist movement as "disagreements between two hostile classes, the proletariat and the bourgeoisie," declaring that the struggle would continue "for so long as classes and the class struggle continued to exist in the world."

Chinese leaders opted for continuing polemics. Open polemics, they stated in an article published March 23, "cannot be stopped in a day, or in a month, or in a year, or in a hundred, thousand, or even ten thousand years. We shall not stop in nine thousand years, we shall criticize for the whole ten thousand years." The Maoists tried doggedly to put words into actions. Central newspapers in the PRC alone published more than 150 anti-Soviet pieces, written to order for Peking leaders, between the CC CPSU October plenary session and the end of March 1965; their henchmen printed over 90 such pieces abroad. The Chinese publishing house Jen Min Ch'u Pan She, in March 1965, published in Chinese and foreign languages a collection of articles entitled *Relative to the Polemics on the General Line of the International Communist Movement,* containing the most malicious anti-Soviet materials published in the PRC since September 1963.

Peking engaged in provocations at the Sino-Soviet border in order to exacerbate tensions between the USSR and the PRC. Attempts to lawlessly seize individual pieces of Soviet territory became more frequent at the end of March. Chinese civilians and military personnel made no attempt to hide border violations. There were 36 incursions into Soviet territory by some 150 Chinese citizens, including servicemen, between October 1, 1964 and April 1, 1965. †And there were 12 such violations by over 500 Chinese civilians and military personnel in the first 15 days of April alone. Border violations became increasingly aggressive. †On April 11, 1965, for instance, some 200 Chinese civilians, with military cover, used eight tractors to plough up Soviet territory. Chinese soldiers, encountering a covering detachment of Soviet border guards, were commanded by their officer to break through using tactics and force.

Peking leaders, in order to justify their anti-Soviet policy, tried to create in China, and abroad, the impression that the Soviet side was following an unfriendly policy toward the PRC, and that an "anti-

Chinese campaign" was under way in our country. The Maoists, in efforts to corroborate this prevarication, submitted crude and unsubstantiated fabrications. Visits to the USSR by any state figure from capitalist countries were attacked immediately by Peking as indicative of a "deal between the Soviet Union and imperialism to fight China." Every item on China appearing in the Soviet press, regardless of nature or content, was characterized as "an attack against the great Chinese people."

Nevertheless, the slanderous fabrications of Peking leaders could not distort the clear-cut, coherent policy of the Soviet Union toward China. This policy was confirmed again at the CC CPSU plenum in September 1965. The First Secretary of the CC CPSU, L. I. Brezhnev, in his speech before the session on September 29, flatly declared that the USSR would "consistently continue to seek ways to adjust the differences and to strengthen friendship and cooperation between the Soviet and Chinese peoples, between our parties and countries."[1]

Peking leaders not only failed to respond positively to this statement, they even went so far as to erect new obstacles along the road to the normalization of relations. Editorials appearing in the journal *Hung Ch'i,* and in the newspaper *Jen Min Jihpao* on November 11, 1965, candidly exposed their splitting, anti-Soviet platform.

Prior to the appearance of this article, CCP leaders, when dealing with Sino-Soviet differences, usually emphasized that "what separates us is but one finger out of ten," that "we have little arguments and great unity." Now, however, they definitively rejected the possibility of adjusting Sino-Soviet differences and stated categorically that so far as the two parties were concerned "there exists that which separates, nothing that unites, there exists that which opposes, and nothing that could be common." The editorial proclaimed the task to be "delimiting politically and organizationally" spheres of activity with the CPSU and other Marxist-Leninist parties.

Chinese leaders unleashed their most vicious attacks against actions by the CC CPSU in domestic and foreign policy after its October 1964 Plenary Session. They repeated their malignant fabrications "about bourgeois degeneration" of the Soviet state, about "collusion" between the Soviet Union and "American imperialism in the name of joint dominion over the world," and publicly announced their ultimatum for our party to reject its general line, to reject decisions of the last congresses and to alter the program of the CPSU.

After the November 11 editorial was published, the Chinese side once again intensified its efforts to interfere in internal affairs of the Soviet Union in order to provoke criticism against the CC CPSU and the

Soviet government. PRC leaders moved closer and closer to open and gross violation of Article 5 of the Sino-Soviet Treaty of Friendship and Mutual Assistance, which obligated the two states to observe the principles of "mutual respect for state sovereignty . . . and non-interference in the internal affairs of the other side."

The Maoists tried to distribute the November 11 editorial, as well as other anti-Soviet materials, in the Soviet Union. Eleven thousand copies of anti-Soviet books and pamphlets were sent to Soviet institutions, organizations, and private individuals from China in 1963; about 45,000 were sent in 1965. A variety of ruses designed to thwart control by USSR state authorities were devised, including insertion of anti-Soviet pamphlets between the pages and in dust jackets of other books, and stuffing them into various corners of the cars on the Peking-Moscow train.

As before the Chinese Embassy acted as the center for dissemination of anti-Soviet literature and provocative rumors among the Soviet people. Particularly in 1966, the Embassy bypassed Soviet organs and began illegal distribution of the journal *Kitay na stroike* (*China in Construction*) in Russian. The USSR Ministry of Foreign Affairs was forced to make necessary representations in the matter to the Chinese Embassy.

†The CC CPSU forwarded a letter to the CC CCP on November 29, 1965, containing a firm denunciation of the pernicious effects the Chinese splitting course was having on Sino-Soviet relations, on socialist cooperation, on the struggle against imperialism, on the liberation of exploited peoples, and on the building of a communist society. That same day, the premier of the PRC State Council, Chou En-lai, made crude anti-Soviet statements at a reception in the Albanian Embassy in Peking.

On January 7, 1965 the CC CCP responded officially to the November 29, 1965 letter from the CC CPSU. The Chinese letter reiterated its slanderous and irresponsible accusations against the CPSU and the Soviet Union, attacked the CPSU program and the foreign and domestic policies of our party and country, repeated continually unsubstantiated phrases concerning "Soviet-American cooperation in the name of world domination," and in every way possible distorted the position of the Soviet Union on the Vietnam question.

The special position of the Chinese leadership on the Vietnam question was an increasing indicator of its hostility toward the Soviet Union and other socialist countries. Peking, while seeking to prolong the war in Vietnam indefinitely, at the same time tried to steer away from involvement in it.

While publicly proclaiming their determination to defend the Vietnamese people against American aggression, Chinese leaders, in fact, repeatedly gave Washington to understand that these warlike declarations were issued only for propaganda effect.

The American journalist Edgar Snow relates that Mao Tse-tung, in an interview with him early in 1965, said he did not believe that the US intended to spread the war into North Vietnam, and that China therefore had no need to enter the war on the side of the Democratic Republic of Vietnam. "And why should the Chinese do so?" asked Mao Tse-tung. "The Vietnamese are quite capable of handling their own problems."

The position of the Chinese leadership on the Vietnamese question did not go unnoticed in the imperialist camp. "The gradual expansion by the United States of the war in Vietnam," wrote the *Washington Post* at the beginning of 1965, "has had a number of favorable political consequences. It has intensified the Sino-Soviet conflict." The British newspaper, *The Observer,* characterized Peking's policy as follows:

> After many months of gradual escalation of the struggle in Vietnam by both sides, the Americans recently indicated serious intentions of attacking North Vietnam. What did Peking do? It gave the Americans a clear hint that if they did attack, China would not come into the war. Mao Tse-tung, in an interview with American journalist Edgar Snow, categorically stated that China would enter the war only in the event America attacked Chinese territory. This means that China would not enter the war if America attacked North Vietnam. When the Americans began bombing North Vietnam, Peking kept its word and did not undertake military countermeasures. At the same time, the Chinese encouraged North Vietnam and the rebels in South Vietnam to oppose negotiations.

In October 1964 the US carried aggression directly to the territory of the Democratic Republic of Vietnam as it began systematic bombing of cities and villages. This act made urgent an increase of aid to the struggling Vietnamese people by socialist countries. Peking leaders, however, remained obstinate in obstructing the solution to this problem.

In February 1965 the CC CPSU and the Soviet government requested that the CC CCP and the PRC take urgent steps to facilitate delivery of Soviet military assistance to the Democratic Republic of Vietnam. This request unexpectedly encountered Peking's opposition.

Beginning in February 1965, the Soviet Union, in the interests of assisting the Vietnamese, repeatedly suggested to the Chinese leadership that there be joint discussions of measures taken to protect the security of the Democratic Republic of Vietnam. †The Soviet side many times took the initiative in proposing a summit meeting of representatives of the Democratic Republic of Vietnam, the PRC, and the USSR, emphasizing the fact that any convenient place for a meeting of all parties was acceptable. Peking stubbornly resisted Soviet proposals, publicly demonstrating its splitting course and lack of desire to cooperate in this most urgent of problems.

Peking leaders took a similar stance with respect to proposals by other socialist countries on coordination of efforts in the Vietnamese cause.

The Chinese position on the Vietnamese question made it all too apparent that the Maoists, for the sake of their divisive, anti-Soviet goals, were ready to sacrifice the interests of the national liberation struggle of the Vietnamese people and to jeopardize the cause of socialism in Vietnam.

5. The outstanding contribution of the CPSU 23rd Congress in the struggle for unity of revolutionary forces

Our party has not only looked at restoring Sino-Soviet friendship and cooperation from the standpoint of relations between the USSR and the PRC and between the CPSU and the CCP, but also as part of the overall problem of strengthening the unity of revolutionary ranks in the struggle with imperialism for peace and socialism. This problem was given special attention by the CPSU 23rd Congress convened in March–April 1966.

The conclusion that the balance of forces in the world arena continues to change in favor of socialism, in favor of the workers' and national liberation movement, was stressed by the 23rd Congress. At the same time, the Congress stated that the contemporary international situation was characterized by an escalation of imperialist aggression and encouragement of reaction. The deepening of the overall crisis faced by capitalism and the aggravation of its contradictions tended to intensify the danger to the cause of peace and social progress of imperialistic adventurism. Imperialism, in seeking an end to impasse, was resorting more frequently to military provocations, and interventions to various conspiracies, and to efforts to exacerbate differences in the world Communist movement.

The 23rd Congress was an international forum for unity of revolutionary forces. It demonstrated the tremendous growth in the trend toward consolidation of revolutionary forces; it further showed itself the greatest factor in strengthening the unity and solidarity of those forces. A significant indicator was broad representation of all detachments of the contemporary revolutionary movement at the Congress.

Eighty-six foreign delegations, including 73 from Communist parties (11 from socialist countries and 62 from capitalist), and 13 from national democratic and left socialist parties, took part in work of the Congress. The central theme of all speeches at the Congress was strengthening the unity and solidarity of modern revolutionary forces. The fraternal parties warmly supported the CPSU conclusion that under prevailing conditions it was necessary to concentrate on unifying and closing revolutionary ranks. They emphasized that it is disloyal and harmful to exacerbate differences, thus creating obstacles to accomplishment of joint actions in the struggle against imperialism.

In conjunction with the 23rd Congress the CPSU undertook a new initiative designed to normalize Sino-Soviet relations.

During a stopover in Peking, shortly before the Congress, a delegation headed by A. N. Shelepin, a member of the Politburo of the CC CPSU, which had visited the Democratic Republic of Vietnam, expressed a desire to meet with CCP leaders. The most prominent leaders declined to meet them. The Soviet delegation nevertheless once again tried to impress upon the Chinese leadership, through the medium of CC CCP representatives with whom they did meet, the steadfast position of our party on elimination of differences, as well as to express the desirability of developing Sino-Soviet interstate relations, particularly in trade and economic cooperation. The Chinese leadership failed to support any of these suggestions.

Because it attached great importance to the CPSU 23rd Congress in strengthening the solidarity of socialist cooperation and the world Communist movement, our Central Committee extended an invitation to the CCP. The podium of the Congress was used to emphasize the readiness of the CC CPSU to consider with CCP leaders, at any time and at the highest levels, outstanding differences and means to resolve them along Marxist-Leninist principles. The Central Committee's line was approved unanimously by the Congress. A resolution contained in the Summary Report of the CC CPSU on the 23rd Congress stated:

> The Congress approves the efforts of the Central Committee of the Communist Party of the Soviet Union and the concrete measures aimed at adjusting the differences with the Communist Party of China on the principled basis of Marxism-Leninism. The Congress expresses confidence that in the end our parties and the peoples of our countries will eventually overcome the difficulties and will present a united front in the struggle for the great common revolutionary cause.[2]

Despite all these efforts, Chinese leaders assumed an openly hostile posture with respect to the 23rd Congress and took the road of further aggravating the struggle with our party and country.

On March 22, 1966, in a letter to the CC CPSU, leaders of the CCP rudely rejected the invitation to send a delegation to the 23rd Congress.[3] Chinese leaders launched malicious, scurrilous attacks against the highest forum of our party, instead of heeding CPSU appeals supported by representatives of the overwhelming majority of Marxist-Leninist parties present. In this disgraceful campaign the opening gun was fired by Chou En-lai on April 30, 1966, at a meeting in Peking attended by a crowd of 100,000.

The refusal of CCP leaders to participate in the work of the 23rd Congress completed the severance of all party line contacts with the CPSU. The CC CCP again failed to respond to an invitation extended in February 1966, for a group of public and state workers to vacation in the USSR. †Greetings sent by the CC CPSU on the 45th anniversary of the founding of the CCP were not published in the Chinese press.

The Maoists simultaneously severed all ties between the young Communist (Komsomol) organizations in the two countries. The Central Committee of the Young Communist League of China published its reply to the March 1966 invitation of the Central Committee of the All-Union Lenin Young Communist League on May 13, 1966, categorically rejecting it and attacking the CPSU and the Lenin Komsomol.

The position of CCP leaders with respect to the 23rd Congress reflected the general line of the Maoists to isolate the CCP from other Marxist-Leninist parties. Leading figures of fraternal parties, in speeches at the 23rd Congress, sharply criticized the anti-Sovietism of Peking leaders and exposed the tremendous damage to the common revolutionary cause wreaked by their irresponsible attacks on the CPSU and the Soviet Union. But it was evident that the hostile reaction of the Peking leaders to the 23rd Congress had deep roots: it was an expression of the same general anti-Soviet line that Maoists tried to reinforce and later expand during the so-called cultural revolution. As events during the second half of 1966 showed, anti-Sovietism became one of the main slogans of the Maoists in attacks against positions of socialism during this counterrevolutionary campaign.

6. Sino-Soviet economic and cultural ties, 1965–1966

The PRC government undertook basic changes in economic relations between the USSR and China in 1965, proposing that they be built in the future on a departmental, rather than an intergovernmental basis; in this way it deliberately downgraded their political importance, and at the same time reduced to a minimum the scope of those relations.

On April 21, 1965, the government of the PRC declared that it was canceling completely all project work established under terms of the June 1961 agreement. This agreement had envisaged technical cooperation with the Soviet Union in the building of 66 large industrial plants. Thus the Chinese side refused to restore economic cooperation between our countries, blocking the main road to its own development. Soviet deliveries to China of complete sets of equipment in 1965 were only one-hundredth of those of 1959.

PRC representatives attending trade talks in the spring of 1965 rejected many proposals advanced by the Soviet side for increasing trade between the two countries. Foreign trade of the PRC was deliberately reorganized to take advantage of capitalist markets. For instance, Chinese exports of tin to capitalist countries increased to between 6,000 and 7,000 tons, and dropped to 500 tons to the USSR. The end result was a reduction in volume of Sino-Soviet trade in 1965 by 7 percent, as compared with 1964.

Since 1966 trade has become the only form of economic tie between the USSR and the PRC, but even it has decreased sharply. Significantly, its volume in 1966 was one-half of that of Sino-Japanese trade.

This situation resulted from the anti-Soviet course adopted by Peking leaders, as well as from their overall policy of severing economic cooperation between China and the socialist community. The share of socialist countries in the PRC's foreign trade dropped to 25 percent in 1966, as compared with 68 percent in 1959. At the same time, the share of capitalist countries in the PRC's foreign trade jumped to 75 percent. It is interesting to note that the PRC trade with the Federal Republic of Germany in 1965 was three times larger than that with the German Democratic Republic.

The Soviet side throughout 1966 took steps to eliminate the grounds for further exacerbation of interstate relations, and sought, at least, resolution of individual problems. The Soviet Union was favorably disposed to requests by Chinese authorities to permit citizens of the PRC to venture onto contiguous islands and into Soviet water areas along border rivers for economic activities, and to permit Chinese peasants to drive their cattle across territory of the USSR. †In March 1966, upon Soviet initiative, the mixed-Sino-Soviet commission on navigation along boundary rivers held its scheduled meeting in Khabarovsk, and in February of the same year representatives of the USSR and the PRC met in accordance with the agreement on joint protection against forest fires.

A new agreement on air traffic between the USSR and the PRC, replacing the December 1954 agreement, was signed in April 1966. This too came about as a result of Soviet initiative. Still, Chinese authorities did everything they could to obstruct cooperation in this area. They unilaterally raised air fares on the Peking-Moscow line, and organized provocations with respect to Aeroflot representatives in the PRC disrupting their normal work. Effective April 1, 1967, upon recommendation of Chinese Aeroflot, the number of flights on the Moscow-Peking run was reduced by one-third.

The scope of Sino-Soviet scientific and technical cooperation in 1965 shrunk precipitously. The 15th session of the Sino-Soviet Commission on Scientific and Technical Cooperation, held in November 1966, clearly showed lack of desire on the Chinese side to expand scientific and technical ties with the USSR. The result was a reduction by more than one-half in the number of obligations undertaken by both sides as compared with those of the preceding session.

Scientific cooperation between the respective academies of sciences also decreased in 1966. The Soviet side (through no fault of its own) sent only one scientist to the PRC to work on a single problem, instead of the 11 scientists for seven problems as stipulated in the plan. The Chinese sent 11 scientists to the USSR to work on three problems, instead of 20 scientists for six problems as planned. †In April 1966 the Academy of Sciences of the PRC made the unfriendly gesture of announcing the "refusal" of two Chinese scientists to accept membership in the Academy of Sciences of the USSR. Needless to say, this "refusal" was the result of raw political pressure. One simply needs to recall that during this period, even scientific correspondence with Soviet colleagues was labeled a "black political offense" by Chinese authorities. This qualification had very definite practical consequences. During the years of the "cultural revolution" thousands of Chinese scientists fell victim to harsh repressions simply because they had studied in the Soviet Union or because they continued subscribing to Soviet scientific publications.

Chinese organizations demonstrated hostility to the Soviet Union in the spring of 1966 by refusing to accept medical supplies and vitamins sent by the Soviet Red Cross to earthquake-stricken regions in the PRC.

Soviet plans for cultural cooperation with the PRC in 1965 called for an expansion in cultural ties of approximately 25 percent as compared with the previous year. This plan was never fully adopted because of Chinese opposition. Still, the number of measures in the plan for cultural cooperation increased somewhat in 1965. Tourist exchanges were restored and agreement reached on student exchanges.

The 1966 cultural cooperation plan between the two countries was signed in Moscow in June under adverse conditions, with numerous procrastinations and difficulties created by the Chinese. This was the smallest of all plans drafted in the history of relations with the PRC in scope of measures included. In sports, a component of the cultural cooperation plan, the 1966 plan called for women's volleyball and basketball teams to go to the PRC, and for men's basketball and table tennis teams to go to the Soviet Union.

But that was only the plan. What actually happened in 1966 was simply an exchange of public health workers, and a tour of the Peking Song and Dance Ensemble, whose program was obviously staged to demonstrate the "great ideas of Mao." The Soviet side repeatedly expressed its readiness to send amateur theatrical groups, as well as groups of specialists, to the PRC, but the Chinese proposed that these events be postponed until 1967 without setting a date. Chinese authorities, pleading lack of space, proposed that "The USSR Today" photographic display, planned for September 1966, also be carried over to 1967.

The Soviet side, on April 22, 1966, proposed the conclusion of a new agreement on cooperation in media communications to replace the old one which had expired (actually, the Chinese had failed to comply with the terms of the earlier agreement, having ceased broadcasting the three half-hour "This Is Moscow Speaking" programs per week forwarded to China for broadcast since 1963). The draft agreement was forwarded to the Chinese side, but the reply from the PRC Ministry of Foreign Affairs (contained in a note December 6, 1966) was replete with slanderous accusations against the Soviet Union. The Soviet proposal concerning cooperation in the field of radio and television was frustrated.

It is easy to understand why Maoists persisted in wrecking cooperation between information services of the PRC and the Soviet Union. They feared the truth about Soviet activities, truth about the successes of Communist construction in our country, and truth about their own perfidious course which inflicted incredible suffering on the Chinese people, destroying their socialist victories one after the other. It was this fear of truth, the attempts to keep their black deed from the bright glare of publicity, that prompted Peking authorities to muzzle foreign correspondents. They were not only forbidden to leave Peking, but their movements were restricted within the city; they could not read newspapers, announcements, or engage in conversation with Chinese. They were subjected to constant insults by officials and often were victims of physical violence by mobs of Red Guards, instigated by Maoists. Representatives of press, radio, and information agencies of socialist countries were particularly hated by the Maoists. They were placed in the most difficult of situations, deprived of information sources, and deliberately terrorized by provocative accusations of "illegal activities."

As part of this practice, the PRC Ministry of Foreign Affairs, on December 16, 1966, gave three Soviet correspondents ten days in which to leave China. Their only "crime" was that they had reported the facts about activities in the PRC.

As previously, Maoists tried to use cultural cooperation for anti-Soviet purposes. There were numerous cases of Chinese tourists, delegations, and students who attempted to collect secret data in the USSR. In July 1966 the USSR Ministry of Foreign Affairs was forced to make an official protest to the Chinese Embassy in Moscow in connection with those PRC military personnel, studying in a military academy, who photographed top secret materials in military installations and forwarded them to their embassy.

Our country, on the other hand, looked at development of cultural ties with the PRC as spiritual intercourse which deepened mutual understanding and strengthened the friendship between Soviet and Chinese people. The Soviet Union, in 1966, solemnly celebrated the 16th anniversary of the Treaty of Friendship, Alliance, and Mutual Assistance between the USSR and the PRC. Many other important dates in the life of China, such as the 17th anniversary of the founding of the PRC, and the jubilees of prominent Chinese revolutionaries and cultural leaders were recognized.

The PRC, in 1966, sharply reduced cultural cooperation with other socialist countries as well. No cultural cooperation plans were signed with Bulgaria, Poland, the German Democratic Republic, Mongolia, or Czechoslovakia in 1967. The plan with Hungary was not signed until December 1967.

The Chinese authorities continued their course of refusing to engage in collective forms of cooperation with the socialist countries. The PRC made the unilateral decision to withdraw from the Dubna Joint Institute of Nuclear Research in the summer of 1965. When, on April 17, 1965, it was invited to join with the socialist countries in mastering space, it failed to respond.

NOTES

1. *Pravda,* September 30, 1965.
2. *Material XXIII s'yezda KPSS* (*Documents from the 23rd Congress of the Communist Party of the Soviet Union*) (Moscow, 1966), p. 185.
3. *Jen Min Jihpao,* March 24, 1966.

CHAPTER EIGHT

Sino-Soviet Relations in the Late 1960s

In the second half of 1966 the Maoist leadership of the CCP launched a frontal attack against the position of socialism in China and openly broke with the principles of Marxism-Leninism in domestic and foreign policy. At the 11th Plenary Session of the CC CCP, convened in August 1966, the leadership initiated the task of launching the so-called "cultural revolution" against the foundations of socialism in the PRC.

The 11th Plenary Session met at a time when Maoists already had succeeded in disorganizing party ranks and eliminating leading party cadres who opposed them. On the eve of the Plenary Session the newspaper *Hung Ch'i,* taken over by Maoists, published the threat that "all who spoke against the ideas of Mao Tse-tung, regardless of the position they occupied, and regardless of their 'prestige' and 'authority,' would be overthrown."

A secret session approved the decision whereby Lin Piao, PRC Minister of Defense and Mao's close comrade-in-arms, was designated "Deputy Commander-in-Chief" of the CCP. Thus Lin Piao became second to Mao Tse-tung in leadership of the "cultural revolution." This indicated clearly that the guiding force in antisocialist attacks of the Maoists was the military. Later on it became known that Mao Tse-tung, at the 11th Plenary Session, promulgated the call to "open fire on the staffs," which was the signal to begin the pogrom of party organs from the top down.

The events unfolded in the PRC under the banner of "cultural revolution" reflected most adversely on Sino-Soviet relations and led directly to further aggravation of relations. Intensification of the struggle with the CPSU and the Soviet Union became a most important trend in the activities of Peking leaders during the "cultural revolution."

1. Origins of the "cultural revolution"

The "cultural revolution" represented no sudden turn in the policy of the Maoists. Although formally initiated at the 11th Plenary Session of the CC CCP, it can in fact be traced to an earlier period, forming the concentrated expression of the deep political crisis resulting from the fatal course followed by CCP leaders.

As has been discussed, after failure of the adventurist policy of "Three Red Banners" (the new "general line," the "great leap forward," and the "people's communes"), Maoists were forced to conduct a so-called normalization of conditions in the country. The main bulwark of PRC economic policy at that time was the policy established by the 1961–62 CC CCP plenary sessions that "agriculture is the basis of the entire national economy."

But a "normalization" failing to restore fundamental principles of socialist economy could not bring the PRC's economy out of crisis completely. The policy of "agriculture is the basis of the entire national economy" acted as a brake on the country's economic development as a whole, and in individual branches of industry (machine-tool building, ferrous and nonferrous metallurgy, and others) led to cutbacks in production, or to significant underuse of productive capacity. In 1965, the last year of "normalization," the gross production of industry was 26 percent below the 1959 level.[1]

Increase in agricultural production was limited, as always, because of the extremely low level of mechanization. The villages had some 100,000 tractors at the end of 1965, whereas the country's minimum requirement was somewhere between 1.2 and 1.5 million units. Machines worked no more than 10 percent of the entire sown area, primarily on army farms. The grain harvest during years of "normalization" barely reached the 1957 level (180 to 185 million tons). What this amounted to was that annual per capita production of grain was 12 percent below the mean for the years of the First Five-Year Plan period, and 20 percent below that prior to the war with Japan. In 1965 the total grain harvest was well below the level called for by the Second Five-Year Plan adopted by the 8th Congress of the CCP in 1956, and set for achievement by 1962 (250 million tons). China had bought between 5 and 6 million tons of grain a year from foreign countries; that is, 30 percent of the cost of the country's total imports,[2] since the end of 1960.

Within the CCP economic difficulties resulted in exacerbation of the struggle over the direction for the country's future development. Antagonisms between two directions in party leadership became even more pronounced. One direction was to apply rational methods to development of the national economy, taking the experience of socialist countries into consideration. The other, advocated by Mao Tse-tung, categorically rejected international socialist experience and insisted on voluntaristic methods of controlling the economy, and on stepping up tempos of economic development.

Those Chinese Communists who continued to support Marxist-Leninist views criticized the Maoist course. At the same time, Mao's adventurist policy created increasing dissatisfaction, even among former adherents who, while generally favoring nationalist positions, doubted the future of the policy. This made the struggle among the CCP leaders particularly keen.

In 1964 and 1965 the Maoists embarked on a systematic attack against all who threatened their supremacy. This attack was carried out through further curtailment of party and state democracy, militarization of society, strengthening the role of the army, arousal of nationalistic passions, and greater exaggeration of the cult of Mao.

Even then principal targets of attacks by the Maoists were intellectuals, for they, more than any other stratum of the population, were capable of exposing the fatal consequences of Mao's foreign and domestic policies. It was among Chinese intellectuals that the so-called campaign to rectify the style of work, the purpose of which was to force the intellectual class to accept the Maoist line unprotestingly, was intensified. The first casualties of the "cultural revolution" were party intellectuals, the leading body of the intelligentsia. Mao Tun, a world-renowned writer, was removed from his post as Minister of Culture. One can unequivocally state that between 1964 and 1966 the flower of the Chinese intellectual class was accused of political unreliability and subjected to repression, which began with degrading "criticism," removal from their posts to the countryside, and ended with physical violence. *Jen Min Jihpao,* in October 1966, admitted that 160,000 intellectuals had been sent into the countryside for "labor reindoctrination" in the previous six months.

The Maoists simultaneously mounted attacks against the progressive cultural heritage of other peoples. The Maoists also attacked the creativity of such famous representatives of world culture as Shakespeare, Rabelais, Stendhal, Balzac, Romain Rolland, Beethoven, Mozart, and others. Peking leaders attempted to hide their hypocritical concern for observance of the "criteria of a revolutionary character" by hit-and-run attacks against outstanding classical works of literature and the arts. Beethoven's Ninth Symphony, for example, was condemned on the ground that it had been written and performed prior to the publication of the Communist Manifesto. Balzac was faulted for "propagandizing the bourgeois theory of humanity" in writing of the love of Père Goriot for his daughters. The operas Carmen, Traviata, Yevgeniy Onegin, and the ballets Swan Lake and Giselle, were said to "stupefy and corrupt the workers."

Soviet literature was a main target of the Maoist campaign to destroy culture. The works of A. Tolstoi, M. Sholokhov, K. Simonov, Y. Ehrenburg, A. Korneychuk, and other Soviet prose writers and poets were not only declared "bad" and "subversive," but were liable to destruction. All who had the temerity to read them were subjected to repression as political criminals.

Marxism-Leninism teaches that it is impossible to build socialism unless ignorance and illiteracy are eliminated. It is well known that during the first years of Soviet power, even while civil war raged, V. I. Lenin made the appeal to "learn, learn, and learn." He believed that the primary task of builders of socialism was that of mastering and critically reappraising everything "of value in the more than 2,000 years of development of human thought and culture."[3] The creator of the world's first socialist state repeatedly insisted: "It is necessary to take all culture capitalism has abandoned and build socialism from it. It is necessary to take all the science, technology, all knowledge and art. Without this we cannot build the life of a communist society."[4]

Lenin's admonitions applied fully to China as well, where the accomplishment of a genuine cultural revolution is imperative. Even today there are over 300 million illiterates. There are not enough schools and teachers in the city or in the country. The national economy of China has a crying need for qualified scientific and technical cadres. It would seem that under such conditions the growth of culture and training of specialists would be of primary importance. Yet Peking leaders deliberately charted a different course. The building of schools and higher institutions of learning was curtailed at the end of the 1950s.

Propaganda campaigns calling for preparation for the so-called revolutionary war were used as a principal weapon to distract the Chinese people from their troubles, and to ensure their unquestioning obedience. The purpose of these campaigns was to strengthen the role of the army in the life of the country, to accelerate the militarization of the economy, the spreading of barracks-like procedures, and to justify the low standard of living of the populace. The following episode is a case in point. In the summer of 1965 a Chinese delegation visiting the Soviet Union was invited to attend a meeting of the Moscow City Soviet of Workers' Deputies, in the course of which they were told about our huge housing construction program. The Chinese representatives, after listening to the discussion, expressed surprise at the expenditure of such huge sums on such "nonsense" as housing, and said that "we in the People's Republic of China are not engaged in housing construction, we are preparing the people for revolution."

The nationalists in the CCP, in militarizing the country's economic life and advancing the army to a commanding position, almost immediately took steps to remove the army from party control by converting it to a tool of their military-bureaucratic dictatorship.

The most politically knowledgeable and active elements of the officer corps were eliminated between 1959 and 1965. The so-called "revolutionization" of the armed forces was carried out in May 1965, when all distinguishing military ranks and insignia were abolished under the pretext of "further strengthening the link between commanders and the masses." In fact, this was an effort to reduce the role of a large segment of military cadres, trained during years of national-liberation and revolutionary war, who sided with enemies of the Maoists. There was simultaneous intensification of propaganda of the thesis that the "ideas" of Mao applied to all spheres of activity, including military. Those who advocated improvement in professional training and equipping of the army, and who ignored indoctrination work among the soldiers and officers devoted "to the ideas of the Great Helmsman," were criticized. This "revolution" served to cloak the new wave of military purges.

"Revolutionization" of the army essentially was preparation for militarization of the country's entire social life. Political sections composed of army cadres were established in plants and institutions in 1964–1965. In other words, it was now possible for the army to exert direct influence over activities of plants and institutions, thus simplifying the transition to a country-wide scale of the "cultural revolution."

CCP nationalists, who knew they couldn't depend solely on the army for staying in power, took action to shatter the moral and political unity of the Chinese people. They resorted to using the slogan "intensification of the class struggle" for setting one stratum of Chinese society against another. The worker, peasant, soldier, intellectual, each was hounded relentlessly by the spectre of the "restoration of capitalism" in China through the "crafty designs of the class enemies."

Long before official proclamation of the "cultural revolution" the Maoists also instigated a struggle against wholesome forces in the party and in government bodies. This struggle, in 1964 and 1965, took the form of the so-called movement to strengthen and clean up party and state apparati. This movement became the excuse to expel from the party all who showed the slightest deviation from the antisocialist course of the ruling faction. Among leading party notables who followed P'eng Teh-huai, a member of the Politburo of the CCP and Minister of Defense of the PRC, into political oblivion were such famous leaders as Ch'en Yun, also a member of the Politburo of the Communist Party of China, Teng Tzu-hui, Hsi Chung-hsun, Wang Chia-hsiang, and others. Active replacement of leading cadres went on as well within ministries and departments. According to incomplete data, some 1,000 ministers, vice ministers, heads of administrations, directors of scientific research institutions and of higher institutions of learning in the country were replaced in 1964 and 1965.

A procedure known as rehabilitation through labor was introduced in 1964 and 1965 for purposes of repressing those with different ideas. This was in addition to "labor indoctrination" practiced in special camps. A system was initiated whereby neighbors shadowed each other, denounced each other regularly and constantly criticized anyone suspected of disloyalty to the "Great Helmsman." Such forms of "indoctrination" as holding "struggle meetings" were widespread. All present at such meetings censured the suspect, "detailing the history of the family," in the course of which all "sins" were exposed and any misconduct on the part of any member of the family was criticized.

The cult of Mao Tse-tung was used on an ever-expanding scale to dupe the Chinese population. Chinese propaganda attempted to create around Mao an aura of "genius," "wise," "great," "infallible," "sagacious," and so forth. His "ideas" were called the "food," "weapon," "compass," and "lighthouse" of the Chinese people. Day in and day out the press and radio insisted that it was not the party, but the hero, standing above the masses, the "great leader" and his "ideas," that lifted and mobilized all the Chinese people for the revolution, and who was organizing and leading the masses toward a new society. The Chinese revolution was described as the creation of the hands of Mao Tse-tung, as the child of his "ideas," rather than of an objective historical process.

The low cultural level of the majority of Chinese, the dominance of petty bourgeois psychology, and the strong vestiges of feudalism and patriarchal principles enabled organizers of the "cultural revolution" to foist their dogma on the masses with comparative ease. The illiterate and semi-illiterate, systematically subjected to ideological indoctrination, were infected with fanatical faith in the leader, thus erecting virtually insurmountable obstacles along the path to their awakening from this mystical trance.

Let us cite one typical example of ugly turns taken in China by the cult of Mao Tse-tung even before widespread development of the "cultural revolution." At the end of 1964 a Soviet delegation visiting a porcelain factory in Ch'angsha (the principal city in Hunan province) witnessed an "explanation" by the secretary of the factory's party committee of elimination of flaws in the plant's products. He said:

> We had been struggling for a long time with the problem of how to eliminate shortcomings. Then we decided to study the works of Mao Tse-tung and, after seeking advice from higher authority, began with his work "On Contradictions." We read it once (everybody in the factory studied it) and understood that the main contradiction in our work was the black spots on the plates. Reading the book the second time we were able to eliminate this shortcoming. Still, the quality of the plates and dishes produced did not meet all requirements. Then we read the book for the third time and understood that only the main contradiction had been eliminated, whereas secondary contradictions remained. Included were rough surfaces and cracks in the glazed layer. These shortcomings gradually were overcome too. So Mao-Tse-tung's work helped us improve the quality of production.

Despite all its effort, the dominant faction in the CCP was unable decisively to strengthen its position. Dissatisfaction with the faction's policies grew among leading party figures and in the broad party masses. Local party and state authorities arbitrarily restored procedures existing prior to the "great leap forward" and the "people's communes." Disregarding intimidation and repression, Chinese writers published works caustically ridiculing the cult of Mao Tse-tung in allegory, and subjected his "ideas" to devastating criticism.

The Maoist domination was threatened not only by the rising tide of discontent in the country, but also by major failures in the international arena.

The Maoists were unable to break down the socialist commonwealth. With the exception of Albania, CCP nationalists were unable to find support for their subversive aims. Despite intrigues of Chinese leaders, the striving for unity and further development of close cooperation became increasingly stronger in the socialist community.

The chauvinist course embarked upon by Peking leaders received no significant support from the world Communist movement. Attempts of Peking to establish hegemony in the movement failed. The overwhelming majority of fraternal parties decisively rejected the anti-Leninist foreign policy platform of the Maoists.

The pro-Peking splinter groups, preaching alien ideas in alien voices, were unable to establish mass organizations and win influence in worker's movements. Appeals for splitting the Communist parties and the collusion of Maoist forces in the struggle against Marxist-Leninist parties with activities of political police organs in capitalist states exposed proponents of the Peking line, making their isolation more complete. Dissension increased in many pro-Chinese groups, leading to their fragmentation and often to their complete disorganization.

The largest Communist party in the nonsocialist world, the Indonesian, figured prominently in the splitting plans of CCP leaders. They succeeded in foisting their political goals on the Central Committee of the Communist Party of Indonesia. They pushed Indonesian Communists into organizing the armed coup in the fall of 1965, the outcome of which is well known. The Indonesian Communist Party and other democratic organizations were virtually destroyed; hundreds of thousands of Indonesian Communists were brutally murdered. Yet even after these tragic events, the Maoists continued to push leftists in Indonesia, now bled white, along the lethal path to civil war. Peking leaders simultaneously made every effort to isolate the Communist Party of Indonesia from the international Communist movement, despite the urgent need of the defeated Indonesian Communists for international help and support.

The tragic events in Indonesia provided a graphic lesson for the world revolutionary movement of dire consequences of practical application of the fallacious, adventuristic concepts of Maoist leadership. The regrettable outcome of events in Indonesia intensified the dissatisfaction smouldering among Communist parties under the influence of CCP nationalists.

Nor were efforts of the Chinese leadership to control such international democratic organizations as the World Peace Council, the World Federation of Trade Unions, and other organizations, successful. Machinations of Chinese leaders also failed with respect to the national liberation movement. The severe defeats suffered by those detachments of the national liberation movement blindly following Peking alerted both governments of developing nations and revolutionary democratic parties to the perfidious goals of the Maoists.

The failure of the attempts to turn Afro-Asian nations against the Partial Test Ban Treaty, the failure of hopes to dominate the 2nd Afro-Asian Conference, the necessity to abandon the establishment of a "revolutionary UN," the failure of plans to wreck the Tashkent Conference convened for peaceful settlement of the Indo-Pakistan conflict, all corroborated the fact that the Maoist foreign policy was rejected by the Third World nations.

Peking leaders proved equally unsuccessful in constructing a separate bloc of Southeast Asian states under PRC hegemony. The Peking-Djakarta axis (the nucleus of the planned bloc) did not materialize. Relations between the PRC and Indonesia deteriorated drastically after the events of September 30, 1965 and reached the point of almost complete rupture.

The weakening of China's foreign policy positions also became apparent in deterioration of relations with a number of Arab countries and in severence of diplomatic relations with Burundi, Dahomy, and the Central African Republic. Nor was Peking successful in pressing its course on progressive organizations in Nigeria, South Africa, Basutoland, and the Portuguese colonies. State leaders in liberated countries, as well as leaders of progressive left-nationalist parties, were fully cognizant of the ruinous foreign policy course of the PRC.

Progressive forces all over the world became increasingly convinced of the hypocrisy of Peking's anti-imperialist slogans. It was apparent that despite their unrestrained "revolutionary" phraseology, Chinese leaders in relations with imperialist states followed mercenary nationalist motives. While accusing the Soviet Union "of collusion with imperialism," they in fact proceeded to unprincipled rapprochement with capitalist countries.

Peking leaders were especially zealous in seeking a "mutual understanding" with the United States. They directed great attention to securing Washington's understanding that their anti-imperialist declarations were without foundation. The response to continuous intrusions by American ships and aircraft into territorial waters and air spaces of the PRC was limited to verbose "serious warnings" by Peking. In August 1964 the PRC Minister of Foreign Affairs declared:

> . . . if American warships do enter the territorial waters of the People's Republic of China they clear out of their own accord. We Chinese do not shoot at them, nor are we going to bomb American military bases on Taiwan, although we could. China does not want war, and the United States knows it.

Peking sought to establish secret economic ties with the United States, particularly via Hong Kong and Macao, buying through them such American goods as petroleum products, chemicals, and others. In turn, as the magazine *The Scotsman* reported on November 12, 1965, China was not reluctant about shipping goods to the United States via third countries.

The Chinese leadership reconciled itself to the fact that Hong Kong was a "military base for the expansion by the United States of the aggressive war against Vietnam." US naval vessels made 340 visits to Hong Kong in 1965, and 390 in 1966. The response to this by the

Chinese was to dispatch formal protests to the British administration in Hong Kong.

The PRC steadily lost stature as a socialist state. Its line proved to sharply contradict the general position taken by socialist countries, the Communist movement, and by all anti-imperialist forces on important questions of international politics.

Domestically, so long as the CCP continued to function, so too did the organs of people's authority; the trade unions, the Young Communists, and the mass workers' organizations. In other words, so long as the political superstructure of the people's democratic system, albeit greatly deformed, continued to function, the Maoists were powerless to turn the country from its socialist path. The ruling faction faced the alternative, either retreat and admit defeat, or try to wreck the political superstructure of the people's democratic system, set up a military bureaucratic dictatorship, and provide conditions needed for undivided domination. As we know, the Maoists chose the latter course.

The most serious obstacle on this road was the CCP, which is why it was the chief target of attack by the Maoists. Here the Maoist faction had to face the issue of finding the forces to support it. The urgency of this issue increased as failures of Maoist policy became evident to active party members, as well as to broad strata of workers and peasants who had been victims of this policy.

The Maoists undoubtedly knew that the struggle with the Communist Party would not be easy. They considered the fact that the older generation of party workers had been indoctrinated, not only on Mao Tse-tung's articles and speeches, but also on Marxist-Leninist theory. Despite the lengthy anti-Soviet campaign, this generation continued to sympathize with the Soviet people and the CPSU. It was more difficult to trick them with statements of "collusion between the Soviet Union and the United States," and of "restoration of capitalism" supposedly taking place in the USSR. And they understood the importance of culture for building socialism, the need to master the heights of modern science and engineering. Better than others, they foresaw fatal consequences in rejecting the experience of socialist construction gathered by fraternal parties. This is why the ruling clique did not trust party activitists, why it did not trust the workers and peasants. Moreover, the Maoists feared this hidden dissatisfaction could trigger an open attack against its policies.

The Maoists found support for their antisocialist course in the army, which was declared to be "the most faithful and obedient weapon of the

Great Helmsman." School children and young students, too, were counted on for support. Youth was indoctrinated in the Maoist spirit, and had only a vague, distorted idea of the ideals of socialism, of Marxism-Leninism, and of current internal and external events. The cynical plan to exploit the emotionalism and instability of youth, its dissatisfactions and ambitions, played no small part in what followed. Significant too was that over half the students in China were of bourgeois and petty bourgeois stock.

The detachments of Red Guards became shock troops attacking party organizations. Moreover, nonparty youth, primarily petty bourgeois, who distinguished themselves during the pogroms, were singled out by the Maoists as the "best," the "most advanced," the "most conscious part" of the Chinese people. It was incumbent on old party members, experienced workers, and outstanding leaders in arts and sciences to learn from these youth and imitate their deeds.

The appearance of the Red Guard detachments, backed by the army and state security organizations, initiated one of the most tragic phases in the history of postrevolutionary China. The ruling clique officially sanctioned mass excesses in the capital and the provinces. These took the form of mockery, assault, and murder of Maoist antagonists, scoffing at cultural values, and destruction of the remnants of socialist law and order.

As they unleashed the "cultural revolution," the Maoists declared that the struggle was against "a handful of counterrevolutionaries, remnants of antiparty, antisocialist elements, who had infiltrated the party and had been cloaked with authority." The mendacity of this version was soon unmasked, however. As early as April and May 1966, when Red Guards began storming Peking committees of the party and the Young Communists, editorial offices of the central party newspapers, the party organization of Peking University, and other party and state authorities, it became clear that dismissal from active political life of a broad stratum of party and state workers was the true goal. By the beginning of September 1966 some 20 party committees in the provinces and in large cities had been charged with following an anti-Maoist line. The publication of over 100 central and provincial newspapers and journals, including organs of the Central Committee of the Young Communists, the Chinese Federation of Trade Unions, and others, was discontinued.

Growing antagonisms among Mao's possible successors inflamed the struggle. The position of PRC Chairman Liu Shao-ch'i was seriously weakened, and members of the CC CCP Secretariat, P'eng Chen, Lu Ting-yi, and Lo Jui-ching, were removed from their posts as a result of clashes within party ranks. Mao's wife Chiang Ch'ing, his closest collaborators, Kang Sheng, Ch'en Po-ta, and others now seized the limelight. These people led the general purge, "the shake-up" of the entire party and state apparatus.

The Maoists dealt savagely with enemies and rivals, subjecting them to torment and torture, and mercilessly belittling their dignity. Graphic evidence is contained in press photographs showing "court" scenes of the trials of P'eng Chen, Lo Jui-ching, Lu Ting-yi, and Yang Sheng-k'un. Photographs of these men, recent comrades-in-arms of Mao, show them to have their heads pushed forcibly downward. Lo Jui-ching's leg is maimed, and he no longer is able to stand and walk. He was carried around the stadium in which his "trial" was held on his "round of shame" in a basket.

Organizers of the "cultural revolution" initiated the destruction of the CCP by removing from the political arena a great many members of the Central Committee, leading workers in party and administrative apparati, and all those Communists who had disagreed with Mao Tse-tung's course. Their methods included repressions, expulsion, and discredit. Over two-thirds of the CC CCP elected by the 8th Congress, the overwhelming majority of leaders of the central offices, the CCP provincial and city committees, the leading workers on ideological fronts, the leadership of creative unions of intellectuals, the leaders of higher institutions of learning and scientific research institutions, and many famous military leaders were persecuted. These people were accused of having approved decisions of the 8th Congress of the CCP and the general line for building a socialist society on the basis of Marxist-Leninist theory in cooperation with other socialist countries. They were persecuted for having censured the "Three Red Banners" policy and for having warned about dangers inherent in repeating the adventuristic "Great Leap Forward."

The ruling clique simultaneously embarked on a course designed to undermine state institutions of people's power. The work of the National People's Congress and the standing committee was completely paralyzed. Over half the deputies to the National People's Congress and members of its standing committee became victims of repression. PRC Chairman Liu Shao-ch'i, without knowledge of the National People's Congress, and in violation of the Constitution, was dismissed. Elected bodies of people's authority in the provinces were disbanded. Military control was established over the State Council of the PRC and over its central offices and ministries. Most of the vice premiers of the PRC State Council, directors of general offices, and ministers were removed from their posts.

At the outset of the "cultural revolution," Maoists counted on replacing party and state bodies by groups or committees of the "cultural revolution," with a central directing system residing in the "Cultural Revolution Affairs Group," ostensibly set up in the CC CCP, but actually placed above it.

Once the "Cultural Revolution Affairs Group" revealed their inadequacies, efforts were made to establish the apparatus of authority in the form of "communes." When results of the Peking, Shanghai, and other communal experiments showed this form of authority to be also unsatisfactory, the Maoists tried to strengthen their hold by using so-called "revolutionary committees," based formally on the "triple alliance" of the army, the "revolutionary masses" (the Red Guards and the agitators), and some experienced workers. These "committees" in fact were completely controlled by the army and were organs of the military-bureaucratic dictatorship of the Maoists.

With the help of the army, the "revolutionary committees" were substituted for dispersed committees of the CCP. Their establishment was backed by the system of military control set up in June 1966, which at once encompassed the central and local state apparatus (the ministries and offices of the PRC State Council, state security, the courts, radio stations, civil aviation, warehouses, plants, ports, railroads, and the like). This enabled the ruling clique, at its discretion, to take charge of state apparatus and departments to issue orders, and to remove and shift cadres all in the name of the State Council. In fact, the country's entire economic and cultural life came under military control. This situation remained even after establishment of "revolutionary committees," the organization of which was not completed until September 1968 (and then only at the provincial level).

The comparative ease with which Maoists destroyed constituted organs of power, paralyzed CCP activities, and established the "revolutionary committees" is explainable in large measure by the peculiarities of Chinese social structure.

Only about 15 million of 300 million gainfully employed people in China, or about 5 percent, were associated with modern production, science, and culture; no more than 10 million were directly engaged in material production (workers, civil servants, engineering and technical personnel). The labor turnover that began in 1958 was created artificially by closing of plants, by laying up building projects, and by administrative resettlement of urban populations. The first to be sent to the country were experienced workers with long records in industry. This policy resulted in serious qualitative changes in the composition of the working class, with a sharp increase in the proportion of political laggards. These elements formed the detachments of so-called "agitators" during the "cultural revolution."

An even more intensive disintegration of the working class resulting from the "cultural revolution" was to set unqualified workers, particularly youth, against experienced workers. The agitators, incited by Maoists, embarked on a wide-ranging campaign to replace the bonus system (which comprised 10 to 15 percent of the wages earned by qualified workers) with a wage reduction. This campaign, called the "struggle with bourgeois economism," was counterattacked by experienced workers. Strikes began in many cities, but were ruthlessly put down with help of the military.

The introduction of the "worker, peasant" system, wherein workers and peasants alternated working in industry and agriculture, also contributed to disintegration of the working class. One purpose of this system was to bring the working class down to the ideological level of the backward peasantry. Workers sent to the country not only were forbidden to bring proletarian, advanced culture and ideology to the peasants, but quite the contrary, were forced to become like peasants in practice, living and working.

2. Anti-Sovietism—the most important aspect of the "cultural revolution"

The most important feature of the "cultural revolution," from its inception, was the clearly distinguishable anti-Soviet bias. The 11th plenum of the CC CCP, convened in August 1966, approved all anti-Soviet measures undertaken by the Maoists during the preceding four years, citing as "entirely correct and necessary" open criticism of the CPSU, and approving all anti-Soviet editorials printed by *Jen Min Jihpao* and *Hung Ch'i*. The plenary session stipulated that "a clear line of demarcation must be drawn" between the CCP on the one hand and the CPSU and other Marxist-Leninist parties on the other, and that the "struggle against them must be carried through to the end."

The 11th Plenary Session did not limit its declarations to a political line hostile to the Soviet Union and the CPSU. In its documents the plenum deliberately distorted the political course of the CPSU, and there were concentrations of slander summarizing all the basic theses of anti-

Soviet propaganda. These documents were additional reminders that the Maoists' most important goal was indoctrinating the Chinese people with a psychological barrier against rapprochement with the CPSU and other fraternal parties holding Marxist-Leninist positions.

The anti-Soviet campaign in the PRC received a new impetus from the 11th plenum. The location of the Soviet Embassy in Peking became the site of unruly anti-Soviet demonstrations. This street was renamed "Struggle Against Revisionism" Street on August 20, 1966. All houses and fences along the street, sidewalks, and roadway were slathered with slogans urging the "smashing" of the CPSU and the Soviet Union and the "destruction of all things Soviet." Wall posters affixed to the Embassy of the USSR by Red Guards threatened Soviet personnel by declaring: "when the time comes, we will skin you, we will strip out your veins, we will cremate your corpses, and we will scatter the ashes to the winds."

On August 22, 1966 an Embassy car flying the national flag of the USSR was detained on this street. In the car were the chargé d'affaires and other Soviet diplomats. Red Guards attempted to force them out of the car and make them walk past a portrait of Mao Tse-tung set up in the center of the roadway.

On August 26, 1966 the Soviet government handed a note to the PRC government containing an emphatic protest against the hooliganism in front of the Embassy and demanding that effective measures to ensure immediate and unconditional cessation of actions interfering with normal activities of the Embassy and staff be implemented. Chinese authorities pointedly ignored these lawful demands.

A new anti-Soviet demonstration was organized near the USSR Embassy on August 29. It lasted through the night and continued into the next evening. The meeting which inaugurated this mass excess had heard the so-called "Appeal to People All Over the Country," where it was declared that "the Soviet Union is our deadly enemy."

In the course of the "cultural revolution" monuments symbolic of friendship between the peoples of the USSR and China (the A. S. Pushkin memorial, the monument to Sino-Soviet friendship in Shanghai, and others) were defiled or destroyed. Soviet citizens residing permanently in China became targets of hooliganism, searches, assault, and outrages.

The Soviet press, on September 1, 1966, published a statement "In the Central Committee of the Communist Party of the Soviet Union," pointing out that decisions reached by the CC CCP 11th Plenary Session "officially confirmed the intention of the Chinese party leadership to implement further their own course, opposing it to the Marxist-

Leninist line jointly worked out by fraternal parties at the conferences of 1957 and 1960," and that the Chinese leadership "is again provoking a sharp deterioration in relations between the USSR and the People's Republic of China." The CC CPSU described Chinese actions and statements as steps "rendering a particularly big service to imperialism and reaction," and stated that responsibility for the renunciation of joint, coordinated struggle against imperialism and reaction, for the unceasing attempts to split the Communist movement, the socialist community, and the anti-imperialist front, rested with the leadership of the CCP and the PRC. In line with its principled course, the CC CPSU stated: "despite the differences created by the leadership of the Communist Party of China, the Communist Party of the Soviet Union will continue to promote further the line of strengthening friendship with Chinese Communists, with the multi-million Chinese people, will resolutely uphold the general line of the world Communist movement, the principles of Marxism-Leninism, and proletarian internationalism."[5]

On September 20, 1966 Chinese authorities announced a decision reached by the PRC government calling a year's halt to study by foreign students in Chinese higher institutions of learning, and requiring the departure of Soviet students for home within 10 to 15 days. Soviet students were forced to return; the USSR reciprocated by calling a halt to study by Chinese students and graduate students in the USSR. At the same time the Soviet side expressed readiness to review the question of restoring student exchanges on a reciprocal basis at the convenience of the Chinese.[6]

CCP leaders used the return of Chinese students to arouse further anti-Soviet hysteria. Yet another demonstration was mounted at the Soviet Embassy in Peking at the end of October 1966. On October 27 the USSR Ministry of Foreign Affairs forwarded a note of protest regarding the event, but Chinese authorities continued their excesses at the Soviet Embassy. Provocations were even organized on November 7, 1966, the 49th anniversary of the Great October Socialist Revolution!

Continual provocations forced a Soviet delegation visiting the PRC, by invitation of the Sino-Soviet Friendship Association, to cut short its visit and return home. By this time the Association had been converted into an organization for conducting propaganda and other hostile activities against the CPSU and the Soviet Union. On September 16, 1966 the Embassy of the USSR in Peking was advised officially that the Sino-Soviet Friendship Association had been renamed the Association for the Friendship of the Chinese and Soviet Peoples. In this way CCP leaders reiterated their unwillingness to conduct friendly relations with the Soviet Union along party and state lines. The renaming of the Association also was dictated by plans to use the slogan of friendship between Chinese and Soviet peoples for the purpose of Maoist demagoguery.

In fact, Peking propaganda strove to persuade everyone, from the lowly to the great, that the Soviet Union was carrying out a hostile, even aggressive policy toward China, and that the PRC "was threatened with the danger of intervention not only by imperialist powers, but particularly by the USSR." The Chinese leadership even dared to make provocative public statements that a military clash between the PRC and the USSR was possible. On September 29, 1965, for example, the PRC Minister of Foreign Affairs, addressing a press conference attended by 400 Chinese and foreign journalists invited to Peking from Hong Kong, Macao, and other places specifically for the purpose, expressed the view that in event of an attack by the United States on China "the modern revisionists" would "coordinate their actions in the north with the United States." The shibboleth of the "threat from the north" then became a permanent theme of Chinese propaganda directed against our country. Propagandistic effort was undertaken among the Chinese people to "explain" that if the United States attacked China the Soviet Union probably "would occupy the northeast immediately"; that the USSR was numbered among the "dangerous friends," without whom China "felt quite safe"; and that "Russian rockets could fly from Moscow to Peking." The populace of the PRC had dinned into it in every way possible that the slightest sympathy for our country was equivalent to treason.

Chinese authorities instigated a violent anti-Soviet provocation in the case of the Soviet ship *Zagorsk,* which called at Port Dal'niy. On December 8, 1966, while the ship was leaving port with a Chinese pilot, he suddenly issued an order which, if executed, would have caused the *Zagorsk* to hit a breakwater, with resulting serious damage and possible loss of the ship. Under the circumstances the master of the *Zagorsk* could not, and of course should not, carry out the order. His failure to do so enabled the ship to continue through the port entrance, after which the master immediately stopped the ship, and upon demand of the Chinese pilot dropped anchor. The *Zagorsk* was boarded immediately by armed Chinese guards and representatives of port authorities. They forbade the ship to proceed and tried forcibly to break into the chart house and seize charts and ship's papers.

On December 10 the Soviet Embassy in Peking requested assistance of the PRC Ministry of Foreign Affairs in obtaining permission for the *Zagorsk* to leave the port of Dal'niy. A representative of the Ministry, deliberately exaggerating charges against the Soviet seamen, stated that the *Zagorsk* had "violated the sovereignty of China." Chinese authorities continued to ignore the requests and the ship with her crew remained under guard in the outer roadstead of Dal'niy.

On December 17, the Soviet side lodged a protest with the PRC Embassy in Moscow in connection with the illegal seizure of the *Zagorsk,* and demanded her immediate release. The statement condemned the fictitious charges lodged by the Chinese authorities against the ship's master and other Soviet seamen. Particularly noted was that in accordance with generally accepted international norms and practice, and reinforced by legislation of maritime nations, the pilot is an advisor (a consultant) to the ship's master. Regardless of whether a pilot is abroad, the ship's master is not relieved of responsibility for the safety of the ship entrusted to him when the ship is maneuvering. This practice is also followed in PRC ports.

The Chinese took no action to release the ship and, in fact, made no reply to the December 17 statement. As a result, the Soviet side on December 24 lodged another vigorous protest against the arrest of the Soviet ship. Not until December 28 was the *Zagorsk* released.

The period after the CC CCP 11th Plenary Session was marked by further hostile activity along Sino-Soviet borders. Armed Chinese units appeared along the Pamir section of the Sino-Soviet border for the first time at the beginning of October 1966 and proceeded to photograph Soviet territory. Numerous detachments of Red Guards materialized in border regions. People's volunteer guards, commanded by PLA officers, conducted military exercises along the banks of border rivers, practicing attacks in the direction of the state boundary of the USSR, and "assaulting" the Amur River.

The Chinese leadership simultaneously moved adaptation of the "cultural revolution" to interfere in USSR internal affairs and to engage in subversive activities. Speaking at the military academy in October 1966, the PRC Minister of Foreign Affairs declared:

> The cultural revolution, led by Chairman Mao Tse-tung himself, is an important innovation in the Communist movement, a great innovation in the socialist revolution. It has had a tremendous influence on the Soviet Union, on the countries of Asia, Africa, and Latin America. We must turn the great cultural revolution on the USSR. The day will finally arrive when there will be Red Guards on the streets in Moscow.

Peking propaganda tried to create the impression that the Soviet people supported the "cultural revolution" and were anxious to follow its example, already looking upon Mao Tse-tung as their leader. On November 16, 1966, in reporting an anti-Soviet meeting in Peking, the Hsinhua Agency asserted that the Soviet people "see the light and hope of the future in the greatest leader of revolutionary peoples of the world, Chairman Mao Tse-tung."

Peking announced for all to hear the necessity of carrying China's "cultural revolution" to the whole world. A Red Guard publication stated seriously their task of "redoing the universe with the help of the ideas of the Great Helmsman," and of "putting the great rebellious spectacle on the international stage, as well as on the domestic one."

These goals led to the instigation of schismatic and anti-Soviet actions by Chinese representatives in international democratic organizations. Chinese representatives made slanderous anti-Soviet statements at the 4th Congress of Latin American Students (Havana, August 1966), at the 12th Conference on the Prohibition of Atomic and Hydrogen Weapons (Tokyo, August 1966), at the 5th World Conference on Trade Unions of Agriculture, Forest, and Plantation Workers (Berlin, November 1966), and others.

The CC CPSU plenum of December 1966 stated that recent events in China, and the decisions of the CC CCP 11th Plenary Session, indicated that the chauvinist, anti-Soviet policy of Chinese leaders had entered a new, dangerous phase. Approving the report of the CC CPSU Secretary General, L. I. Brezhnev, on "The International Policy of the USSR and the Struggle of the Communist Party of the Soviet Union for the Solidarity of the Communist Movement," the plenum pointed out:

> The course upon which the leaders of the Communist Party of China are now embarked in the international arena, their policy with respect to relations with the socialist countries, their hostile campaign against our country and against the Soviet people, and their splitting actions in the international Communist movement, all have nothing in common with Marxism-Leninism. This policy and these actions are harmful to the interests of socialism, of the international workers' and liberation movement, to the socialist victory of the Chinese people and objectively lend aid to imperialism. . . .[7]

The Plenary Session of the Central Committee confirmed the firmness of our party's course in terms of friendship and international solidarity with the CCP and the PRC. At the same time it considered it necessary to expose, once and for all, the anti-Leninist views and chauvinistic, nationalistic course of present Chinese leaders and to intensify the struggle to defend the general line set down by the Moscow conferences of 1957 and 1960.

3. Mounting difficulties of the "cultural revolution" and intensification of the anti-Soviet line of the Chinese leadership

The "cultural revolution" encountered new difficulties in 1967, showing that the Maoists were unable to solve their problems in one fell swoop.

First, the "cultural revolution" resulted in a recession, worsening the country's economic crisis. It undermined industrial and agricultural production, reduced state income, and disrupted transportation. Tremendous numbers of man-hours were lost, and vast quantities of materials and money were expended unproductively. Of equal loss to the national economy was the destruction of administrative bodies, and repression against the cadres of experienced business executives and economists.

The coal, metallurgical, petroleum, and power industries suffered particularly severe losses. In one of the largest coal basins in the PRC, the Tatung Basin, mines worked at only half capacity for the greater part of 1967. Confusion reigned in the Fushun and Tsinsi mines.

The work load on large metallurgical plants dropped to 65-70 percent in the first half of 1967, as compared with a work load of 90-95 percent in 1966. The main metallurgical combines, Anshan, Yunnan, Paotow, and Shihchingshan, were idle for several months. According to the *Far Eastern Economic Revue* of August 24, 1967, "half of the oil refineries in Lanchow had ceased production; the chemical plant and the plant engaged in the repair of machinery and rolling stock were closed." Even in Peking, where order was maintained by faithful Maoist troops, clashes between the different factions of Red Guards and militants resulted in fulfillment of only 55 percent of industrial plans. Electric power plants operated sporadically. For example, the supply of electric power to plants and the populace of Yunnan was cut off in April. The same thing happened in May in Kunming, Tsinan, Chungking, and T'aiyuan; and in July in Lanchow, Changchun, and other cities.

Difficulties in light industry at the end of 1966 caused conflicts in many plants. The source of the problem was replacement of the piece-work and bonus systems accompanied by a reduction in wages of at least 10 percent. *Jen Min Jihpao,* on June 4, 1967, reported that armed clashes had occurred in the 6th Chenghsien Textile Mill. Disturbances and strikes occurred in the 2nd Peking Textile Mill, and in many plants in Shanghai, Tsingtao, Canton, Yshe, and other cities.

The defense industry alone, and particularly those branches engaged in production of nuclear missiles, was a special case. These plants were placed under strict army control from the start and were protected against excesses of the "cultural revolution." According to estimates in the Western press, military expenditures by the PRC in 1967 were larger than all capital investments made in the national economy as a whole.

Overall, the gross industrial production in the PRC dropped by 15 percent in 1967. Coal production comprising 90 percent of the country's fuel balance fell 40 percent, electric power production fell 30 percent, steel fell 25 to 30 percent.[8] Premier Chou En-lai was forced to state publicly that "one had to pay a price in productivity for the cultural revolution."[9]

Transportation was badly disorganized during the "cultural revolution," and this is understandable. Railroads were forced to carry over 20 million Red Guards and other "representatives of the revolutionary masses" between the fall of 1966 and February 1967 alone, resulting in total disruption of railroad schedules. Freight failing to reach its destination clogged warehouses and spur lines at plants and railroad stations. Disturbances, strikes, and, finally, armed clashes periodically led to complete breakdowns in communications between different parts of the country. Railroad construction ceased entirely with the onset of the "cultural revolution." Disorganization of transportation reached proportions where hostile Red Guard factions seized weapons and equipment moving by rail to Vietnam.

At first the "cultural revolution" did not involve the countryside. But by the end of 1966 its disorganizing influence was felt even in agriculture. Between January and March 1967 peasants began the arbitrary appropriation of the commodities which were public property, the raiding of food warehouses, and the slaughter of commonly owned livestock.

Peking leaders, unable to depend on organization of the peasants and on experienced agricultural workers for the spring sowing season of 1967, were forced to send regular army units to the country to supervise work in the fields. Even the official Chinese press acknowledged that peasants in a number of main agricultural provinces, such as Shansi, Hunan, Hopeh, Shensi, Szechwan, and Hupeh had left their villages, migrating to cities in order to take part in the "struggle for power." The exodus of peasants to the cities reached so enormous a scale that Hsieh Fu-chih, speaking to the Peking "revolutionary committee" on August 13, 1967, said "the tendency for the countryside to surround the cities is not a deviation but a reactionary phenomenon."

The result of breakdowns in production and transportation and disorganization of trade was a deterioration in quantity and quality of the food supplies reaching the cities. Prices of certain items (rice, pork, tomatoes, cucumbers) were raised at the end of 1966. Ration cards were issued for bread, rice, vegetable oil, sugar, cotton cloth, shoes, and tobacco; this was soon followed by rationing of meat, vegetables, fuel, and kerosene. Special chits even were needed to visit public baths.

The severe shortage of basic commodities and consumer goods induced black market speculation of major proportions. The Chinese press, at the end of 1967 and beginning of 1968, reported that speculators "had large quantities of scarce industrial goods, cement, building materials, fuel, gold, weapons, and ammunition." Special groups were set up in the "revolutionary committees" to "control markets and destroy speculation." Mass round-ups took place in many cities. In Shanghai, for example, 10,000 soldiers, security workers, and "revolutionary cadres" took part in such round-ups. The scourge of speculation was accompanied by a sharp increase in crime. Gross violations of social order by all types of "left revolutionary organizations," actually gangs of hooligans and robbers, became a general phenomenon. The streets of Peking, Shanghai, Kwangchow, Yunnan, and other large cities in China were festooned with reports of sentences meeted out to thieves and exposures of hooligans and other criminal organizations.

The 1967 political situation in the PRC was characterized by a general weakening of centralized authority, an increase in anarchy, an intensification in disagreements between factions of Red Guards and militants, and an aggravation of bickering within the ruling clique.

Armed clashes broke out in virtually every region of the country by the fall of 1967. Whereas it had been youth involved in earlier skirmishes, now such skirmishes involved large masses of workers. Kwangchow (Canton), for example, was for a long period divided into hostile sections, and thousands of its inhabitants took part in the struggle. Even the official Chinese press reported that during fighting in Anshan on August 10, 1967, over 2.000 "revolutionary rebels" were killed or seriously wounded. Mao Tse-tung was forced to recognize that the working class in the PRC "had split into two large opposing factions." The actions of the Red Guards, often uncontrollable, escalated to anarchy.

The reduction in the people's standard of living stirred deep discontent. A wave of mass strikes hit the country at the beginning of 1967. Plants, factories, and whole industrial complexes shut down for long periods of time. Disorders in the plants often were accompanied by destruction of buildings and equipment.

The army became the sole support of the regime, for the Maoists had destroyed the party, the trade unions, and the constituted system of organs of authority. Lin Piao, in September 1967, declared that "the party and administrative authority in the country has been toppled. Military authority must not be allowed to collapse." He was seconded by the Minister of Public Security, Hsieh Fu-chih, who said, "if the army is stricken with disorders the country will have no government."

But even the army was not united. There were many areas where military authorities refused to support the Maoists, and the threat of an open split in the army, and of local armed clashes turning into civil war, was very real.

The development of the situation in China exposed the real nature of the "cultural revolution" as deeply inimical to interests of the Chinese people, hostile to the cause of socialism, and detrimental to friendship and cooperation between the PRC, the Soviet Union, and other socialist countries.

It had become increasingly apparent, not only in China but abroad as well, that the pseudorevolutionary Maoist slogans were lies. The adventurist plans and intentions of the ruling clique and its unscrupulous attempts to move China off the socialist road were exposed with increasing clarity. L. I. Brezhnev, on March 10, 1967, said that the legend of the "proletarian cultural revolution" is only a clumsy disguise for a policy alien to Marxism-Leninism, that it looks more like the suppression of the socialist revolution, and a reactionary military coup d'etat.[10]

Faced by extreme aggravation of domestic political crises, instigators of the "cultural revolution" once again attempted to improve their position by intensifying anti-Soviet agitation. They attempted to distract the attention of the Chinese people from their grave domestic problems, to encourage nationalism, and to unite the warring factions on a nationalistic platform by further aggravating anti-Soviet hysteria.

Propaganda weapons employed by Peking leaders were no longer successful in inflaming anti-Soviet tendencies in the PRC. The malicious propaganda, endlessly repeating the same primitive, slanderous concoctions about the CPSU and our country, ceased to have significant effect on the Chinese populace. Recognizing this, ringleaders of the "cultural revolution" resorted to additional methods for promoting anti-Sovietism in China. They organized a series of crude demonstrations both on Soviet territory and against Soviet representatives in China.

Their objectives were several. First, to provide the possibility of obtaining "concrete material" for propaganda, the shortage of which was quite obvious. The Maoists had so isolated the populace from all things Soviet that discussions about the Soviet Union, completely divorced from facts, had ceased to have reality for the Chinese. The last remnants of plausibility had vanished. Thus, despite Peking's assertions concerning the threat "from the north," or the Soviet-American deal on the struggle against the PRC, the Chinese public remained calm; in practice it was persuaded of the friendly policy of the Soviet Union and perceived no signs of change. The meaningless mouthings of anti-Soviets concerning "bourgeois backsliding" of the Soviet society, "restoration of capitalism in the USSR," and the like, became increasingly unpopular.

Second, Peking anticipated that its crude acts would provoke the Soviet Union into drastic countermeasures, up to and including severance of diplomatic relations. This not only would provide the Maoists with fodder for a new anti-Soviet campaign, but also would make their efforts to shirk responsibility for disruption in Sino-Soviet relations more credible.

The hooliganistic demonstration by Chinese students and personnel of the PRC Embassy in Moscow's Red Square on January 25, 1967 was the first in a series of anti-Soviet provocations. They created a disturbance among visitors to Lenin's tomb and brawled with Soviet citizens who happened to be there. The First Secretary of the Chinese Embassy openly led the hooligans. The USSR Ministry of Foreign Affairs lodged a strong protest against these disgraceful tactics with the Embassy of the PRC on that same day.

But it soon became clear that the provocation in Red Square was not an isolated episode in the overall objectives of CCP leaders. The next day Chou En-lai and Chen Yi, in a telegram representing Mao Tse-tung and Lin Piao, not only approved the hooliganism, but even went so far as to send the provocateurs enthusiastic greetings. On January 28, the PRC Embassy in Moscow called a press conference on the "assault" committed against Chinese citizens in Red Square. Chinese diplomats proceeded to use the conference to distort the incident, offering anti-Soviet concoctions to representatives of the bourgeois press. Appealing for imperialistic cooperation in attacking the CPSU and the Soviet Union, instigators of the provocations even presented "material evidence" in the form of students and Embassy personnel, the supposed victims. This fraud, however, was so crude and primitive that even the Western anti-Soviet press refused to take it up. Despite the outpouring of protests of other Communist parties, CCP leaders stubbornly held to their planned line. On February 1, 1967 the acting PRC chargé d'affaires in the Soviet Union approached the USSR Ministry of Foreign Affairs for permission for reading of Mao Tse-tung's quotations by Chinese students at Lenin's tomb, to be accompanied by speeches and propaganda handouts. Permission denied, the PRC Embassy used its photographic display window for anti-Soviet propaganda. On February 3 the USSR Ministry of Foreign Affairs demanded that the Chinese Embassy remove all anti-Soviet materials from its window and cease anti-Soviet propaganda activities of any description. The PRC Embassy pointedly ignored these demands. Moreover, on February 7, 1967 loudspeakers installed on the Embassy building were used to broadcast hostile, inflammatory slogans directed against the Soviet people, the CPSU, and the government of the USSR.

On February 9, 1967, during the departure of a group of Chinese citizens, the PRC Embassy attempted to provoke a new incident, this time in the Yaroslavl' Railroad Station. Embassy personnel, upon arriving at the station in violation of rules governing traffic regulations, stopped their cars in the middle of the street, interfering with traffic, and holding up pedestrians.

On March 18, 1967, the USSR Ministry of Foreign Affairs made a statement to the Embassy of the PRC in connection with the incessant provocations of Chinese diplomats, pointing out that the Embassy "was deliberately ignoring conditions and norms prevailing throughout the world in permitting actions completely incompatible with the status of a foreign diplomatic mission." Two Embassy people whose conduct was particularly obnoxious were declared *persona non grata*.

The Ministry of Foreign Affairs made nine official protests to the Chinese Embassy in 1967, all dealing with its provocative activities. Travel limitations within the USSR were imposed on personnel assigned to the PRC Embassy in retaliation for hostile acts to Soviet diplomats and correspondents accredited to China. †The ever-increasing tendency of Chinese leaders to interfere in the internal affairs of the USSR forced the Soviet government to abolish its practice of permitting PRC citizens to enter the Soviet Union without visas.

The Maoists also used the Chinese crew of the Peking-Moscow train to organize varied provocations on Soviet territory. Crew members attempted to distribute anti-Soviet literature within our country, deliberately violating rules and procedures established for our railroads.

Chinese train crews in March, April, and May 1967 organized provocative demonstrations rehearsed in advance with a most unoriginal scenario, in connection with Soviet authorities' seizure of illegal propaganda. The trainmaster and conductors on the Peking-Moscow Chinese train refused to permit customs authorities at Naushki station to inspect their personal belongings, proceeded to organize an anti-Soviet demonstration in the station, and insulted Soviet authorities. As a result the train departed quite late. On December 17, in Novosibirsk, a Chinese train crew forcefully dragged a Soviet passenger into a compartment, accused him "of insulting a portrait of Mao Tse-tung," and demanded written apologies. This escapade also resulted in upsetting train schedules.

Chinese authorities organized a total of 40 anti-Soviet provocations in transportation in 1967, 17 on the railroads, 15 on the airlines, and 3 in river and maritime transportation. The result was 18 protests by the USSR Ministry of Foreign Affairs and other Soviet agencies.

The January 1967 provocation in Moscow's Red Square signaled new outrages at the Soviet Embassy in Peking. They were prepared in advance, and began promptly the following day.

This time anti-Soviet demonstrations around the Embassy assumed a particularly widespread and malicious aspect. They lasted over two weeks, continuously, day and night. The Soviet citizens within Embassy grounds literally were subjected to assault by noise. Loudspeakers set up around the Embassy blasted away, twenty-four hours a day. No Soviet newspapers or journals were delivered to the Embassy between January 26 and February 13. Chinese workers left the Embassy, saying they were going on "strike." When the Chinese were advised that the Embassy no longer had need of their services they tried to return by force. On February 3 those Chinese citizens who had been fired burst into the Embassy's consular section and issued an ultimatum that they be reinstated. They detained the chief of the consular section in his office for almost a day and threatened him with physical violence.

On January 29, the USSR Ministry of Foreign Affairs lodged a strong protest against these anti-Soviet outrages and demanded, on behalf of the government of the USSR, that the Embassy be protected against hostile demonstrations interfering with its normal activities and threatening the personal safety of its personnel.

The outrages persisted. This led the USSR to evacuate families of Soviet representatives, Embassy personnel, trade delegation personnel, economic advisors, and TASS correspondents from Peking.

On February 2, A. N. Kosygin, Chairman of the Council of Ministry of the USSR, sent the Premier of the State Council, Chou En-lai, a letter requesting a guarantee of safety for families of staff members of Soviet institutions during their return.

But PRC leaders failed to provide a normal departure for the Soviet citizens. Quite the contrary, Soviet women and children leaving Peking confronted an atmosphere of humiliation, flagrant violence, and the flouting of the most elementary norms of international law and morals. All this was coordinated and encouraged by Chinese authorities. Representatives of Soviet Aeroflot were advised that the safety of the special aircraft being flown to Peking, with official permission of the Chinese authorities, to evacuate the families of USSR delegations in the PRC could not be guaranteed. Our Embassy in Peking appealed three times to the PRC Ministry of Foreign Affairs for assistance in getting the women and children out of the country, but each time the stereotyped answer came back, "the safety of Soviet people cannot be guaranteed."

On February 5, when returning Soviet citizens and accompanying personnel from the Soviet and other socialist embassies arrived in Peking airport, they were surrounded by a crowd of Red Guards and agitators. Alternating malicious anti-Soviet taunts and curses with readings from the works of Mao, unrestrained provocateurs terrorized the defenseless people for eight hours. The jeering continued even during boarding. The Red Guards made the people run the gauntlet; they shook their first at women and children, struck their feet and pulled their hair. The same thing happened upon departure of succeeding groups of Soviet citizens.

La Stampa, the Italian newspaper, in describing these events wrote:

... the disgusting, unprecedented hooliganistic actions of the "Red Guards" with respect to the Soviet Union definitely surpassed all bounds. They are absolutely intolerable to all foreigners living in Peking. One gets the distinct impression that the government of Mao Tse-tung also wants to force the USSR to break its official relations with China, and at the same time wants to arouse in its country fanatical hatred for the Soviet Union. The Soviet citizens behaved splendidly, demonstrating firmness and retaining their dignity in this disorderly and howling crowd, ready for any baseness. Women and men, pressing the smallest of the children to their breasts, stood with their heads held high among the howling crowd.[11]

On February 4, 1967 the Soviet government issued a statement elucidating the crude anti-Soviet actions by Chinese authorities and lodging a stern protest with the PRC government. The statement noted that provocations directed against Soviet institutions in Peking indicated intentions of the Chinese leadership to further exacerbate relations with the Soviet Union. It stressed that outrages around the Soviet Embassy in Peking, arbitrary humiliation of staff members of Soviet institutions, appeals "to overthrow" the Soviet government, and "to take care of" state and political leaders in the USSR, all were just causes of indignation to the Soviet people, whose self-restraint and patience were not inexhaustible. The Soviet government demanded that the Chinese authorities take most urgent measures to ensure the safety of workers and their families assigned to Peking, and to punish severely organizers of provocations. The statement emphasized that the Soviet Union reserved the right to take whatever measures were dictated by the situation to protect the safety of its citizens and of its lawful interests.[12]

Chinese leaders continued to inflame the situation around the Soviet Embassy in Peking. On February 6 the PRC Ministry of Foreign Affairs officially advised the Embassy of the USSR that the safety of Soviet personnel leaving the Embassy grounds "could not be guaranteed."

The USSR Ministry of Foreign Affairs on February 9 dispatched a note to the PRC government demanding that the safety and mobility of the staff members of the Soviet Embassy be guaranteed. The note stated:

> ... the Ministry of Foreign Affairs of the USSR, upon the request of the Soviet government, declares that the steps taken by the Chinese authorities can mean either a deliberate attempt to undermine relations between the People's Republic of China and the USSR, or the inability of these authorities to provide in the country elementary conditions for the life and activities of representatives of a state maintaining normal diplomatic relations with the People's Republic of China. The Soviet government demands the immediate cessation of the arbitrary measures taken by the Chinese authorities directed against the Soviet Embassy in Peking and the freedom of its staff members to move about. If this is not done in the shortest time possible, the Soviet side reserves to itself the right to take the necessary retaliatory measures."[13]

Two days later the PRC Ministry of Foreign Affairs advised the Embassy of the USSR that the February 6 notification was retracted.

The chaotic events at the Embassy of the USSR would remain forever a disgrace to their instigators and organizers; even so they could not help the Maoists reach their objectives. *Pravda,* in an editorial published on February 16, 1967, wrote:

> The anti-Soviet campaign by the Chinese leaders is being carried out in the most provocative, truly hooliganistic forms. But this outward aggressiveness should not delude anyone. In fact, the actions of the Mao Tsetung faction are based not on its strength but on its weakness, by fear of its own party, its own people.

The fraternal parties were unanimous in observing that anti-Soviet actions by CCP leaders played into the hands of imperialism. As one example, *Nuestra Palabra,* the newspaper of the Argentine Communists, on February 27, 1967 wrote:

> ... Mao intends to show the world that no one is more anti-Soviet, more anti-Leninist, more anti-Marxist, than he, and in this he has been successful. Yankee imperialism should be deeply indebted to him for this. Needless to say, it is no accident that the Yankees began their bombing of Vietnam at precisely the moment the unlimited anti-Soviet campaign on the part of the Chinese leaders was unleashed. The aggressive anti-Sovietism of the clique we are talking about is a tremendous gift to the imperialist aggressors.[14]

A leader of the CP USA, James Jackson, expressed the same thought in the newspaper *The Worker:*

> ... This spectacle of how far behind the leaders of China have left even the sworn enemies of Communism in their slander of and attacks against the fraternal party cannot help but attract the attention of the strategists of imperialism. Anti-Sovietism is what currently unites the adherents of Mao Tse-tung and the imperialists.[15]

The imperialist camp expressed unabashed satisfaction over the anti-Sovietism of the Maoists. A columnist for *The Washington Post,* Joseph Kraft, commented:

> Officials in Washington think that Mao is serving American interests because his efforts to galvanize the Chinese masses are drawing China into conflict with Russia to a greater degree than with the United States.

American officials, in the words of the columnist, "even are thinking of cultivating Maoism as a means of putting pressure on Moscow."

It was openly said in Washington that US ruling circles were interested in keeping Mao Tse-tung in power. In February 1967 a directive sent to all centers by the Director of the United States Information Service (USIS), pointed out that members of the service should "take every opportunity to strengthen the positions of Mao's adherents," because the United States wanted "Mao and his faction to remain in power" since their activities were directed against the CPSU and other Communist parties. "The United States is betting on Mao," wrote the journal *U.S. News and World Report,* continuing:

> American officials are inclined to prefer a Mao Tse-tung victory in his struggle to eliminate the more moderate elements, because this would mean a continuation of the unpleasantness for Soviet Russia.

The journal noted with satisfaction that the anti-Soviet campaign in China exceeded all Peking's anti-American campaigns in its "maliciousness."[16]

Instigators of the "cultural revolution" continued efforts to incite anti-Soviet provocations in other countries. They staged a meeting of Chinese citizens in the Ulan Bator railroad station under the pretext of greeting those Chinese students responsible for the Red Square demonstrations. This led to the Ministry of Foreign Affairs of the Mongolian People's Republic lodging a strong protest with the acting chargé d'affaires for China. The Chinese Embassy was given a stern warning that any further "rallies" or any other provocative acts directed against a sister nation, and occurring on the territory of the Mongolian People's Republic, would be suppressed as an illegal act. Two weeks later the Ministry of Foreign Affairs of the Mongolian People's Republic also lodged a stern protest with the PRC Embassy in Ulan Bator in condemning propaganda efforts of the Chinese Embassy on Mongolian territory directed against the USSR and other socialist countries.

This was also the period when Chinese citizens living in Algiers, acting upon instructions from Peking, engaged in hooliganistic acts with respect to diplomatic personnel attached to the Embassy of the USSR and Soviet citizens in the Algerian People's Democratic Republic. On February 2, 60 Chinese grossly violated the generally accepted norms of international law and diplomatic immunity by stopping a Soviet Embassy car containing the First Secretary and his daughter. Hooligans surrounded the car, hammered on windows, roof, and doors, then tried to open the doors and get into the car. All the while they screamed threats against the Soviet Union and insulted the Soviet people, their party and government.

It should be noted that Chinese authorities organized numerous hostile acts against representatives of other socialist countries in the PRC during the "cultural revolution." The wife of the First Secretary of the German Democratic Republic Embassy, for instance, was attacked and seriously injured in Peking on April 29, 1966. Military attachés of the GDR, their wives and children, were beaten on August 28, 1966. Red Guards, the same day, attacked the correspondent of the Polish news agency. Hooliganistic demonstrations were held near the Embassies of the People's Republic of Bulgaria and the Hungarian People's Republic.

While the outrages near the Embassy of the USSR in Peking in January and February 1967 continued, and Soviet evacuations were in progress, Chinese authorities also permitted hostile actions against personnel attached to the Embassies of Bulgaria, Hungary, the German Democratic Republic, the Mongolian People's Republic, Poland, Czechoslovakia, and the Korean People's Democratic Republic. On January 26, 1967 Red Guards in Peking attacked two Czech diplomats and damaged an official car belonging to the Embassy of Czechoslovakia. On February 5, fanatical groups of youths, in the presence of police, abused the Ambassador of the Polish People's Republic, Rodzinski. The crowd detained the Polish diplomats for several hours, cursed them, threw paint, and pasted placards with hooliganistic inscriptions on the Ambassador's car, which flew the Polish national ensign. The Ambassadors of the Mongolian People's Republic, the German Democratic Republic, Hungary, Bulgaria, and Czechoslovakia were grossly insulted on that same day. The car carrying the deputy trade counselor from Bulgaria and his family was almost overturned by Red Guards, who threatened to "execute" the passengers.

On August 9, 1967 there occurred an infamous provocation in Peking involving Mongolian representatives. A group of Red Guards attacked the car belonging to the Ambassador of the Mongolian People's Republic in China, turned it over, and set it on fire. The driver, a Mongolian citizen, was rudely jeered at and then arrested. On that same day a crowd of hooligans broke into the official premises of the Mongolian People's Republic Embassy, committing outrages which continued for several hours.

The line aimed at maximum exacerbation of Sino-Soviet relations was not limited to staging outrages before the Embassy of the USSR in Peking. The whole of 1967 literally was full of provocations directed against Soviet representatives in the PRC. For purposes of illustration, we have compiled a short incomplete chronology of these disgraceful actions.

On January 28, Red Guards engaged in a hooliganistic attack on a bus en route to the USSR Embassy carrying a group of Soviet railroad men working on the Moscow-Peking train.

The following day Red Guards spewed their venom at our diplomats arriving at a hotel for a meeting with the Soviet train brigade. They were surrounded by an unruly crowd for four hours. Police witnesses said they "were not responsible for the actions of the revolutionary masses."

Another provocation occurred at the Peking airport on January 31, when aircraft carrying our specialists en route to the Democratic Republic of Vietnam to help the Vietnamese people landed. Soviet personnel were not permitted to disembark and, in violation of safety regulations, the aircraft was required to refuel with passengers on board. After take-off, representatives of Soviet Aeroflot in Peking were detained and suffered vulgar insults.

A group of Soviet diplomats and personnel assigned to other Soviet institutions in Peking was detained in the vicinity of the Chinese Civil Aviation Adminstration building on February 2. They were held until about 3 A.M. on the 3rd of February, when energetic protests on the part of the Soviet Union resulted in their release. The Soviet people had been subjected to insults, blackmail, and threats for 16 hours. Physical force had been used on some. Soviet Embassy cars were defaced with vandalist graffiti. The chief of the Embassy's consular section and several other Soviet diplomats proceeding to the scene were also detained on a city street. On that same day, there was an attack on a group of Embassy personnel and on the trade representative of the USSR near the Embassy. Hooligans surrounding them chanted anti-Soviet slogans under the very eyes of the police.

A crowd of Red Guards detained a group of Soviet specialists and diplomats just returned from Hanoi for six hours on February 3. Rocks, clumps of dirt, and the like were thrown at their bus.

Two Soviet passenger trains, arriving in Zabaykal'sk Station from Peking on January 30 and February 6, were plastered with anti-Soviet posters, covered with provocative slogans, and daubed with paint.

On February 21 the Soviet Embassy in Peking was forced to protest the gross discrimination of Embassy personnel to the PRC Ministry of Foreign Affairs. Normal functions of the Embassy staff were constantly disrupted. They were forbidden to eat in public places, their hotel was saturated with anti-Soviet graffiti, and stores refused to take their orders. But provocations against Soviet representatives in China continued. On March 11, the PRC Ministry of Foreign Affairs declared two second secretaries of the Embassy *persona non grata* on the trumped-up charge that they interfered in PRC internal affairs. On May 6, the press section of the PRC Ministry of Foreign Affairs, without reason, declared the *Pravda* correspondent in Peking undesirable and demanded his immediate departure. There were incidents in April and May when Soviet diplomats going about the city on official business were detained by hordes of Red Guards for several hours. Their cars were plastered with anti-Soviet slogans, daubed with paint, and efforts made to thrust anti-Soviet materials upon them.

PRC officials refused permission for USSR Embassy personnel to travel in Yunnan, Harbin, Mukden, Dal'ny, and Port Arthur; they were also forbidden to place wreaths in honor of the 49th anniversary of the

Soviet Army and Victory Day on graves of Soviet soldiers fallen in battles for liberation of the Chinese people.

Personnel of the Soviet trade delegation in the PRC arriving with Chinese permission on business in Mukden on June 17, were met by a provocation. Efforts were made to try them for "espionage"; they were subjected to interrogation; the farce of "judicial process" was indulged. The outrages ceased only after protests by the Soviet Embassy.

Ringleaders of the "cultural revolution" missed no opportunity to demonstrate their hostility toward our country. They even went so far as to organize anti-Soviet demonstrations outside China's boundaries. On July 20 and 21, a naval vessel and armed fishing vessels of the PRC engaged in threatening actions against the Soviet ship *Gidrograf* in international waters in the Yellow Sea, 150 kilometers off the China coast.

The August 1967 provocation against the Soviet ship *Svirsk* in the port of Dal'niy occupies a special place in the chain of premeditated actions organized by instigators of the "cultural revolution."

A large party of armed Chinese border guards boarded the *Svirsk* on August 8. They accused the second mate, S. V. Ivanov, who refused to accept a badge bearing the image of Mao Tse-tung, of "violation of the sovereignty of China," and demanded that he be turned over to Chinese authorities. The ship's master, V. A. Korzhov, naturally refused.

On August 11, Chinese authorities unceremoniously flouted the generally accepted norms of international law and arrested the skipper. Despite protests, he was subjected to a humiliating search and was locked up in a cell containing a loudspeaker blasting full force.

At the same time, Red Guards stormed the *Svirsk,* used cutting torches to cut down the door to the radio room, broke portholes, pipelines, and ventilators, tore down antennas, and clogged the ship's stack. They entered the cabins, seized S. V. Ivanov, and placed him under arrest. Both V. A. Korzhov and S. V. Ivanov were subjected to humiliating interrogation. They then were hauled to the city stadium where "court" was convened.

On August 11, the Soviet government lodged a strong protest in connection with provocative actions against the Soviet ship and crew, demanding immediate release of the ship's master, a guarantee that the ship would be permitted to leave port without further interference, and full accountability by those responsible for authorizing the arbitrary actions.[17]

The Trade Union of Maritime and River Fleet Workers of the USSR, in a statement condemning outrages perpetrated in the *Svirsk* case, stated:

In the name of the many thousands of Soviet seamen, we hold up to shame the organizers of this filthy provocation, and all those who are trying to sow enmity between the Soviet and Chinese peoples.[18]

Numerous meetings were held in Soviet ports and aboard Soviet ships to protest the *Svirsk* incident, but Chinese authorities continued their provocations. This led A. N. Kosygin, Chairman of the Council of Ministers of the USSR, on August 12, 1967, to address a letter to the Premier of the State Council of the PRC, Chou En-lai, containing the categorical statement:

The Soviet government expects the immediate adoption of appropriate measures by the government of the People's Republic of China to ensure the safety of the crew, the return of the captain and other crew members to the ship, as well as to ensure the unhindered departure of the motorship *Svirsk* from the port of Dal'niy. . . .[19]

The Soviet seamen were released on August 13, and the *Svirsk* departed Dal'niy for Vladivostok. The workers of Vladivostok held a huge rally for the Soviet seamen, who had conducted themselves with great courage and patriotism throughout the disgusting incident.

The *Svirsk* provocations were used by Maoists to organize new outrages at the Embassy of the USSR in Peking. On August 14, Red Guards surrounded the Embassy, threw rocks on the grounds, and broke glass and windows in the living quarters. The Embassy was ringed with powerful loudspeakers, just as in February, spewing streams of obscene anti-Soviet abuse day and night.

On August 17, 1967 anti-Soviet agitators raised Chinese flags on the fence of the Soviet Embassy, after which almost a hundred hooligans broke into the grounds, destroyed the sentry box and consular section, broke the glass in the Embassy's office building, and burned two vehicles. Another Soviet vehicle was burned that same day in the center of the city. The result of such outrages was material damage to the Embassy estimated in the tens of thousands of yuan.

Anti-Soviet demonstrations and hooliganistic brawling at the Embassy of the USSR continued. They were even organized on November 7, 1967, the 50th anniversary of the Great October Socialist Revolution.

In all, some eighty provocations with the PRC were committed during 1967, either instigated by or on direct orders of the ruling clique, against the Embassy, other Soviet missions and institutions, their personnel and families. Another 120 or more outrages took place more or less "spontaneously." The Ministry of Foreign Affairs of the USSR and the Soviet Embassy lodged 90 protests with Chinese authorities as a result of these events.

The activization of provocations by Peking was fully apparent in the increase in frequency and scope of Sino-Soviet border violations. Violations in 1967 more than doubled as compared with 1966, now numbering over 2,000. Noteworthy is the fact that border violations occurred most frequently precisely when general anti-Soviet hysteria in China peaked, that is in January-February, August-September, and December. In August-September, for example, Chinese violators, in groups of 13 to 20, tried more than 30 times to land on the Soviet island of Kultuk in the Amur river. Actions of the Chinese in the vicinity of Kirkinskiy Island in December 1967 were openly provocative. Throughout the month, groups of military and civilian Chinese trespassed on the island several times a day.

The Ministry of Foreign Affairs of the USSR lodged nine protests in 1967 as a result of border violations. All Chinese border violations, without exception, bore the appearance of premeditation, and all followed the same pattern. Here is but one example. A truckload of Chinese drove onto a Soviet island in the frozen Ussuri river at the beginning of February 1967. Soviet border guards suggested that the violators leave Soviet territory. But the provocateurs, many of whom were drunk and armed with clubs and crowbars, tried to force a fight with the border guards. In about 30 minutes new groups moved out from the Chinese shore, where they had been hiding. Military uniforms were visible under their sheepskin coats. The Chinese screamed curses at the Soviet border guards, trying to force them aside with crowbars, axes, and poles, and force their way into our territory. The bandits then beat up one of their own people, put him on a litter and a photographer, fortuitously on the scene, took pictures of this "victim of the atrocity" committed by the Soviet border guards. That same day, representatives of Chinese border authorities lodged a protest with Soviet border guards against molesting a "Chinese fisherman on Chinese territory."

So-called "self-defense detachments" were organized among Chinese fishermen during the fishing season. Their task was to organize confrontations with Soviet border guards. Local Chinese authorities decorated with honors border violators who had been turned out of Soviet territory, and used such occasions to organize anti-Soviet meetings and demonstrations. Attempts also were made to broadcast anti-Soviet propaganda in Russian by mounting loudspeakers on military cutters. On October 19 the Embassy of the USSR in Peking delivered a verbal protest to the PRC Ministry of Foreign Affairs in connection with the massive provocations by Chinese authorities along border rivers. On October, 26 the Ministry of Foreign Affairs of the USSR handed the Chinese Embassy in Moscow a note of protest on this same matter.

The border violations perpetrated by the PRC reflected a policy geared toward unleashing major border conflicts. This was made quite clear in statements by leading Chinese officials. In February 1967 the Minister of Foreign Affairs, Chen Yi, referring to the future of Sino-Soviet relations, said that "a severance of relations is possible; so is war." Chou En-lai, on March 26, 1967, in a speech before representatives of bourgeois democratic parties, flatly stated that in addition to large wars, there are "border wars as well," and that "a border war between China and the USSR will begin sooner than a war with the United States."

One characteristic feature of Peking's anti-Soviet policy was evidenced quite clearly in 1967: The attacks of Chinese leaders against our party and country intensified with the expansion of US aggression in Vietnam. Organizers of the "cultural revolution," stirring up hatred of the Soviet Union and rejecting any joint action on the part of socialist states to frustrate US tactics, gave American imperialists to understand that they could escalate the Vietnam war without any obstacles, and without risking confrontation with the combined front of the USSR, the PRC, and other socialist countries. In a January 1967 speech M. A. Suslov said:

> The struggle to curtail American aggression in Vietnam, to increase assistance to the Vietnamese people, is intensifying all over the world. Solely because of the leadership of the People's Republic of China we cannot achieve the unity of action we need in this struggle of the socialist countries and of all progressive forces to completely isolate the American aggressors. By their rejection of unity of action in supporting Vietnam, and by their criminal policy of anti-Sovietism and splinterism, the leaders of the People's Republic of China are actually aiding imperialism.[20]

Our party in 1967 continued efforts to mobilize all forces in support of the heroic struggle of the fraternal Vietnamese people. The Secretary General of the CC CPSU, L. I. Brezhnev, in statements at the Seventh Congress of the Socialist Unity Party of Germany on April 18, 1967, and in speeches to the conference of Communist and workers' parties in Karlovy Vary on April 24, 1967, and to the meeting of Soviet-Bulgarian friendship on May 12, 1967, steadfastly emphasized the need for united action, to include the Soviet Union and the PRC, in defending the Demo-

cratic Republic of Vietnam against aggression by American imperialism.
L. I. Brezhnev, at the Karlovy Vary conference, said:

> ... the Central Committee of the Communist Party of the Soviet Union
> and the Soviet government are ready for unified action with China in
> planning and providing practical assistance to struggling Vietnam. We
> are ready for such unified action on the broadest scale.[21]

And how did Peking leaders react to this appeal, supported by the
entire revolutionary movement? On April 30 *Jen Min Jihpao,* which
calls itself the organ of the CC CCP, flatly stated that Chinese leaders
"of course, would not in any case" consider unity of action for "this is
what was the case in the past, is now, and this is how it always will be
in the future."[22]

The ruling faction in Peking disgraced itself by this statement; people
aspiring to the title of revolutionaries certainly could not do a more
odious thing than refuse to carry out their international duty.

The anti-Soviet schismatic course of the Peking leaders was flagrantly obvious in connection with Israel's aggression in the Middle East
during June 1967. Chinese leaders unleashed filthy, slanderous attacks
against the Soviet Union and other socialist countries which decisively
supported the struggle of the Arab peoples against Israeli aggressors
and their imperialist accomplices. CCP leaders did everything possible
to disrupt the friendly relations enjoyed between the USSR and the
Arab states, disseminating for this purpose provocative rumors about
Soviet foreign policy.

Events in the Middle East emphasized how vital it was for the Communist and workers' parties, the international workers' movement, and
the national liberation movement of the Third World to unite in their
actions. At the same time these events once again exposed the adverse
effects of Maoist policy on the interests of unity and solidarity of revolutionary forces.

In June 1967 the plenary session of the CC CPSU heard and discussed a report by L. I. Brezhnev "On the Policy of the Soviet Union in
Connection with the Aggression of Israel in the Middle East." The
plenary session pointed out the need:

> ... to carry on the struggle against the slanderous campaign and splitting
> activities of the Mao-Tse-tung group, the purpose of which is to divide
> the anti-imperialist forces and to destroy the trust that exists between the
> peoples of the Arab states and peoples of the socialist countries. . . .[23]

The anti-Soviet course of the Peking leaders was particularly apparent during celebration of the 50th anniversary of the Great October Revolution. This historic event, celebrated by all revolutionary forces of the world, was exploited by Peking to unleash an even more unbridled anti-Soviet campaign. *Jen Min Jihpao,* the mouthpiece of the "cultural revolution," devoted whole columns to slanderous attacks against the CPSU, against its foreign and domestic policies, and all Soviet actions over the past 50 years.

In order to forestall improvement of Sino-Soviet relations, the ruling clique rudely refused to send a PRC delegation to Moscow for the celebration of the 50th anniversary of Great October. Thus once again this clique demonstrated its alienation from the Chinese people's vital interest in strengthening friendship and cooperation with the Soviet People.

Nevertheless, our party, as part of the celebration of the 50th anniversary of the Great October Socialist Revolution, once again confirmed the immutability of its internationalistic course with respect to China:

> The Soviet peoples [asserted the theses of the CC CPSU for the 50th anniversary of the October Revolution] always have considered the great Chinese people as friends and allies in the struggle for the revolutionary transformation of society. A breaking away of the Communist Party of China from its present fatal policy, a strengthening of relations between the People's Republic of China and the Soviet Union and the other countries of socialism, would be in the interests of world socialism and above all in the interests of China itself.[24]

Our party and the whole Soviet people expressed great confidence that the future of China belongs to forces which champion the ideas of Great October and are steadfastly true to Sino-Soviet friendship. L. I. Brezhnev, in a report devoted to the 50th anniversary, emphasized the fact:

> We believe that the present events in China are historically a transient stage in its development. We believe that despite all the difficulties the cause of socialism will triumph in the People's Republic of China.[25]

4. The 12th Plenary Session of the CC CCP. The beginning of a new stage in the political course of the Peking leaders

The anti-Soviet policy of the organizers of the "cultural revolution" developed further in 1968.

Propaganda hostile to our party and country became even more widespread in China. *Jen Min Jihpao* alone published over 600 verbose articles full of unbridled, slanderous attacks on the CPSU and the Soviet Union in 1968.

At the end of March and beginning of April 1968, Chinese authorities perpetrated a gross provocation in the case of the Soviet tanker *Komsomolets Ukrainy* upon its arrival in the port of Whampoa (near Canton) with cargo for struggling Vietnam.

Soviet ships ceased calling at Chinese ports after the *Svirsk* incident in Dal'niy. However, at the end of 1967, by request of Hanoi, the Soviet Union agreed to deliver certain cargoes for Vietnam through Chinese ports providing that PRC authorities guaranteed the safety of ships and crews. This promise was not kept. In fact, the first time the Soviet tanker *Komsomolets Ukrainy* arrived in Whampoa (December 1967) Chinese officials who boarded the ship to complete port formalities lined up on deck and organized a reading of Mao Tse-tung's sayings, including those anti-Soviet in nature. The tanker also was flooded by quantities of anti-Soviet literature. The Chinese persisted in trying to give Soviet seamen books of Mao Tse-tung's sayings and buttons with his picture. The same thing happened during the second call of *Komsomolets Ukrainy* in Whampoa.

On March 27, 1968 Chinese authorities organized a more serious provocation involving the Soviet tanker. This time they demanded that the ship's master turn over to them the second mate, A. P. Ponomarchuk, whom they accused of having photographed the Chinese port. This slanderous accusation was used as a pretext for still another anti-Soviet provocation. On March 30, Chinese authorities once again tried to arrest Ponomarchuk. Soviet seamen attempting to protect their comrade were abused. Then, during the night of April 3, an armed Chinese detachment boarded the tanker and organized a pogrom, using force to seize the ship's papers and arrest the ship's master and his mate. The bandits broke down cabin doors, damaged watertight bulkheads, broke hatches in the aft superstructures, cut the antenna and radio-telephone line, and smashed the standby receiver. They twisted the arms of Soviet seamen and beat them. Eleven crewmen were seriously injured. The ship's master was seized and thrown in jail. Throughout the entire shocking affair, the tanker's crew performed courageously. A hunger strike was organized to protest the arrest of the ship's master.

The Embassy of the USSR in Peking requested permission to send Embassy personnel to Kwangchow to look into events on board the *Komsomolets Ukrainy*. Chinese authorities refused to approve this legitimate demand.

On March 31 and April 3, the Soviet government lodged strong protests with the PRC government, demanding that it take steps to guarantee the safety of the crewmen and to remove the ban on the tanker's departure from the port of Whampoa. The Soviet government was emphatic in placing full responsibility for the consequences of the unwarranted violence aboard the tanker and against Soviet seamen squarely on the government of the PRC.[26]

These measures forced the Chinese authorities, on April 4, to release the master of the Soviet ship and to give the ship permission to leave port.

The provocation instigated by the Maoists involving the *Komsomolets Ukrainy* caused deep indignation among Soviet seamen and our entire populace. Protest meetings were held in Soviet ports with participants branding actions of the provocateurs as disgraceful. Speeches at these meetings stressed that Soviet seamen were ready to make every effort to continue delivery of cargo to heroic Vietnam.

The Trade Union of Maritime and River Fleet Workers sent an appeal to the government of the USSR which stated:

Soviet seamen consider it to be a matter of honor to deliver to the Vietnamese people the cargo they need to repel American aggression. Their journey to Vietnam is not an easy one. United States naval and air forces simulate attacks on our ships on the high seas, and they are subjected to bombing and strafing in ports in the Democratic Republic of Vietnam. But Soviet seamen are also concerned with the bandit attacks on the crew of the tanker *Komsomolets Ukrainy* in the port of Whampoa in the People's Republic of China, and resolutely condemn the Mao Tsetung faction, which, hypocritically declaring itself to be a friend of the Vietnamese people, in fact is interfering with the rendering of aid to it by the Soviet Union."[27]

The Chinese side continued its attempts at hostile actions on the territory of the Soviet Union as well. In April 1968 a citizen of the PRC, Chen Tsi-hsian, on official business in Tashkent, violated existing laws, photographing the airport and engaging in an altercation with a Soviet official. As a result, competent Soviet organs took decisive and immediate action to expel him from the Soviet Union and to forbid his ever returning.[28]

The Chinese authorities continued to hamper the normal activities of the Embassy of the USSR in the PRC. In February 1968 the delivery of provincial periodicals to the Embassy and to the TASS bureau in Peking was stopped and future subscriptions to them were refused. Soviet representatives in the PRC have ever since received only two

Chinese newspapers, *Jen Min Jihpao* and *Kungmin Jihpao*. Similar discriminatory measures were carried out by Chinese authorities with respect to the embassies of other socialist countries in Peking.

Provocative outrages against Soviet representatives were common occurrences in Peking. On May 20, 1968 a crowd of hooligans, incited by soldiers, detained TASS correspondents on a street for seven hours, giving them no opportunity to communicate with the Soviet Embassy or to summon official representatives to the site. Red Guards wrote anti-Soviet slogans on the sidewalks around the detainees and threatened the correspondents with physical violence.

The police illegally detained an Embassy chauffeur on August 3, 1968. He was taken to a police station and subjected to ten consecutive hours of interrogation, blackmail, and threats. The employee of the Soviet Embassy was forced to make false statements, and to slander his own country. He was told flatly that if he refused he would have to deal with the "revolutionary masses." In other words, he would be turned over to Red Guards for summary justice.

The anti-Soviet policy of the Maoists created untenable conditions for Soviet citizens permanently residing in China. They became open victims of rude humiliation and oppression, from the outset of the "cultural revolution." Soviet citizens had their property illegally confiscated; they were dispossessed from their quarters, discharged from their jobs, excluded from schools and forbidden to correspond with their families in the USSR, or to appeal to their Embassy. Many such citizens were arrested, yet Chinese authorities did not advise the Soviet Embassy in Peking.

In its external relations, Peking, at the height of the counterrevolution in Czechoslovakia in August 1968, joined West German revanchists and the other reactionaries and right revisionists. In company with them the Maoists began a malicious, slanderous campaign in connection with measures taken by five sister nations to help the Czechoslovak people defend socialism in the Czechoslovak Socialist Republic. Peking leaders undertook an intensive propaganda campaign based on the thesis that a socialist camp, as such, no longer existed, so there really could be no talk of common interests of the socialist community.[29]

The Maoists, with this position as point of departure, intensified attacks against collective organizations of the socialist countries and actively tried to destroy them. They disseminated the slanderous assertions that the Warsaw Pact and the Council for Mutual Economic Aid, ensuring the security and successful development of socialist states, were being used to bring about the "restoration of capitalism in the countries of Eastern Europe." Mao Tse-tung, in a telegram to Enver Hoxha on September 17, 1968, openly called for a struggle against the Warsaw Pact and the Council for Mutual Economic Aid. In this same telegram he declared that Peking was beginning a "new historic period of struggle" against the CPSU and the Soviet Union.

The ruling faction continued efforts to hammer into the Chinese populace an awareness of the possibility of armed conflict between the USSR and the PRC. Leaders began to participate directly in intensification of anti-Soviet hysteria. Premier Chou En-lai, at a state reception of October 30, 1968, said that "we can expect anything, including an attack on China,"[30] from the Soviet Union.

In resorting to such provocative statements, Peking attempted to reinforce the fabrication of fantasies about "the hostile actions of the USSR with respect to China." Included among such fantasies was the PRC Ministry of Foreign Affairs' note of September 16, 1968 complaining about so-called intrusions of Soviet military aircraft into China's airspace. This assertion was totally unfounded. A thorough investigation established beyond doubt that Soviet military aircraft had not flown into China's airspace, and had not violated China's sovereignty. Inventing numerous "intrusions" by Soviet military aircraft into China's airspace and accusing the Soviet Union of "serious incidents," of "reconnaissance," "military provocations," "aggravating tensions along the border," "infringing on the territorial integrity and sovereignty of China," and so on, obviously were necessary primarily to disguise the anti-socialist essence of Peking's position regarding Czechoslovakia. These actions merged, for all practical purposes, with the position of imperialist circles which had started a noisy anti-Soviet campaign. The Ministry of Foreign Affairs of the USSR lodged a strong protest against actions of PRC authorities so clearly hostile to the Soviet Union, the purpose of which was to further complicate relations between the two states.[31]

The provocative concoctions concerning alleged violations of PRC borders by Soviet military aircraft were convincingly demolished in an interview with the Deputy Chief of the General Staff of the Soviet Armed Forces, published in *Izvestiya* on November 2, 1968.

The Chinese press deliberately suppressed all such materials which exposed the falsity of their accusations. As in similar cases, Peking cynically counted on success in concealing the truth from its people, thus extracting some benefit from its provocative lies.

Actually, it was the Chinese side that had committed grossly provocative border violations. Ninety such cases were recorded in January-February 1968 alone. This number had increased to 164 by mid-May 1968.

Instigators of the "cultural revolution" tried to strengthen their anti-Soviet policy at the CC CCP 12th Plenary Session, convening in October 1968.

The 12th plenum marked a new phase in China's political development. Though they had completely discredited and destroyed the original CCP, Maoists suddenly found it necessary to convene a plenary session of its Central Committee. An extremely dangerous situation encountered during the "cultural revolution" forced this paradoxical action.

Organizers of the "cultural revolution" soon were persuaded that without a mass political party they would not long be able to lead. Even with military assistance, the Red Guards and Chinese militants were unsuccessful in creating a stable system of new authority. At the same time, the ruling clique feared to remain alone with the army, whose power had conspicuously increased. What worried those in power was that party cadres and millions of rank and file Communists remained discontented. Resumption of CCP activity was also necessary in order to strengthen results of the "cultural revolution" and to cover up the scandalous lawlessness which accompanied reprisals against its enemies.

A cloak of the party also was needed because of the problems created in the international Communist movement by their splitting actions. Despite the bravado of their propaganda, Chinese leaders feared the consequences of condemnation and criticism by the international Communist movement. Had they completely repudiated the role of the party, it would have been difficult for them to consolidate into an independent movement various pro-Peking factions and renegade groups, who as a result of the destruction of the original CCP found themselves in a most ridiculous situation.

Under pressure of these circumstances, the Chinese ruling group by the end of 1967 had begun work on creating a qualitatively different political organization, "the Maoist party," which, borrowing the authority of the CCP, would become the blind instrument of the "cultural revolution." This work was camouflaged under the slogan of "rectification and reorganization of the party," although it was openly stated that the topic under discussion was the creation of a qualitatively new political organization. Directives issued in connection with its establishment emphasized the fact that it would be incorrect to speak of the "restoration" of the party organization in its previous form, that the "renewal of the organizational life of the party in no way meant the restoration of the old order existing prior to the "cultural revolution."

The struggle to convert the Communist Party into an obedient instrument of the Maoists was waged in many directions.

Basic changes were effected in the composition of the CCP. "Rectification and reorganization" were accompanied by a mass purge of the party, by checking the loyalty of each former member of the CCP, by expelling all who showed the slightest doubt or vacillation with respect to present leadership and policies, or who had not been active in the "cultural revolution" proving their devotion to anti-Sovietism. Steps were taken simultaneously to inject "fresh blood" into the party in the form of the most rabid Maoists. Directives dealing with the "rectification of the party" urged "devoting special attention to acceptance into the party of activists from among Red Guards and militants." The press collaborated, steadfastly emphasizing the decisive role of the "revolutionaries outside the party" that is, nonparty people. Included among the leadership of party groups in lower echelon organizations were nonparty militants "co-opted" into the party, bypassing the candidate stage. Any attempt by party members to defend the thesis that "rectification of the party is the business of Communists" was considered incorrect and harmful.

The ideological base of the new party was Maoism, which replaced completely Marxist-Leninist ideology. The December 10, 1967 resolution of the CC CCP and the "Group for Cultural Revolution Affairs" emphasized that "the thought of Chairman Mao should be at the basis of the new program theses and the party constitution." The criterion for "party worthiness" was personal devotion to Mao Tse-tung, faith in his "thought" and in his political line. "Only devotion to Chairman Mao Tse-tung and mastery of the thought of Mao Tse-tung give one the right to speak and to leadership," declared Lin Piao.

Anti-Sovietism was a main plank in the ideological and political platform of the new party. The ruling group inspired proposals that appeals for struggle against the Soviet Union and the CPSU be written into program documents. The Chinese press reported that the new party "should become a bastion of a fierce struggle" with the CPSU and other parties not sharing Mao's "thought."

The CC CCP 12th Plenary Session revealed that the leadership of the "cultural revolution" had moved far along the path of "rectification and reorganization." The Plenary Session occurred after the constitution of the CCP was dismantled. All that need be said is that more than

130 of 173 members and candidate members of the CC CCP were already discredited and repressed when the session convened. Losses suffered by the Central Committee were so extensive, and the demand of Maoists for obedience so adamant, that it was necessary to import people who were not members of the Central Committee, who in fact were not even members of the party, in order to constitute a quorum for the convention.

The Plenary Session officially sanctioned the antisocialist, antidemocratic, and unconstitutional acts of the Peking leaders from the outset of the "cultural revolution." It approved Mao Tse-tung's directive "Fire on the Staffs" of August 5, 1966, which signaled the pogrom of party organizations and elected organs of government; confirmed the "Decree on the Great Proletarian Cultural Revolution" of August 8, 1966, as well as all of Mao's "instructions" and Lin Piao's statements; noted the important role of the "Group for Cultural Revolution Affairs" in the struggle for realization of the "Great Helmsman's" policy. The Plenary Session officially announced plans for convening the 9th Congress of the CCP "at a suitable time," an act destined by Maoists to complete the creation of the new "Mao Tse-tung Party."

All documents of the 12th Plenary Session were permeated with livid anti-Sovietism. They officially confirmed the policy of open struggle with our party and country. The Plenary Session's communiqué and the approved draft of the Constitution of the new CCP demonstrated that an antisocialist, anti-Soviet policy was the basis for long-term PRC domestic and foreign policies.

The magazine *Kommunist,* appraising the significance of the 12th Plenary Session in an article "The Situation in China and Conditions in the Communist Party of China at the Contemporary State," wrote:

> The staging of the 12th "Plenary Session" was necessary to the Maoists to once again justify the "cultural revolution," to isolate them from the policy line of the 8th Congress of the Communist Party of China, and at the same time cancel the period of development of the People's Republic of China along the socialist path, and ideologically prepare the country for the formation of a new system of authority.[32]

5. Armed provocation by Chinese authorities along the Soviet border in March 1969

Peking leaders, constantly escalating anti-Sovietism, organized an armed provocation on the Sino-Soviet border in March 1969 on the Ussuri river, in the Damanskiy* Island area.

* Translator's note: called Chenpao (Treasure) by the Chinese.

During the night of March 1–2 a specially trained detachment of the Chinese army numbering some 300 men violated the Soviet state boundary and intruded on Damanskiy Island. This detachment was joined by another group of 30 armed soldiers on the morning of March 2. Concentrated in advance on the Chinese bank were reserves and fire power, including a battery of antitank guns, mortars, grenade launchers, and heavy machine guns.

When Soviet border guards approached the border violators, planning to protest and demand immediate withdrawal from Soviet territory as had been previous practice, the intruders treacherously and without warning opened fire, literally mowing down the Soviet soldiers point-blank. Another group of Soviet border guards was fired on in simultaneous ambushes on the island and from the Chinese bank.

Soviet border guards, together with reserves from neighboring border posts, formed a battle line boldly, valiantly repulsed the surprise attack, and drove the intruders off Soviet territory.

The armed provocation in the Damanskiy Island area undertaken by the PRC was planned in advance and carefully prepared. Inspection of the battle site on Soviet territory turned up Chinese infantry weapons and military equipment discarded when the Chinese fled; also field type telephones, communication lines leading to PRC territory, mine fins, shell and grenade fragments were discovered. The result of this bandit raid organized by Chinese authorities was 45 Soviet casualties: 31 dead and 14 wounded.

On March 2 1968 the Soviet government sent the PRC a strong note protesting the impudent armed incursion into our territory and demanding immediate investigation and the stringent punishment of the persons responsible. The government of the USSR stated that it "insists that immediate steps be taken which would preclude any violation of the Soviet-Chinese frontier." The note further asserted that the Soviet government in relations with the Chinese people, was guided by sentiments of friendship and was going to continue this line in the future.[33]

The Chinese authorities paid no heed to these proposals. Quite the contrary, steps were taken to further increase tensions. Beginning on March 3, 1969, specially trained groups once again subjected the Soviet Embassy in Peking to organized siege. An unruly anti-Soviet campaign began in China, during which territorial claims were openly made against the USSR, and all methods used to cultivate an atmosphere of chauvinistic intoxication and military hysteria.

Meanwhile, Chinese authorities were preparing a new armed provocation along the border with the USSR, which took place on March 14–15, 1969.

On March 14 a group of armed Chinese soldiers made another attempt to invade Damanskiy Island. The following day a large Chinese detachment, supported by artillery and mortar fire from the bank, attacked Soviet border guards protecting the island. But the provocateurs were repulsed.

The Soviet government, in its statement of March 15, 1969, severely condemned the new Chinese provocations. The statement stressed that "if the lawful rights of the USSR are flouted, if further attempts are made to violate the integrity of Soviet territory, the Union of Soviet Socialist Republics and all its peoples will resolutely defend it and give a crashing rebuff to such violations.[34]

Armed provocation along the Soviet-Chinese border was undoubtedly conceived as a multipronged action. It was used to incite nationalist and chauvinist feelings in the PRC, and once having created this situation, to strike new blows against their internal enemies, yet another step along the road of assuring Maoist supremacy.

The armed conflict on the Soviet-Chinese border was deliberately organized to coincide with preparations for the 9th Congress of the CCP. The Maoists, fanning anti-Soviet hysteria and rousing chauvinist intoxication, tried to create an atmosphere that would permit them to use the congress for officially establishing anti-Sovietism as a general line of PRC foreign policy.

The inflaming of anti-Soviet psychosis in China and attempts to exploit armed provocation on the Soviet-Chinese border to discredit our country in the international arena also served to intensify the schismatic activities of the Maoists with respect to the socialist commonwealth and the world Communist movement. One of their short-term goals was to impede and disrupt the convening of an international conference of the Communist and workers' parties, preparations for which had already reached the final stage.

At the same time, armed border provocations instigated by Chinese authorities created conditions necessary for Peking's unprincipled political flirtation with the imperialist states. By organizing criminal intrusions on the Soviet-Chinese border, Peking was in effect making overtures to extreme imperialist reaction and laying claim to cooperation with it. Hence it was no accident that Chinese authorities coordinated the attack on the Soviet border guards with Bonn's provocative undertaking of presidential elections in West Berlin.

The provocation in the Damanskiy Island area was an important link in Maoist efforts to force radical reorientation of PRC foreign and domestic policy, a shift into a posture openly hostile to socialist countries.

The Marxist-Leninist Communist and workers' parties and progressive world public opinion sharply condemned these provocations playing into the hands of international imperialism. This provocation caused grave concern among Communists and progressive forces all over the world.

The Soviet Union, while dealing a crushing rebuff to the armed Chinese provocations, still remained true to its unchanging policy of achieving normalization of relations between the USSR and the PRC, including issues concerning the Soviet-Chinese border. This policy was clearly expressed in the statement made by the Soviet government on March 29, 1969.

The statement offered convincing proof of how groundless were attempts of the Chinese leadership to support its territorial claims by using historical references to "prove" the unequal nature of treaties establishing the present boundary between the Soviet Union and the PRC.

Peking leaders, in their efforts to "justify" their territorial claims, had the audacity to declare themselves heirs of Genghis Khan, including him among "emperors of China." But these chauvinist falsifications of history had long since been scoffed at by Lu Hsün. In 1934 he wrote:

I was 20 when I heard that "our" golden era had been when "our" Genghis Khan had conquered Europe. Not until I had reached 25 years of age did I know that in fact in the so-called golden era of "ours," the Mongols had conquered China and that we had become slaves. In August of that year I leafed through three books on the history of Mongolia in order to refine certain historical facts, and only then did I understand that before having conquered all of China, the Mongols had conquered the "Rus" and had invaded Hungary and Austria. He was not yet our Khan at that time. The Russians had been enslaved before us, and it was they who should have said that "when our Genghis Khan conquered China our golden era began."[35]

Worth recalling is another opinion of this great revolutionary and internationalist Chinese writer, which, while directed at imperialists, could be a direct indictment of the provocateurs in the Damanskiy Island area. In a 1932 article, "We Shall No Longer Be Tricked," he wrote:

We are against attacking the Soviet Union. We shall strive to destroy the dark forces attacking it, whatever the honeyed speeches they make, whatever the pretence at justice they use as a cover. This and only this, is our own path to life!

Chinese leaders, in attempting to provide a semblance of justification for their assertions as to the "unequal nature" of the border treaties, go so far as to juggle citations from works of the founders of Marxism-Leninism, even those of V. I. Lenin! But it is well known that not a single statement by the first head of the Soviet state ever asserted that the treaties dealing with the Chinese border were supposedly unequal, or among those subject to review. The principled position of V. I. Lenin is well known. He emphasized that "we reject all points concerning pillage and violence, but we gladly accept all points containing conditions for good neighborliness and economic agreements. These we cannot reject."[36] V. I. Lenin left no doubt about the fact that the Maritime Provinces were Soviet soil. Lenin's words are well known: "Vladivostok is a long way off, but this city is ours. . . . our Republic is here, and it is there."[37]

The Soviet people, under the leadership of V. I. Lenin, between 1918 and 1922 freed at great cost their Far Eastern lands from foreign interventionists who tried to wrench from the young Soviet Republic the Maritime Provinces, Chabarovsk Region, and Eastern Siberia.

Japanese militarists and their accomplices frequently tried to test the strength of Soviet frontiers in the Far East in following years. After the occupation of Manchuria, they planned the seizure of Soviet islands in the Amur and Ussuri rivers but suffered a crushing rebuff. Their anti-Soviet adventures at Khasan and Khalkhin-Gol ended the same way. The aggressors were completely routed and dislodged from Soviet territory.

The Chinese government, after the foundation of the PRC, repeatedly emphasized its obligation to respect the state sovereignty and territorial integrity of the USSR. This obligation was confirmed in the Treaty of Friendship, Alliance, and Mutual Assistance between the USSR and the PRC, signed in 1950. Article 5 of this treaty envisages observance of the principles of "mutual respect for state sovereignty and territorial integrity." This same obligation is embodied in joint declarations of the Soviet and Chinese governments of October 12, 1954[38] and January 18, 1957.[39]

Early in the 1950s, at China's request, the Soviet Union handed over complete sets of topographic maps showing the line of demarcation in accordance with the Russo-Chinese treaties. At that time, Chinese authorities made no comments on the border shown on the maps; this line was observed in practice.

After the conclusion of the Soviet-Chinese Treaty of Friendship, Alliance, and Mutual Assistance, both sides agreed to joint study and use of the Amur and Ussuri Rivers. The population living on both sides maintained friendly relations and developed trade, cultural, and other relations. A Soviet-Chinese agreement on navigation on the Amur, Ussuri, Argun', and Sungari rivers, and on Lake Khanka, was signed in 1951. It included provisions for the establishment of aids to navigation on these waterways. An agreement on complex joint utilization of water resources of the rivers in the Amur basin, and on conduct of joint research, was concluded in 1956.

Soviet and Chinese border guards dealt with issues in a businesslike manner and settled misunderstandings in a good-neighborly spirit. There were no conflicts or misunderstandings along the border.

Deterioration in these comradely relationships began when those in authority in the CCP set out along the road to exacerbation of Sino-Soviet relations. As already has been said earlier, the violations of the Soviet border by the PRC became more and more frequent after 1960, taking on an ever-increasingly aggressive and provocative nature. It is no accident that Chinese leaders opposed the very principle of peaceful settlement of border disputes. They violently attacked and rejected the Soviet government's December 1963 proposal that an international agreement outlawing use of force by states in settling territorial disputes and boundary questions be concluded. Significantly, Chinese leaders vented their anger on the efforts of the Soviet Union and other countries to arrive at a peaceful settlement of a conflict between India and Pakistan. The Tashkent Declaration, ending that conflict, was violently attacked in Peking. In fact, Chinese leaders continue to ignore the initiative of the Indian side in proposing a settlement of the Indo-Chinese border dispute.

On its part, the government of the USSR attempted from the beginning to settle disputes with the PRC by bilateral consultations. This position was clarified in the March 29, 1969 statement by the government of the USSR.[40] The statement once again proposed that consultations on border questions which had begun in Peking in 1964 be resumed in the near future. Guided by an earnest desire to ensure lasting peace and security and to maintain friendship and cooperation with the Chinese people, the government of the USSR emphasized the need for immediate practical steps to normalize the situation on the Soviet-

Chinese border. It urged the government of the PRC to refrain from any border actions that could cause complications, and further urged the Chinese to resolve differences, should they arise, in an atmosphere of calmness.

The USSR Ministry of Foreign Affairs, on April 11, 1969, addressed a note to the PRC Ministry of Foreign Affairs proposing renewal of consultations between plenipotentiaries of the two governments, and expressing readiness to begin them in Moscow on April 15, 1969, or at an approximate date convenient to the Chinese side.[41]

On April 26, 1969 the Soviet Union, in order to normalize conditions along boundary rivers and to ensure normal conditions for navigation, proposed that the PRC call, in May 1969, the 15th session of the Soviet-Chinese Commission on Navigation, which had been established in accordance with the intergovernmental agreement of 1951 on rules for navigation on the boundary rivers.

Efforts of the Soviet Union to solve differences through discussions in a calm atmosphere were reaffirmed in statements made by Soviet leaders. L. I. Brezhnev, Secretary General of the CC CPSU, in a Red Square speech of May 1969, emphasized that the Soviet Union was in favor of resolving unsettled international differences by discussions. Secretary of the CC CPSU I. V. Kapitonov, in a report during the Kremlin ceremony on April 22, 1968, pointed out the need for immediate practical steps to normalize the border situation and repeated the appeal of the Soviet government to the government of the PRC to refrain from any action that could cause complications, and to solve differences, should they arise, in an atmosphere of calm discussion.

On April 14, 1969, in response to the USSR note of April 11, the Chinese side stated that Soviet proposals for the settlement of the border situation "were being studied," and that a reply would be forthcoming. However, practical actions of Chinese authorities on the border and the overall political course of the leadership not only did not diminish their anti-Soviet nature, but in fact became even more hostile.

6. Anti-Sovietism—the most important component of the political program of the 9th Congress of the CCP

Armed provocations on the Soviet-Chinese border formed a background of preparation for convocation of the 9th Congress of the CCP, held in Peking between April 1 and 24, 1969. The Congress assembled under conditions of further aggravation of the domestic policy crisis and of intensification in the factional struggle in the Maoist camp. The CCP ruling faction decided to hold the Congress on a wave of chauvinist intoxication and anti-Soviet hysteria, in order to divert the Chinese people from failures in domestic and foreign policies.

The 9th Congress was held in an atmosphere of complicated internecine struggle within the CCP. Finally the Maoists successfully imposed their policy on the Congress.

The Congress "summed up" the "cultural revolution," and directed PRC policy for the next few years. Materials of the Congress—the report by Lin Piao, and the new by-laws of the CCP—reaffirmed that internally this policy mitigated against socialist gains of the Chinese people, and that internationally its purpose was to engage in a struggle against socialist countries and the world Communist movement.

The 9th Congress in the official party constitution approved the Mao Tse-tung cult of personality, envisaging conditions ensuring the triumph of the "thought" of Mao on a long-term basis. The constitution states that Mao Tse-tung is the "leader of the Party" and that Lin Piao is "his successor." The main standard of internal party life, as set forth by the 9th Congress, is the requirement of loyalty to Mao Tse-tung. "Those who dare oppose Mao Tse-tung's thought, regardless of when, and under what circumstances, will be condemned by the entire party and punished by the entire country."[42]

The goals of the 9th Congress with respect to internal development of China were to create a militaristic, bureaucratic state suited to the conduct of an adventurist, great-power policy in the international arena. The Congress made no effort whatsoever to advance a positive program for economic construction, social development, or improvement in the material well-being of the people. Instead the task assigned was that of a "continuous revolution, to prepare for war, prepare for famine." The ruling faction divested itself in advance of responsibility for deterioration in workers' living standards, for a breakdown in the national economy, and for foreign policy adventures.

Lin Piao's major report to the Congress gravely distorted the picture of contemporary world development. He lumped into one category the imperialist states and all socialist countries opposed to Peking. These countries were declared to be "revisionist" or "social-imperialist," and were numbered among forces hostile to revolution. This breakdown was not based on class analysis, but simply on postures of the particular countries with respect to Peking's policies. The Congress essentially proclaimed the socialist countries the main enemy of China.

Anti-Sovietism formed the foundation of foreign policy as planned by the 9th Congress. The new constitution established it as the party's official policy. Lin Piao emphasized that "a new historical period had begun" as of that time, one that was to be a struggle with the USSR; stated the task of setting up an international anti-Soviet front; emphasized territorial claims; once again commented on "unequal treaties" and on "seizures of Chinese territory" by our country; and propagandized a false version of the Damanskiy Island incidents. The report attempted to twist the meaning of the Soviet government's statements in the 1920s relative to the Soviet-Chinese border and asserted that our country supposedly failed to keep its "promises" to return everything "seized from China" by the Tsarist government.

The policy laid down in the report concerning Sino-Soviet relations completely reversed the spirit and the letter of the Sino-Soviet treaty of 1950. Peking's leaders evidenced no interest in cooperation with the USSR or in normalizing relations. The Congress failed to put forth a single constructive proposal designed to achieve this goal.

In his report to the 9th Congress Lin Piao spoke of the Chinese leadership's desire "to settle territorial questions through diplomatic channels by conversations," but that "until they are settled the situation existing on the border must remain and conflicts must be avoided." In fact, however, the Chinese side engaged in provocative violations of the Soviet border while the Congress was still in session, as well as after its adjournment.

At the end of April 1969 a large body of Chinese landed on the Soviet Union's Kultuk Island in the Amur river and, covered by military detachments, made ostentatious attempts to engage in economic activities. This led the USSR Ministry of Foreign Affairs to send a strong note of protest to the Chinese side on April 25. On May 2, 1969, PRC soldiers, over 300 strong and armed with machine guns and mortars, violated the state boundary of the USSR along the western sector of the Soviet-Chinese border. The provocative nature of this action is all too apparent from the fact that Chinese authorities used the civilian population, shepherds with their flocks, to cover the violators. A large group of Chinese citizens landed on a Soviet island near the city of Blagoveshchensk on May 14. The intruders responded to demands of Soviet border guards that they depart Soviet territory by attacking them with axes and iron bars. It took decisive action to clear the provocateurs from our territory.

In the first half of 1969 alone, representatives of Soviet border troops lodged over 20 protests with the Chinese side in connection with gross violations of the Soviet border.

The Chinese government, on May 24, 1969, after a two-month

delay, responded to the USSR's March 1969 statement. The response demonstrated that its authors were not at all interested in settling disagreements. Quite the contrary, its purpose was to exacerbate further Sino-Soviet relations. The absurd demand was again advanced that the "unequal nature" of the treaties establishing the border between the USSR and the PRC be acknowledged, and attempts were made to justify claims of the present leaders of China to age-old Soviet lands. The PRC government did not formally reject the idea of discussion, but the possibility of engaging in such talks was based on a series of obviously unacceptable conditions. In his speech to the international conference of Communist and Worker's Parties (June 1969), L. I. Brezhnev, discussing the Chinese reply, said:

> . . . the statement of the government of the People's Republic of China can in no way be said to be constructive, either in its content or in its spirit. This verbose document is full of historical falsifications, of perverted facts of the present time, and full of hostile attacks against the Soviet country. It repeats unfounded claims of a territorial nature against the Soviet Union, and we decisively reject these claims.[43]

The May 24 statement of the PRC government not only confirmed the hostile statements of the 9th Congress with respect to our party and country but also justified the actions of Peking, actions designed to exacerbate Sino-Soviet interstate relations. The Chinese government, talking as an accuser, which is impermissible in relations between sovereign states, attempted to judge the Soviet government and its domestic and foreign policies. The Soviet Union was officially included among countries hostile to China. In this way Peking attempted to justify its expansionist aims, and to represent anti-Sovietism as a struggle with "social-imperialism," thereby masking their own renegade and backsliding nature.

The issuance of the May 24 statement served to signal further incitement of anti-Soviet hysteria in the PRC. Anti-Soviet propaganda took on an increasingly belligerent character, emphasizing the inevitability of war between China and the Soviet Union. *Kungmin Jihpao,* on June 6, 1969, for example, published an article containing an appeal for "readiness to fight a conventional, as well as a large-scale nuclear war with the Soviet revisionists." *Jen Min Jihpao* alone published 653 anti-Soviet articles in the first five months of 1969, more than in all of 1968.

Interwoven with provocative anti-Soviet attacks in the Chinese press were prophecies of the imminence of a new world war. *Chiehfang Jih-*

pao, on May 14, 1969, wrote that 22 years had passed between the first and second world wars, that 23 years had elapsed since the end of the Second World War, and that now "we already smell powder. The question of a world war is in essence a question of the future of the proletarian revolution, the future of mankind." *Jen Min Jihpao,* on May 25, 1969, urged the world proletariat not to worry about a new world war, "because the result would only be loss of its chains and acquisition of the whole world."

On June 13, 1969 the Soviet government issued a new statement responding to the May 24 document which once again set forth a positive program for settling border disagreements.[44] Confirming its proposal to resume discussions on the issue of refining the border line along certain sections on the basis of existing treaties, the Soviet side suggested:

> ... by agreed opinion of the sides, those sections of the border about which there is no disagreement be fixed; that where there are disagreements about individual sections, mutual discussions be held to reach an understanding of where the border runs, using the treaties as a basis for so doing; and that where natural changes have occurred the existing treaties be used to determine the boundary line, observing the principles of mutual concessions and economic interests of the local populace in those sections; and that once agreement is reached, that the countries sign the corresponding documents."

The Soviet government proposed that the Peking talks, interrupted in 1964, be resumed within two to three months in Moscow, and named P. I. Zyryanov as plenipotentiary of the USSR with rank of Deputy Minister to head the Soviet delegation. The Soviet government in its statement emphasized:

> The policy of the USSR with respect to the Chinese people has been, and continues to be, the same. It is built on the basis of the long-term future. We remember that the interests of the Soviet and Chinese peoples coincide. The Soviet Union is for good neighbor relations and friendship with China, for eliminating everything that can complicate relations between our two states.

7. The decisive rebuff to the schismatic, anti-Soviet course of Peking at the international conference of fraternal parties

The anti-Soviet course of Peking provides the most important link in its conflict with all contemporary revolutionary forces. The Maoists had long hoped to convince these forces that their disagreements lay solely with the CPSU. They resorted to all sorts of maneuvers to conceal the fact that their position was hostile to the entire world revolutionary movement. But as time passed, it became evident that Maoism was actually warring with all Communist parties. In 1967, for example, in an article dealing with the Karlovy Vary conference of the European Communist and Workers' Parties, the Maoists openly designated as implacable enemies and "cliques" such detachments of the world Communist movement as the Communist and Workers' Parties of Hungary, the German Democratic Republic, Poland, Bulgaria, Italy, France, England, Spain, Finland, and other countries. At the 9th Congress the Maoists generally referred to the socialist community and the world Communist movement as "nonexistent." They condemned the Warsaw Pact, which serves as a dependable shield, providing security for socialist countries and a stronghold of peace in Europe; they railed against the Council for Mutual Economic Assistance, the most important tool for providing mutually advantageous cooperation between fraternal peoples.

Peking's conflict with the socialist community and the world Communist movement, and their anti-Soviet schismatic activities, were severely criticized at the June 1969 Conference of Communist and Workers' Parties in Moscow.

The CPSU and other parties continually tried to persuade the CCP to take part in preparations for the conference. The CC CCP received invitations to participate in all preparatory measures; it was given timely news of progress in preparations; and it had every opportunity to familiarize itself in good time with documents that would be presented for discussion.

But Peking leaders held stubbornly to their hostile position with respect to the international Conference of Communist and Workers' Parties and rudely rejected the idea of participating in its work.

The convening of the Conference caused extreme irritation in Peking, signifying itself that Maoist plans to isolate the CPSU and other parties firmly and consistently holding to Marxist-Leninist positions had failed. The Conference fully emphasized the key trend in development of the world Communist movement as that of strengthening the unity and solidarity of its ranks.

The Conference adopted a document entitled "Tasks of the Struggle against Imperialism in the Current Stage and Unity of Action of Communist and Workers' Parties, of All Anti-Imperialist Forces." This document provided a comprehensive analysis of the world situation and completely refuted the distorted presentations on the same subject rendered by Lin Piao to the CCP 9th Congress. Not one of the 75 Communist parties active in the Conference expressed support for the insular views which Peking had attempted to foist upon revolutionary forces.

Peking propaganda attacked the Conference with impotent fury, attempting to distort its goals and tasks, to disparage its historical significance, and to prevent the dissemination of its documents. Chinese leaders declared the slogans of unity of action against imperialism advanced by the Marxist-Leninist parties to be "rotten banners," and the idea of alliance between the international working class and the peasantry "shopworn."

The need to consistently expose and then to criticize in principle the theory and practice of Maoism, particularly in connection with the CCP 9th Congress, was emphasized repeatedly in speeches by representatives of a great many parties.

Representatives of fraternal parties stressed that condemnation of Peking's disruptive tactics in no way signified interference in CCP internal affairs. The chief of the delegation from the Communist Party of Czechoslovakia, First Secretary of the Central Committee of the Communist Party of Czechoslovakia, Gustav Husak, said:

> One cannot consider the efforts of the Mao Tse-tung faction to undermine relations between socialist countries, to support and expand separatist nationalistic tendencies and anti-Soviet feelings, to weaken and disrupt friendly relations and ties of alliance between the Soviet Union and other socialist countries as internal affairs of the Communist Party of China.

The convincing analysis of the anti-Leninist aims of Maoist leaders presented to conferees by the head of the Soviet delegation, the General Secretary of the CC CPSU, L. I. Brezhnev, met with great attention by conferees. He stated:

> The combination of the political adventurism of the Chinese leaders and their constant incitement of an atmosphere of war hysteria has introduced new elements into the international situation, and these we have no right to ignore.

Thus the CPSU, which initially had no intention of dragging before the conference the problem of Sino-Soviet relations, was forced to do so. The head of the delegation from the CPSU delineated the principled position on China of our party and the Soviet government, a position based on long-term perspective, and stemming from the fact that root interests of the Soviet and Chinese people coincide.[45]

The conferees made statements concerning the break the present-day leaders of China had made with Marxism-Leninism and emphasized the particularly pernicious nature of the line taken by the Chinese leadership in the struggle against the socialist community. Sharp criticism of this criminal line was heard in the speeches made by the heads of the delegations from the Communist parties of Bulgaria, Hungary, the Mongolian People's Republic, the German Democratic Republic, France, Denmark, the United States of America, Uruguay, and many other countries.

Many speakers cited numerous facts of gross interference in internal affairs of fraternal parties by CCP leaders and their stooges. For example, the head of the delegation from the Brazilian Communist Party, the General Secretary of its Central Committee, Luis Carlos Prestes, said that his party was:

> ... one of the first parties to experience the consequences of factionalism, instigated and openly supported in our country by Chinese leaders from the Mao Tse-tung faction. ... In the interests of the unity of our party we have been forced to come out in the open against the antiproletarian and anti-Marxist positions of the Maoists."[46]

The conferees pointed out that in their struggle the Maoists did not hesitate to employ terrorism. The head of the delegation from the People's Party of Panama recounted how since 1964 CCP leaders had waged a hostile campaign against his party differing in no way from actions of the ruling oligarchy. In fact, Peking went even further, deciding it would be acceptable to physically eliminate opponents. The leader of the Federation of Students and the head of the anti-imperialist movement, Victor Avila, suffered a head wound inflicted from a shot fired by a Maoist lackey. Later on, another Communist youth leader suffered two bullet wounds in the leg.[47]

The conferees severely condemned the disruptive, schismatic activities of Peking and its agents in the national liberation movement. The Chairman of the South African Communist Party, John B. Marx, told the conference that the Chinese leaders had not only cut off aid to the Afrikaans National Congress but were in fact subsidizing and protecting groups of right-wing renegades who undertook their activities upon insistence and support of the CIA.[48] It was emphasized that activities of the Maoists played directly into the hands of imperialism in its struggle against revolutionary forces. As the head of the Hungarian Socialist Workers' Party delegation, Janos Kadar, put it:

> "Objectively, the present policy of the Chinese leadership is the greatest gift that could be made to international imperialism, for it gives it advantages, and inspires it with hope."[49]

The consequences of Maoist treachery impacted particularly on fraternal parties leading the revolutionary struggle in places that world imperialism considers its bridgehead. The head of the delegation of the West Berlin Communists, G. Danelius, said:

> In West Berlin, "Maoism" is a direct weapon of the bourgeoisie. It undermines the unity of all adversaries of the latter-day capitalist system, binds the democratic and socialist movement to an ultra-left and adventurist line and confuses young people who are entering the movement."[50]

The First Secretary of the Central Committee of the Communist party of Germany, M. Reiman, also noted that while the Communist Party was outlawed in the Federal Republic of Germany, the Bonn government encouraged officially existing Maoist factions, using them for its own purposes. "The West German imperialists," he said, "consider the Chinese leaders to be their strategic reserve."[51]

The anti-Marxist thesis of the Maoists concerning the inevitability of a new world war was severely criticized during the conference. Acceptance of this thesis, it was emphasized, would imply rejection of the struggle for creating conditions most favorable to settling the main conflict of our epoch, the conflict between socialism and capitalism; it would infer doubts in the strength of the socialist system, the international working class, and the national liberation movements. Participants in the conference also convincingly demonstrated the fallaciousness of Maoist assertions that, so far as war was concerned, there exist two possibilities, namely, that "war either will lead to revolution, or revolution will avert war."[52]

Representatives of the Communist and workers' parties stated concern that CCP leadership, headed by Mao Tse-tung, was attempting to subordinate China's entire development to warlike goals; the militarization of the country, and the generating of war psychosis.

The armed border provocations instigated by Chinese authorities roused deep indignation among the conferees. Walter Ulbricht, head of the delegation from the Socialist Unity Party of Germany, said that "these acts of military aggression directly support the global strategy of the United States and the expansionist policy of West German imperialism."[53]

The CC CPSU plenum, convened at the end of June 1969, having heard and discussed a report by L. I. Brezhnev, "Results of the International Conference of Communist and Workers' Parties," fully and completely approved activities of the Soviet Politburo directed at strengthening the solidarity of the world Communist movement, as well as work accomplished by the CPSU's delegation to the conference. The Plenary Session declared that our party would carry on an unrelenting struggle against the anti-Leninist goals of China's leadership against its schismatic policy and great-power, nationalistic course, and would do everything necessary to protect the interests of the Soviet people against infringement. The resolution of the Plenary Session noted that:

> ". . . the Communist Party of the Soviet Union is proceeding on the basis that the root interests of the Soviet and Chinese peoples coincide. The Communist Party of the Soviet Union henceforth will endeavor to preserve and support the friendly feelings the Soviet people have for the Chinese people and which the Chinese people unquestionably also have for the Soviet Union and the other socialist countries."[54]

8. Meeting of the heads of state of the USSR and the PRC in September 1969

At the beginning of July 1969 a session of the Supreme Soviet of the USSR discussed the issues of the international situation and the foreign policy of the Soviet Union. In his address, the USSR Minister of Foreign Affairs, A. A. Gromyko, devoted great attention to problems of Sino-Soviet relations, once again stating that, with regard to China, the basic policy of the Soviet state remained that of restoring and developing friendship without encumbering preliminary conditions.[55] The Soviet government expressed readiness to discuss a wide range of questions of mutual interest with the Chinese leadership in order to achieve this goal.

However, Peking leaders continued stubbornly to disregard Soviet proposals directed at normalizing relations. Furthermore, on July 8, 1969, they instigated a new action calculated to increase tension along the Soviet-Chinese border. Chinese authorities organized an armed attack on Soviet river workers on Gol'dinskiy Island.*

The Ministry of Foreign Affairs of the USSR strongly protested this latest incursion and demanded that the PRC government punish the guilty and take steps to insure that such actions were not repeated. The note further emphasized that the Soviet side, in order to protect its legal rights, would be forced to take additional measures against Chinese actions directed at violating the state border of the USSR and jeopardizing the security and lives of Soviet citizens.[56]

At the end of July 1969 the Soviet government took the initiative in suggesting a bilateral Soviet-Chinese meeting, in which to discuss prob-

---

* Translator's note: this is referred to by the Chinese as Pacha Island, and as being part of Fuyuan county in Heilungkiang province.

lems of principle in relations between the USSR and the PRC on a state level, to exchange views on ways to ease tensions in relations, and to discuss questions of trade, economic, scientific-technical, and cultural cooperation.

The PRC State Council gave no reply to this initiative. The extremist wing of the ruling Peking clique, striving to consolidate fully China's position of implacable hostility toward the Soviet Union, continued its policy of exacerbating relations with the USSR, resorting to the organization of direct armed provocations on the border.

An obstacle in the path of Peking's designs was a meeting between the USSR Chairman of the Council of Ministers, A. N. Kosygin, and the Premier of the PRC State Council, Chou En-lai. This meeting, taking place by Soviet initiative, occurred in Peking on September 11, 1969, during A. N. Kosygin's return from the funeral of the President of the Democratic Republic of Vietnam, Ho Chi Minh. Representing the Soviet side were Secretary of the CC CPSU, K. F. Katushev, and the Deputy Chairman of the Presidium of the Supreme Soviet of the USSR, M. A. Yasnov. The Chinese side was represented by Vice Premiers Li Hsien-nien and Hsieh Fu-chih.[57]

Certain questions of Sino-Soviet relations were discussed. The exchange of views was then continued in official correspondence. The most important result was the resumption of discussion of border disagreements in Peking in October 1969. The governmental delegation assigned to attend this discussion was headed by First Deputy Minister of Foreign Affairs V. V. Kuznetsov. The Chinese delegation was led by the PRC Vice Minister of Foreign Affairs, Chiao Kuan-hua.

The Soviet Union attached great importance to discussions of border questions with the PRC. L. I. Brezhnev, in a speech on October 27, 1969, said:

> The Central Committee of the Communist Party of the Soviet Union and the Soviet government would like to hope that a positive, realistic approach will prevail at these discussions.
>
> There is no lack of good will on the Soviet side. We favor a solution to the border and to other differences between the USSR and the PRC on a firm and just basis, in a spirit of equality, mutual respect, and consideration of the interests of both countries. If the Chinese side demonstrates good will too, there is no question but that this will all be possible.[58]

The Soviet side strove to create an atmosphere favorable to successful progress of the discussions. The press ceased critical remarks about the policies of CCP leaders, and all possible steps were taken toward normalizing the border situation and toward resolving differences by friendly consultations.

The Chinese side took the opposite tack. Shortly before discussions began, the PRC government published documents repeating earlier, unfounded assertions that Sino-Soviet treaties establishing the present border were unequal, and attempting to place responsibility on the Soviet Union for the aggravation of the border situation.

Anti-Soviet propaganda in China intensified as discussions began. The very day the delegations started their work, anti-Soviet brochures in Chinese, Russian, and other languages, containing malicious attacks on the Soviet Union, territorial claims to our land, deliberately distorted historical facts relating to the Soviet-Chinese border, and inflammatory assertions that the USSR was nurturing plans to seize Chinese territory went on sale in state stores.

Chinese cinema again showed so-called documentary films designed to inflame hostility and hatred for the Soviet people. Anti-Soviet photographic displays appeared in store windows, in parks, and other public places; slogans appealing for "cracking the heads, spilling the blood, and burial" of the Soviet people were common. Such slogans were propagandized in the official Chinese press as well.[59]

In the fall of 1969 a campaign to "prepare for war" began in China. This campaign, constantly fed by provocative warnings of a Soviet attack on the PRC, encompassed virtually the whole of the populace, and subordinated to it the country's entire political and economic life. Preparation for war was declared to be "the fundamental purpose of economic construction in China."[60] Mass movements of industrial plants deep into the interior were initiated, and stockpiles of goods, medicines, and the like were established. The populace, preparing for a "state of siege," was mobilized on an emergency basis in cities and in agricultural regions to build defenses and bomb shelters. Air raid drills accompanied by simulated enemy attacks were held constantly.

The Maoists created this atmosphere of war psychosis in the country to sustain anti-Soviet feelings during discussions of border disagreements between the USSR and the PRC, to dispel hopes of the Chinese people for normalization of relations, to suppress the rising tide of political discord, to rally the broadest possible strata of the populace against the so-called "Soviet threat," to justify economic difficulties, and to establish reasons for further increasing military production.

To justify its military preparations, Peking took a clumsy step by declaring that the PRC supposedly was under military pressure from the Soviet Union. Chinese propaganda frantically disseminated provocative fabrications to the effect that the Soviet Union was preparing an "attack on the PRC," and was conducting "large-scale military actions." The Soviet-Chinese territorial situation was deliberately distorted, the Maoists asserting that Soviet troops were being massed along borders.

A TASS statement published in the Soviet Union on March 14, 1970 decisively refuted attempts to distort the policy of our country with respect to China:

> ... distortions such as these are utterly groundless. Anti-Communist propaganda (in the West) is attempting to use them to interfere with the Soviet-Chinese discussions now going on in Peking, "to throw in" material designed to increase tension in relations between the USSR and the PRC. The Soviet Armed Forces are carrying out their routine, everyday duties and are improving their combat proficiency within the framework of conventional plans and programs, strengthening the defense of the Soviet state throughout its territory. . . .[61]

The TASS statement emphasized that the permanent policy of the USSR and of its government was one of attempting to normalize Sino-Soviet relations, to develop cooperation, to restore and strengthen the friendship between the two countries.

Even so Chinese leaders continued to distort the foreign policy of the Soviet Union, representing it as a force hostile to the PRC. The "prepare for war" campaign, encouragement of militarism, and anti-Soviet diatribes continued unabated. The statements of a "Soviet threat" to China, clearly provocative in nature, were necessary to the devious purposes of Peking. These purposes were to influence the USSR by subjecting it to military blackmail, and to put pressure on our country at the discussions of border disagreements.

These efforts were fruitless. The position of the Soviet Union was set forth in no uncertain terms by the General Secretary of the CC CPSU, L. I. Brezhnev, in his April 14, 1970 speech in Khar'kov. Regarding the Soviet-Chinese border discussions he stated:

> The Soviet Union's position at these discussions is clear-cut and unambiguous. We believe that it is necessary to reach an agreement that will turn the Soviet-Chinese border into a line of good-neighborly relations, not enmity. Maintaining our legal, principled position, upholding the interests of the Soviet motherland and the inviolability of its frontier, we shall do all we can to normalize interstate relations with the People's Republic of China. Of course, all are well aware of the fact that this depends not on us alone.
>
> We firmly proceed from the fact that long-term interests of the Soviet and Chinese people do not conflict, they coincide. At the same time, we

do not close our eyes to the fact that the atmosphere that is artificially created around the talks now going on in China cannot promote their success. As a matter of fact, who can seriously assert that the fanning of anti-Soviet military psychosis and the calls to the Chinese people to prepare for "war and hunger" promote the success of the talks? If this is being done to bring pressure to bear on the Soviet Union, then it can be said in advance that these efforts are wasted. Our people have strong nerves, and this is what the organizers of the war hysteria in China should know. And in the final analysis, the People's Republic of China is as interested in clear-cut regulation of the border question as is the Soviet Union, which has everything that is needed to uphold the interests of the Soviet people, the builders of communism.[62]

9. Sino-Soviet economic ties, 1967–1969

The Chinese side, in the second half of the 1960s, took steps to close all channels of economic and interstate cooperation with the Soviet Union, and with the majority of other socialist countries.

On June 24, 1967, Peking issued a statement that the agreement on cooperation for rendering assistance to ships and aircraft in distress at sea signed July 3, 1956 by the governments of the USSR, the PRC, and the Korean People's Democratic Republic would cease as of January 1, 1968. This was the third multilateral agreement between socialist countries abrogated by the PRC.

In 1967 the Chinese continued sabotaging multilateral agreements between socialist countries on international rail shipments and passenger traffic (Agreement on International Railroad Freight Traffic, and Agreement on International Railroad Passenger Traffic). Chinese representatives engaged in splitting tactics within the organizing committee for the conference of ministers of the Railroad Cooperation Organization, trying to paralyze its efforts.

Chinese authorities, despite numerous Soviet appeals, refused passage through the PRC of food and medicines for Soviet specialists in the Democratic Republic of Vietnam. On June 9, 1967 they officially canceled the existing agreement on Soviet flights en route to Vietnam via Chinese territory.

Peking's policy of rupturing Soviet-Chinese state-to-state cooperation was graphically demonstrated by activities of the Soviet-Chinese navigation commission on boundary sections of the rivers in the Amur basin. The 14th session of this commission, which was to have discussed unresolved problems of improving conditions for navigation along the Amur and Ussuri rivers, convened in Harbin at the end of July 1967. The Chinese side ignored constructive proposals advanced by the Soviet section of the commission and resorted to unfounded political attacks against the Soviet Union. The goal of disrupting the work of the conference was planned in advance, resulting not only in a gross violation of the 1951 agreement, but also in further increasing tensions between the USSR and the PRC.

On April 27, 1968, the Soviet section of the Mixed Commission on Navigation proposed to the Chinese section that the next scheduled session be held in Khabarovsk in May 1968, in order to exchange views and jointly draft measures to maintain normal navigation conditions along border sections of the Amur and Ussuri rivers. The Chinese were given a draft of the preliminary agenda, and the field work plan for 1968. The plan envisaged completion of a number of projects during the 1968 navigation season necessary to maintain normal depths and ensure safety of navigation. On August 16, 1968 the Chinese side rudely rejected this proposal for another meeting.

This step was but a link in overall Chinese policy. For several years it had demonstrated its disinclination to cooperate in solving practical navigation problems on border sections of the rivers. For example, natural processes result in changes taking place in the bed of the Amur river. This in turn makes it necessary to update systematically the direction of the navigable channel by changing the positions of the aids to navigation. Yet the Chinese side responded with stubborn refusals, despite the repeated proposals made by river workers along the Amur river that corresponding re-establishment of many of the aids to navigation established along the bank take place in order to mark the channel with the greatest depths. The Chinese side would not agree to the route work planned for 1968, thus wrecking the extremely necessary plans designed to clear out the shoals and bars that were limiting shipping. Failure to do so resulted in artificial reductions in the quantities of cargo carried in Soviet ships, inflicted substantial losses on transportation, and created danger for shipping.

In 1967 the greater volume of deliveries occurred in the second half of the year as a result of the tardy signing of the goods exchange protocol. These deliveries became very complicated because of the position of the Chinese authorities. Their provocative actions deprived Soviet merchant ships of the possibility of conducting transportation and commercial operations in Chinese ports. In August 1967, for example, the motorships *Turkestan* and *Kamchatskles* were forced to depart the port of Dal'niy without the cargo called for under the existing trade agreement. Actions of Chinese authorities with respect to Soviet ships and crews in Dal'niy were an integral part of the anti-Soviet campaign waged in the PRC. Their actions created a real threat to commercial shipping because Soviet ships, under such abnormal conditions, were deprived of the possibility of calling at Dal'niy.[63]

According to protocol, Soviet-Chinese trade for 1967 had been set at 228 million rubles, or 58 million rubles less than the actual 1966 trade. In fact, however, it was 96 million rubles, about one-third of the 1966 amount. The Soviet Union dropped to fourteenth place on the PRC's foreign trade list.

Trade between China and other socialist countries also dropped off sharply in 1967. Compared with 1966, trade between the PRC and countries participating in the Council of Mutual Economic Assistance decreased from 528 million to 313 million rubles.

The year 1967 marked the first time that the USSR and the PRC failed to sign a plan for cultural and scientific exchange and cooperation through the medium of friendship associations and tourist organizations.

A similar situation evolved in the field of tourist exchanges. There was correspondence in 1967 between the "Intourist" and its Chinese counterpart, "Lu Hsing She," exchanges. The Soviet side, on August 9, 1967, declared that given a guarantee of normal conditions for Soviet tourists in the PRC, to include banning anti-Soviet provocations, trips by Soviet tourists could be arranged under conditions of equal exchange for the remainder of 1967, and in 1968. "Lu Hsing She," the Chinese tourist agency, in its September 1 letter of reply to "Intourist," rejected this initiative.

Nor was a trade protocol signed in 1968. This was the first year without such a protocol since 1949 and the blame falls on the Chinese. Trade between the USSR and the PRC was conducted on the basis of individual contracts covering specific commodities. The actual trade in 1968 was 10 percent below that of 1967, totaling 86 million rubles.

A. A. Gromyko, USSR Minister of Foreign Affairs, in his report to the session of the Supreme Soviet of the USSR on June 27, 1968, referred to the condition of Sino-Soviet interstate relations:

> Let me say bluntly that these relations are a long way from what relations can and should be between two socialist countries, and even simply between neighbors. Our side is doing everything it can to see to it that state relations with China do not worsen. This year the Soviet government has made concrete proposals to the government of the People's Republic of China on questions of trade, joint use of the border rivers for navigation, and on some others. But Peking remains deaf to any initiative reflecting concern for current and future Sino-Soviet relations.... The Mao Tse-tung faction is carrying on hostile, disruptive activities against our state. Peking newspapers and radio, in their vile attempts to defame the in-

ternal life of the Soviet Union and its foreign policy, are competing with imperialist propaganda.[64]

The Soviet side, in 1969, advanced a number of proposals for activating economic ties between the USSR and the PRC. These included plans for expanding trade in 1969, for more than doubling trade in 1970 as compared with 1969, and for resuming border trade.

The Chinese side failed to respond to any of these proposals. Soviet-Chinese trade in 1969 fell 41 percent as compared with 1968, to a figure of 51 million rubles, the lowest level in the entire history of mutual trade relations.

A clear expression of the neighborly and cooperative policy of the Soviet Union is the fact that indoctrinating our populace in a spirit of friendship and respect for the Chinese people and for their glorious history and revolutionary progress never ceased. The Soviet-Chinese Friendship Association engages in a great deal of fruitful activity. It systematically stages programs devoted to the most important events in the life of the Chinese people, celebrates jubilees of outstanding Chinese revolutionary leaders, world-renowned leaders of Chinese culture and literature, and famous dates from the history of Soviet-Chinese friendship and cooperation. In the last three years the association celebrated the 100th anniversary of the birth of that great son of the Chinese people, the revolutionary democrat Sun Yat-sen; the 80th birthday of a founder of the CCP, Li Ta-chao; the 70th birthday of the famous Chinese Communist-internationalist Ch'ü Ch'iu-pai; the 80th birthday of the father of modern Chinese literature, Lu Hsün; the 60th birthday of the famous Chinese writer Chou Li-po; the 70th birthday of the famous scientist and writer Cheng Chen-do; the 1,200th anniversary of the birth of the Chinese humanist and classicist of Chinese literature, Han Yung; the 40th anniversary of the death of the famous leader of the CCP, P'eng P'ai; and the 60th birthday of the Chinese poet In Fu. Public meetings in the capital, held in the House of Friendship with the Peoples of Foreign Countries, were devoted to these dates. Central newspapers printed special articles on the life and activities of these famous sons of the Chinese people. The Far East Institute of the Academy of Sciences of the USSR has been making a great contribution to research on the problems of Sinology and to popularization of knowledge about China. Its scholars have published a great many fundamental works on China in recent years.

Unfailingly friendly attention to China and the dissemination of propaganda on friendship and cooperation between the Soviet and

Chinese peoples are elements of our Leninist foreign policy. The Soviet-Chinese Friendship Association and the Far East Institute of the Academy of Sciences of the USSR held a jubilee conference, "Lenin and China," in Moscow on February 24–25, 1970, to honor the 100th anniversary of the birth of V. I. Lenin. Participants included representatives of the public, activists in the Soviet-Chinese Friendship Association, sinologists, and distinguished military leaders and specialists who had helped the Chinese people in their revolutionary struggle and in building a new society. Speeches stressed the role of Leninist ideas in the national liberation and revolutionary struggle of the Chinese people and in the founding of the CCP, noted the fruitful nature of friendship and cooperation between the USSR and the PRC at different stages of the Chinese Revolution, and affirmed the great importance of friendship between these two great peoples as a crucial factor in the struggle against imperialism, and for the unity of revolutionary forces of our time.[65]

NOTES

1. B. Zanegin, A. Mironov, Ya. Mikhailov, *K sobytiyam v Kitaye* (*Events in China*) (Moscow, 1967), p. 25.

2. Ibid., pp. 25–26.

3. V. I. Lenin, *Complete Collected Works,* Vol. 41, p. 337.

4. Ibid., Vol. 38, p. 55.

5. *Pravda,* September 1, 1966.

6. *Pravda,* October 3, 1966.

7. *Pravda,* December 14, 1966.

8. *Kommunist,* No. 4, p. 93, 1969.

9. *Korni nyneshnikh sobytiy v Kitaye* (*The Roots of Today's Events in China*) (Moscow, 1968), p. 31.

10. *Pravda,* March 11, 1967.

11. *Pravda,* February 7, 1967.

12. *Pravda,* February 5, 1967.

13. *Pravda,* February 10, 1967.

14. *Pravda,* February 28, 1967.

15. *Pravda,* February 6, 1967.

16. *Pravda,* February 15, 1967.

17. *Pravda,* August 12, 1967.

18. *Pravda,* August 13, 1967.

19. Ibid.

20. *Pravda,* January 6, 1967.

21. *Pravda,* April 25, 1967.

22. *Jen Min Jihpao,* April 30, 1967.

23. *Pravda,* June 22, 1967.

24. *50 let Velikoy Oktyabr'skoy sotsialisticheskoy revolyutsii. Postanovleniye Plenuma TSK KPSS.* (*50 Years of the Great October Socialist Revo-*

lution. Resolution of the Plenary Session of the CC CPSU) (Moscow, 1967), p. 54.

25. L. I. Brezhnev, *Pyat'desyat l'et velikikh pobed sotsializma* (*Fifty Years of Great Victories of Socialism* (Moscow, 1967), p. 41.

26. *Pravda,* April 4, 1968.

27. *Trud,* April 13, 1968.

28. *Pravda,* April 9, 1968.

29. *Jen Min Jihpao,* September 2, 1968.

30. *Jen Min Jihpao,* November 1, 1968.

31. *Pravda,* November 1, 1968.

32. *Kommunist,* No. 4, p. 87, 1969.

33. *Pravda,* March 4, 1969.

34. *Pravda,* March 16, 1969.

35. Lu Hsün, *Sochineniya* (*Works*), Vol. 6, Peking, p. 109.

36. V. I. Lenin, *Complete Collected Works,* Vol. 35, p. 20.

37. Ibid., Vol. 45, p. 303.

38. *Izvestiya,* October 12, 1954.

39. *Izvestiya,* January 19, 1957.

40. *Pravda,* March 30, 1969.

41. *Pravda,* April 12, 1969.

42. Lin Piao, *Otchetnyi doklad na IX Vsekitayskom s'yezde KPK* (*Report to the 9th All-China Congress of the Communist Party of China,* hereinafter referred to as *9th All-China Congress*) (Peking, 1969), p. 64.

43. *Mezhdunarodnoye Soveshchaniye kommunisticheskikh i rabochikh partiy* (*The International Conference of Communist and Worker's Parties,* hereinafter referred to as *Communist and Worker's Parties*) (Moscow, 1969), p. 199.

44. *Pravda,* July 14, 1969.

45. *Communist and Worker's Parties,* p. 195–200.

46. Ibid., p. 473.

47. Ibid., p. 852.

48. Ibid., p. 862.

49. Ibid., p. 422.

50. Ibid., p. 270.

51. Ibid., p. 226.

52. Ibid., p. 118–120.

53. Ibid., p. 290–291.

54. *Kommunist,* No. 10, 1969, p. 6.

55. *Pravda,* July 11, 1969.

56. *Pravda,* July 9, 1969.

57. *Pravda,* September 12, 1969.

58. *Pravda,* October 28, 1969.

59. *Jen Min Jihpao,* December 13, 1969.

60. *Hung-chi,* No. 10, 1969.

61. *Pravda,* March 14, 1970.

62. *Pravda,* April 15, 1970.

63. *Pravda,* August 22, 1967.

64. *Pravda,* June 28, 1968.

65. *Pravda,* February 26, 1970.

Conclusion

A twenty-five year history of Sino-Soviet relations, as set forth in this survey, seems an extremely short segment in the chronicles of such great nations as the Soviet Union and the PRC. Nevertheless, these years cover an unusually critical period in the life of the Chinese people, a period of the birth and building of the new, socialist China.

Study of the history of Sino-Soviet relations between 1945 and 1970 leads to the indisputable conclusion that friendship and cooperation between the USSR and China are in the basic interest of peoples of both countries, as well as in the interests of peace, democracy, and socialism throughout the world. The help and support provided by the Soviet Union at all stages of China's most recent development played an important role in the national liberation and revolutionary struggle of the Chinese workers. Each time Sino-Soviet relations drew closer, revolutionary forces in China strengthened their position, the progressive movement received additional impetus, and reaction suffered a setback. Conversely, weakening of such ties reflected very negatively on the political climate in the PRC, led to a reduction in revolutionary ardor, encouraged development of nationalism, and opened the way for internal reaction to collude with imperialism.

The help given revolutionary forces by the Soviet Union continued to retain its high order of importance even after the founding of the PRC in 1949. With a relatively small and politically divided industrial proletariat, the transition from the bourgeois democratic stage of the revolution to the socialist stage required special conditions for strengthening the leading role of the working class, and for increasing the proportion of its membership in the party. The relative political weakness of the working class in China was compensated by its close alliance with the international workers' and Communist movement, and in particular by its alliance with the most powerful country of socialism—the Soviet Union.

The reactionary,.anti-socialist forces in China are well aware that an obstacle in the path of their dominance is friendship and cooperation

347

between the Chinese and Soviet peoples. That is why the struggle against revolutionary, socialist development in China has always been and continues to be waged under the slogan of anti-Sovietism. It is no accident that anti-Sovietism became the banner of the organizers of the "cultural revolution," who set themselves the task of converting the PRC into a military bureaucratic dictatorship. Anything reminiscent of the Soviet Union stirred hatred and fear in the instigators of the "cultural revolution," because, so far as the broadest masses of Chinese people were concerned, the concept of "Soviet" was unequivocally associated with the concept of "socialist."

The history of Sino-Soviet relations confirms yet another irrevocable truth: the open transition of today's leaders of the PRC to a position of anti-Sovietism was neither unexpected nor random in nature. From its very inception, the CCP has been torn by a sharp struggle between two lines; the international Marxist-Leninist, and the nationalist petty bourgeois. The champions of the latter line are today's Peking leaders. Those leaders who seized power in the party and the country as a result of the "cultural revolution" have foisted on the PRC an anti-Soviet course, which they had long favored, but had previously found impossible to implement.

The CPSU has never been an indifferent observer of the development of Sino-Soviet relations. The history of these relations is a history of an active, aggressive, and uncompromising struggle by the CPSU for friendship and cooperation between our countries and peoples. Our party has exhibited a sincere interest in settling disagreements on the basis of Marxist-Leninist principles at all stages of disagreements between the CCP, the CPSU, and other Marxist-Leninist parties. It has made every effort to prevent transference of ideological disputes into interstate relations. The fraternal parties have repeatedly pointed out that the policy of the Soviet Union in relations with the PRC during its transition to the present leadership has been a model of self-restraint, deep understanding of its historical responsibility to the cause of world socialism, and detailed consideration of interests of both Soviet and Chinese peoples. Attempts of Maoist and bourgeois historiography to burden our party and country with responsibility for exacerbation of Sino-Soviet relations are refuted by reality.

The consistent course of the CPSU, aimed at development and strengthening of Sino-Soviet friendship, encouraged the influence of internationalist forces in the CCP. It was no secret that there were forces among the CCP leadership capable of assuming positions hostile to the Soviet Union at the opportune time. However, our party proceeded from the position that the help rendered the CCP would achieve its primary intents, those of assisting the struggle of the Chinese people and of indoctrinating Chinese Communists in a spirit of Marxism-Leninism and proletarian internationalism. It can be confidently asserted that without this help nationalist elements would much earlier have imposed their will on the CCP.

Moreover, the history of Sino-Soviet relations consistently confirms how dangerous nationalism is to the cause of friendship and cooperation between socialist countries, particularly in the case of a country recently embarked on the road to socialism and not yet rid of the rejection by current leaders of the principles of proletarian internationalism. This anomalous situation clearly recalls Lenin's instruction that the struggle:

> . . . with the most ingrained petty bourgeois, national prejudices, the more it is pushed to the forefront, the more essential becomes the task of converting the dictatorship of the proletariat from a national one (that is, from one existing in but a single country and incapable of setting world policies) into an international one (that is, into a dictatorship of the proletariat including at the very least several advanced countries capable of exerting a decisive influence on world policies).[1]

The imperialist camp does not disguise its satisfaction with the exacerbation of Sino-Soviet relations. The ideologues of anti-Communism are trying to prove that this course of events is "natural and inevitable," that a return to friendly and cooperative relations between the USSR and the PRC is impossible because they supposedly cannot overcome contradictions in their national interests. This provocative thesis also appears in the arsenal of Maoist propaganda, which is trying to impress on the Chinese people that there is a threat "from the North."

However, as the history of Sino-Soviet relations attests, there can be no objective reasons for alienation, let alone for the peoples actually fighting each other. Quite the contrary, all prerequisites for friendship and cooperation are present, based as they are on the requirements for the successful development of the USSR and the PRC, as well as the needs of the world revolutionary process.

Our party constantly educates the Soviet people in a spirit of friendship and deep respect for the Chinese people, for their history and culture, for the heroic deeds of their workers in the struggle for liberation from foreign oppressors, and for the revolutionary transformation of their motherland. The Soviet Union consistently champions the interests of the PRC in the international arena and decisively rebuffs any imperialist attempts to exacerbate relations between our countries.

Our party's affirmative course concerning friendship with China is combined with its decisive struggle against the anti-Leninist, antipopular nature of political and ideological aims of the current Peking leaders. It condemns the PRC's schismatic, anti-Soviet activities. This is a component of overall efforts of other Marxist-Leninist parties, and the entire world Communist movement, in their struggle for the Communist Party of China, for a socialist China, and for a bright future for the Chinese people.

NOTES

1. V. I. Lenin, *Complete Collected Works,* Vol. 41, p. 165.

Index

Academies of Sciences, 161–62, 245, 275, 344–45
Aeroflot, 275, 304
African countries, 248–50, 285
Afrikaans National Congress, 335
Afro-Asian conferences, 248–49, 262
agriculture: socialist transformation of, 142; great leap forward and crop expectations, 145; communization of, 169; limited by low level of mechanization, 279; disorganized during cultural revolution, 298
air lines, 66, 275, 304
airspace violations, 319
Albanian issue, 182–87, 190–96, 232–36
Algiers, 307
All-Chinese Congress of Communist Youth, 237
America. *See* United States
Amur River, 100, 326–30, 341–42
anti-Sovietism: CCP launches, 95; and emerging nationalism of CCP leadership, 108–33; in 1945–1949, 121–23; as basis for new CCP ideology, 321–22; of 9th Congress of CCP, 328–30; as official policy of PRC, 328–30; international socialist movement rebuffs, 332–37; conclusions on, 348
Argentine Communists, 306
army, Chinese: role in CCP, 112–13; role in cultural revolution, 281–82, 287–88; power under Maoists, 320, 339–40; *see also* Red Guard
artists: Soviet groups visiting PRC, 165; Chinese used for propaganda purposes, 244–46; *see also* cultural cooperation

Asian countries, 248–50, 262, 285
atomic bomb, China's, 254, 256
atomic energy, Soviet assistance on, 82
Avila, Victor, 335

bacteriological warfare, 44
Bandung Conference, 156
Baroyan, O. V., 58
"Basic Provisions of the Program," 88–90
black market, 299
Blagoveshchensk, 330
"blind faith" in foreign experience, 148–49
Blum, Léon, 15
books, Soviet gifts of, 162
border disputes: Chinese-Indian, 156–58; PRC foments on Sino-Soviet border, Sinkiang mass exodus, 219–25; Chinese encouraged to violate borders, Sino-Soviet talks fail, 239–42; territorial claims of PRC, 263, 325–31; PRC attempts to seize Soviet territory, 267; Soviet concessions on boundaries, 274; PRC hostile activity during cultural revolution, 295; increased violations in 1967, issue of border war raised, 312–13; PRC claims violations of airspace by Soviet aircraft, 319; armed provocation at Damanskiy Island, 322–25; Indo-Chinese, 324; USSR attempts at bilateral settlement of, 327–28; further PRC island landings, 329–31; 9th CCP Congress' twisted statement on, 330; Soviet program for settlement of, 332; attack on Gol'dinskiy Island, 337; PRC prepares for war over, Brezhnev's stand on, 338–41; naviga-